The Book of Sculthorpe

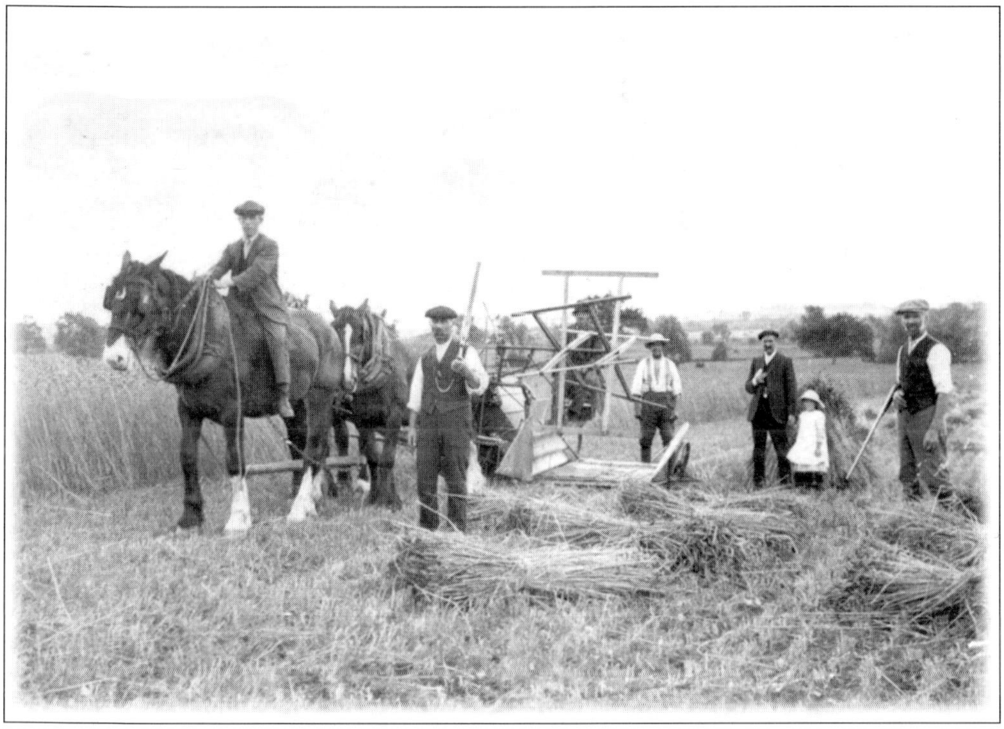

A Pictorial and Historic Celebration

Gary T. Windeler

HALSGROVE

First published in Great Britain in 2003.

This book is dedicated to the memory of the late Mrs Eleanor Crane and her sister, the late Mrs Marion Howard, who knew and loved the village of Sculthorpe better than anyone.

British Library Cataloguing-in-Publication Data.
A CIP record for this title is available from the British Library.

ISBN 1 84114 250 6

HALSGROVE

Halsgrove House
Lower Moor Way
Tiverton, Devon EX16 6SS
Tel: 01884 243242
Fax: 01884 243325
email: sales@halsgrove.com
website: www.halsgrove.com

Frontispiece photograph: *A pre-First World War photograph of harvest time in Sculthorpe on the north side of the village. John Woodhouse is seated on the horse at the head of the sail reaper and binder.*
(Reproduced by kind permission of Mr Richard Land)

Printed and bound in Great Britain by Bookcraft Ltd, Midsomer Norton.

Foreword

To understand the village and its people well, it is not enough for us to read of their traditions, legends and history; we must also study contemporary accounts that bring out their ways of life and strongest characteristics. *The Book of Sculthorpe* has been some 25 years in its assembly. The successful completion of a quarter-century of dogged ferreting and persistent high-grade research is a triumph worth trumpeting.

A blend of historical fact, inspired detection, logical argument, intuitive guesswork backed by irrefutable evidence, and much 'local knowledge', this book about a Norfolk village and its people is outstanding. Gary Windeler has brought many threads together to weave a readable, jocular, learned and enjoyable chronicle. Sometimes the recollections of parishioners even agree with the records – within a century or two!

Deciding what to leave out is often a problem for an historian. For Sculthorpe Mr Windeler gathered much more material then he could accommodate, both textual and graphical. His selection of photographs, obtained from many archives and family albums, depicts nearly 200 years of village life.

From settlements on the upper reaches of the Rivers Wensum and Burn, priceless relics from the Bronze Age have been found near Sculthorpe. These, with Viking jewellery and a Norman church whose famous font has for more than 900 years been used in celebrating Holy Baptism, bear testimony to three millennia of constant occupation of the higher ground. The fourteenth-century church, with its Victorian additions an example of Norfolk's finest, is just 28 feet above the water-mill more than a mile distant.

Born 'furren' in nearby Burnham Thorpe, I was brought up in Sculthorpe after the Second World War. Like my father Peter and aunt Manie, son and daughter of the Revd Jack Labouchere, my brother Henry was born at the Old Rectory, and he and I both live near our 'home' to this day. In 1947, at the age of ten, I stayed with Willie Woodhouse in Rose Cottage, while the house was redecorated – just as my clerical grandfather had done 45 years earlier. Many friends and retainers welcomed father's return to his birthplace.

I have done no more for the author and his project than to provide encouragement. I am grateful for the compliment he pays me in asking me to contribute this foreword. My grandfather spoke upon his deathbed of his high regard for the parishioners of Sculthorpe and the Norfolk character. Gary Windeler has with this book proved himself to be one of those people.

John Labouchere
North Elmham
April 2003

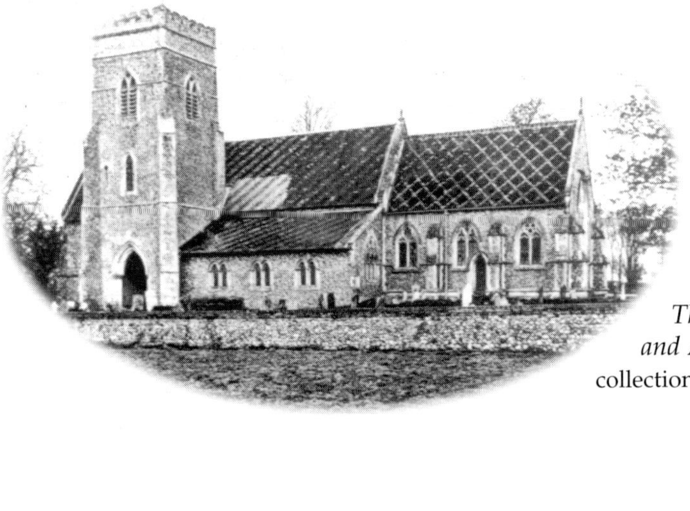

The Parish Church of the Blessed Virgin Mary and All Saints, Sculthorpe, c.1910. (From the collection of Audrey Jordan)

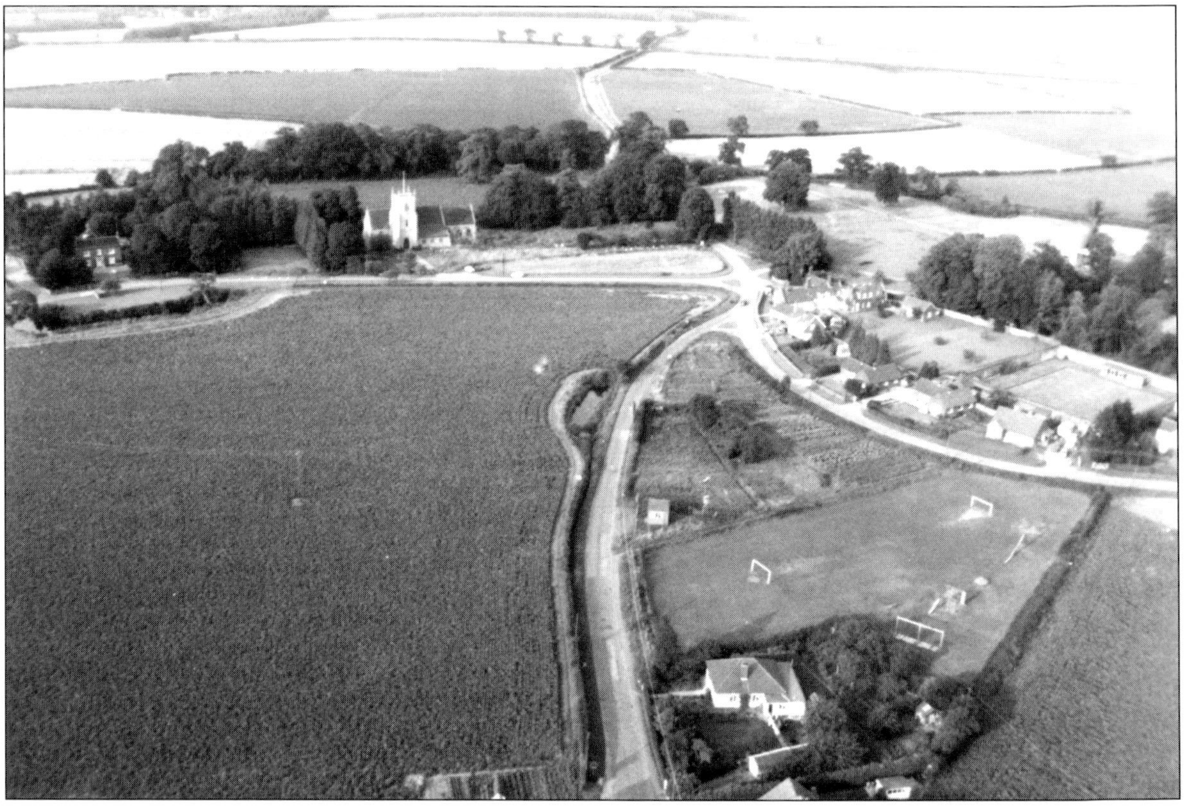

An aerial view of Sculthorpe taken by John Labouchere from the Tiger Moth piloted by his brother, Henry Labouchere, during the summer of 1984. This photograph shows the village playing-field, a former allotment, which was officially opened by Anthony Duckworth-Chad in 1976. The village had attempted to raise funds for a playing-field ever since 28 young people had petitioned Sculthorpe Parish Council in 1933 to make provision for one. Next to the church is Manor Farm, built c.1809 on the site of the late-fourteenth-century manor-house of Sir Robert Knollys who died here in August 1407.
(Reproduced by kind permission of John and Henry Labouchere)

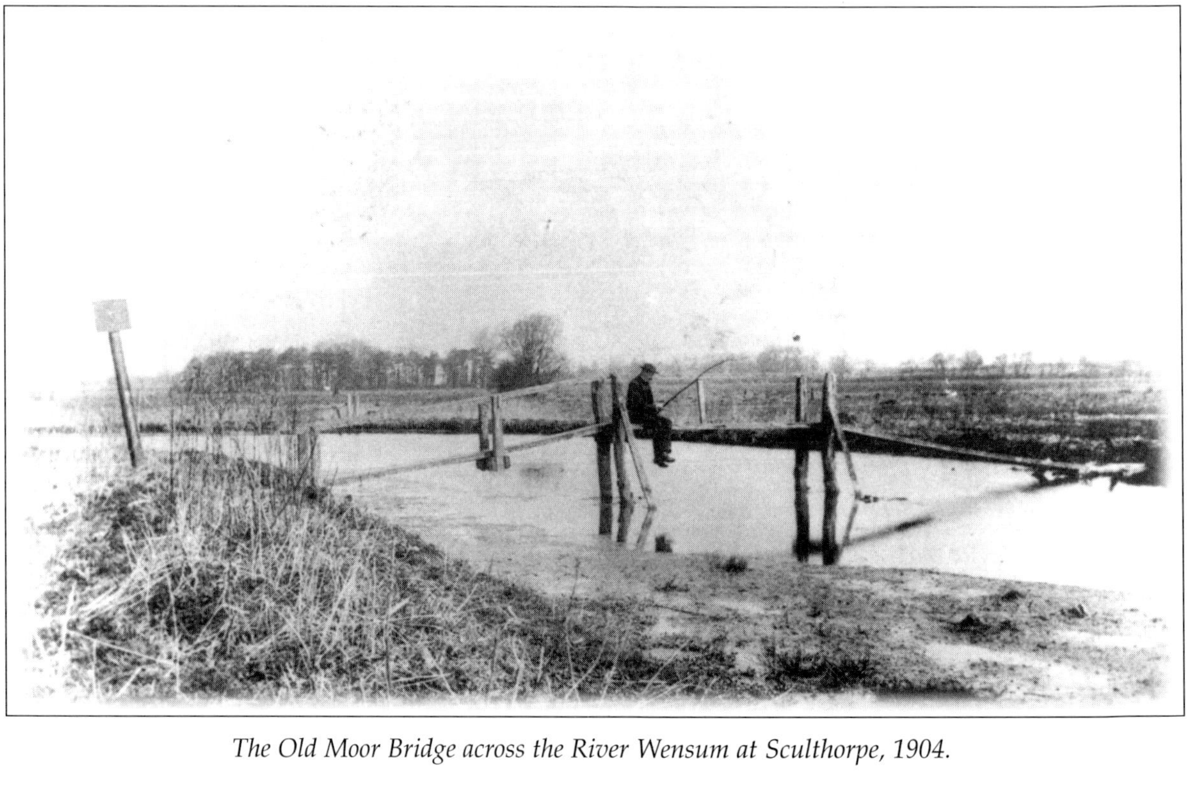

The Old Moor Bridge across the River Wensum at Sculthorpe, 1904.

Contents

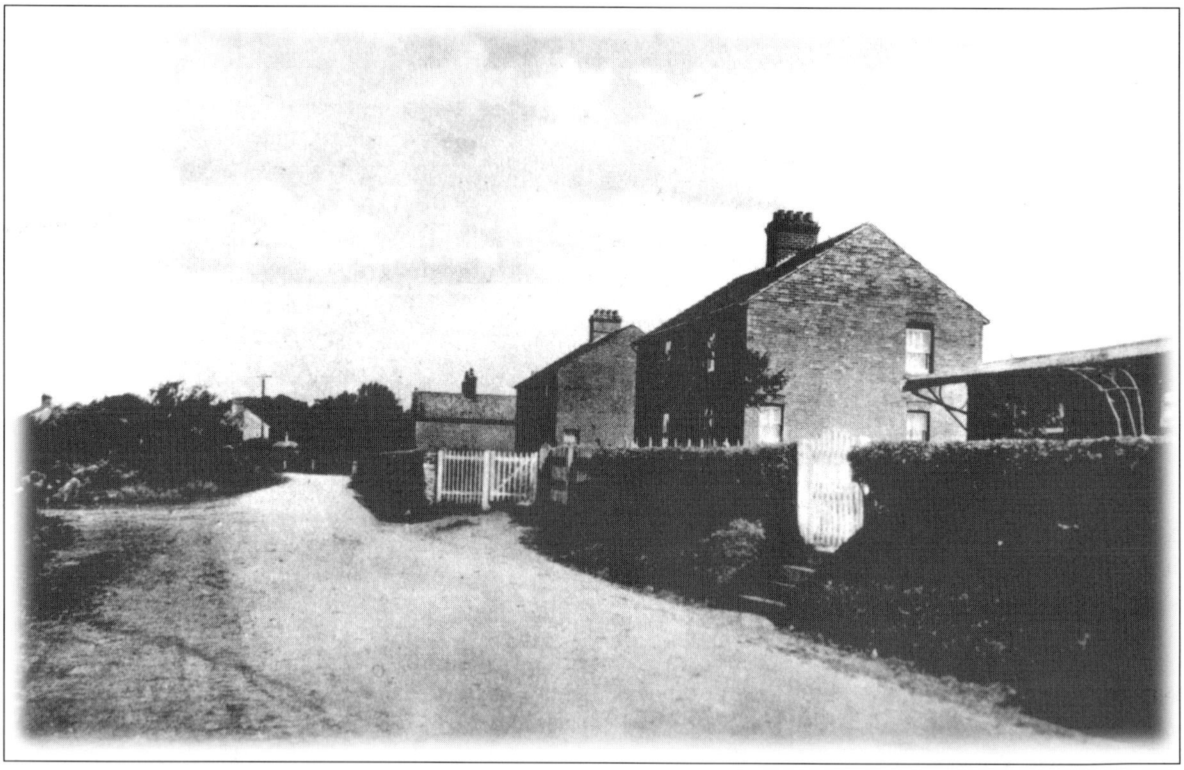

Creake Road, Sculthorpe, early 1930s. The two cottages on the right were built in 1925 and 1927 by Sir Lawrence John Jones. The bungalow was a former railway carriage and was the home of the Sturman family.
(From the collection of the late Mr William Sewter. Reproduced by kind permission of Mrs Jean Benstead)

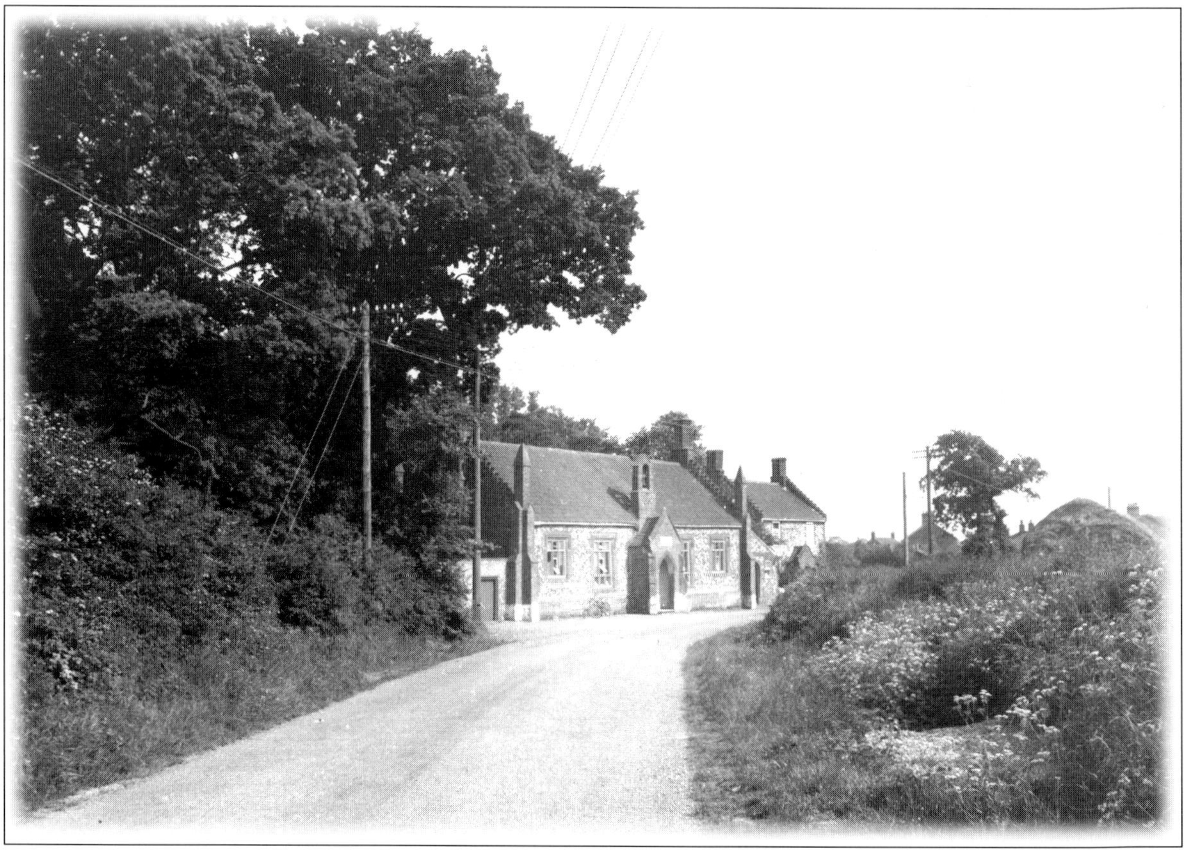

Creake Road and the school during the 1940s.
(Reproduced by kind permission of the Norfolk Rural Life Museum at Gressenhall)

AUTHOR'S NOTE

As children my sister and I loved to hear the wonderful stories which our beloved grandmother, Mrs May Lingwood, told us about her 'Upstairs, Downstairs' existence in domestic service during the Edwardian period, particularly the years before the First World War when she was employed by Mr and Mrs Charles Reid as their cook housekeeper at Sculthorpe Lodge Farm.

We burrowed through the drawers of her ancient eighteenth-century bureau of Norfolk oak, rooting out faded sepia photographs of our family and our village from the past.

In 1977 I started to research the history of Sculthorpe, visiting various libraries, museums and art galleries, collecting village memories and assembling a vast collection of old photographs. Mrs Eleanor Crane and her sister, Mrs Marion Howard, whose father, Willy Woodhouse, had been land agent for the Cranmer Hall estate from 1886 until 1946, took a particular interest in this project and so did Mr Stanley Gathercole, the verger and gravedigger, Mr Willy Sewter and Mrs Rose Applegate. I am deeply grateful to these kind friends for their generous support during the early period of my research.

In recent years my interest in studying the history of Sculthorpe has involved the active participation of so many different friends and supporters and I am particularly indebted to the following people and organisations for their assistance with this book:

The British Library – Zoë Stansell from the department of manuscripts and Ivor Kerslake, the British Museum studio manager of photography and imaging; the Carnegie Library at King's Lynn; the Church of England Record Centre – Sarah Duffield, National Society Archivist; Fakenham Library; Fakenham Town Council; the Institution of Royal Engineers and its secretary, Lt-Col David Hamilton; Lambeth Palace Library staff; the Norfolk & Norwich Archaeological Society, Roger Bellinger, hon. general secretary; the Norfolk and Norwich Millennium Library, Clare Agate at the Norfolk Heritage Centre; the Norfolk Record Office and the county archivist, Dr John Alban; the Norfolk Rural Life Museum at Gressenhall and its inspiring collections officer, Frances Collinson, also Dr Edwin Rose of the Norfolk Archaeological Unit at Gressenhall; Norwich Castle Museum and Art Gallery – Norma Watt, assistant keeper of art; the Public Record Office (The National Archives) at Kew – T.R. Padfield, copyright officer; the Royal Botanic Gardens at Kew; Sculthorpe Church of England Primary School and its head teacher Leslie Whitehead; the South Australian Genealogy and Heraldry Society; State Library of South Australia staff; Tattersalls of Newmarket and its director, Paul Ryan; the Uniting Church of Australia Historical Society; York City Archives staff and D.R. Apperly, city solicitor at York Guildhall.

The *Daily Mail* and Rebecca Barnard at their agents, Atlantic Syndication; the *Dereham & Fakenham Times*, Norfolk weeklies editor, Terry Redhead; the *Eastern Daily Press* – Dennis Whitehead, picture editor, and the staff of the *Eastern Daily Press* picture library at Prospect House, Norwich; David & Charles Publications Ltd – Pat Bence; the *Illustrated London News* picture library manager, Elaine Hood; the Larks Press – David and Susan Yaxley; the *Lynn News* editor, Malcolm Powell.

Mrs Jean Allison; Verily Anderson; the late Claire Anley; the late Harry Apling; Mary Barham-Johnson; Mrs Jean Benstead; Kenneth Boast; Mr John Burnside; Austin Cornwall; Mrs Josephine de Bono of

Cranmer Hall; His Grace the late Duke of Norfolk and the staff at Arundel Castle Library; Mrs Jean Edge; Mrs Evelyn Gibson; Don Goldney, pastor of the Wesleyan Methodist Church of Australia; the late Revd Fred Gunn, rector of Sculthorpe, 1955–64; Rachel Gurney; Richard Gurney; John Harper; Mrs Joyce Harrison; Lady Harrod; Mr Bob Hood; Dr Arnold Hunt; Mrs Louise Hurst; Mrs Audrey Jordan; Miss Sue Kimbley; John Labouchere, his brothers Henry and Colin Labouchere and their cousin, Ursula Clifton Brown; Jack Land; Richard Land; the Revd William Leary; Harold and Anne Lingwood; Leslie and Joyce Lingwood; the late Ronnie Lingwood; Mr Nigel Middleton; Mrs Lavinia Monaco, Mrs Vivien Asquith and their late sister the Hon. Nancy Morse, daughters of Sir Lawrence and Lady Evelyn Jones of Cranmer Hall; Mrs Doris Mitchell; the late Mrs Doris Norman; the Very Reverend Stephen Platten, Dean of Norwich Cathedral and now Bishop of Wakefield; the Rochester Bridge Trust; Mr Peter Rix; Mr and Mrs John Savory of Thorpland Hall; the late Mrs Violet Skippon; Mr John Smith; Father Andrew Thomson, rector of Sculthorpe; Marquess Townshend and his secretary, Scilla Landale; Nan and Joe Tuck; Mrs Rita Tuck; the late Mrs Ellen Van Damme; the late Mrs Minnie Woodhouse; Miss Patricia Wright of Glen Osmond, South Australia, and her cousin Mr David Wright of Salisbury East, South Australia, descendants of the Revd John Gibbon Wright.

Finally I wish to thank my mother, Mrs Gwen Windeler, and my sister, Tracey Waters, who typed the manuscript and put up with my constant demands!

Gary T. Windeler
November 2003

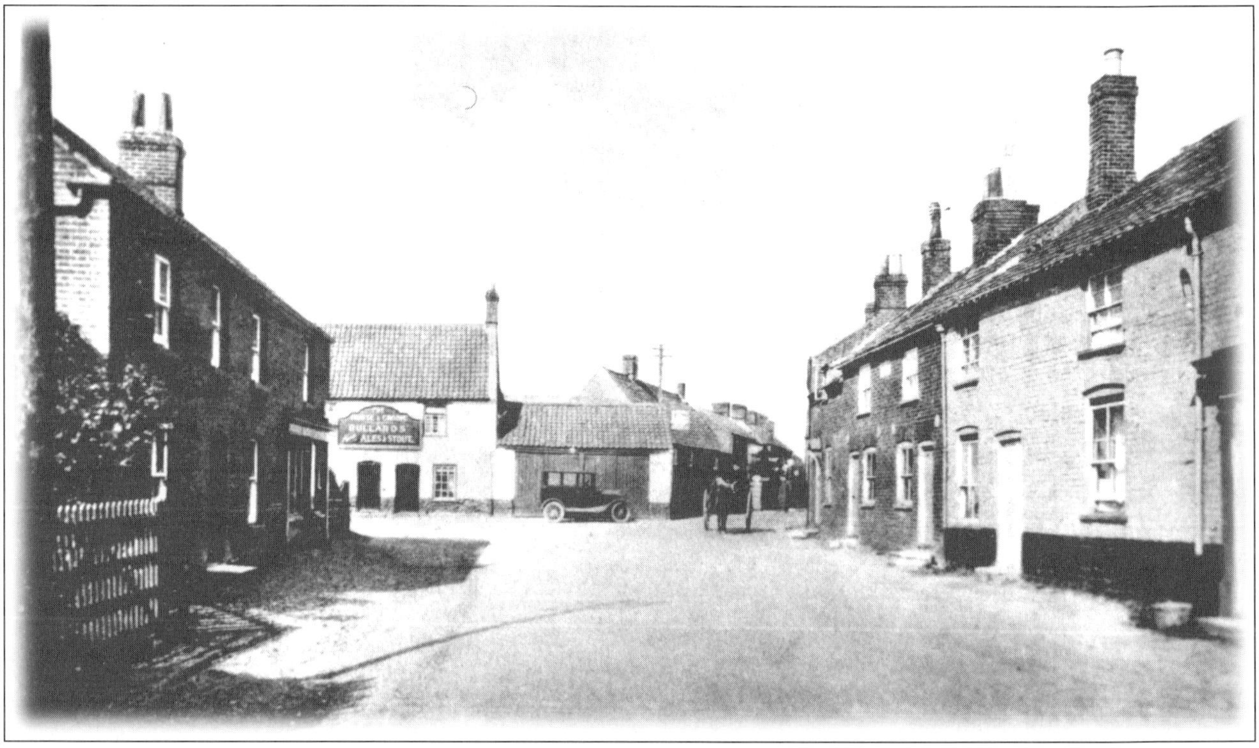

The Horse & Groom in The Street, Sculthorpe, mid-1920s. To the left is Aunt Bessie Sewter's Post Office and General Stores and to the right the Foundry Cottages and the Greyhound pub. 'Sweep Armiger' is in his pony and trap. The Horse & Groom belonged to Bullards brewery in Norwich from the mid-nineteenth century and ceased trading in 1968. Restored by Peter Wright, it reopened in 1975. It is now a flourishing village pub with a very popular licensed restaurant, patronised by both holiday-makers and residents from much of the surrounding locality.
(From the collection of the late Mr William Sewter. Reproduced by kind permission of Mrs Jean Benstead whose father, Mr Leonard Dennis, was landlord of the Horse & Groom in 1934)

Acknowledgements

The author acknowledges with thanks the following who have allowed him to quote and reproduce from source material:

The British Library (department of manuscripts) for permission to quote from Robert Kemp's entry about the heraldic arms in Sculthorpe Church (Ref: The Harleian Manuscript, 901, folio 103, dated c.1575) and passing reference to the famous Lewes Chartulary originally held in the British Museum.
The British Museum for permission to use a drawing of Sculthorpe Church by Elizabeth Turner, c.1841.
The *Daily Mail* (agent: Atlantic Syndication) for permission to quote from Anthony Brown's article dated 13 December 1954, entitled 'Atom Bomb Village'.
David & Charles Publications Ltd for permission to quote from *A General View of the Agriculture of the County of Norfolk*, 1804, Arthur Young.
The *Dereham & Fakenham Times* (Archant Norfolk Ltd) for permission to quote from newspaper articles dated 1891 and 1928.
The *Eastern Daily Press*, the *Dereham & Fakenham Times* (Archant Norfolk Ltd) and the *Lynn News* (Anglia Newspapers Ltd) for permission to use press photographs in the book.
Fakenham Town Council for permission to use the portrait of Sir Lawrence John Jones of Cranmer.
The *Illustrated London News* picture library for permission to use the engraving of the Great Oak at Bale from the May 1845 edition of the *Illustrated London News*.
The Institution of Royal Engineers for permission to use the portrait of Major-General Sir John Thomas Jones of Cranmer.
The Larks Press and the Norfolk Record Office for permission to use extracts from Faden's map of Norfolk (1797) and Bryant's map (1826).
The Norfolk & Norwich Archaeological Society for permission to use drawings from *Notes on Sculthorpe Church* by Mrs Herbert Jones, published by the Norfolk & Norwich Archaeological Society, 1872, and for consulting transactions published by the Society.
The Norfolk Record Office and the County Archivist, Dr John Alban, for permission to quote from: the Parish Registers of Sculthorpe (Ref: PD214/1–1726); the Church Terriers (Ref: PD214/29); the churchwarden's accounts 1729–1865 (Ref: PD214/46); the Sculthorpe Poor Rate Book 1831–67 (Ref: PD214/53–57); 'Church Notes' by Tom Martin of Thetford from the *Rye Manuscript*, Vol. VII, p.321; John Weever's *Funerall Monuments* (1631), p.538; a ground plan of Sculthorpe National School, c.1841; the calendar of wills and administrations/Norwich Court of Probate; Cotman's *Architectural Remains, Vol. I*; the Inventory of Effects at Cranmer Hall, 1783 (Ref: NRS 20768, 41D6); Sculthorpe Inclosure Award, 1829 (Ref: MS 18623/91, 365x5); Sculthorpe Field Book of 1766 (Ref: NRS 8803); Sculthorpe Chapel secretary's book (Ref: FC18 – Sculthorpe); and passing reference to the Manor Court Rolls, Cranmer Hall estate maps and family papers deposited with the Norfolk Record Office by Major (later Sir Lawrence) Jones of Cranmer in 1946.
The Norfolk Rural Life Museum at Gressenhall for permission to use historic photographs from their Roots of Norfolk collection.
The Norwich Castle Museum and Art Gallery for permission to use the civic portrait of Sir Willoughby Jones of Cranmer.
The Dean and Chapter of Norwich Cathedral for permission to use Dean Goulburn's drawing of the cloister boss in Norwich Cathedral.
The Public Record Office (The National Archives) for permission to quote from the Inventory of Church

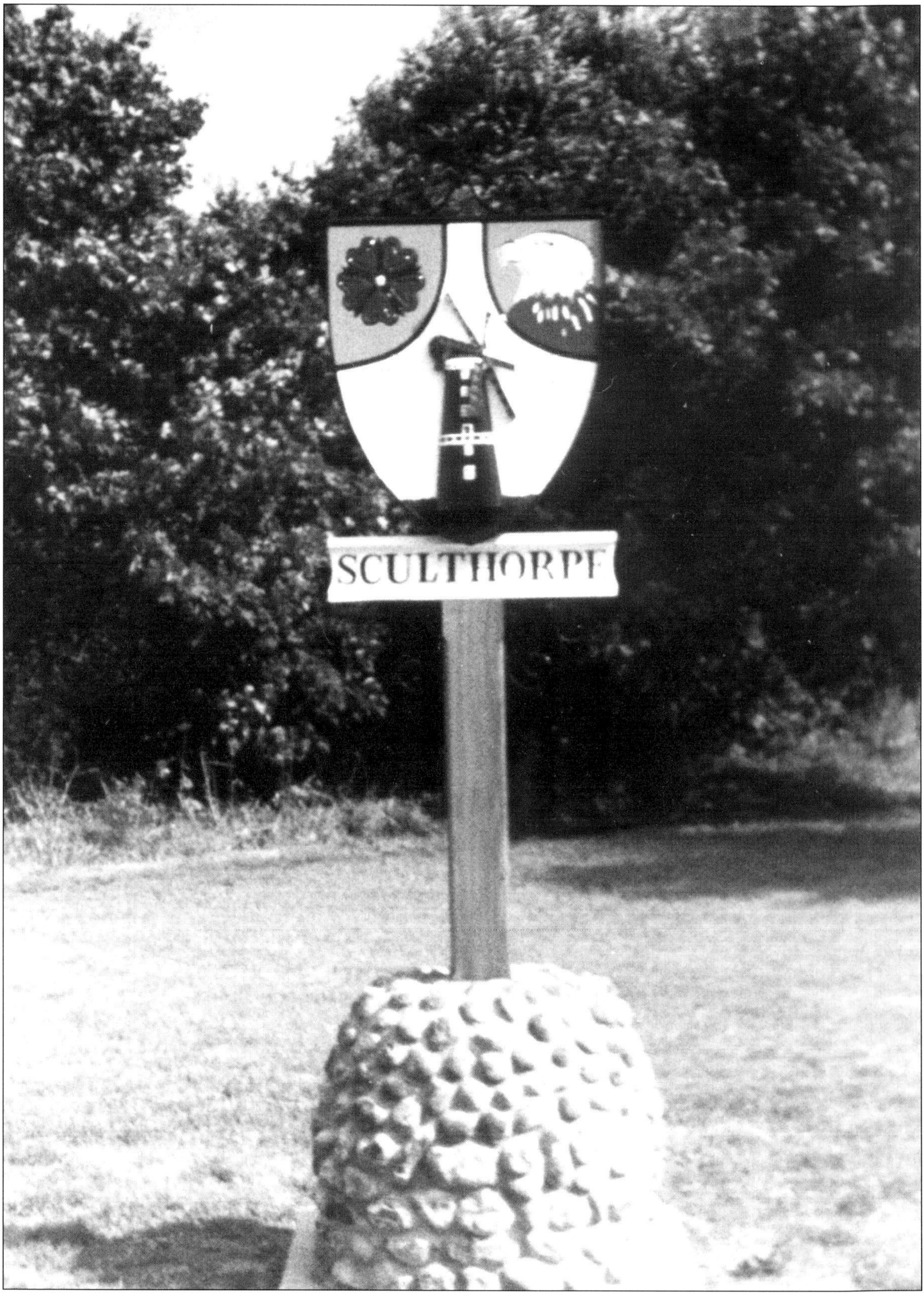

The village sign was unveiled by local schoolchildren in September 1994. Designed by Julie Pearce, a talented art student from Sculthorpe, the sign depicts the Knollys Rose, the Tower Windmill and an American Bald Eagle, symbolic of both the US Air Force based at RAF Sculthorpe during the last century and Eagle Iron Works, the agricultural foundry established by the Blackett family in 1862.

Goods at Sculthorpe in 1552 (Ref: The Public Record Office: E315/505, No.15) and for consulting the Trust Deed of Foundation of Sculthorpe National School (Ref: Close Roll: 1840, Part 155, No.3), the Coal Fund for the Poor of Sculthorpe (Ref: Close Roll: 1856, Part 45, No.6) and the Star Chamber Records (Ref: PRO STAC 2/15 CP/3204).
Sculthorpe Church of England Voluntary-Aided Primary School for permission to use quotes from the school log-book, dating from 1870.
Tattersalls Ltd of Newmarket for permission to use the portrait of Edmund Tattersall.
The Marquess Townshend for permission to use the portrait of George, 4th Viscount and 1st Marquess Townshend.
The York Archives for use of brief quotations from the Assembly Room Records, the Director's minute-book (Ref: M32:2 and M23:2) and the account ledger (M23:5).
Norfolk County Council Library and Information Service for permission to reproduce photographs.
The Coronation bookmark (1953) is reproduced by gracious permission of Her Majesty the Queen.

The author is especially indebted to the following for the inclusion of photographs and pictures:

Mrs Jean Allison
Mrs Vivien Asquith
Mrs Jean Benstead (the collection of the late Mr William Sewter)
Mr Kenneth Boast
Ursula Clifton Brown
Mrs Jean Edge
Mrs Evelyn Gibson
Mr John Harper
Mrs Joyce Harrison
Lady Harrod
Mr Bob Hood
Mrs Louise Hurst
Mrs Audrey Jordan
Colin Labouchere
John and Henry Labouchere
Mr Jack Land
Mr Richard Land (the collection of the late Mrs Eleanor Crane)
Mrs Joyce Lingwood
Mrs Doris Mitchell
Mrs Lavinia Monaco
Father Andrew Thomson
Mr and Mrs J. Tuck
Mrs Gwen Windeler
Miss Patricia Wright

Individual acknowledgements appear within the picture captions in the book.

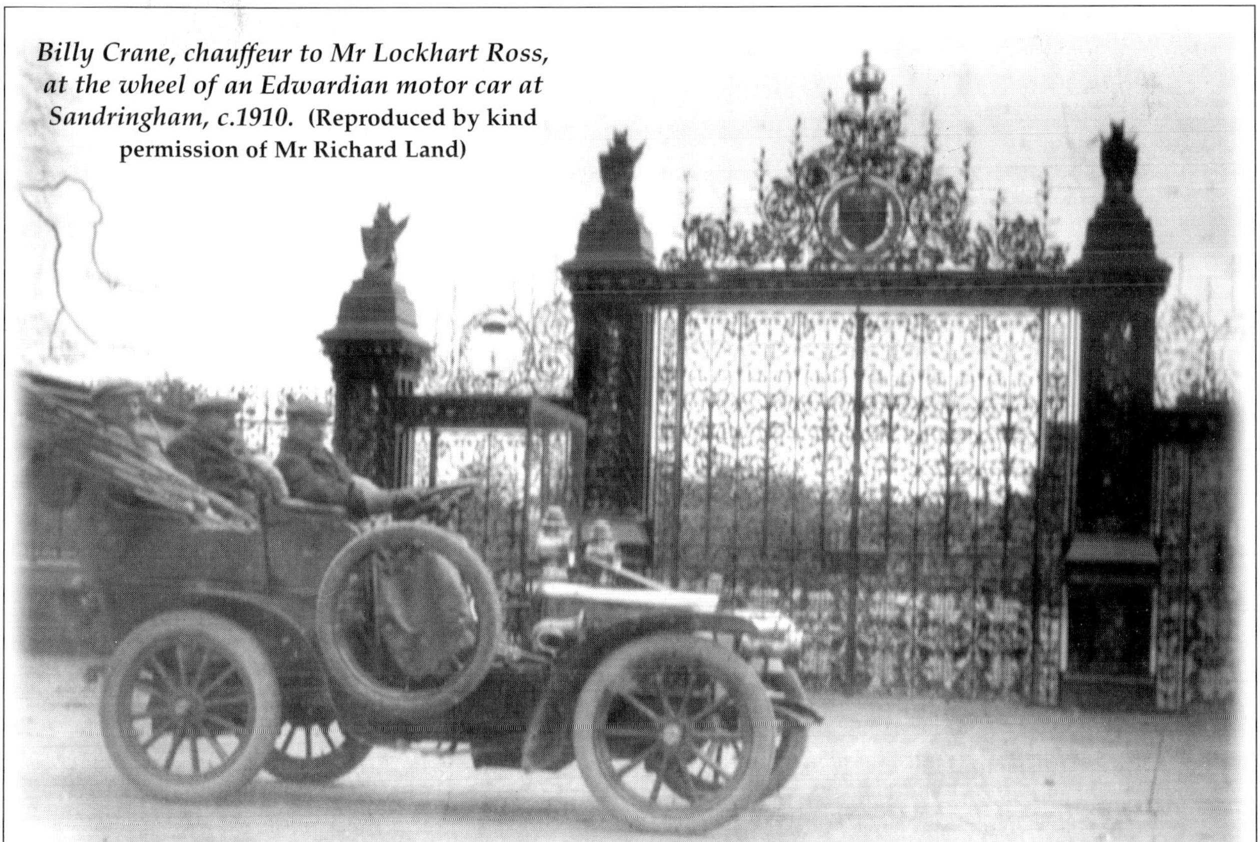

Billy Crane, chauffeur to Mr Lockhart Ross, at the wheel of an Edwardian motor car at Sandringham, c.1910. **(Reproduced by kind permission of Mr Richard Land)**

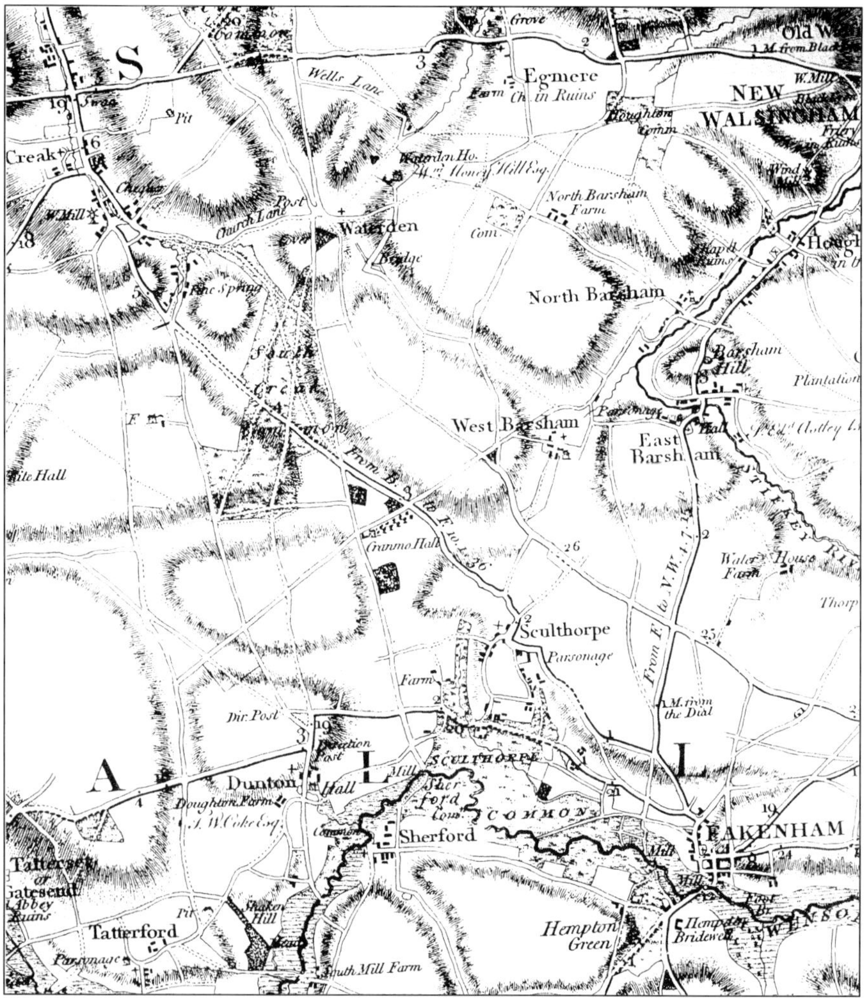

Left: *Sculthorpe as it appears on Faden's map of Norfolk, 1797. The vast expanse of Sculthorpe Common is clearly visible and flowing through this is the Old Soak Drain, or Main Drain, to the River Wensum. The Moor Plantation, Sculthorpe Water-mill, Grange Farm, the parsonage house and Cranmer Hall, with its Avenue and Old Square Wood by the Roman road, all feature on this map.* (Reproduced by kind permission of the Larks Press Ltd/the Norfolk Record Office)

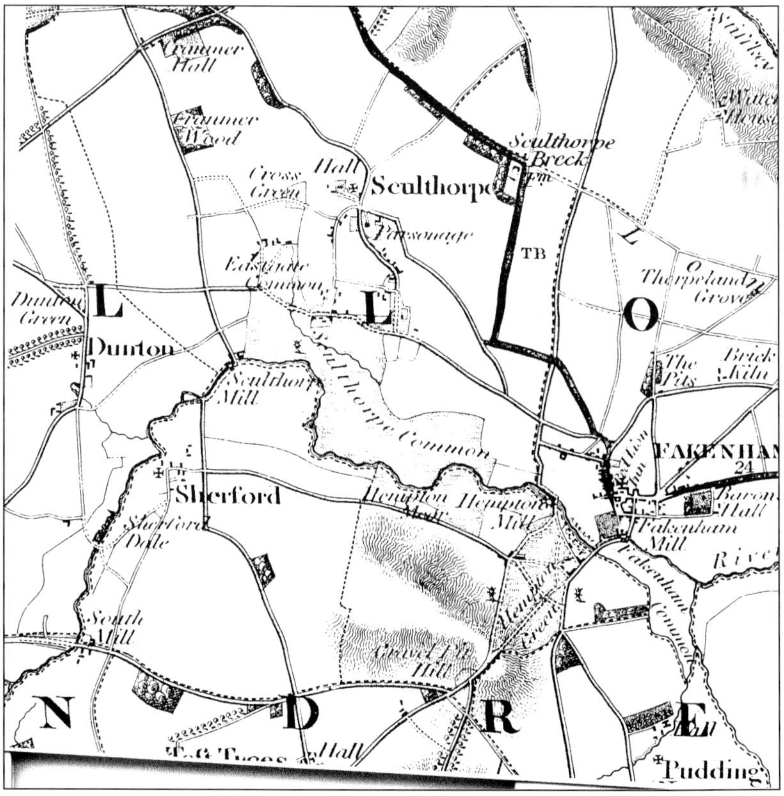

Right: *Sculthorpe as it appears on Bryant's map of Norfolk, 1826. Compare this to the earlier map by Faden* (above). *Sculthorpe Common, Eastgate Common and Cross Green, where a medieval stone cross once stood to mark the Walsingham Green Way, all appear on this map. The Old Soak Drain and Cranmer Wood (Old Square Wood) are also prominently marked. The original road to Creake was replaced by the 'New Road' in 1829. This map also shows Breck Farm (now Lodge Farm), which is reputedly the birthplace of Edmund Tattersall.* (Reproduced by kind permission of the Larks Press/ the Norfolk Record Office)

Chapter One

THE ORIGINS OF A NORFOLK VILLAGE

Archaeological discoveries in Sculthorpe have revealed much about the early history of the village. Perhaps the most spectacular find to date has been the middle- to late-Bronze-Age gold torc, dated c.1000BC, which was discovered by a farmer in a sugar-beet field in 1984. This superb piece of Bronze-Age jewellery was possibly a coiled bracelet or a decorative girdle which is on display, at the time of writing, in Norwich Castle Museum. Other finds in the vicinity of Sculthorpe have included five late-Bronze-Age socketed axes, discovered near Home Farm at Cranmer, and Bronze-Age pot-boiler mounds in Cranmer Park. Aerial photography has also revealed a circular mark in the fields near the perimeter fence of RAF Sculthorpe; was this the site of a Bronze-Age burial mound or a later Iron-Age earthwork enclosure?

There are several Roman remains in existence in Sculthorpe, including the well-known Roman road and the Romano-British smother-kiln, which are discussed in more detail in the chapter about Cranmer Hall *(see page 103)*. The ancient ford at Sculthorpe Mill has yielded vital evidence of three important river crossings on this lower stretch of the Roman

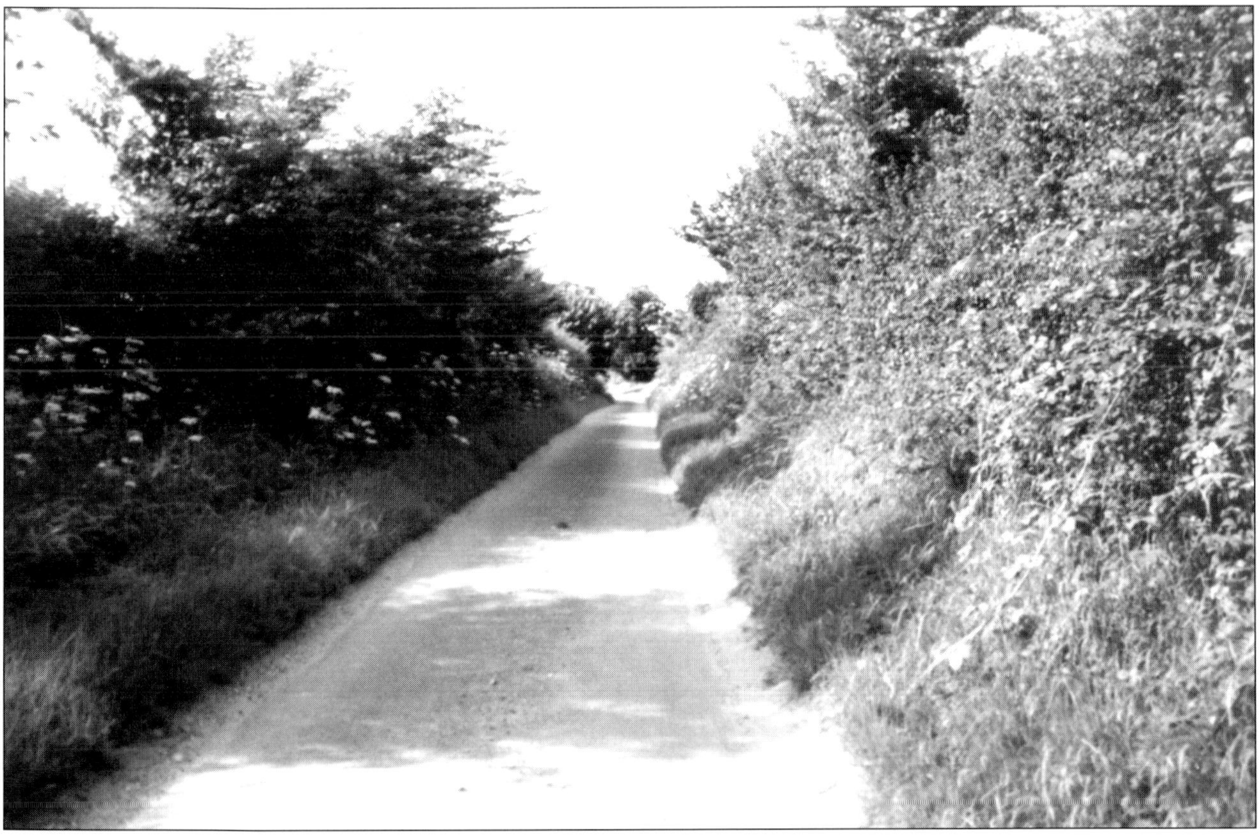

The Roman road, once called Greengate Way, near Sculthorpe Mill. Much of this road, which heads inland from the North Norfolk coast at Holkham, can still be traced. Magnus Magnusson believed it to be an important Roman military road dating from after the famous Boudicca Revolt of AD61.

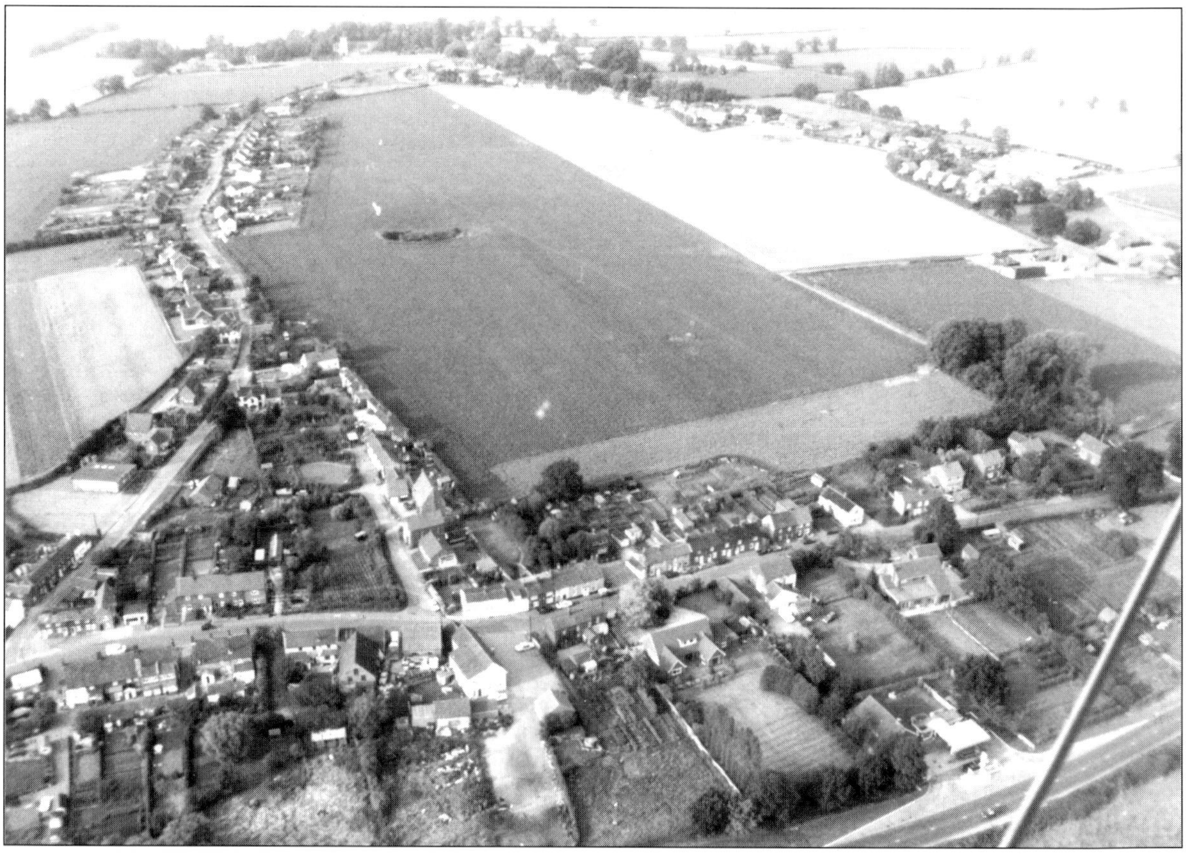

Sculthorpe from the air, 1984. Mill Field Pit perpetuates the memory of the six-sail Tower Windmill, which once dominated the skyline of the village. (Reproduced by kind permission of John and Henry Labouchere)

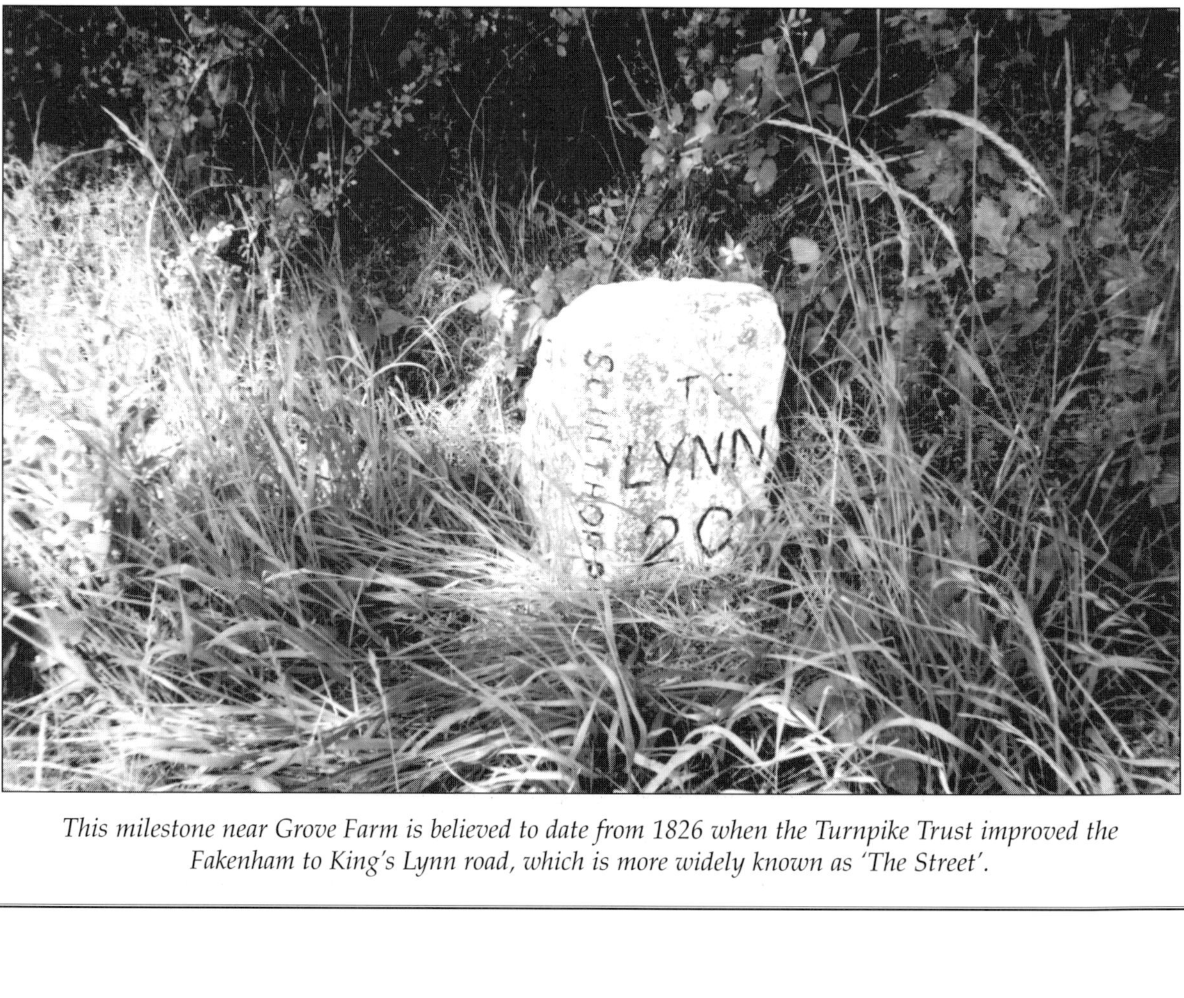

This milestone near Grove Farm is believed to date from 1826 when the Turnpike Trust improved the Fakenham to King's Lynn road, which is more widely known as 'The Street'.

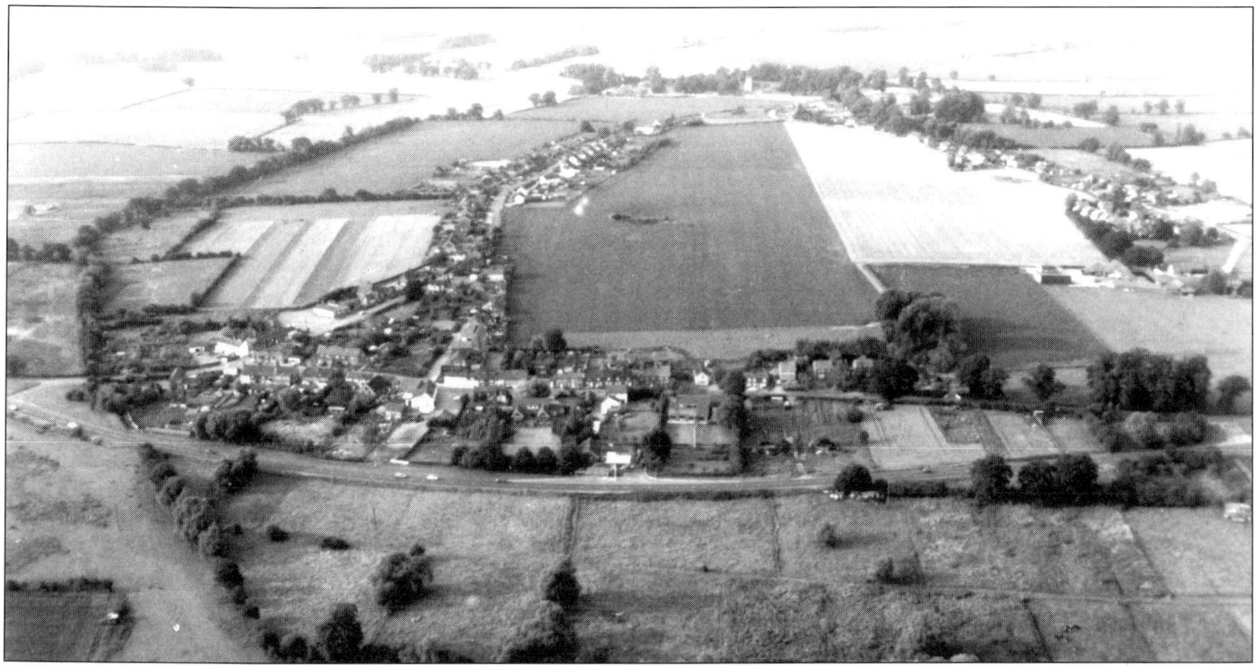

Sculthorpe from the air. The line of trees and hedgerows to the left of the picture shows the course of the Main Drain, or Old Soak Drain, which appears on all the old maps of the village. In the foreground is the 1968 bypass, which effectively separated the village from the moors, originally the Great Common. (Reproduced by kind permission of John and Henry Labouchere)

road. When the River Wensum was dredged during the autumn of 1954 a substantial causeway of flints was exposed on the north side of the river bank whilst on the south side a strip of hard chalk was discovered. Archaeologists have also located some large boulder flints in the ford which date from the first century AD when the road was an important *Via Militare* for Roman soldiers.

A number of Roman coins have been discovered in the village itself; these have included a *sestertius* from the reign of the Emperor Vespasian who founded the Flavian dynasty in AD69. The coin, inscribed *judaea capta*, was issued by Vespasian to commemorate the fall of Jerusalem and the destruction of Herod's Temple in AD70 by his son, the future Emperor Titus, 40 years after the Crucifixion of Christ. Another bronze Roman coin, dated c.AD350, is from the reign of the Emperor Constans who visited the *Coloniae Britannia* in AD343 and increased the defences of Hadrian's Wall against the Picts and the forts of the Saxon shore against Anglo-Saxon piracy.

The name Sculthorpe is derived from strong Scandinavian influences although the best authorities on place names never seem to quite agree on the real meaning! The *Concise Oxford Dictionary of English Place Names* states the combination of an Old Norse personal name 'Skuli' or 'Skule's thorp', roughly translated as 'the outlying farmstead or hamlet of a man called Skuli or Skule.' Certainly the popular spelling of the village name for much of the Middle Ages – in legal documents and on historic maps of Norfolk surveyed during the seventeenth and eighteenth centuries – is

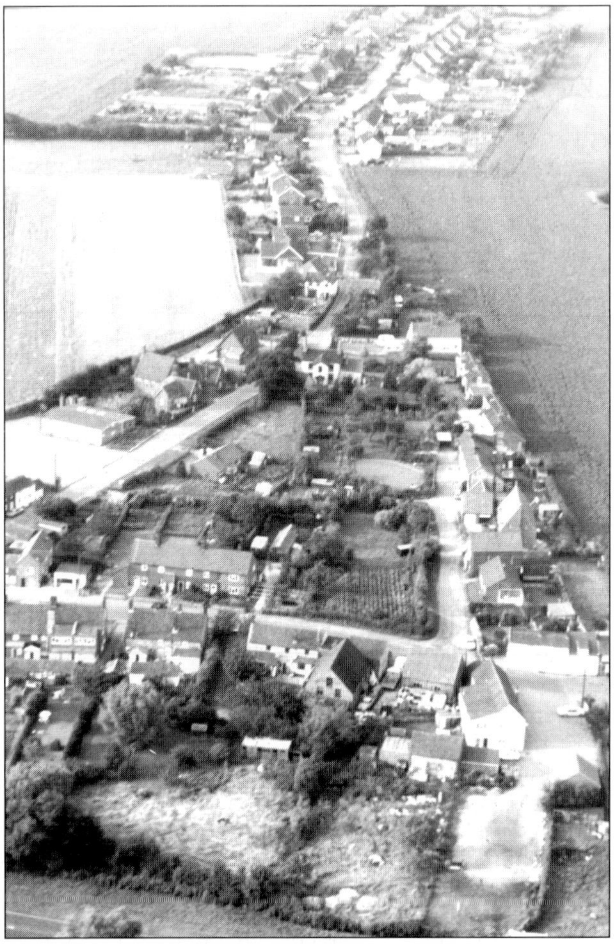

An aerial view of Sculthorpe showing The Street, Chapel Lane, Mill Field and Moor Lane. (Reproduced by kind permission of John and Henry Labouchere)

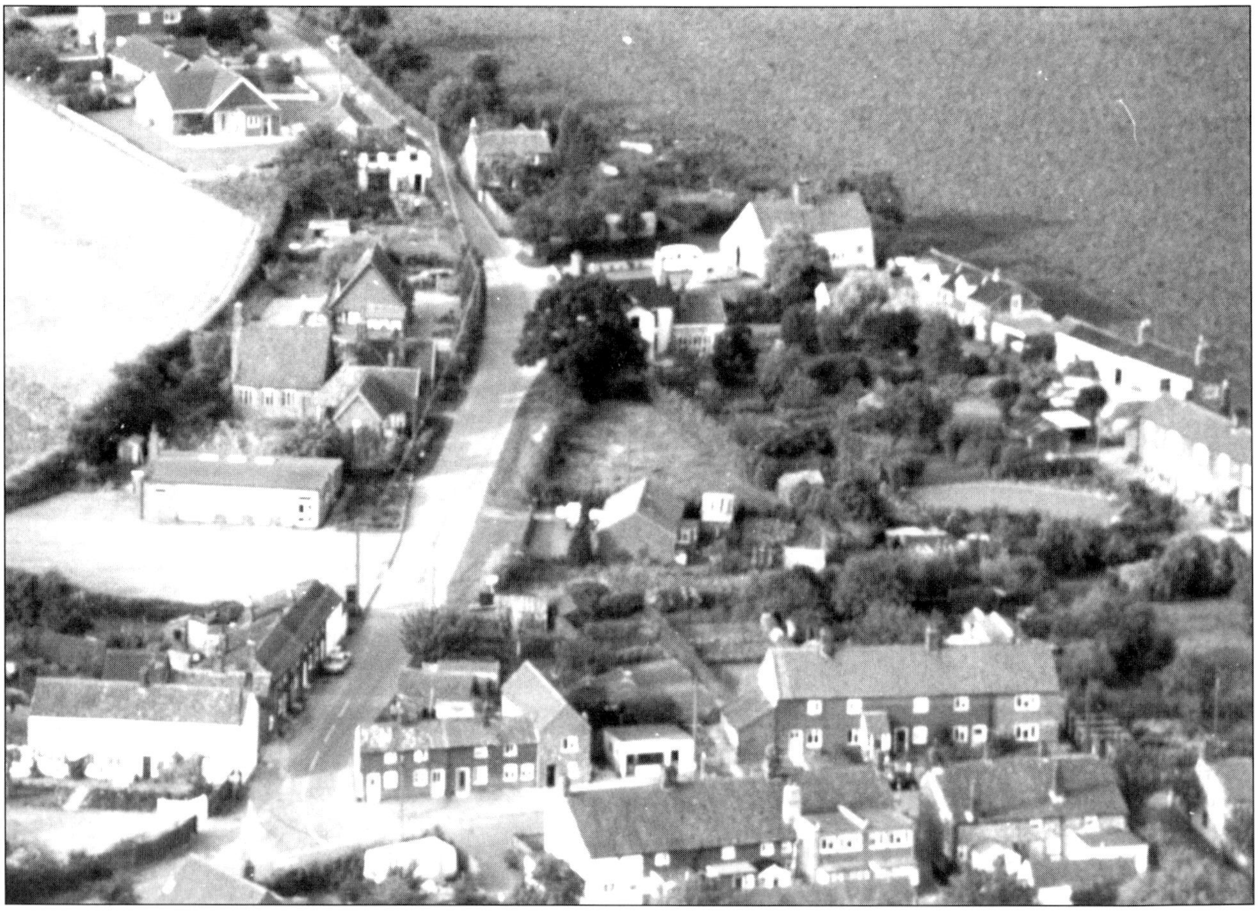

This aerial view of Sculthorpe shows part of Moor Lane and The Street. Also visible is the Olde Forge (1785), the Village Hall, built in 1966 on the site of the old parish pound, the Beckham Almshouses, rebuilt in 1859, and the lecture room, originally built as a church mission room and infants' school in 1865.
(Reproduced by kind permission of John and Henry Labouchere)

'Skulthorp', reflecting the Scandinavian personal name.

However, a number of historians, including the Revd Francis Blomefield in his eighteenth-century *History of Norfolk*, advocate the alternative theory of 'Sculatorpa'. This version of the place name appears in the Domesday Book (1086), 'scula' meaning a 'schoal' or 'narrow stream of water' which could relate to either the River Wensum itself or its tributary stream – the Old Soak Drain or Main Drain. This tributary flows through the south-western edge of the parish, under Rumbelow's Bridge and the 1968 bypass of the main A148 road, down to the River Wensum across the moors. In 2003 this water theory, which is also of Scandinavian origin and suggests a 'floating village', is the most popular in Sculthorpe. The water table has always been high in the village and flooding is a frequent problem, even in the parish churchyard which is on high land above the flood plain of the Wensum valley.

The present village originated following the Danish settlement of the region during the late-ninth century or early-tenth century AD. The early settlers followed the Great Heathen Army into East Anglia after AD865 and during that time Sculthorpe would doubtless have been a small but flourishing farming community drawing people with its plentiful supply of water. The numerous natural springs which can be found in the area might well have been regarded as sacred to religious customs. Ancient Viking lore involved belief in the god Mimir, guardian of the Fountain of Knowledge, and the watering of the roots of the magic ash tree, Yggdrasil. The people made offerings to their deities by casting jewellery into natural springs and streams. Several examples of Viking jewellery dating from the ninth and tenth centuries AD have been discovered in Sculthorpe, including brooches, a lead weight adorned with a gilded animal ornament and a superb tenth-century Viking buckle of Scandinavian origin. Additionally there is ample evidence of Old Norse words in Sculthorpe such as 'gata' or 'gate' for 'way' or 'road'. For example, Falgate Farm, Eastgate Common, Greengate Way, Churchgate, Creake Gate Way and Through Gate or Rudham Road Gate can all be found in the village and are indicative of the Scandinavian origins of this ancient Anglo-Danish community.

Chapter Two

SCULTHORPE WATER-MILL

The Little Domesday Book of 1086 cites the presence of three water-mills within the manor and lordship of 'Sculetorpa'. This property was held after 1066 by the Anglo-Danish thegn Toki from the fee of Frederic de Warenne. Following Frederic's treacherous murder in 1070 during the Fenland Rebellion of Hereward the Wake, the manor was inherited by Frederic's brother, William de Warenne, Earl of Surrey.

The mills, all water-driven in the period prior to the advent of windmills, were not only essential for grinding the corn produced on the manorial estate but also vitally important as fisheries. During that period the Catholic Church, which controlled the land, strictly prohibited the eating of meat on Fridays, the proscribed days of fasting and abstinence and during the penitential season of Lent. On such days fish was the sanctioned alternative to meat. The upper reaches of the River Wensum have long been home to an abundance of brown trout, roach and eels. These shoals of fish and eels could easily be trapped and caught in the mill stream to supply the demand.

William de Warenne and his Countess Gundrada had effectively introduced the Order of Cluniac Monks into England through the foundation of the

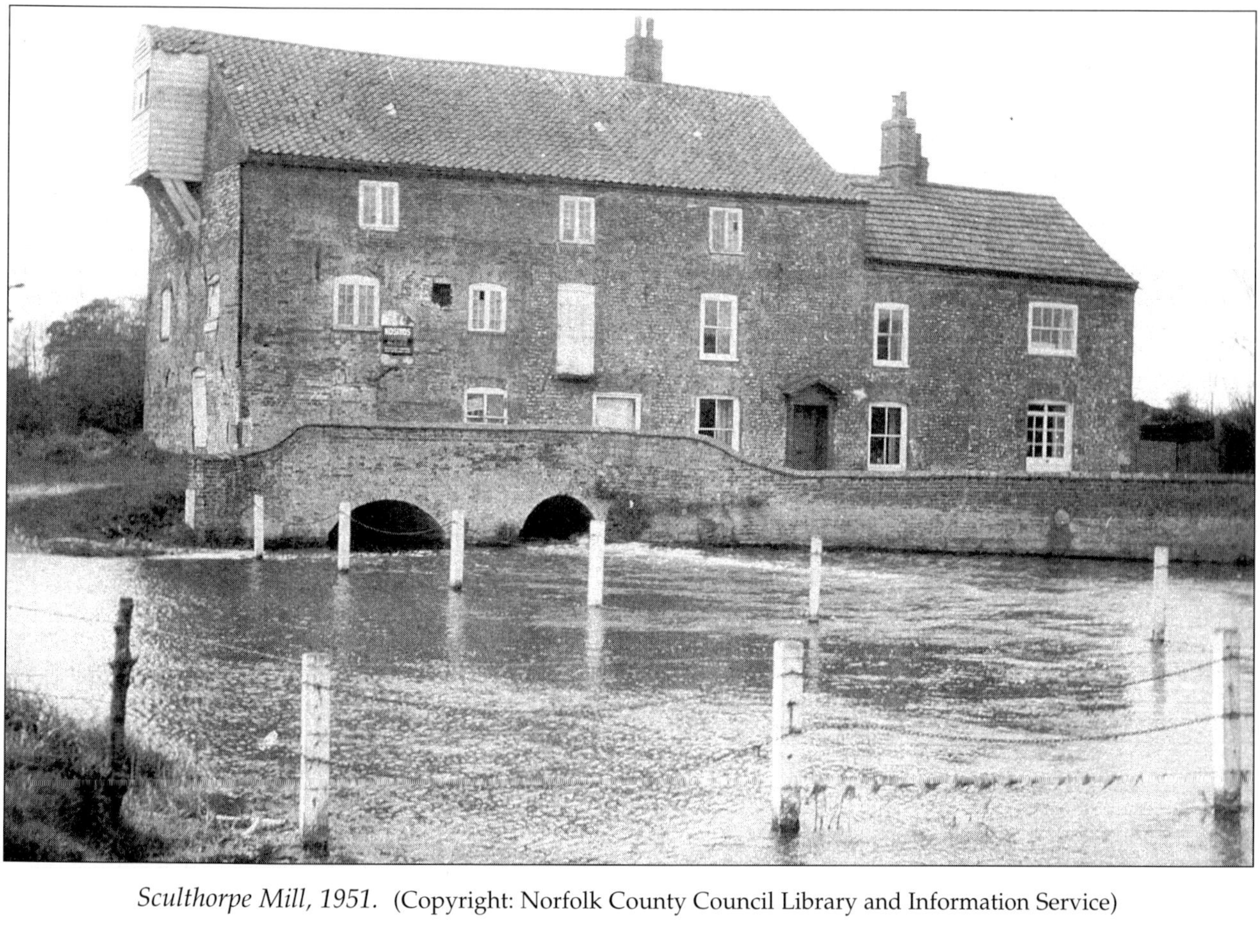

Sculthorpe Mill, 1951. (Copyright: Norfolk County Council Library and Information Service)

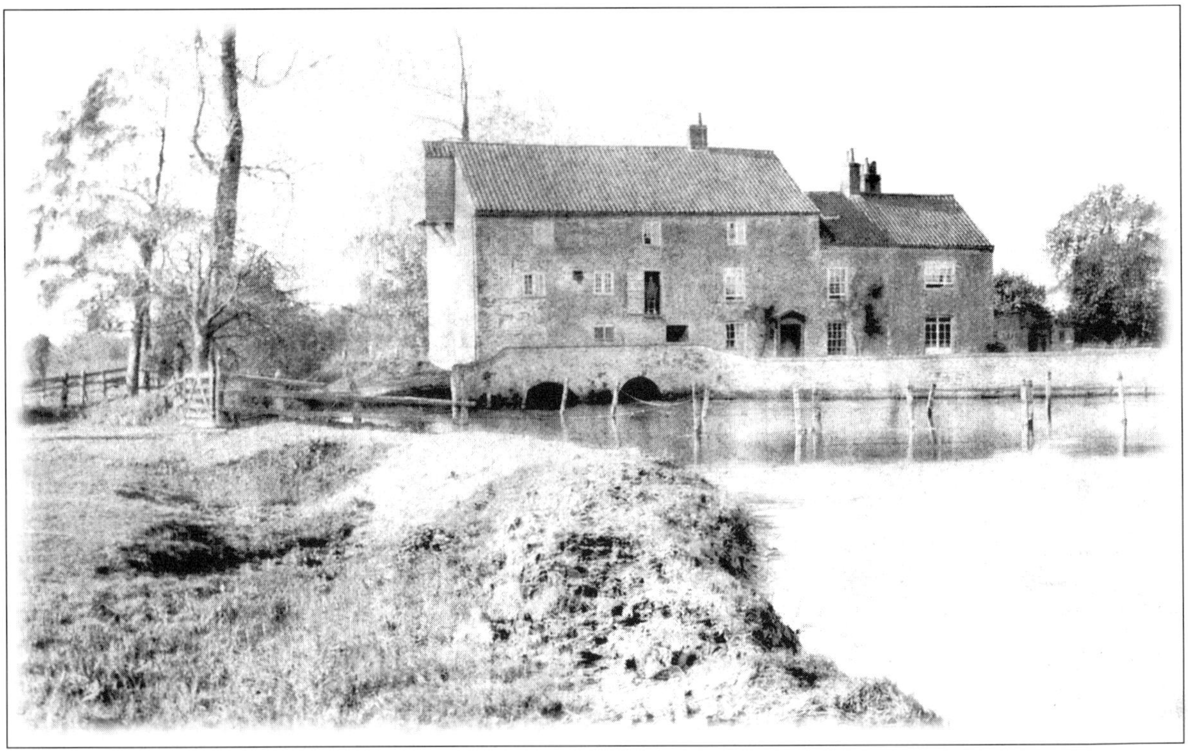

Sculthorpe Water-mill from a photograph dated c.1900. The figure standing in the doorway is thought to be Alfred Handcock the miller. Coes of Norwich digitally restored and enhanced this faded sepia photograph, which was given to the author by Mrs Janet Edge.

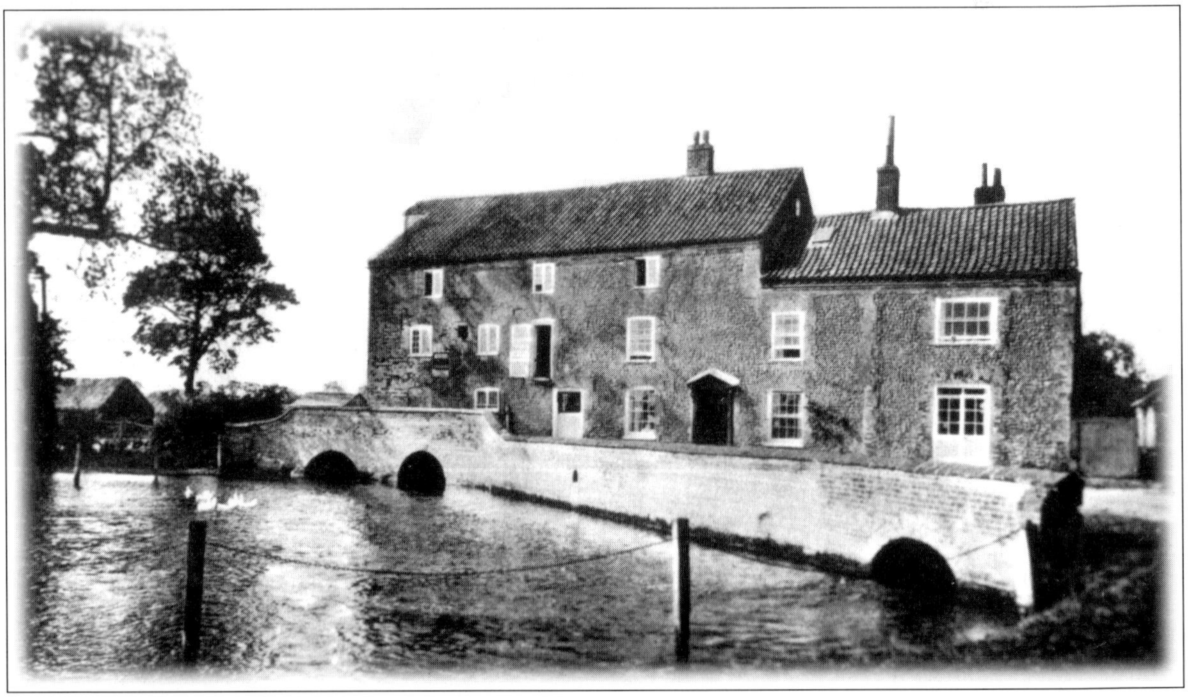

Sculthorpe Water-mill during the 1920s. This photograph is from the collection of the late Mr William Sewter.
(Reproduced by kind permission of Mrs Jean Benstead)

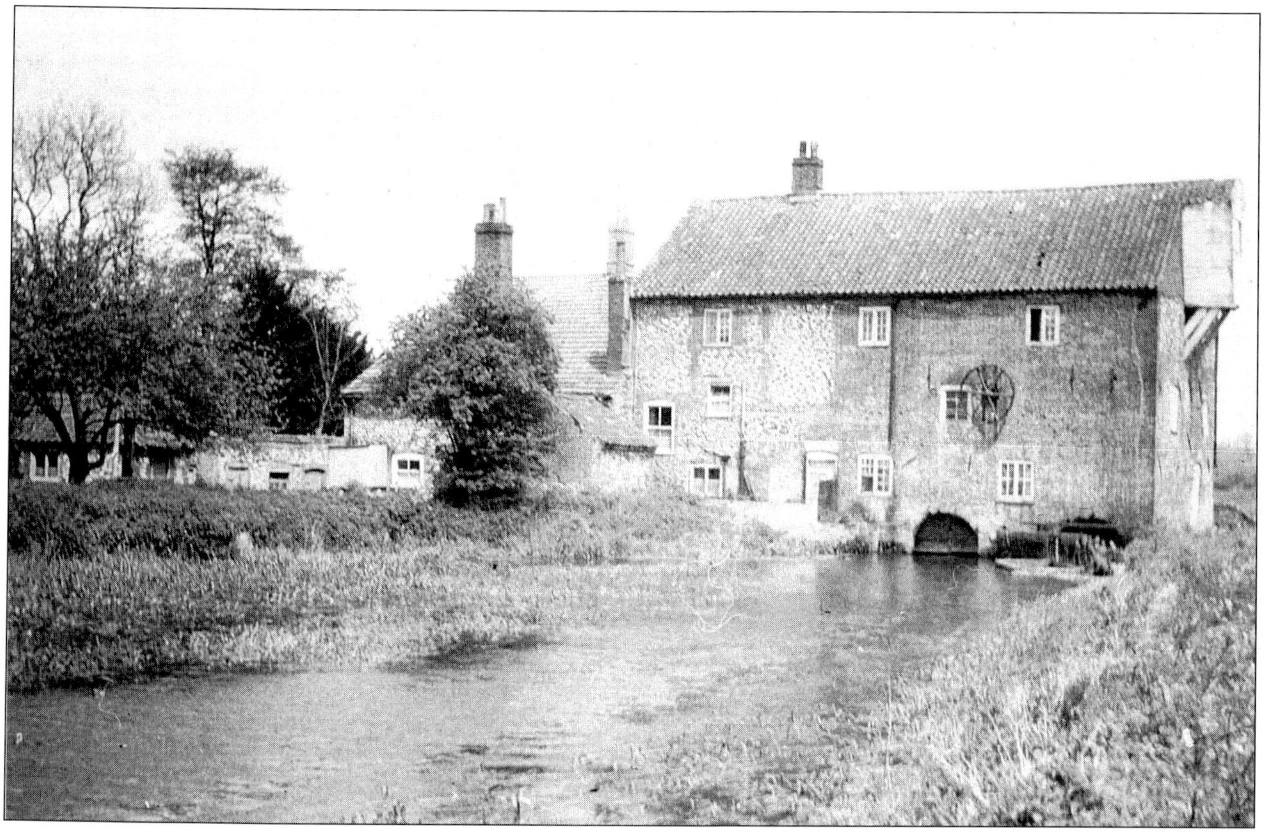

Sculthorpe Water-mill, 1951. This image shows the mill from the rear on the Shereford side of the River Wensum.
(Copyright: Norfolk County Council Library and Information Service)

Cluniac Priory of St Pancras in Lewes and, for much of the thirteenth century, there were frequent and heated disputes between the Cluniac monks from Lewes and Castleacre and successive parish priests of Sculthorpe about the monks holding tithes at farm within the lordship of Sculthorpe.

The Norfolk portion of the well-known Lewes Chartulary in the British Museum sheds light on the water-mills in Sculthorpe, which belonged to Richard Botte and the de Hasseneye or de Hasseneia family. There are records dating from 1225 describing land belonging to Hasseneia Mill, ten acres in total, and records of 'Lemerin' or 'Lennard the miller' and also of 'Simon the miller'.

In 1257 John Earl Warenne – renowned as the opponent of William Wallace at the Battle of Stirling Bridge in 1297 – held the manor here, including a water-mill and a fish-pond.

In 1375, upon the death of Sir John De Norwich, a water-mill in the 'Manor of Sculethorp' was valued at 26s.8d. Little more is recorded until 1478 when, in the Manor Court Rolls for 'Skullthorppe', held by the Norfolk Record Office, there is evidence of Valerianus Shragger and Johannes Barsham confirming in their deed of 29 acres 'the freedom of one water-mill with staith and fishpond pertaining to the same mill formerly once called Bottemylle.'

This medieval 'Bottemylle' was obviously associated with the thirteenth-century family of Richard Botte but it is the Hasseneia Mill which must now occupy our attention. By the eighteenth century it was the only one of these ancient water-mills to have survived, standing on a prominent strip of gravel and silt above an ancient ford. This ford was the former river crossing for the Romans on the upper reaches of the Wensum.

A number of papers stored in the attic and library of Raynham Hall have been unearthed by the present Marquess Townshend, dealing with the more recent history of the mill. These papers include the documentation of a lease, dated 28 September 1757, from Mary Chaplin of Tattersett to the Hon. George Townshend of Sculthorpe – the well-known General George Townshend, then resident as tenant at Cranmer Hall. Apparently much of the present building of flint, rubble and brick dressings dates from this time, incorporating the core of an earlier structure. A date-stone marked 1757 was, until recently, still visible on the rear wall, and the adjoining mill house, with its ancient beams and old panelling, probably dates from the same period. The rebuilding of the mill may have been as a direct result of the major alterations made to the course of the river here during the 1750s; the ancient cut can still be clearly identified in 2003 and is marked prominently on the Inclosure Award Map of 1830.

The Sculthorpe Field Book of 1766, held in the Norfolk Record Office, shows the mill as the

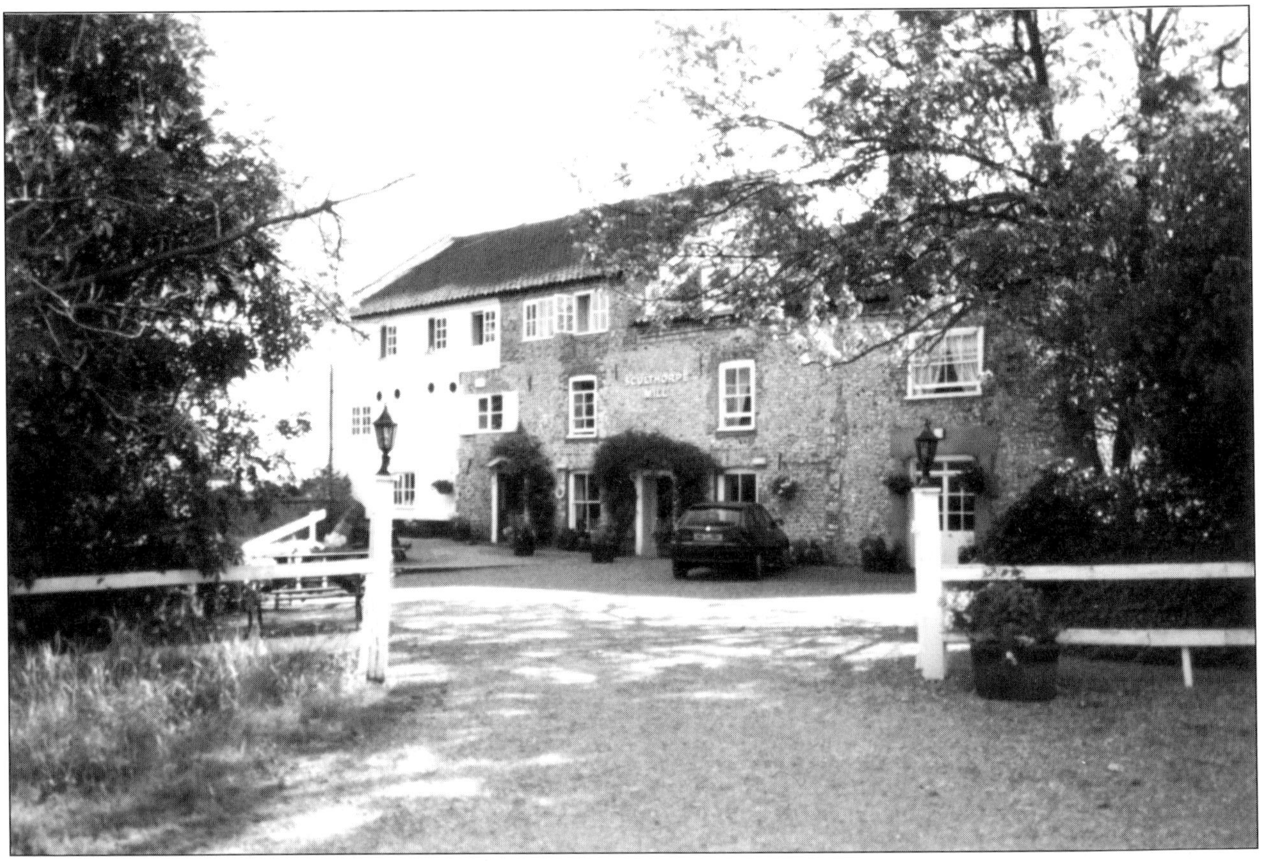

Sculthorpe Mill. In July 2002 a fire caused serious damage to the interior but the Norfolk Fire Service prevented the flames from spreading to the listed section of the building and guests were guided to safety. The owners at the time of writing, Greene King, undertook a magnificent restoration and the mill reopened for business in January 2003.

property of George Townshend 'next the Mill Dam... one Watermill called Hastney Mill otherwise Sculthorp Mill...'. The name Hastney is probably a derivation of the ancient family name of de Hasseneia, as is Hastneygate Green in the village, and the Sculthorpe Field Book describes the nearby surroundings in some detail – the mill pool, the mill dam or causeway, the mill moor and the adjacent 'small pightle' or enclosure of land. It also gives us the name of the resident miller, Osman Lowder. Osman Lowder's gravestone can be found in Sculthorpe churchyard – he died on 21 April 1771, aged 74 years, and is buried with his wife Elizabeth. The charming inscription on his gravestone reads:

Weep not for me my children dear
I am not dead but do rest here.
My debt is paid
My grave you see
Wait but awhile
You will follow me.

Arthur Young, the celebrated general secretary of the Board of Agriculture, mentions Sculthorpe Mill in his *General View of the Agriculture of the County of Norfolk*, which was published in 1804 at a time when land improvements, particularly drainage, were increasingly being regarded as an important responsibility of the landowner. He writes:

In going from Waterden to Rainham, passed by Sculthorpe Mill, and there enter a region that must make a farmer's heart ache. Of the nuisances that a country can be plagued with, certainly water-mills class very high in the black catalogue: for the sake of this beggarly mill, which apparently cannot be worth more than from £20 to £30 a year, here is a noble tract, from a furlong to a mile wide, of what, ought to be rich meadow, poisoned with water, and producing rushes, flags, sedge, and all sorts of aquatic rubbish.

Who would not suppose the two sides of the river belonging to little proprietors, as beggarly as the mill, who could meet over their tankard to wrangle, but never agree? No such matter.

Marquis Townshend and Mr Coke on the other. It would not be amiss to couple the two stewards of the estates up to the chin in one of these overflowing dykes, till they settled the matter, for the benefit of the public.

Obviously such scathing criticism soon reached the ears of both Lord Townshend and Coke of Norfolk with whom Young was acquainted. To modern ears the description of 'rushes, flags, sedge, and all sorts of aquatic rubbish' confirms why this stretch of the

Wensum valley has always been such an important wetland habitat for the rarer species of wildlife.

During the nineteenth and early-twentieth centuries the mill remained the property of the Townshend family and was thus a part of the Raynham estate. It proved to be a flourishing concern, grinding corn for the tenant farmers and smallholders on the neighbouring Cranmer Hall estate and selling flour to the village bakeries. According to the Inclosure Award of 1829 the corn miller was William Santy, who was succeeded by Joseph Fyson, miller, maltster and shopkeeper, who remained until the late 1860s. By 1888 William Handcock was the miller.

Tragedy struck both in the summer of 1903 when William's 15-year-old son, Alfred Handcock, was caught and crushed to death in the water-wheel and, two years later, in 1905, when (whilst Philip Goulder was based at the mill as miller, seed and artificial manure agent) young Nellie Goulder drowned. The popular village pastime of swimming in the river and the mill-pool declined from this period.

After 1905 Richard Harris of Grange Farm, Sculthorpe, hired the lease on the mill but it was his miller, George Gostling Gray, through his marriage to Caroline Fairbairn, who eventually acquired the money from the Fairbairn family to buy it from the Townshends of Raynham in 1923. Following the death of her husband in 1934 Mrs Caroline Gray continued the business and is remembered by many in the village with great affection.

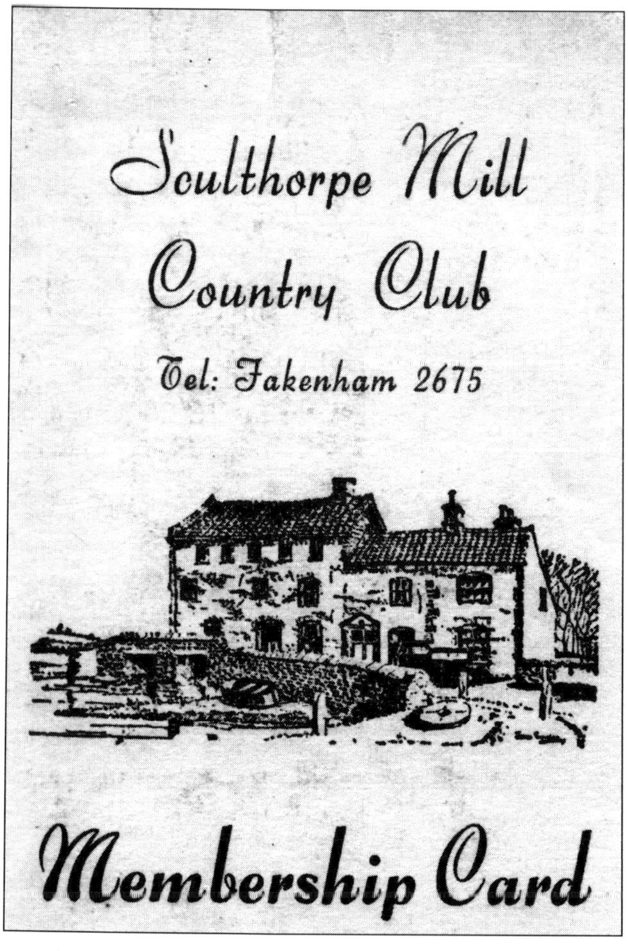

A membership card for Sculthorpe Mill Country Club dating from the 1970s.

The picturesque nature of Gray's Mill, with its ancient ford and eighteenth-century bridge over the flow of the mill-stream, made it a favourite subject for artists and brownie-box photographers. In 1938 Claude Messent sketched the mill for inclusion in his book *Old Norfolk Water Mills*.

Gray's Mill finally ceased operating as a flour mill in 1946 and the old water-wheel and interior machinery were removed. The water rights on this particular stretch of the Wensum were purchased by the former East Suffolk and Norfolk River Board. In 1963 the mill and its adjoining mill house, cottage and pightle of nine acres was put up for sale by public auction at Fakenham Corn Hall and purchased by William Collins. The partially derelict building underwent a thorough and extensive conversion into the extremely successful Sculthorpe Mill Hotel and Country Club, which opened for the first time in 1965. Most of the interior panelling and ancient beams from the eighteenth century had fortunately survived and were tastefully adapted in the conversion, glass panels being inserted in the floor of the old wheel room, allowing guests to observe the flow of the mill-race.

In 1969 William Collins sold the Mill Hotel and Country Club to Ken and Jean Parrish who successfully maintained the original charm and character of the place whilst expanding on its enormous popularity as a country venue. There were dangers too – the River Wensum frequently burst its banks and affected areas beyond its flood plain, and there were also bad periods of flooding in November 1974 and January 1978 when livestock had to be rescued by boat from the surrounding fen meadows.

It was a sad day when Ken and Jean Parrish finally retired in 1985 – they had brought much fun and laughter to the mill and had ensured its continued popularity in the local area.

No longer a country club, the mill has continued as a very fashionable licensed restaurant and hotel, popular for conferences, weddings and social receptions. The more recent refurbishment by successive owners including Thornham Lifeboats and Old English Inns have seen the development of a charming riverside garden.

In July 2002 the interior of Sculthorpe Mill was severely damaged by fire and much of the first-floor restaurant and ground-floor bar were ruined. Eighteenth-century beams and panelling dating from its heyday as a working water-mill were left blackened and badly charred.

At the time of writing the building is undergoing extensive restoration in an heroic bid to return it to its former glory.

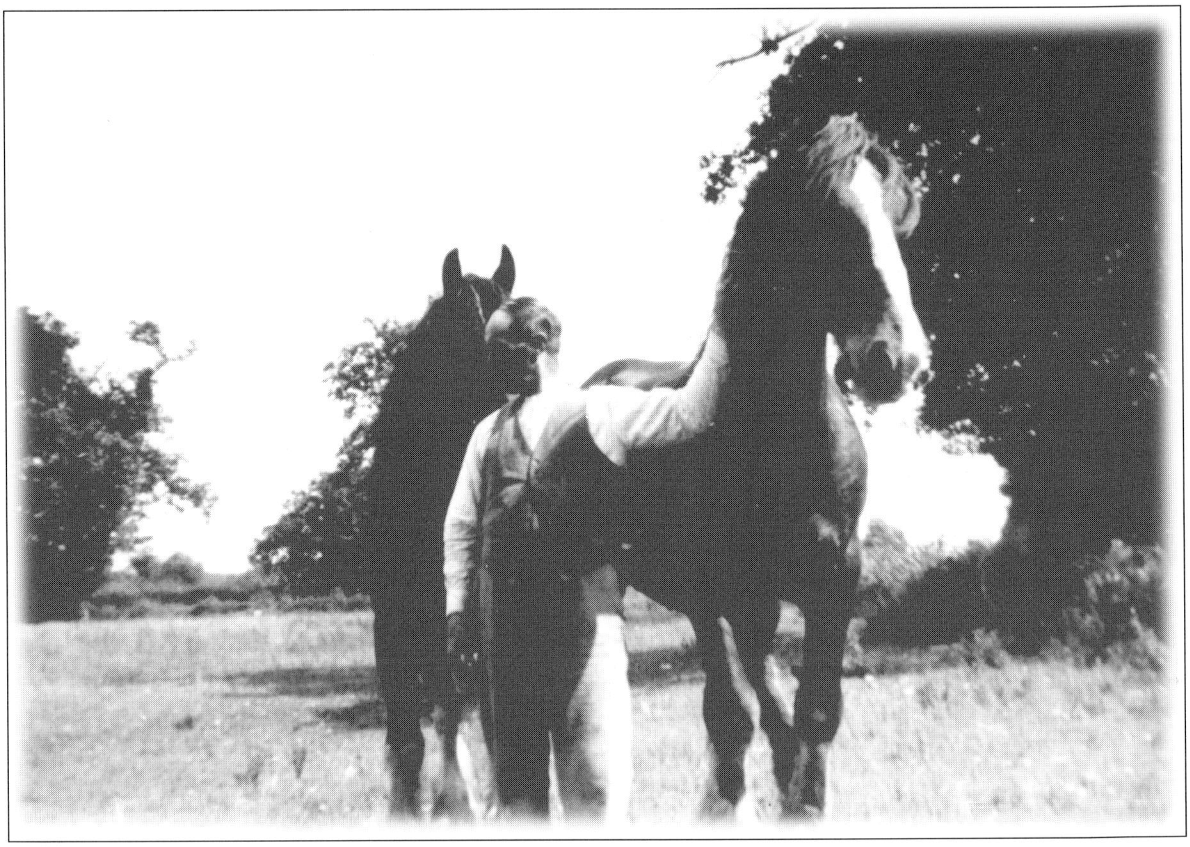

Fred Lingwood at Haydikes on the Glebe during the 1920s.

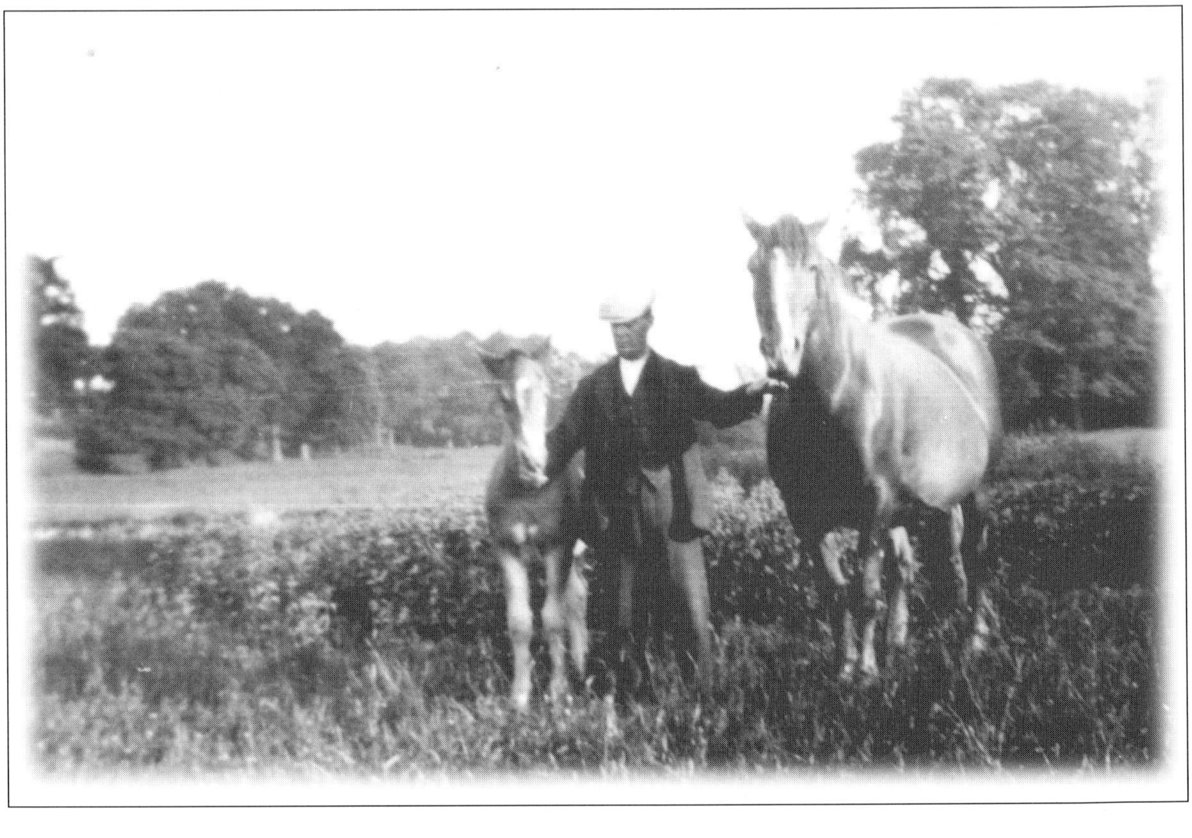

Fred Lingwood with some of his farm horses at Haydikes near the Old Rectory during the 1920s.

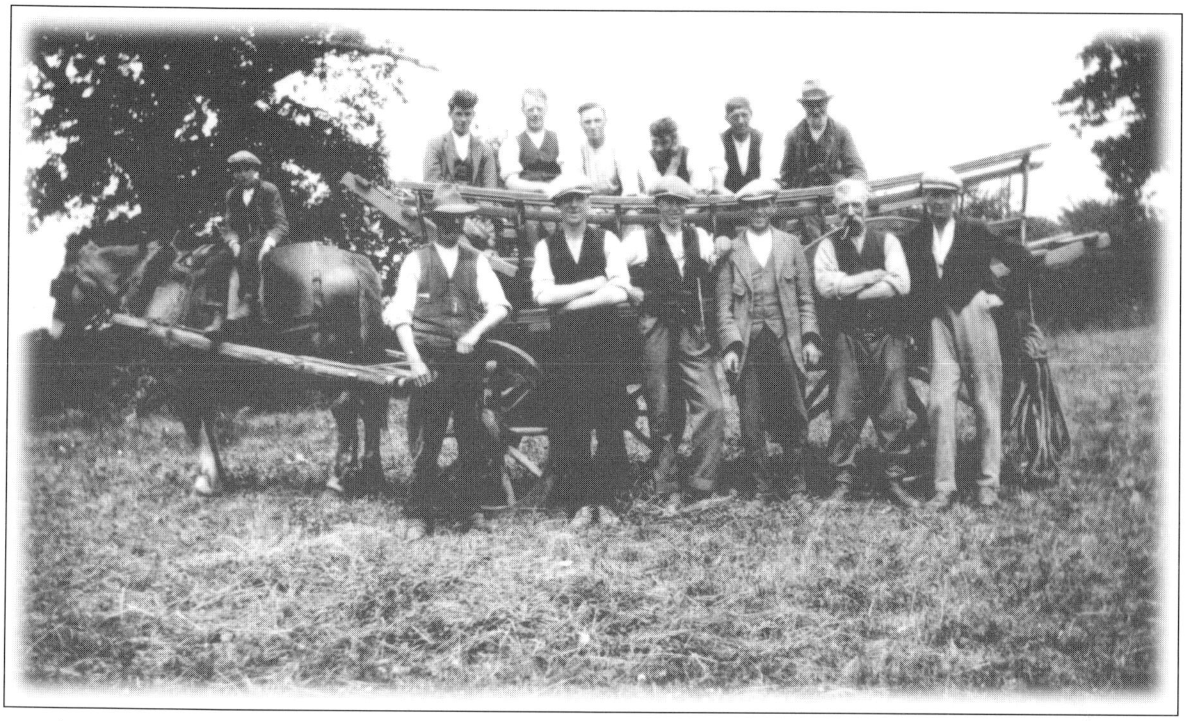

This photograph captures members of the Lingwood family with friends from the village on a hay cart on Haydikes off Barsham Road (John Lingwood's Lane), late 1920s. John Lingwood's smallholding is still remembered today. On the cart, first from the right: *John Lingwood with his son Jack beside him;* first from the left: *Jack's eldest son, Albert;* standing, first from the left: *Bob Lingwood (John's son) who was 'captain of the tower' for Sculthorpe's bell-ringers;* second and third from the right: *Louis Owen and Fred Lingwood. The little boy sitting on the cart-horse is young Arthur Lingwood, Bob's eldest son.*

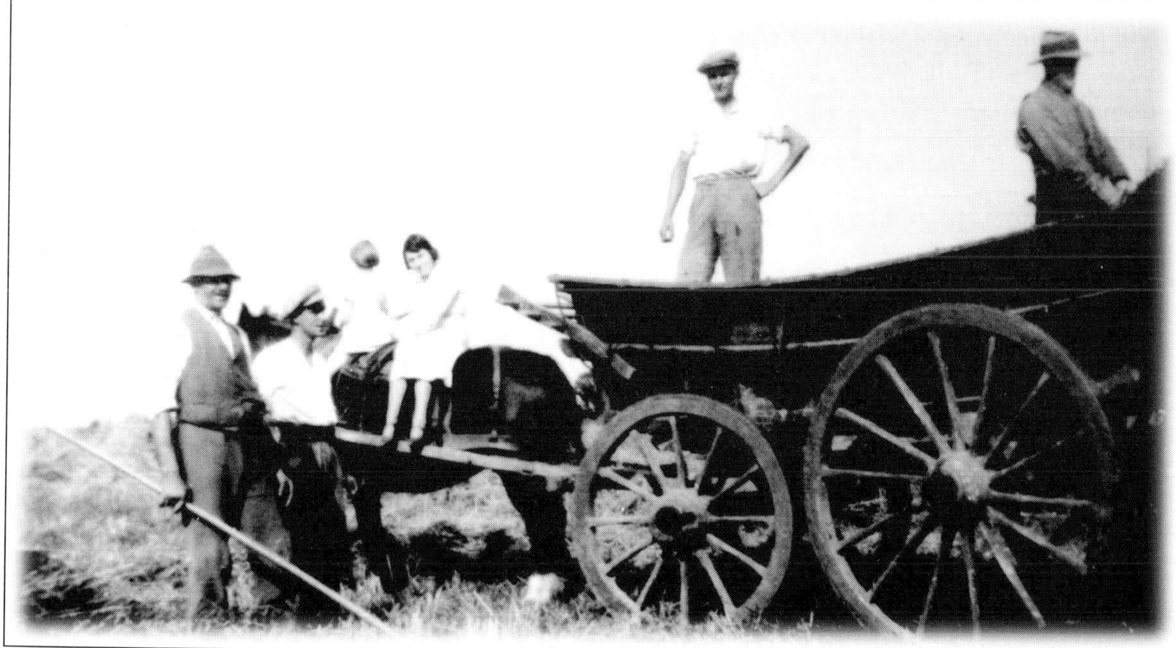

Harvest time in Moor Lane, Sculthorpe, late 1920s. Standing with his pitchfork obscuring the head of the horse is Mr George Howes, a Primitive Methodist lay preacher and a great friend of Sir George Edwards. The young lady sitting on the horse is Violet Lingwood, Fred Lingwood's eldest daughter. The two men on the farm cart are Dick Yallop and 'Tu'penny' Howell. Fred Lingwood had a smallholding of 40 acres in Moor Lane and a small dairy at Guywelles Cottages on Bird's Hill which moved to his new home in 1920 at No.1 Council Houses (later No.60 Moor Lane).

During the First World War Miss Mary Alcock of Sculthorpe was the oldest member of the Women's Land Army in Norfolk. This photograph, dated c.1915, shows Miss Alcock topping mangolds in a field at Mr Thistleton-Smith's farm in neighbouring West Barsham.
(Reproduced by kind permission of the Norfolk Rural Life Museum at Gressenhall)

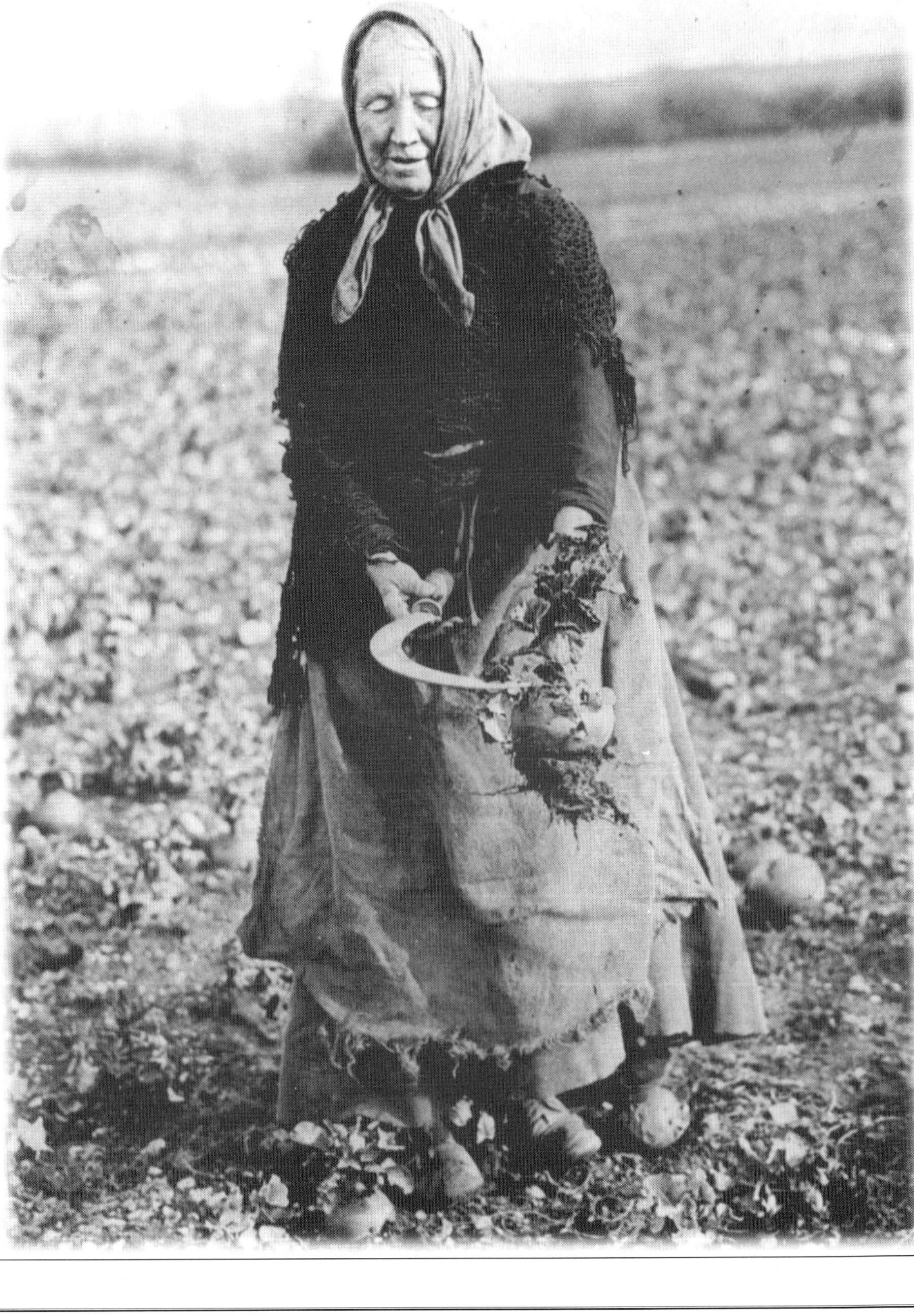

FARMING IN SCULTHORPE

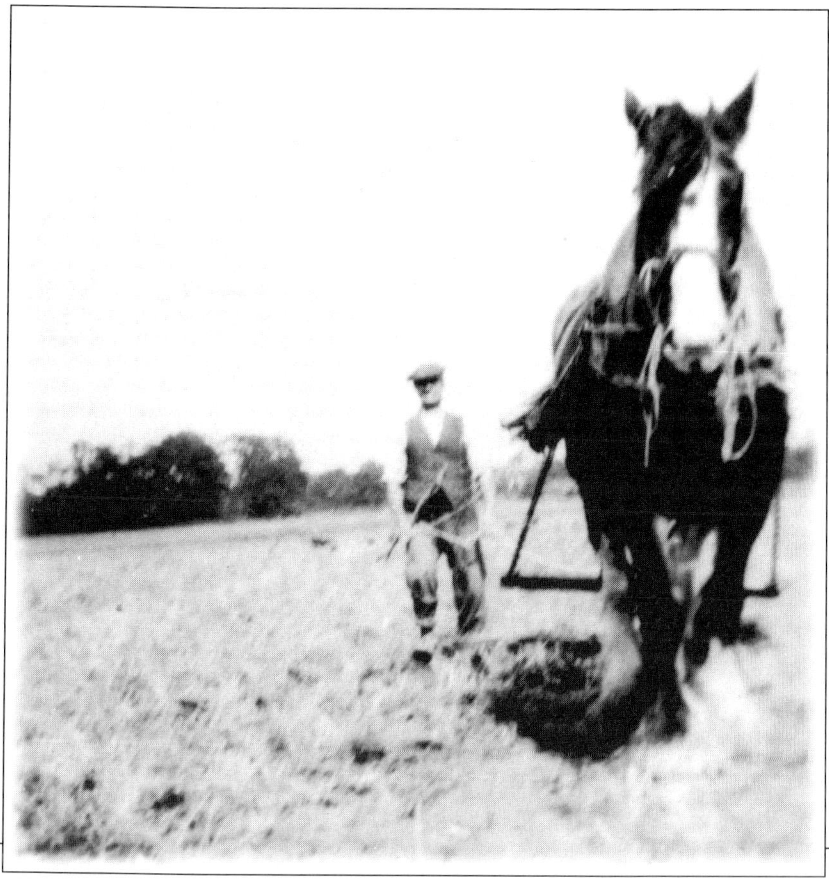

Left: *Fred Lingwood with Rosie the horse, Moor Lane, Sculthorpe, 1 September, 1928.*

Below: *Harvest time at Sculthorpe Lodge Farm, 1966. Donny Lake is standing to the right of the cart-horse.* (Reproduced by kind permission of the *Eastern Daily Press*, Archant Norfolk Ltd)

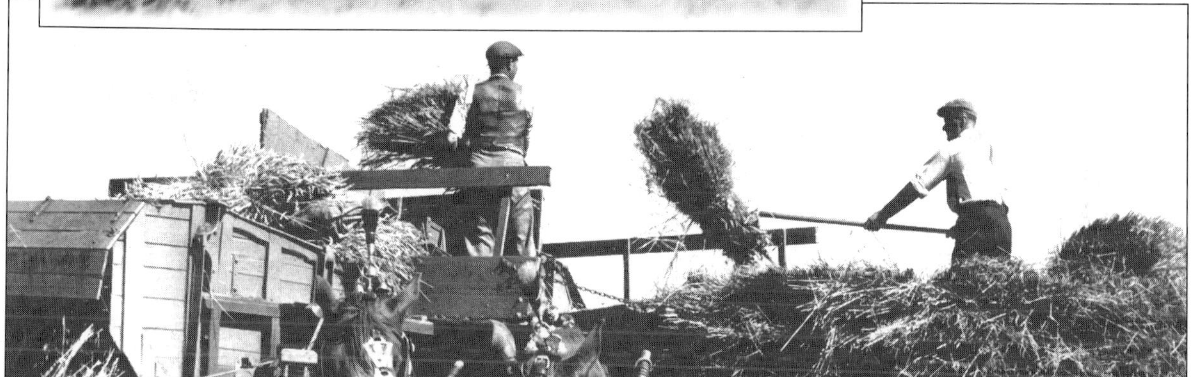

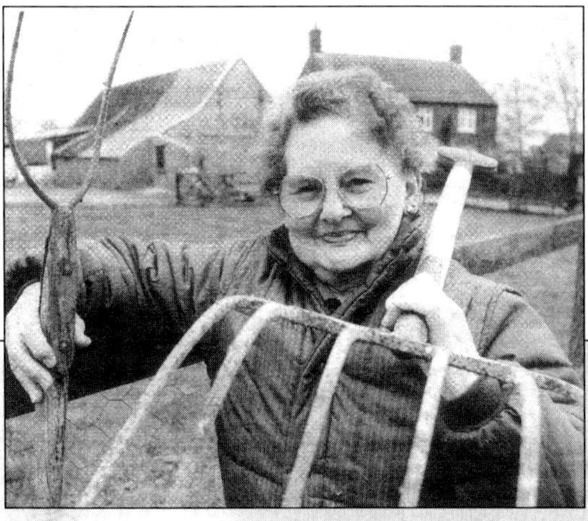

Left: *Mrs Jean Allison outside Glebe Farm in Creake Road where she first came to live with her parents, Horace and Mabel Boyce, and her brother Derrick in 1940. Jean vividly recalls hand-milking the cows and undertaking the milk round in Sculthorpe and the neighbouring hamlets of Shereford and Dunton-cum-Doughton.* (Reproduced by kind permission of the *Lynn News*)

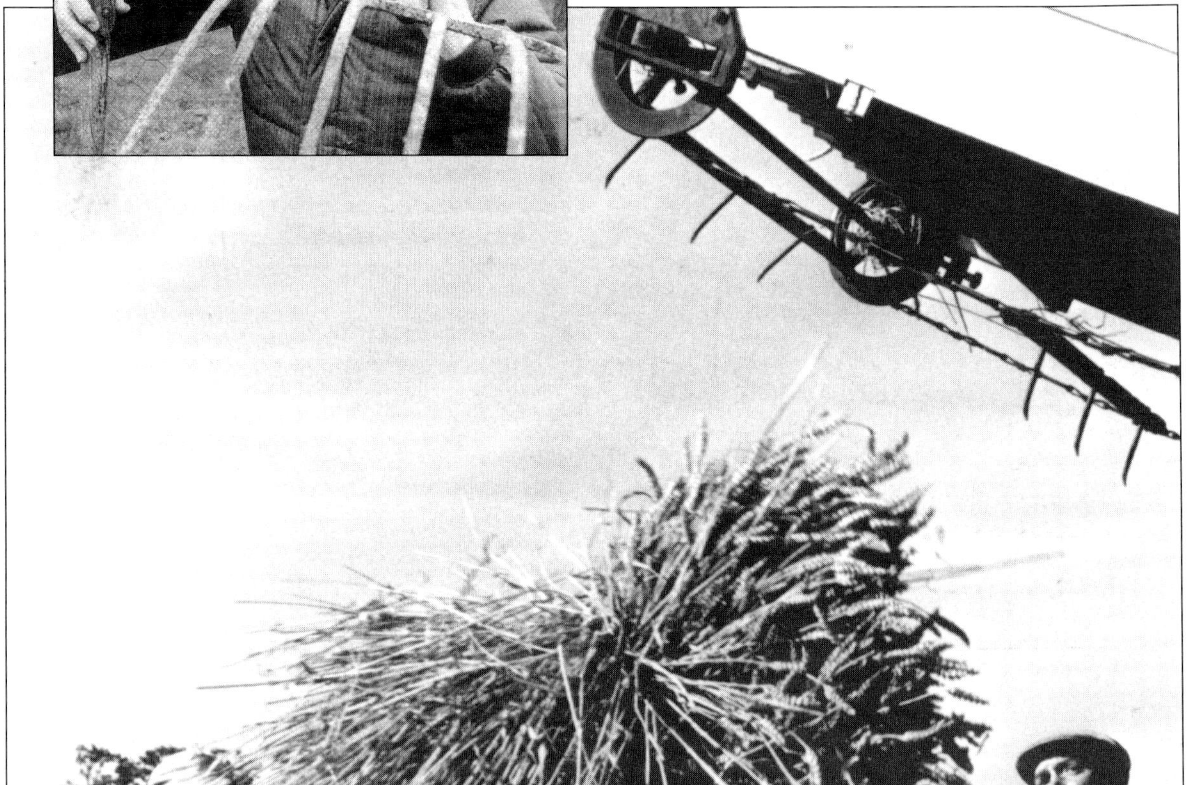

Harvest time at Grange Farm, Sculthorpe, near the Roman road, c.1965. On the right is Mr Jack Framlingham. (Reproduced by kind permission of the Norfolk Rural Life Museum at Gressenhall)

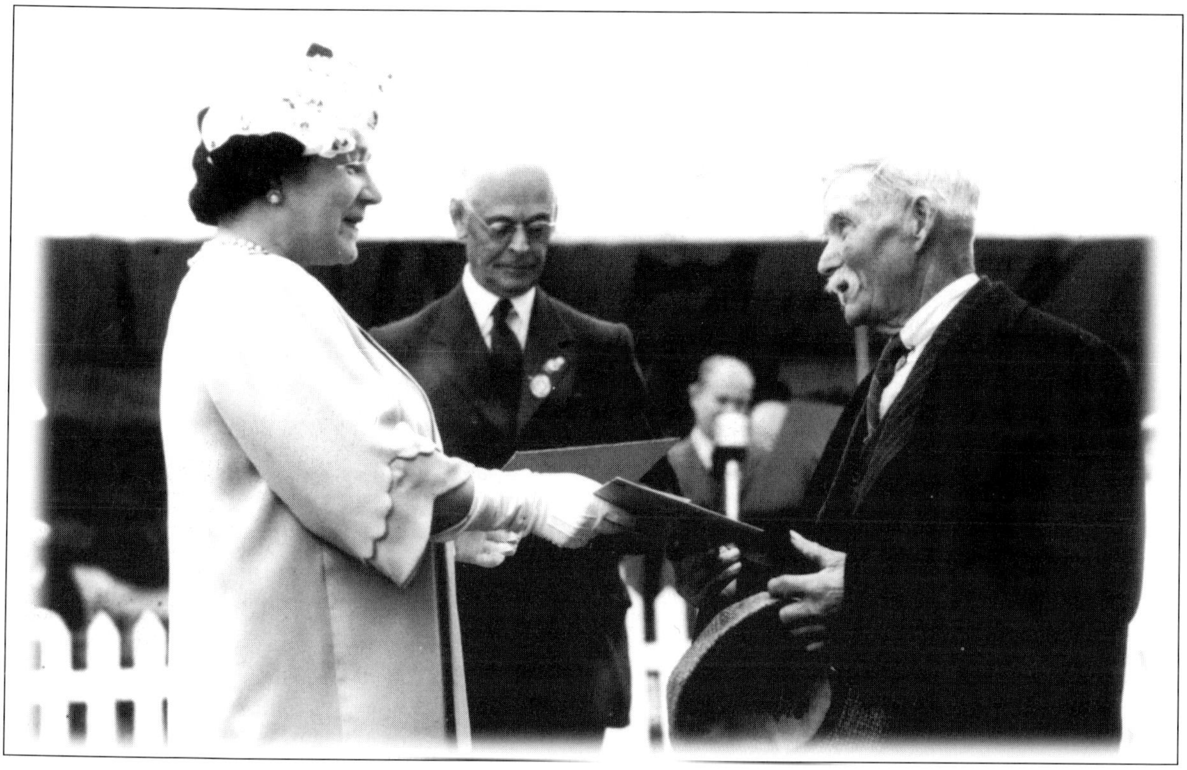

The Royal Norfolk Show, Anmer, June 1950. Her Majesty Queen Elizabeth (later the Queen Mother) presents Jimmy Wicks with a certificate to mark 50 years' loyal service at Grange Farm, Sculthorpe. Jimmy had first worked on the farm as a young shepherd at the end of Queen Victoria's reign. He was one of the great village characters and is still remembered with affection by many. (Reproduced by kind permission of the *Lynn News*)

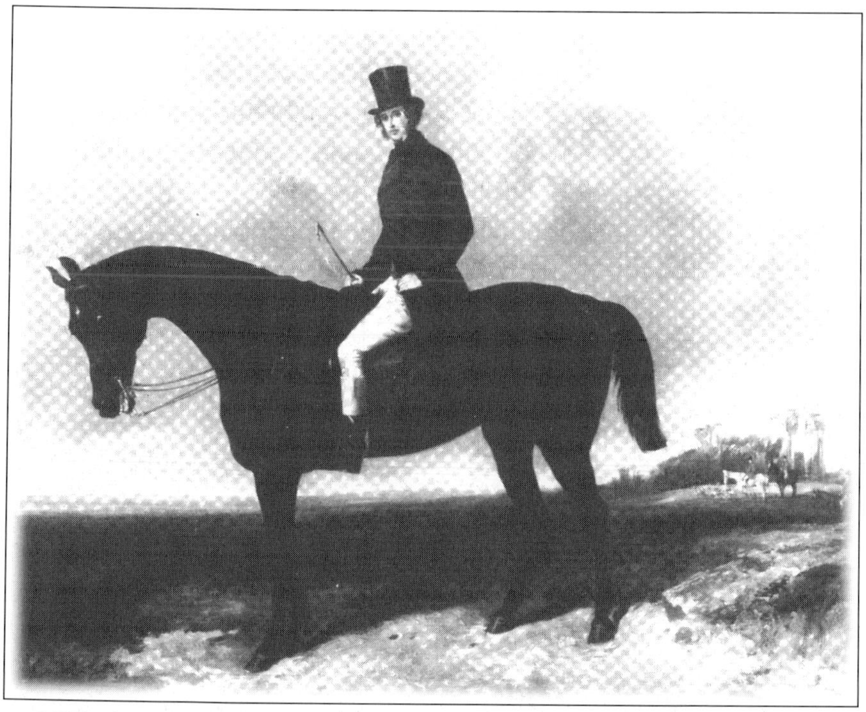

Left: *Edmund Tattersall (1816–98) was largely responsible for establishing the prestige of the House of Tattersalls as Europe's leading bloodstock auction house and was also a native of Sculthorpe. The eldest son of George and Elizabeth Tattersall, Edmund was born on 9 February 1816 at Sculthorpe Lodge Farm (formerly Breck Farm), which was reputedly built to the design of the architect Samuel Wyatt in c.1800. Edmund's father rented it from Sir Jacob Astley of Melton Constable Hall. Here Edmund grew up with his younger brothers and sister: George, John, Henry and Elizabeth Tattersall. He learnt to ride a horse before he was seven years old and in his youth rode to hounds with the Norfolk Harriers and the West Norfolk Foxhounds. The family prospered at Sculthorpe as a result of the agricultural boom during the Napoleonic Wars but later faced financial difficulties and moved to the Tattersalls' stud farm at Dawley near Uxbridge during the late 1820s.* (The portrait of Edmund on 'Black Bess' by Byron Webb is reproduced by kind permission of the Board of Directors of Tattersalls Ltd, Newmarket.)

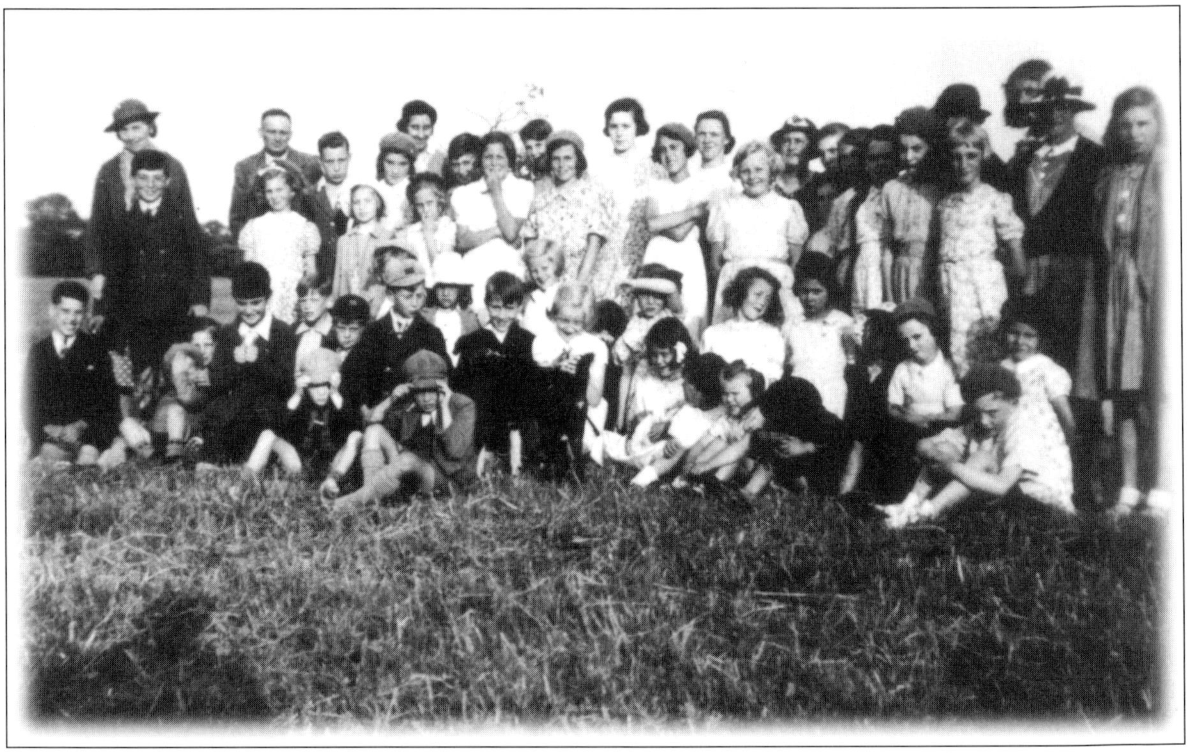

Sculthorpe Methodist Sunday school, early 1940s. Among those pictured are: *Miss Annie Sayer, Mr George Boast, Mrs Flo Greeves, Betty Howes, Gwen Lingwood and Molly Fuller.*
(Reproduced by kind permission of Mr Kenneth Boast)

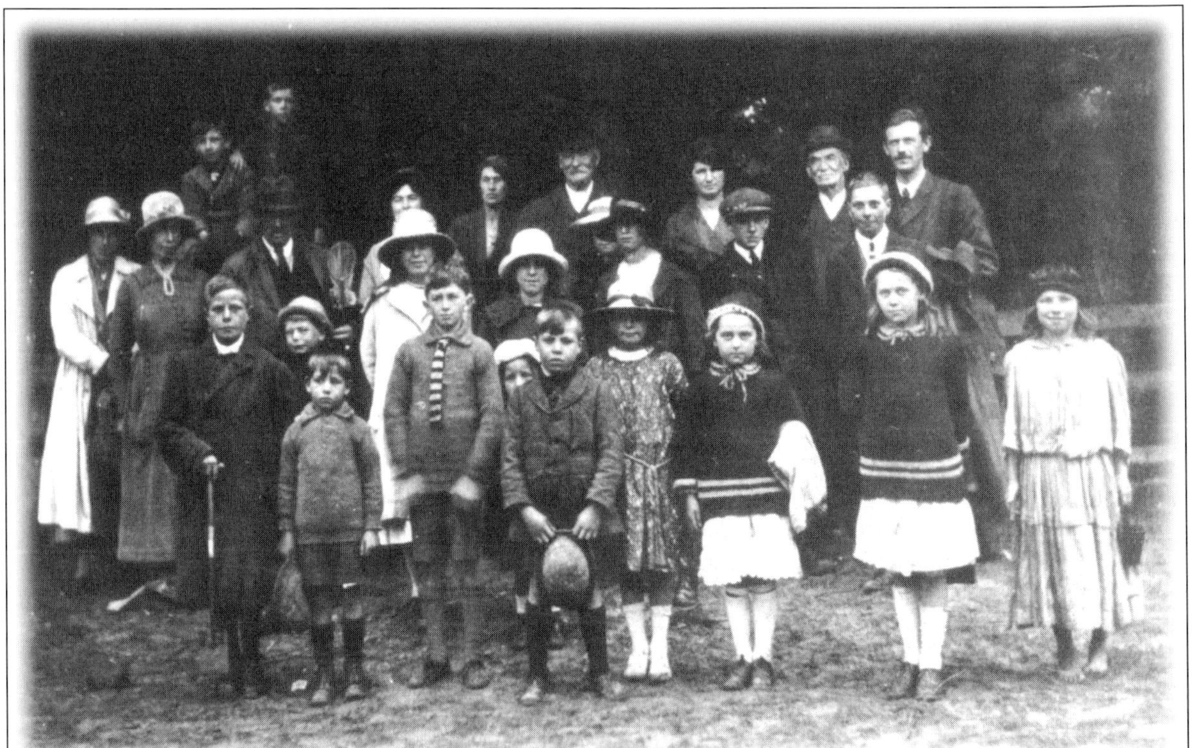

The Sunday school on its annual outing to Wells beach, early 1920s. Among the adults are Robert Tuck, his son Charles Tuck and his daughter Winifred (Mrs George Boast). The little girl holding her shoes on the sand is Daisy Cox. (Reproduced by kind permission of Mr Kenneth Boast)

Chapter Three

THE PRIMITIVE METHODISTS

On 30 October 1781 John Wesley skirted Sculthorpe Parish, bound for the port of Wells, having spent the previous day preaching to the people of Fakenham. However, it was not until the early-nineteenth century that Sculthorpe actually began to experience the growing influence of the Methodist movement which posed a serious challenge to the dual strength of the landed squire and parson and provided an alternative form of worship for the agricultural poor.

The Primitive Methodists, a splinter church founded during the Napoleonic Wars, reached Norfolk in the early 1820s and, by 1825, a Primitive Methodist Chapel had been erected in Fakenham, resulting in widespread evangelising of surrounding villages by various travelling preachers.

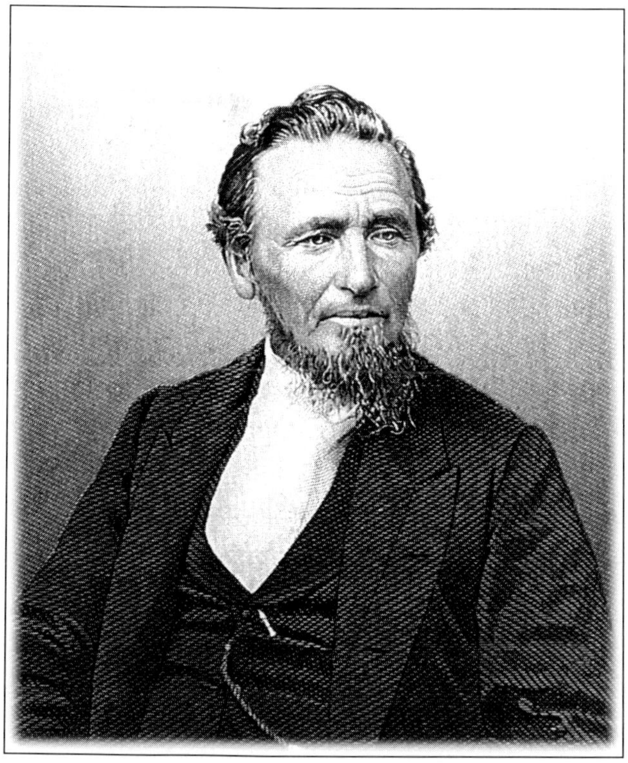

The Revd John Gibbon Wright (1822–1904) was born in Sculthorpe and became one of the founding fathers of the Primitive Methodist Church in South Australia.
(Reproduced by kind permission of the Reverend's great-great-granddaughter, Miss Patricia Wright of Glen Osmond, South Australia)

In Sculthorpe, despite initial opposition, the climate of the times fuelled success. Poverty and disease, coupled with an increasing indifference to the Established Church and the loss of common lands as a direct result of the 1829 Inclosure Award, had heightened a sense of grievance amongst the labouring classes. Primitive Methodism, with its strong sympathies for the social and moral welfare of the poor, its vocal proclamation of the gospel and its unpretentious simplicity of worship, won a considerable number of converts.

William White's Directory and Gazetteer of Norfolk, 1845, indicated the presence of a Methodist Chapel in Sculthorpe. The building stands, at the time of writing, in the yard to the rear of the former Greyhound pub and has been converted into a modern chalet. The deeds of the Greyhound contained frequent references to the 'Chapel Stable', the 'chapel late barn' and its early association with the Wright family. Mrs Annie Jarmany recalled childhood memories of worshipping at the 'Chapel Stable' in the 1880s. The stable continued in use as a Primitive Methodist Chapel and reading room, complete with pews, lectern and gallery, until it was replaced in 1888.

Later generations recalled its use as a cart house and plucking shed.

THE REVEREND JOHN GIBBON WRIGHT (1822–1904)

The first Primitive Methodist missionaries to seek a preaching place in the village of Sculthorpe were welcomed by Mr and Mrs George Wright who lived with their children in one of the cottages in the vicinity of the Greyhound; the Wright family were widely regarded as 'godly people'.

George Wright, a farm labourer, attended Sunday worship at the Parish Church whilst his wife was a

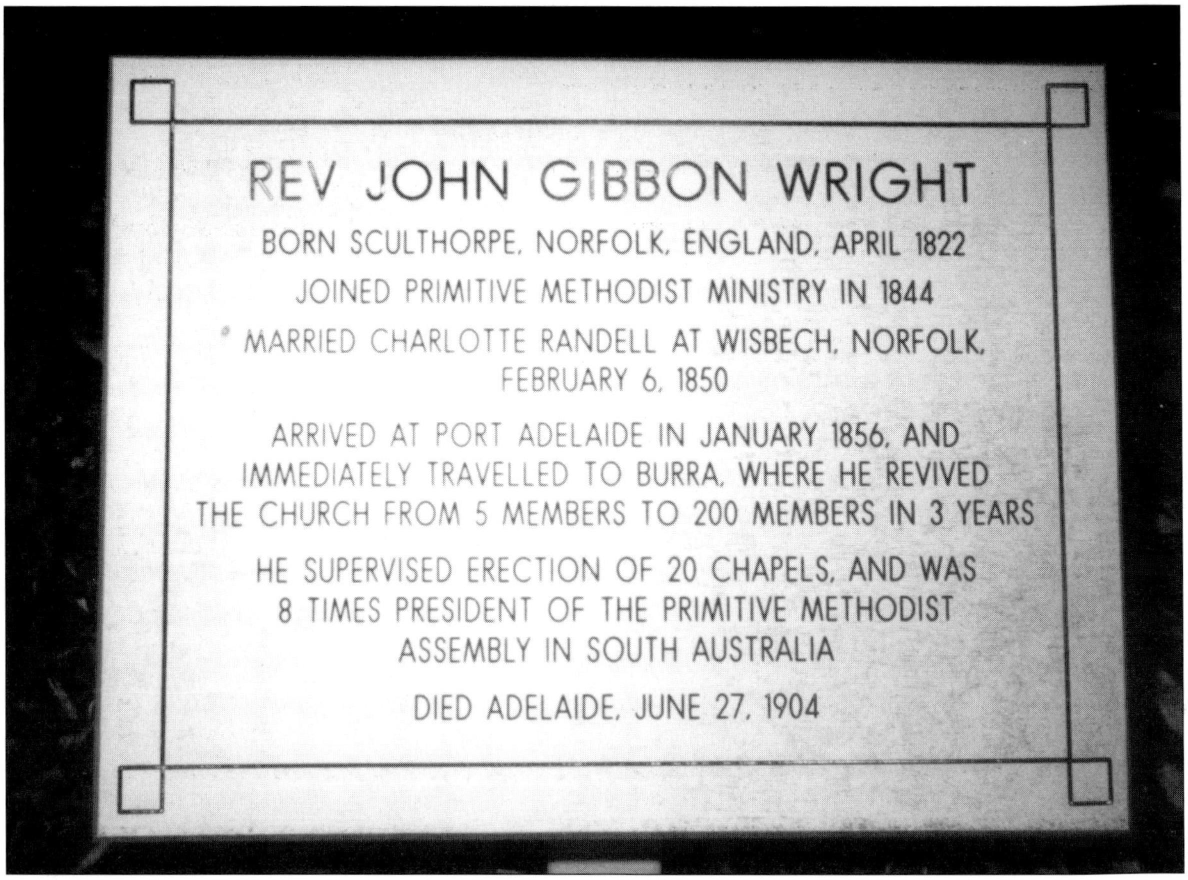

The memorial plaque to the Revd John Gibbon Wright in the cemetery at East Payneham, Adelaide, South Australia. (Reproduced by kind permission of Miss Patricia Wright, from Glen Osmond, South Australia, great-great-granddaughter of the Revd John Gibbon Wright)

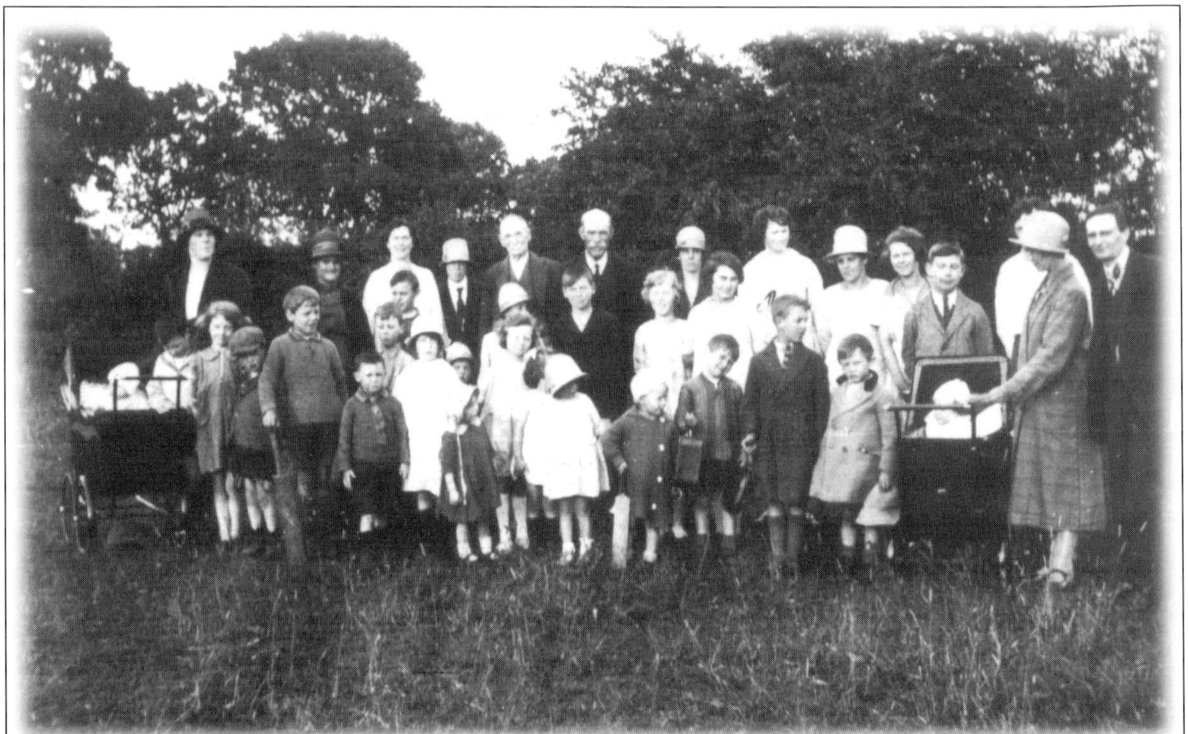

Sculthorpe Methodist Sunday school, late 1920s. Among the adults are Mr Robert Tuck, Mrs Sarah Tuck and Mr George Boast. (Reproduced by kind permission of Mr Kenneth Boast)

Baptist. They gladly opened their cottage door to receive the Primitive Methodist preachers and were both subsequently converted. George's son, John Gibbon Wright, born in Sculthorpe on 30 April 1822, had received some education at a Congregational school – possibly in Fakenham – and in 1839, at the age of 17, was also converted. A farm labourer like his father, John Gibbon Wright became an enthusiastic local preacher, walking many miles into neighbouring villages to address evening gospel meetings. He soon offered himself as a candidate for the Primitive Methodist ministry and in 1844 was sent to the North Walsham Circuit. Here, barely existing on a meagre stipend of £3 per quarter, John Gibbon Wright suffered hardship and near starvation. He almost returned to his parents' cottage in Sculthorpe but, hiding in a ditch, he prayed for guidance and underwent a profound religious experience which inspired him to continue with his evangelistic mission.

In 1846 he moved from the North Walsham Circuit to Bury St Edmunds and then, in 1848, he went to Wisbech where he met and married Charlotte Randell. In 1850 he moved to the Swaffham Circuit where he bravely faced violent mobs in his bold opposition to 'Sabbath breakers' and to cricket matches being played on the Lord's day. Moving as a superintendent within the Briston Circuit in 1852, John Gibbon Wright was increasingly successful in winning converts. At Edgefield he gained the admiration of local farmers in his conversion and pacification of 'stack burners', 'housebreakers' and 'barn robbers'. He travelled extensively around Norfolk villages, both inland and along the coast, and large crowds gathered to hear him preach – many people became converts.

The popular style of his revivalist preaching made the Revd John Gibbon Wright an ideal candidate for the overseas mission. Although he had hoped to be sent to Africa, the London Mission Committee finally decided to send him to South Australia where another Primitive Methodist missionary was urgently required. The Australian gold-rush in the state of Victoria had decimated the population of mining towns in South Australia and the Primitive Methodist Church was attempting to revive its depleted membership there.

In September 1855 the Revd John Gibbon Wright, together with his heavily pregnant wife and two daughters, left England on the Dutch ship *Walvisch,* thus commencing their 16-week voyage to Port Adelaide. In the English Channel off Dover Mrs Charlotte Wright gave birth in her cabin to a baby son, John George Wright. The Revd Wright would later communicate this and other eventful stories of their long and often turbulent sea voyage in a pastoral letter to the Briston Circuit in Norfolk.

Arriving in South Australia on 4 January 1856, the Revd Wright took the mail cart from Adelaide 110 miles north to the copper-mining town of the Burra where he helped to rebuild the Burra Chapel. His revivalist preaching led to the conversion of hardened miners and a boxer. The Revd Wright frequently slept in the bush or under a gum tree with only his horse's saddle for a pillow. The missionary work at the Burra led to the foundation of a flourishing Primitive Methodist Society and the beginnings of the Revd Wright's 47 years in an active ministry in South Australia. His postings ranged from Adelaide, where the famous Morphett Street Church was built, to Mount Barker, Mount Lofty and to Callington and Springfield where further churches were constructed. By the end of the nineteenth century the Revd John Gibbon Wright was popularly called the father of Primitive Methodism in South Australia. He had been instrumental in the building of some 20 Primitive Methodist Chapels and was credited with the conversion of some 800 people, adding greatly to the membership roll of the Primitive Methodists.

The Revd Wright did not return to England but his love for his native county of Norfolk never diminished; he continued to correspond with old friends and took a particular interest when he heard that a new Primitive Methodist Chapel was going to be built in Sculthorpe. The income accounts from the secretary's book of the Sculthorpe Chapel, held in the Norfolk Record Office, reveal that a donation of £2 was received from the Revd John Wright in January 1888 and a further receipt of £1 from J.G. Wright in March 1889. The Reverend John Gibbon Wright spent his final years with his wife Charlotte at 4th Avenue, St Peter's, in East Adelaide – one of the small Wesleyan Methodist cottages built by the Revd Edward Spicer for elderly ministers and their wives.

A supernumerary minister, he continued preaching twice on Sundays at the East Adelaide Wesleyan Church and became an enthusiastic supporter of Methodist Union in Australia, which was finally achieved in 1900.

On 27 June 1904 'dear old Father Wright' died in East Adelaide and was buried at East Payneham cemetery *(see photograph opposite).* Numerous tributes were paid to his pioneering spirit and revivalist preaching which had paved the success of the Primitive Methodist Church in South Australia. Present-day Australians, some of whom bear the surname Sculthorpe, still cherish the name of the Revd John Gibbon Wright and frequently pay visits to the native Norfolk village of this remarkable man.

The Wright family helped to establish the presence of the Primitive Methodists in Sculthorpe and contributed to their success.

The foundation of the National School in 1840 was followed in 1859 with the induction of the Revd Herbert Walsingham Jones to the living of Sculthorpe. This marked the beginning of a considerable revival in the fortunes of the Church of England in the village. The restoration of the Parish

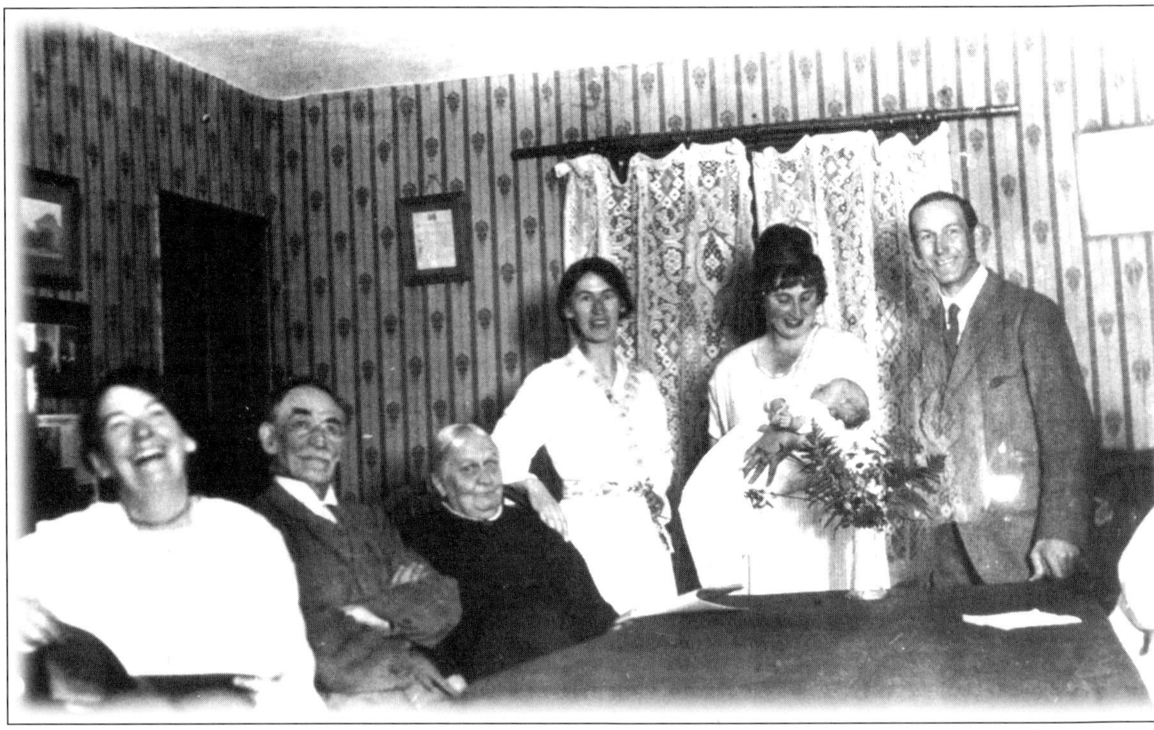

Above: *Members of the Tuck family inside Bay House, late 1920s.* Left to right: *Charlotte Tuck, Mr and Mrs Robert Tuck, Winifred Tuck (Mrs George Boast), Detective Inspector and Mrs Willy Tuck with their baby.*

Right: *Mrs Winifred Boast (née Tuck) at Bay House during the late 1920s.*

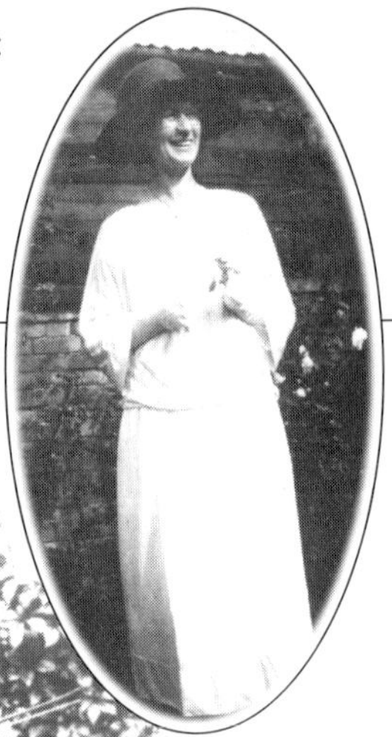

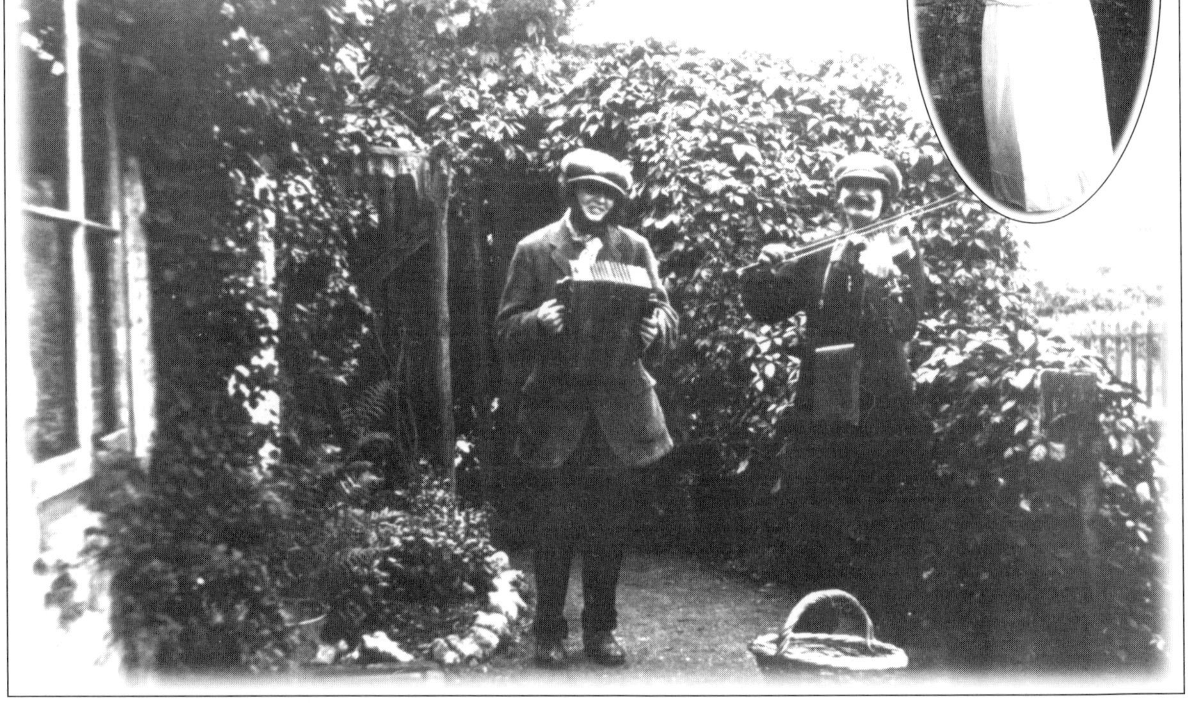

Music time at Bay House, The Street, late 1920s. The characters in costume, playing the accordion and violin, are thought to be May and Charlotte Tuck. Mr Robert Tuck, a talented violinist, was affectionately known as 'Fiddler Tuck' by many in the village. (All images reproduced by kind permission of Mr Kenneth Boast)

Church in 1860–61 and the building of the church mission room and infants' school to the rear of the almshouses in Moor Lane in 1865 are the visible signs of this revival. However, the strong presence of the Primitive Methodists continued to strike the balance of power and for much of the nineteenth century there was an uneasy tension and an emerging rivalry between the supporters of church and chapel which frequently bred suspicion and resentment.

Mrs Eleanor Crane and Mrs Marion Howard recalled their childhood memories of the 1890s and described how their uncle, Fred Plane, tenant of Falgate Farm and later farm bailiff at Home Farm at Cranmer, had complained bitterly when his sister had abandoned the Parish Church and joined 'them old ranters down in the village!'

The Street, a largely Victorian development along the old main high road improved by the Turnpike Act of 1826, was now a hive of shops and village industries forming the new centre of parish life. Here, amidst the growing prosperity of tradesmen and shopkeepers, the Nonconformist presence was particularly strong and virtually unchallenged.

Robert Tuck and his Legacy

The name of Robert Edward Tuck will long be cherished by the Methodists of Sculthorpe. A vigorous local preacher and founder superintendent of the Sculthorpe Methodist Sabbath School, he was the main instigator behind the building of the present chapel. To the wider village he is remembered as a much-loved baker and confectioner who enjoyed playing the violin.

In 1862, aged only 14, the young Robert Tuck moved with his father and younger brother George from Norwich and settled in Fakenham, finding work at Mr Sly's bakery and confectionary in Oak Street. The elder Mr Tuck was both a baker and sugar boiler by trade and had taught Robert and George these skills.

By the 1870s Robert Tuck had moved to Sculthorpe and, at Bay House in The Street, commenced his business on a small scale, specialising in boiled sweets, rock, biscuits and iced cakes, besides bread. The small bay-fronted shop with its little bakehouse next door subsequently flourished and older inhabitants in the village recall their visits to Tuck's Bakery with its warm, inviting smell of freshly-baked bread, Mr Tuck's delicious custard tarts and the horse-drawn baker's cart for deliveries.

The Street's Methodist background enabled Mr Tuck to use his skills as a lay preacher to form a thriving congregation which was beginning to outgrow the Chapel Stable, unfavourably sited in the Greyhound yard. The drinking and dancing in the pub offended the strict piety of those pledged to temperance societies like the Band of Hope and by the mid-1880s many of the services and prayer meetings were being conducted in private houses.

The provision for the building of a new and larger chapel to serve the spiritual needs of the Methodist faithful was largely met when Robert Tuck gave a plot of land in what was then Jodrell's Drift (now Chapel Lane), only a stone's throw away from his bakery.

Naturally there was opposition and Robert's daughter, Winifred Tuck, later Mrs George Boast, often recounted the story she had heard as a child of the trouble caused in the village when the Revd Herbert Walsingham Jones attempted to persuade the Methodists not to build their chapel, fully realising that it would invariably draw more people away from the Parish Church. Entries from the secretary's book of Sculthorpe Chapel reveal details of donations and fund-raising penny bazaars to meet the building costs.

After obtaining several estimates from various local contractors, the Primitive Methodist Society of Sculthorpe finally commissioned Mr William Priest, a builder from Oak Street, Fakenham, to build the

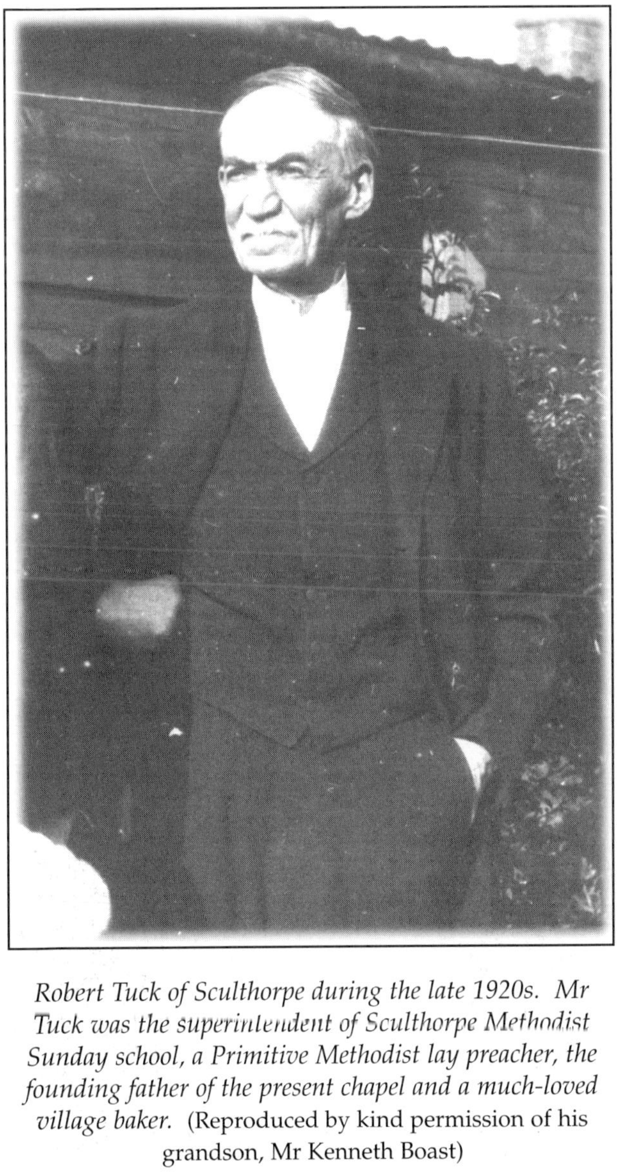

Robert Tuck of Sculthorpe during the late 1920s. Mr Tuck was the superintendent of Sculthorpe Methodist Sunday school, a Primitive Methodist lay preacher, the founding father of the present chapel and a much-loved village baker. (Reproduced by kind permission of his grandson, Mr Kenneth Boast)

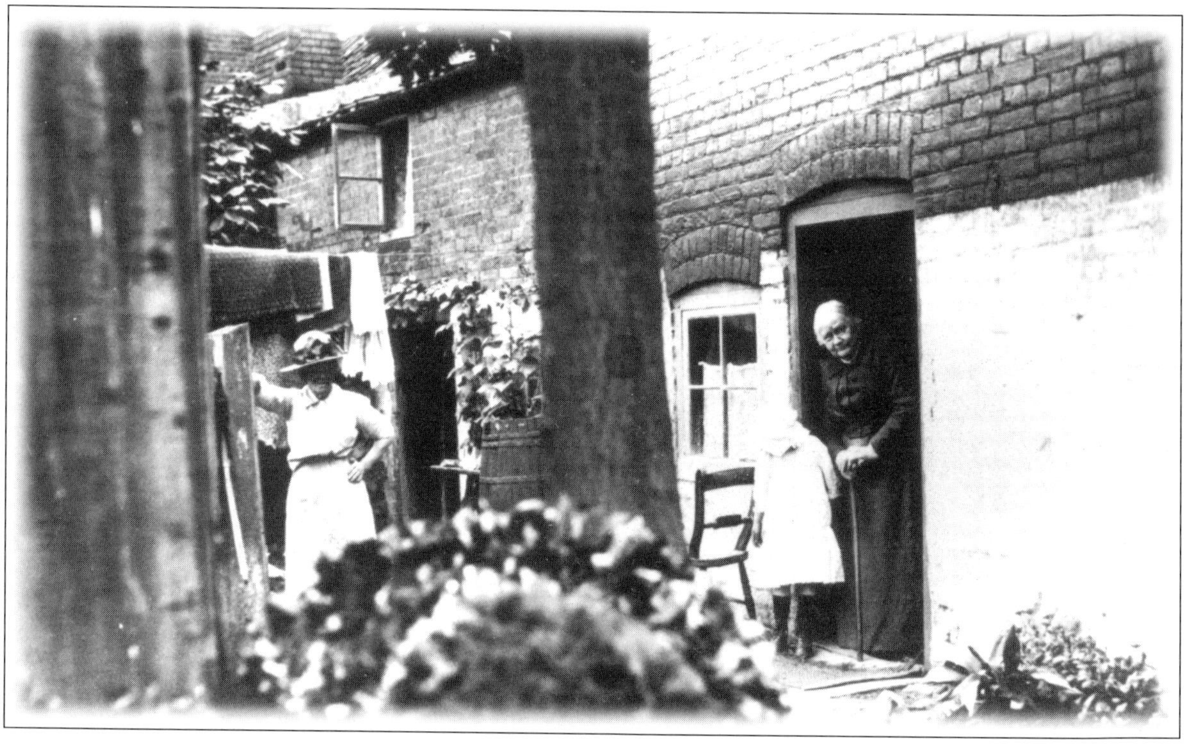

A rear view of Bay House Cottage and the neighbouring Foundry Cottages in The Street, Sculthorpe, 1920s. Mrs Robert Tuck is at the cottage door. (Reproduced by kind permission of Mr Kenneth Boast)

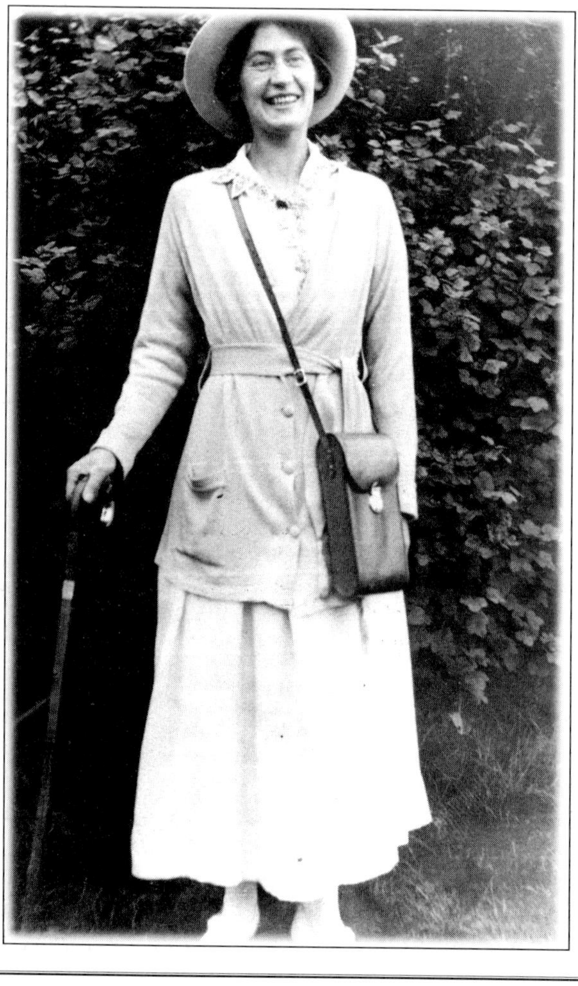

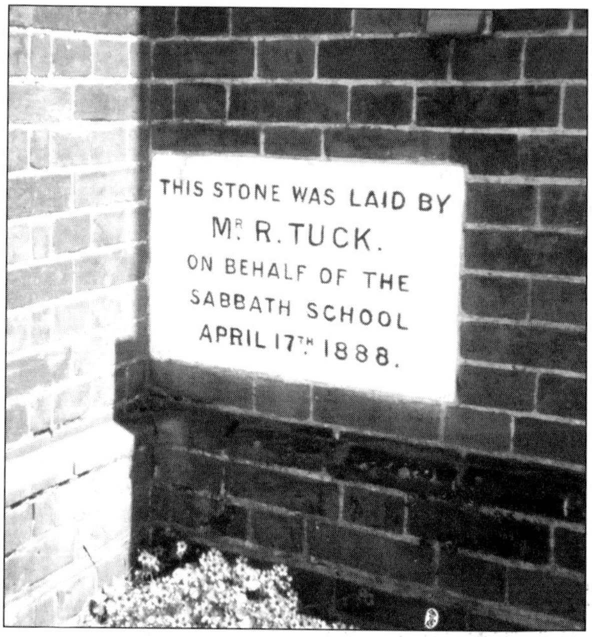

Above: *The foundation-stone laid by Robert Tuck at the Primitive Methodist Chapel in April 1888.*

Left: *Mrs George Boast (the former Miss Winifred Tuck).* (Reproduced by kind permission of Mr Kenneth Boast)

new chapel in Sculthorpe according to plans drawn up by the surveyor, Mr R.J. Turner.

A special service took place on 17 April 1888 at which Robert Tuck laid the first of four inscribed foundation-stones 'on behalf of the Sabbath School' *(see opposite)*. The service, which was concluded by a celebratory tea, marked the start of the new chapel's construction, a momentous occasion for Sculthorpe's Methodist congregation. In April 1988 – 100 years later – the grandchildren, great-grandchildren and great-great-grandchildren of Robert Tuck, together with present-day members of Sculthorpe Methodist Chapel and Sunday school, celebrated the centenary of this event.

The construction of the new chapel provoked fresh support for Methodism in Sculthorpe and there was a corresponding increase in the number of villagers aiding the Primitive Methodist movement. Mr Elijah Walker, under-gardener to Sir Lawrence John Jones at Cranmer Hall, was a staunch Methodist lay preacher; another faithful supporter was Mr Edward Sayer, later the Parish Council Clerk.

Mr Sayer, like his near neighbour Mr Tuck, was a prosperous tradesman, baker, confectioner and pork butcher. His bakehouse and butchery was at No.1, The Street and was originally Providence House, the gable-end of which still has a plaque fixed to it inscribed 'Hygenic Bakery'. Mrs May Wright remembered the traditional Norfolk 'hollow biscuits' sold in Mr Sayer's shop and, during the 1920s, Doris and Joyce Lingwood particularly enjoyed their visits to 'the shop across the road' from their cottage door. They admired the huge, succulent hams strung up on gleaming metal hooks and also recalled the ritual killing of the butcher's pig just before Christmas, a major event in the village calendar which always attracted a large crowd as Mr Sayer, helped by Mr Jimmy Antingham, held the squealing boar over a drain to catch the blood.

The availability of regular weekday worship in addition to the four Sunday services drew large numbers to the new chapel. The early practice of pew rents – 'seat money at one shilling and sixpence' – to raise extra funds to meet building costs was swiftly eradicated but a donation of £4, made by the builder William Priest in June 1888, paid for the new lamps and the stove. In 1897, the year of Queen Victoria's Diamond Jubilee, a donation of £6 paid for a new harmonium.

During the summer months the farm wagon on the meadow opposite the chapel served as a venue for traditional camp meetings, services of song and tea and harvest home. Adults attended prayer meetings and Bible classes, and there were visiting ministers and lay preachers from within the Fakenham-Wells Circuit as well as much vigorous hymn singing. The annual summer anniversary was always something of an occasion for the Primitive Methodists, particularly for the young members of

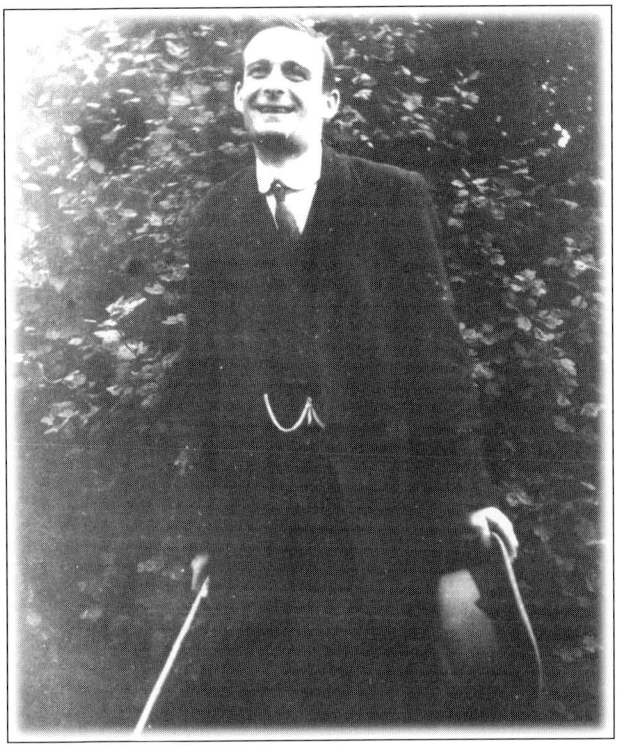

Mr George Boast, late 1920s. A Primitive Methodist lay preacher in the Fakenham-Wells Circuit, he succeeded his father-in-law, Mr Robert Tuck, as superintendent of Sculthorpe Methodist Sunday school. His grocery store and Post Office are still remembered in the village.
(Reproduced by kind permission of his son, Mr Kenneth Boast)

the Sabbath school; in Sunday best they would be expected to give a public recitation of appropriate religious verses learned by heart. A touch of finery was the order of the day so it was 'best bib and tucker' for the boys and straw hats trimmed with ribbon and new frocks for the girls. By 1910 Mr Tuck, as superintendent of the Sabbath school, had enlisted the active support of his young daughters, Winifred and May, and Mr Sayer's daughters, Annie and Bessie, as Sunday-school teachers to instruct the younger children.

An important event in the Sunday-school year was the annual treat, usually a trip to the seaside. During the 1890s this journey had been made in a horse-drawn, flower-decked farm cart but by the 1920s had been considerably modernised – farm lorries covered in tarpaulin being hired from Ernest Hannant, the motor engineer based at the former Red Lion public house in The Street.

Methodist Union, the decisive unification of Primitive Methodism with the Wesleyan and United Methodist Churches to create the Methodist Church of Great Britain, became an issue during the period between the First and Second World Wars and was finally accomplished in September 1932. In Sculthorpe the move brought relatively little change but old loyalties die hard and to this day the commemorative inscription 'Primitive Methodist

Chapel' survives over the entrance to the building, a perpetual reminder of a rich past.

Trade Unionism was also an important feature of these times, winning the active support and participation of many Methodists in the village. Sir George Edwards, the pioneering leader of what was then the National Union of Agricultural Workers, was based in Fakenham and often addressed meetings in Sculthorpe. His powers of oratory had been acquired during his active ministry as a local Primitive Methodist lay preacher. Leslie Lingwood vividly remembered walking up to Hannant's garage as a small child in the 1920s and seeing Sir George Edwards preaching to assembled people from a farm cart sent from Grange Farm by Dick Harris.

In 1928 Robert Tuck celebrated his 80th birthday; still remarkably robust he continued to work at his bakery in partnership with his son Charles Tuck well into the mid-1930s, being dubbed Sculthorpe's veteran baker by the *Norfolk Chronicle* newspaper. When interviewed by the correspondent about how he spent his birthdays his reply was suitably direct and to the point, 'What do I do on my birthday? Why, work hard and forget it. That's how to keep young!'

Mr Tuck remained superintendent at the chapel almost until the end of his long life – he died in 1941, his 93rd year, having been succeeded a while earlier by his son-in-law, George Boast, who had married his daughter, Winifred Tuck, soon after the First World War. As a young man George Boast had worked at Horsley's General Stores in The Street and in 1934 opened his own grocery business with a little prefabricated wooden shop. This was upgraded to accommodate the new village Post Office in 1946 when Mr Boast was appointed sub-postmaster, a position he continued to hold until he retired in 1965.

A fully-licensed lay preacher in the Fakenham-Wells Circuit for 60 years, George Boast proved to be a most popular superintendent. He was ably assisted in this work by George Girdlestone, George Howes and George Titmarsh, causing the Sculthorpe Chapel to be known locally as the Chapel of the Four Georges.

Since the end of the Second World War considerable changes have been witnessed in the life of Sculthorpe Methodist Chapel. Great emphasis has been placed upon achieving a warmer relationship with the Parish Church and in a modern ecumenical age a developing exchange of mutual ideals has been pursued successfully together with shared worship. Old rivalries have been largely eroded in the new atmosphere of reconciliation.

Family ties are still important; Eric Boast succeeded his uncle George as superintendent and Tina and Trudi Armiger – the great-granddaughters of Robert Tuck – became Sunday-school teachers. Faithful witness to the spiritual life of the chapel can be seen in the dedicated service of people such as Milly Girdlestone, Dorrie Pearson, Joan Banham and the chapel organist Avril Temple.

In 2003, more than a century after Robert Tuck and the Primitive Methodists boldly resisted the persuasive blandishments of the Revd Herbert Walsingham Jones, a strong Methodist presence still remains in the village.

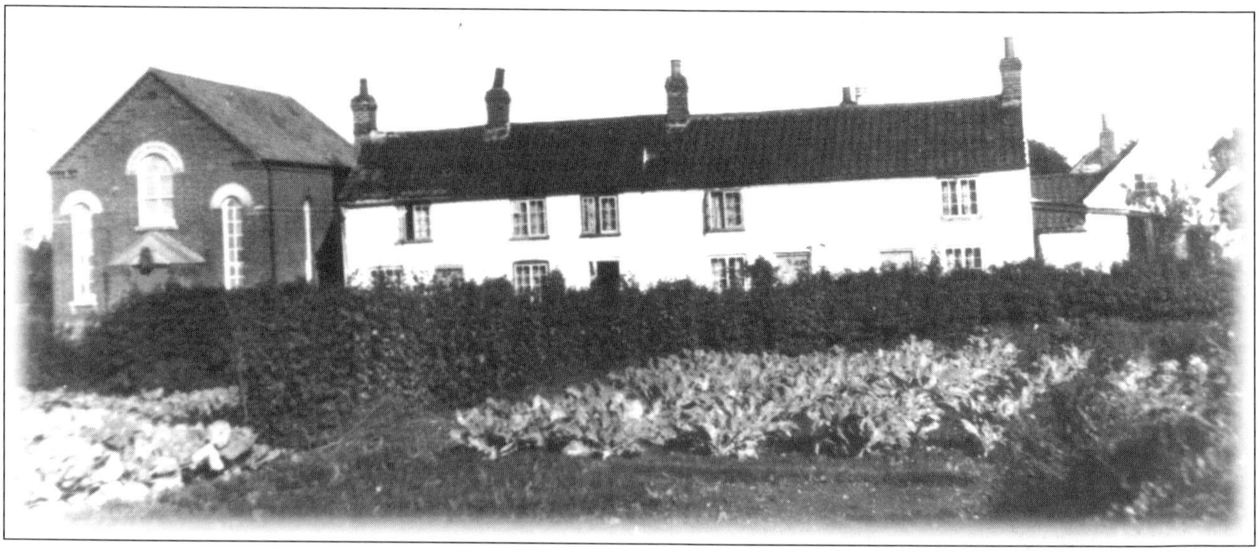

Chapel Lane, c.1920. This photograph shows the Primitive Methodist Chapel (1888) with the Drift Cottages, which have since been demolished, and Robert Tuck's bakehouse. To the left of the chapel (not visible in the image) are the cottages built by the Revd Sir Edward Repps Jodrell of Salle Park in 1865. The Jodrell family, of Salle Park and Bayfield Hall in Norfolk, Lewknor in Oxfordshire and Syon near Kew, were great landowners. Their acquisition of properties in Sculthorpe came about through a family link with the Revd Edward Marsham, rector of Sculthorpe (1811–59), whose aunt, Vertue Hase, had married into the Jodrell family. The Jodrell Laboratory at the Royal Botanic Gardens in Kew and the Jodrell Bank Telescope are associated with this family. Chapel Lane was previously known as Jodrell's Drift because of these cottages built in 1865. (Reproduced by kind permission of Mr Kenneth Boast)

Chapter Four

THE BAPTIST CHAPEL

The Primitive Methodist Church was not the only Nonconformist group to be found in nineteenth-century Sculthorpe. In 1838 a small chapel and meeting-room was built in Moor Lane at the bottom of Bird's Hill, bordering the old orchard near the almshouses. It was affiliated as a branch of the Baptist Chapel in Fakenham and appears, in its early days at least, to have been very well supported. The returns from the National Census of church attendance, taken on Sunday 30 March 1851, revealed that 62 people attended the morning service and 66 people the evening service. The pastor was the Revd S.B. Gooch, based at Fakenham, who preached at the Sculthorpe Baptist Chapel on Tuesday evenings, worship on Sundays being led by visiting preachers. The resident deacon at Sculthorpe was Mr James Bassham. *Craven's Trade Directory of Norfolk*, 1856, also indicated the provision of three Baptist services on Sundays at 11a.m., 2.30p.m. and 6.30p.m., with the Baptist ministers being given as 'various'.

The increasing popularity of Primitive Methodism coupled with the great revival in the Parish Church ensured that support for the Baptists began to wane. The opening of the Primitive Methodist Chapel in 1888 sounded the final death knell and, by the early 1900s, the Baptist Chapel had been closed and appropriated for use by Fred Plane as a cattle shed for his dairy herd. Mrs Crane and Mrs Howard recalled how their uncle Fred often christened his livestock 'holy cows' in mock-reference to the former chapel!

The building survived into the late 1940s, derelict and decaying, until the roof finally collapsed. Mr Ernest Syder, the cattle dealer at Shrublands in Moor Lane, claimed that this was caused by the intense vibration of the big, low-flying American bombers coming in to land at nearby RAF Sculthorpe.

The Independent or Congregationalist Church, which traced its origins from the separatist movement founded at Norwich in 1581, also had its supporters in Sculthorpe during the mid-nineteenth century. The 1851 Census Returns showed that 23 people attended evening service at a 'licensed cottage' in the village; they appear to have been supported by members from the Independent Chapel in Fakenham including a theological student, Mr Henry Goward, then resident at the home of the Revd W. Legge, the independent minister in Fakenham.

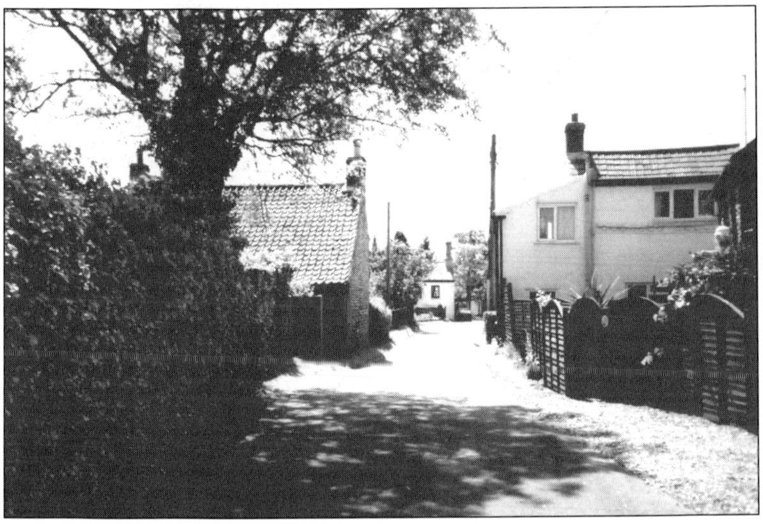

Bird's Hill in Moor Lane derives its name from the family of village blacksmiths who once worked at the Old Forge. To the left of this photograph is eighteenth-century April Cottage, once the home of the village carpenter Samuel Woodhouse (1825–1912). Sam Woodhouse made coffins in his cart shed here, often working by candlelight into the early hours. As a young boy during the early 1830s he once travelled on the stagecoach from the Crown Yard, Fakenham, to London. To the right of the picture are the Guywelles Cottages where Fred and May Lingwood ran a small dairy after the First World War. This photograph was taken in June 2002.

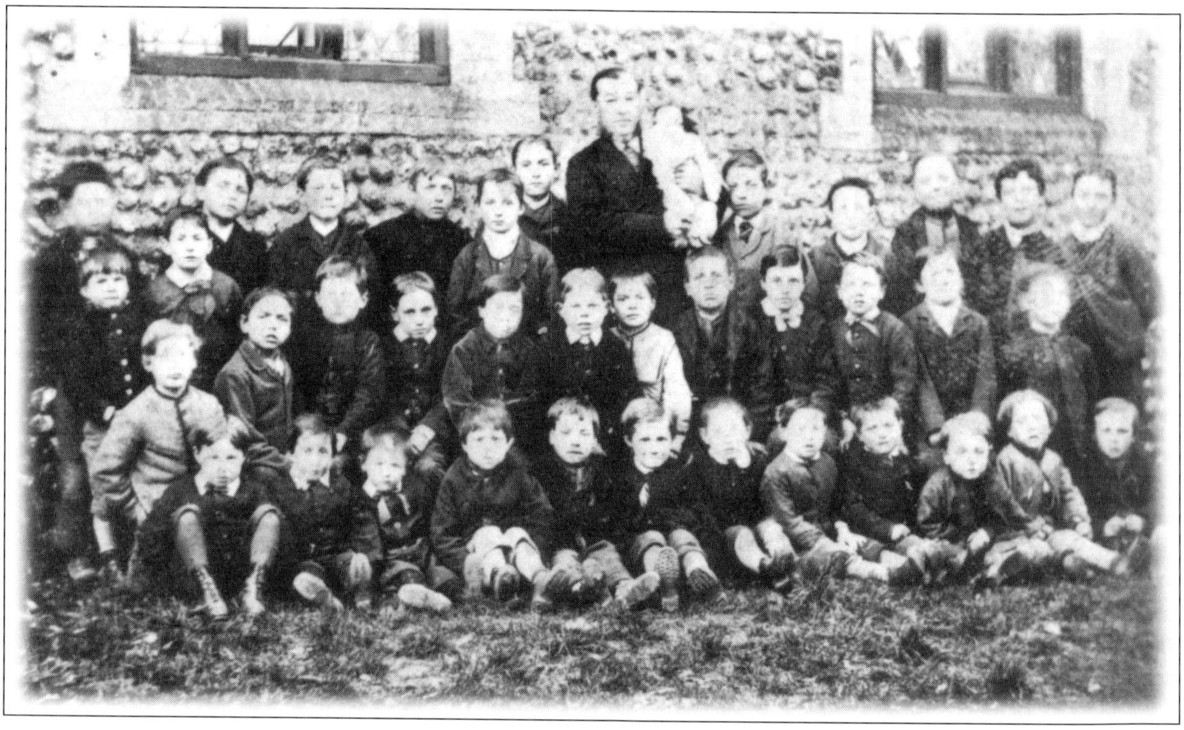

Sculthorpe National School, c.1875. The teacher is Mr Alfred Chalker and to his right is the young Willy Woodhouse. (From the collection of Willy's eldest daughter, the late Mrs Eleanor Crane. Reproduced by kind permission of Mr Richard Land, Willy Woodhouse's great-grandson)

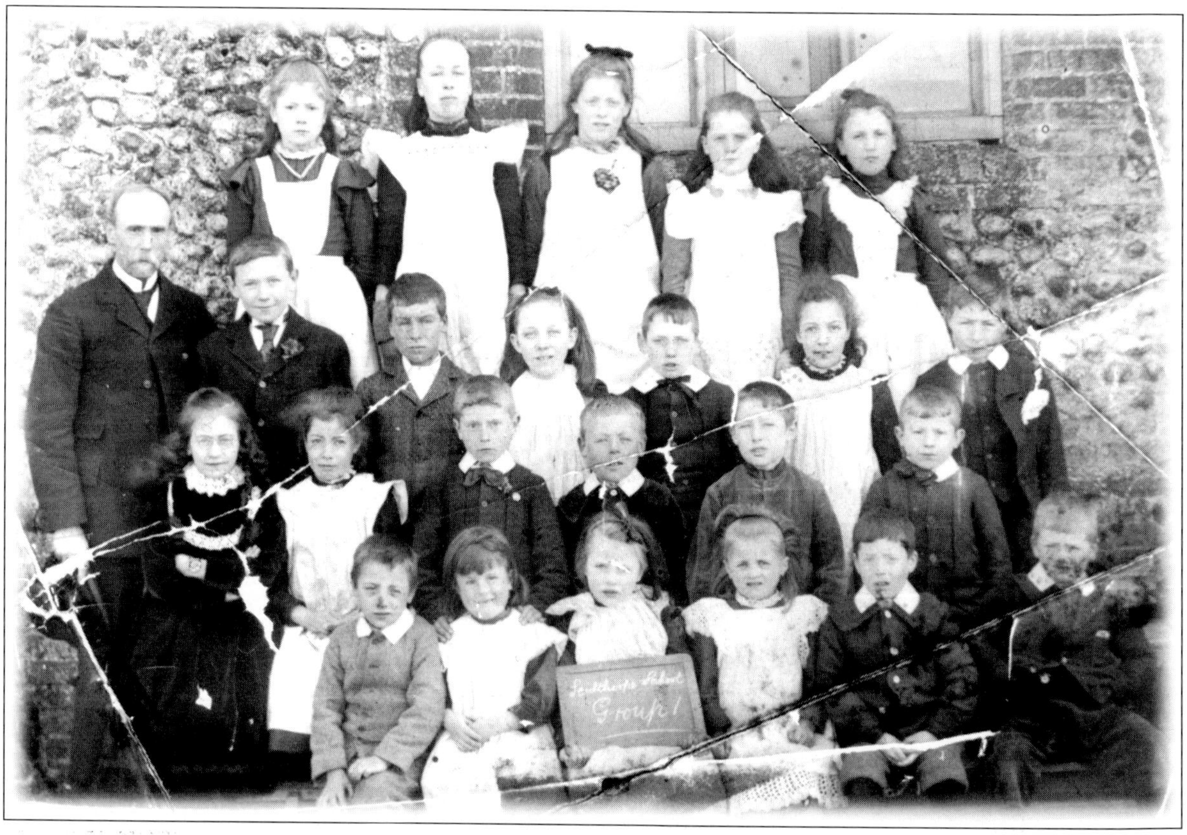

Sculthorpe School, 1902. This photograph was taken to mark the coronation of King Edward VII and Queen Alexandra. The headmaster is Mr William Fawcett. Back row, second from the left, is Nellie Winn. Next to Mr Fawcett and wearing a carnation in his buttonhole is Jack Lingwood. In the same row, second from the right, is Eleanor Woodhouse (Mrs Eleanor Crane). In front of Jack Lingwood are Winifred Tuck (Mrs George Boast) and Marion Woodhouse (Mrs Marion Howard). (Reproduced by kind permission of Mr Richard Land)

Chapter Five

SCULTHORPE SCHOOL

In May 1839 Edward Stanley, Bishop of Norwich, and Edward Marsham, Sculthorpe's rector, formally signed an application to obtain a grant in an attempt to establish a Church school in Sculthorpe affiliated to the National Society for Promoting the Education of the Poor. Prior to this date some perfunctory education had been provided by the rector, particularly in the preparation of candidates for confirmation by the bishop and at the Sunday school. By 1836 there had been a small day school of sorts with John Pleasants listed in *White's Directory and Gazeteer* as 'schoolmaster', but this position was obviously privately funded and regarded as only a temporary measure. A more permanent foundation was now envisaged – a Church day school designed to accommodate 60 boys and 60 girls and to be financially supported by voluntary contributions, including the sum of one penny per week to be paid for each child.

The lord of the manor, Major-General Sir John Thomas Jones, apparently shared Edward Marsham's concern for promoting the education of poor children on his estate and was instrumental in providing a flint barn to be converted into the new village schoolroom.

The Stone Barn, situated by what was East Gate Green and Creake Road on the boundary of the ancient glebe lands, is mentioned in the Sculthorpe Field Book of 1766 as being part of the landed property belonging to the elder Daniel Jones of Cranmer and later to his son, the Revd Matthew Jones, rector and lord of the manor of Sculthorpe at the end of the eighteenth century. The re-roofing of the schoolroom in 1990 revealed a splendid old beam carved with Matthew Jones' initials and the date: 'M.J. 1787', obviously commemorating a period of past restoration. The Stone Barn is marked on the Inclosure Map of 1830. The old and now virtually-forgotten pathway running to the rear of Creake Road and the village bowling green (then a walled kitchen garden) and ending at the school also appears on this map and is called Stone Barn Lane.

The trust deed of foundation for the school, dated 16 October 1840, is now kept at the Public Record Office at Kew and was made between Sir John Thomas Jones and the Revd Edward Marsham and his churchwardens, Edward Sherringham and William Santy. From this fascinating document it is possible to evaluate the extent of the building work taking place at this time – the Stone Barn undergoing its transformation into a schoolroom together with the construction of an adjacent schoolhouse for a resident master.

The newly-converted schoolroom exhibited many features of the fashionable Tudor-Gothic style, incorporating tall chimney-stacks, crow-stepped gables and buttresses with a well-proportioned Gothic porch and bell cote, and mullioned windows with diamond-leaded panes adding to its ecclesiastical flavour. The starkly functional interior featured in a draughtsman's detailed ground-plan of the school dating from this period (held in the Norfolk Record Office) which depicts the ordered ranks of desks and benches in 'best American birch stained 1¼ inches thick' and 'inkstands with brass covers', the floors of 'best yellow deal 1¾ inches thick' and the wall partitions – 'dwarf walls with oak sleepers' – dividing boys from girls in the days of carefully segregated classrooms.

The surviving date-stone, set into the coped Gothic porch, is boldly lettered:

NATIONAL SCHOOL
ERECTED TO THE GLORY OF GOD
AND WELFARE OF MAN
1840

However, the school did not officially open until early in the following year, a detail revealed by an entry in the church baptismal register inscribed by the Revd Edward Marsham:

22 March 1841 – Opened a National School in the parish, under the instruction of – Francis Humphrey –

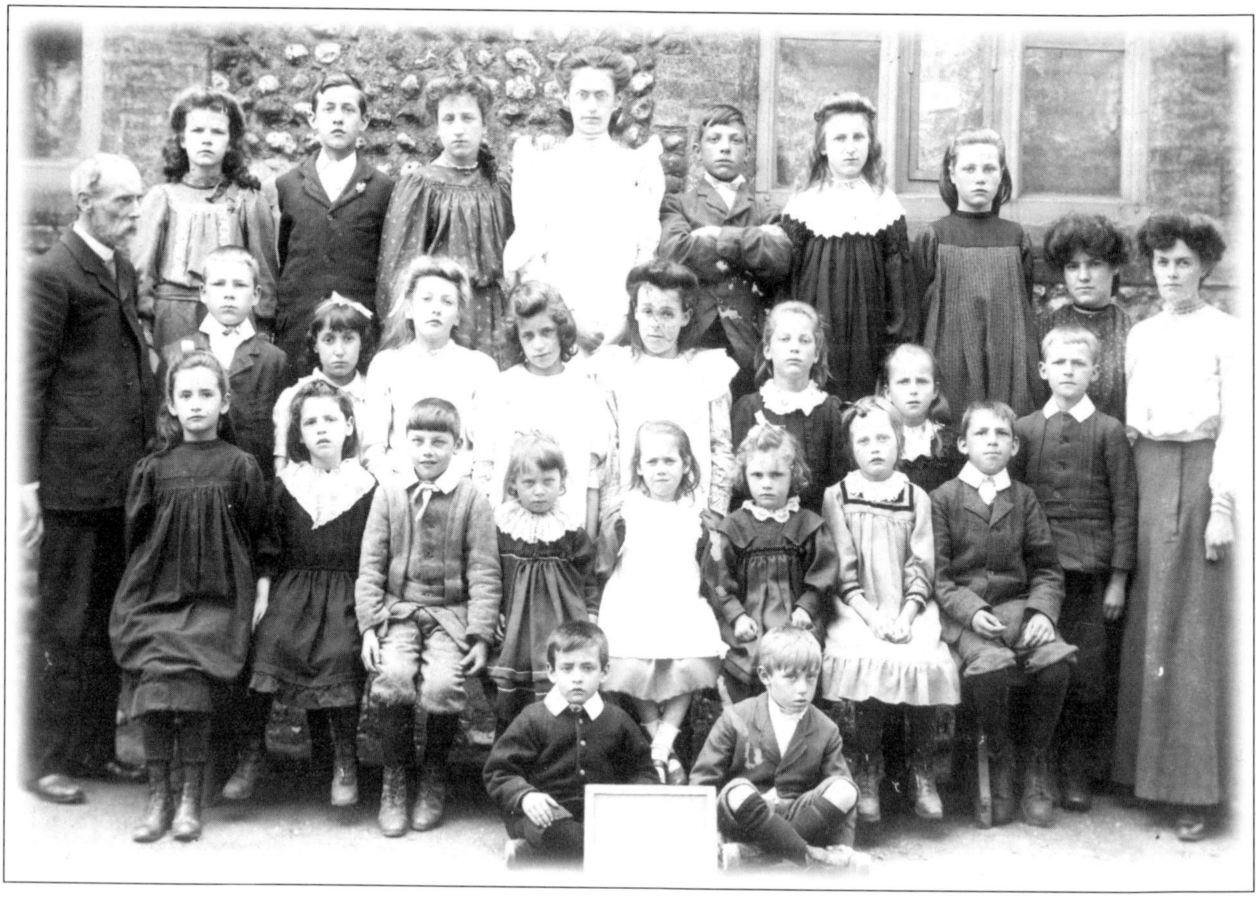

Sculthorpe School, 1909. The headmaster, Mr William Fawcett, stands on the left of the picture. To the right are his assistant teachers, Miss Lewis and Miss Nudds. The tall girl in the centre of the back row is Winifred Tuck (later Mrs George Boast). On her right is Sidney Lingwood. Middle row, third and fifth from the left: *Ivy Sands and Minnie Mallom.* Front row, third, fourth and fifth from the left: *Jimmy Lingwood, Daisy Lingwood and May Gathercole. The little boy holding the chalk slate on the left is Elvi Masters.*

Master, Alice Plane, Mistress of sewing, etc – 71 children attended at first opening.

The school's early years were particularly difficult; education for poor children was not as yet deemed compulsory and attendance was often very low. The constant outbreak of epidemics in the village at this time claimed several young lives and prevented many children from attending their lessons. According to the baptismal register there were periods of whooping cough in 1841 and 1842, measles in February 1844 and scarlet fever in July 1844. Additionally, haymaking, turnip-thinning and the lure of work in the harvest field kept others away. Most poor families, fearing being carted off to the workhouse, thought it rather more important for their offspring to work for their daily bread than attend school.

By 1856 John Chalker was master and was held in high esteem by the Revd Edward Marsham who bequeathed five guineas to him in his will. Despite this the average attendance at the National School was only some 40 pupils, a small figure considering the building was large enough to accommodate 120 children – obviously improvements were necessary.

The remarkable incumbency of the Revd Herbert Walsingham Jones from 1859 until his death in 1889 saw far-reaching changes in the standard and development of the establishment. From 2 July 1860 the school became an alternative place of worship whilst the Parish Church underwent restoration. The entry in the baptismal register, recorded in the elegant hand of the new rector, stated: 'The services were held in the Schoolroom from this time until Whit Sunday May 19 1861.' Also attached to the register is a fascinating little notice on black-edged paper, again in the rector's hand, which was obviously put up in the church porch:

Notice is hereby given, that in consequence of this building undergoing repair, for the next few Sundays Divine Service will be held in the Schoolroom.
Morning – 1/4 before 11 punctually.
Afternoon – at 3 ocl.
Evening at 7 ocl.
It is intended that each service shall not occupy more than an hour and a quarter. *H.W.J.*

In 1865 the Revd Herbert Walsingham Jones together with his elder brother, Sir Willoughby Jones of

Cranmer Hall, built a church mission room to the rear of the almshouses in Moor Lane, screened by a wooden partition from the adjoining men's reading room. It was to be used primarily as the infants' school, accommodating children from the age of 5 to 7 years. By 1883 Miss Alice Warner was the infants' schoolmistress.

Eleanor Crane and her sister, Marion Howard, were amongst the last Sculthorpe children to attend the infants' school at the end of the nineteenth century. Both of them cherished fond memories of walking almost two miles from their home at Cranmer Lodge, across the little gravel footpath through the trees of Cranmer Park and down into the village, often arriving late for their lessons which were taken by their aunt, Miss Edith Woodhouse, as acting mistress together with her assistant, Miss Susan Winn. The standard fee in 1896 was tuppence a week and the average attendance approximately 24 children. By 1900 the school had closed, the infants being admitted to the National School and the building increasingly used as a lecture room.

Forster's Education Act of 1870 attempted to introduce the concept of compulsory education and to improve teaching standards. Sculthorpe National School, although remaining a voluntary-aided Church school, soon found itself subject to these statutory requirements. The first entry in the newly-kept school log-book is dated 3 April 1871 and records that 'The Regulations for the Conduct of a Public Elementary School (extracted from the Education Act of 1870 – Clause 7) were fixed to the School Walles [sic]', and we find that for Tuesday 4 April, when the number of pupils present was 80, 'the school was taught for the first time according to the Regulations of the Education Act of 1870.'

The Revd Herbert Walsingham Jones visited the school regularly during this formative period and kept a weekly attendance register, frequently taking many of the lessons himself. The school log-book recorded that the senior class were examined in 'scripture, the history of England and spelling' and the lower standards were examined in 'reading, writing and arithmetic', the basic three Rs at the very core of the Victorian curriculum.

Religious instruction, particularly the prayer book catechism and Bible study, were high on the agenda and regular attendance at church services was an important part of the school year.

In addition to the two day schools, the rector held a successful night school for the young men of the village between 7p.m. and 8p.m. The entry in the school log-book on 25 April 1871 stated that he gave 'the lads of the night school a supper at the rectory at 6 o'clock. The number of scholars present – 24.'

Mrs Herbert Jones shared her husband's enthusiasm for the schools and frequently inspected the girls' sewing class. It is recorded in the journal of her niece, Laura Troubridge, that Mrs Herbert Jones started the school's first lending library as well as organising special treats for the pupils, including an annual distribution at Christmas of iced gingerbread cakes, decorated with pink sugar mice – an event which was always thoroughly enjoyed.

The school participated in Sculthorpe's celebrations to mark the recovery of Albert Edward, Prince of Wales (the future King Edward VII), from a serious attack of typhoid fever. The entry from the school log-book on 27 February 1872 reads:

The rector and Mrs Jones visited the school in the afternoon and gave the children buns, oranges, etc., it being a thanksgiving day for the recovery of the Prince of Wales.

The headmaster was still Mr John Chalker, now ably assisted by members of his own family: Alfred Chalker teaching the second class and Harry Robert Chalker the third class. In 1876 it became legally binding for parents to ensure their children attended school and an interesting entry from the school log-book stipulated a new system of payments to be introduced:

Sculthorpe National School. Monday Sept 7th, 1877. It has been decided to abolish payments by instalments altogether henceforth and to substitute a uniform school fee of 2d. a week, for every child whose name is on the register.

By 1880 the average attendance had risen to 87 pupils and the diocesan inspectors were able to report that the school was in 'excellent order'.

The last day of December in 1883 saw the departure of John Chalker and the arrival, on 27 January 1884, of John William Savage and his wife, Annie-Maria, as master and assistant teacher.

The festivities to mark Queen Victoria's Golden Jubilee in the summer of 1887 were not entirely appreciated by Mr and Mrs Savage, especially when the event affected the conduct of their pupils: 'June 24th 1887. The children appear very much excited over the Jubilee. It has given us much trouble in consequence.'

Mrs Horsley and Mrs Garood visited the school to supervise arrangements for the Jubilee celebrations; there was a series of tea parties and a week's holiday, during which the choirboys went to the seaside.

The Revd Herbert Walsingham Jones died on 9 February 1889; he was noted as being 'Hon. Canon of Norwich, rector of this parish and also correspondent of this school.' Mr Savage provided a suitably solemn entry in the log-book regarding the Reverend's funeral:

February 13th – Burial of the rector in the Parish Churchyard. The school children were permitted to stand round the coffin while in church were each

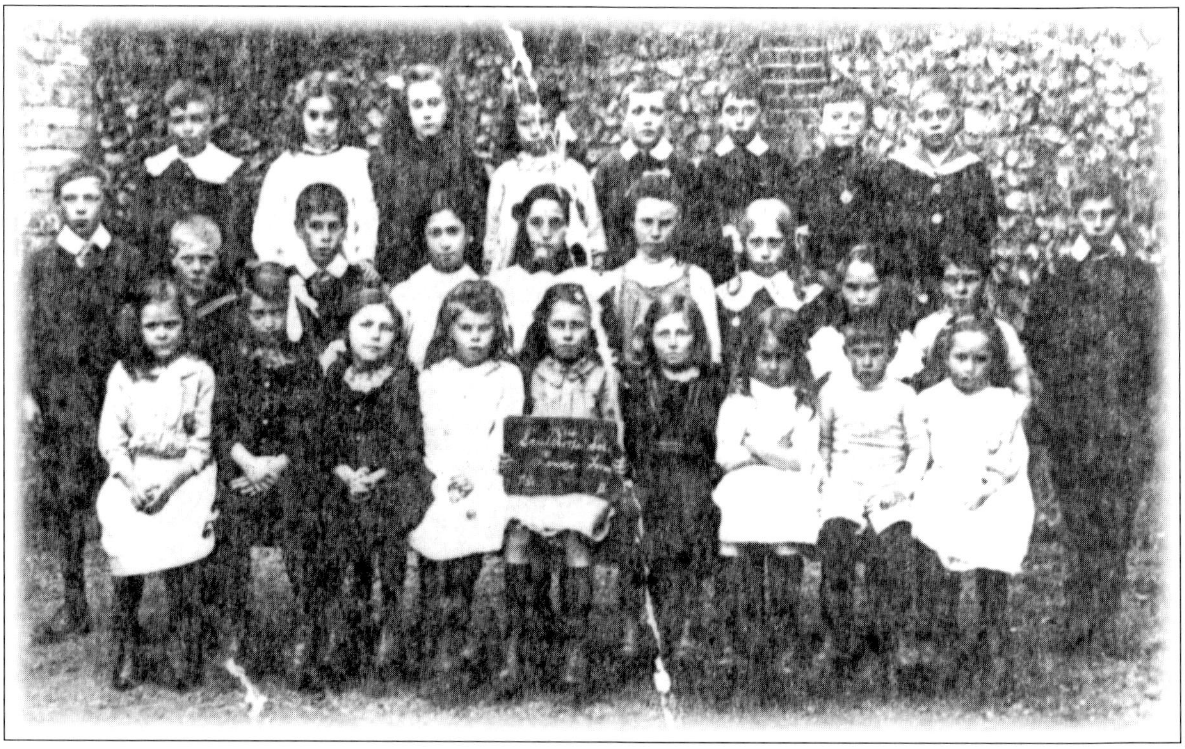

The lower form of Sculthorpe National School, 1914. Back row, third from the right: *Stanley Gathercole;* front row, second and third from the left: *Lily and Violet Lingwood (sisters). The tall boy standing on the left is Tom Sewter.* (From the collection of the late Mr William Sewter. Reproduced by kind permission of Mrs Jean Benstead)

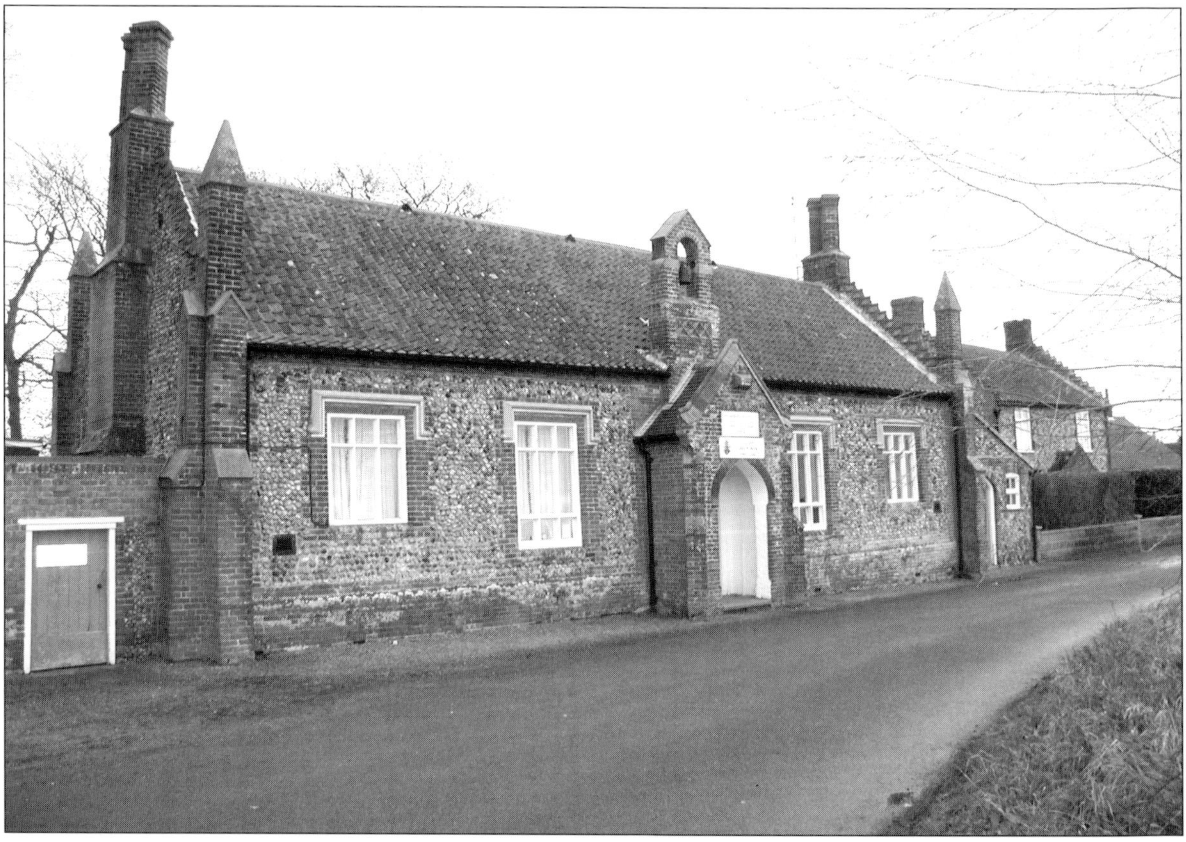

Sculthorpe Church of England Primary School, 2002. The school is rightly proud of its long history from the early years of Queen Victoria's reign. (Photograph: Mr Richard Land)

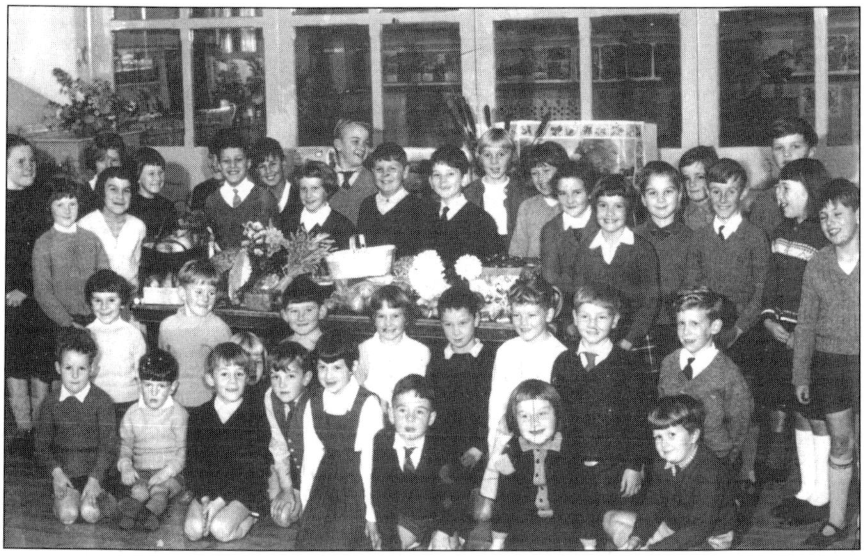

Sculthorpe Primary School, 1965. The harvest festival thanksgiving service. Among the children in this photograph are: *Theresa Mackay, Paul and David Jarrett, Carol and Diane Matless, David Gibson, Kelvin Rowley, Carol Sharpin, Aidan and Desmond Mackay, Bruce Webster, Christine Edge, David Cubitt, Peter and Valerie Futter and Terry Yarham.*
(From the collection of Mrs Jean Edge. Reproduced by kind permission of the *Eastern Daily Press* and the *Dereham & Fakenham Times)*

presented with a Black Rosette. It was fearfully cold with driving storms of sleet and snow. At least 600 persons present without the children.

Walter George Hedgethorne became headmaster in 1890 and began a decade of many changes. An article from the *Dereham & Fakenham Times* describes a particularly charming performance staged by the schoolchildren on 24 December 1891:

The children of the National School gave a contata on Christmas Eve called A Bundle of Sticks. *The stage was tastefully arranged as a room with a Christmas tree in the middle, while a funny old elf, Santa Claus by name, came with his sack full of presents for the children. The parts were nicely acted, the singing both of solos and choruses being of superior merit. The master (Mr Hedgethorne) deserves much credit for having trained the children so well. Mrs Hedgethorne accompanied on the piano, which she kindly lent for the occasion. Sir Lawrence and Lady Jones and family were present besides a fair number of parents. Christmas carols concluded a pleasant evening.*

The early 1890s saw further problems with attendance owing to many local events which included the arrival of the circus at Fakenham in July 1892, the annual September sheep fair on Hempton Green and market day.

The school log-book noted that Queen Victoria's birthday was another occasion when truancy was common. Mrs Crane and Mrs Howard recalled the children singing the following in unison:

The 24th of May
Is the Queen's birthday,
If you don't give us a holiday
We'll all run away.

Evelyn Mary, Lady Jones, visited the school in August 1893 and 'gave prizes in the shape of new boots to those who had attended regularly', doubtless to encourage those truants who had not!

In 1894 William Fawcett replaced Walter Hedgethorne as headmaster. Many of the older generation of villagers, including Mrs Crane and Mrs Howard and their sister-in-law Mrs Minnie Woodhouse, remembered him with great affection. Considerable improvements were made to the school curriculum at this time, including the introduction of recreative and conversational letters, music drill and singing in Sonic Sol-fa. There were drawing classes for the boys and in gardening classes the children cultivated tiny plots and planted seedlings. Mr Fawcett's sister, Eliza, was appointed the new sewing mistress for the girls.

Patriotic observance was marked by saluting the Union Jack and wearing, on Oak Apple Day (29 May), the traditional spray of oak leaves to commemorate the hiding of King Charles II in an oak tree after the Battle of Worcester. Lessons were given on the great British Empire upon which 'the sun would never set' and in July 1897, as a commemorative souvenir of Queen Victoria's Diamond Jubilee, each child was presented with a copy of the Revd E.J. Hardy's book *The People's Life of their Queen.* The outbreak of the Boer War in South Africa elicited further loyalist demonstrations and several of the schoolchildren went to Fakenham where they heard the town band playing 'Soldiers of the Queen' in the market-place. On 1 March 1900 Mr Fawcett recorded in the school log-book: 'News of the relief of Ladysmith received. Cheers given for our soldiers.'

During February 1901, with the country in deep mourning following the death of the Queen on 22 January, the schoolchildren were marched in line from the school to attend a special memorial service at the Parish Church. The Royal Arms on the south wall of the nave were draped in swags of black crêpe and the children sang hymn 537 from *Hymns Ancient and Modern*: 'Peace, perfect peace, in this dark world of sin, the blood of Jesus whispers peace within.'

The rector, the Revd Arundel Glastonbury St John Mildmay, had visited the school in order to teach the children the words and explain the meaning.

The annual visits by His Majesty's Inspectors occasionally proved a strain for Mr Fawcett, particularly when criticism was levelled at the 'lack of adequate books', at certain children being 'talkative and unresponsive' or at the academic conduct of the assistant teachers, Miss Nudds and Miss Lewis, but a sympathetic entry by one school inspector in the log-book for September 1901 appreciated that:

The master shows much interest in his duties and works very diligently and it is much to his credit that the older scholars have in some respects made good progress. The task of teaching 88 children ranging from 4–15 years of age with very little assistance is, however, hopeless and depressing.

The Revd and Mrs Jack Labouchere proved stalwart friends of the National School during the early years of the twentieth century; the older generation remembered Mr Labouchere's talent as a conjurer and magician, pulling rabbits out of top hats and holding magic lantern shows besides taking scripture and catechism class. The schoolchildren were often invited to afternoon tea in the parish room at the rectory and were allowed to gather apples in the orchard there.

The outbreak of the First World War in August 1914 invariably brought about great changes in Sculthorpe. The absence of able-bodied men in the village meant that children were needed to work on the land and thus they were forced to leave school earlier than expected; as a result attendance again became problematic. The school register from this time carries a common entry, 'father called up'. The Revd Labouchere led the schoolchildren in singing national songs and gave frequent addresses on the British Empire to boost morale. Coal became scarce and firewood was sent from the wood yard at Cranmer Hall by Mr George Lockhart-Ross, providing much-needed fuel to heat the cold and draughty classrooms.

Acts of wartime bravery and heroism were magnified by newspaper reports and it was during this period that the National School in Sculthorpe honoured its own heroine – Miss Edna Rutland. Mr Fawcett's entry in the log-book for Friday 9 March 1917 was as follows:

At the close of school today the children assembled in the main room, and there were also present the rector and Mrs Labouchere and several parishioners. The occasion was the presentation of a certificate awarded to Edna Rutland (13) by the Royal Humane Society for conspicuous bravery on January 30th in saving the life of a school fellow, Mabel Lusher, from drowning. Several children were sliding on a pond on the Glebe just before morning school and Mabel Lusher ventured on a dangerous part near the middle of the pond. The ice broke and the child fell into very deep water. She would have drowned but for the presence of mind of Edna who very bravely crawled to the edge of the bending ice and rescued her. The Reverend J.A. Labouchere recounted the circumstances and also gave a brief history of the RHS after which Mrs Labouchere handed the certificate to Edna, and the children gave hearty cheers for their brave schoolfellow.

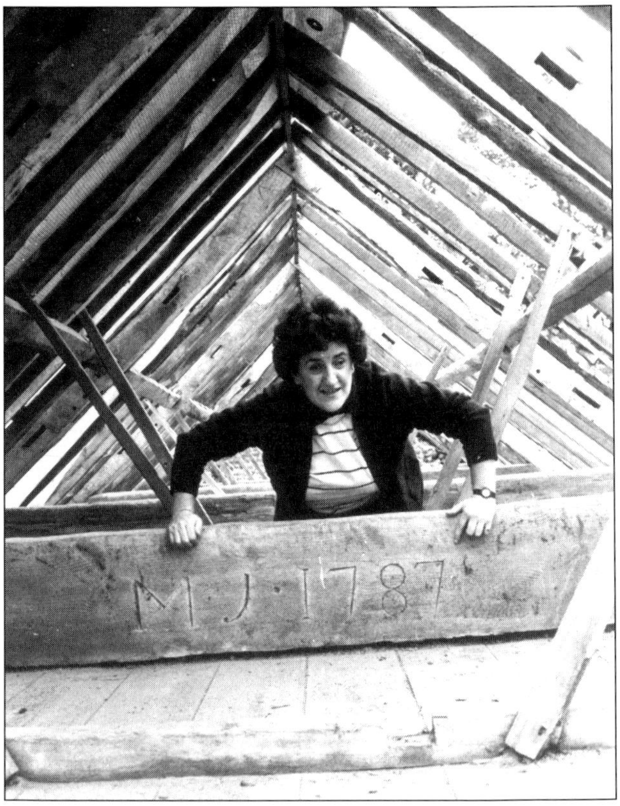

During the autumn term of 1990 the roof of Sculthorpe School was being renewed when an historic beam was discovered, bearing the inscription 'MJ – 1787'. This referred to the Revd Matthew Jones who was both rector and lord of the manor of Sculthorpe at the end of the eighteenth century and owned the building, then the Stone Barn. The head teacher, Miss Sue Kimbley, is pictured with the beam. (Reproduced by kind permission of the *Eastern Daily Press*, Archant Norfolk Ltd)

William Fawcett retired during September 1917 ending 23 years' devoted service as headmaster. Mrs Sarah Frances Bowles was appointed as the school's first headmistress.

The Armistice in November 1918 was shortly followed by a serious outbreak of the Spanish influenza epidemic, spread by the troops returning from the Front. The school was closed from 31 January until 7 February 1919 as a result of the infection.

During the 1920s the children's horizons were considerably widened; the availability of cookery and carpentry classes at Fakenham Central helped to break down parochial insularity and, towards the end of the decade, secondary education became a possiblility through the scholarship exam at the age of 11. The Christmas treat for 1923 was an outing to Fakenham to see the silent film *Oliver Twist* which proved to be most popular.

Mrs Bowles was a stickler for discipline and the short service held annually in the schoolroom on Armistice Day stressed the need for the children to observe the two minutes' silence. The Revd Dundas Harford usually paid a visit on Empire Day to read the messages sent 'to the children of the Empire' by King George V and Queen Mary.

Educational standards continued to improve and by 1925 Mr Harford was able to report in the log-book that 'evidence of the children's pride in their school is seen in the tasteful arrangements of flowers in the classrooms.'

In 1929 a number of schoolchildren stood in the field opposite the school looking up into the sky. The R101, then the largest airship in the world, filled with hydrogen gas, was passing over Sculthorpe on a test flight from Cardington in Bedfordshire. Joe Tuck, Austin Cornwall, Harold Lingwood and Joyce Lingwood (now Mrs Joyce Harrison) vividly remember standing in the field and watching the ill-fated craft. Less than a year later, in October 1930, the R101 crashed into a hillside near Beauvais in France whilst on its maiden flight to India and exploded into flames, claiming 48 lives.

The 1930s witnessed further changes in the life of the school, including a new headmistress in the shape of the redoubtable Mrs Brown. The year 1935 saw greater emphasis being placed upon hygiene and nutrition with the introduction of the School Milk Scheme. There were also visits from the school nurse and the dentist, the formidable Miss Howe in her mobile caravan. The infant teacher, Miss Mary Bacon, is still affectionately remembered by former pupils and for several years she acted as the church choirmistress. A village girl and former pupil, she was popular with parents and children alike.

The religious atmosphere of Sculthorpe during the '30s was still largely divided between the unwavering traditions of church and chapel but Miss Bacon eventually embraced the Roman Catholic faith and became the first native of Sculthorpe since the Reformation to practice the 'old religion'. Many recall her early-morning walks along the old medieval green ways to Houghton St Giles, rosary beads in hand, to hear Father Bruno Scott-James offer the Holy Sacrifice of the Mass in the fourteenth-century Slipper Chapel; surprisingly she was always back in Sculthorpe before the ringing of the school bell!

The Second World War overshadowed the school's centenary celebrations and on 10 April 1940 gas masks were issued to the children and a regular drill initiated. Low-flying German planes became a familiar sight, seeming, to the children at least, to almost touch the tops of the tall trees in the playground. Major Jones, as the local Home Guard commander, gave his lectures in the schoolroom on a weekly basis, carefully observing the blackout in case of air raids.

Despite these necessary precautions there were still occasions when the school was able to celebrate. In December 1940 Lady Evelyn Jones attended the performance of the school's Christmas play *The Princess and the Dragon* with Gwen Lingwood and Herbert Woodhouse in the starring roles.

The school bell, silenced for almost six years, tolled once again with rejoicing on VE Day in May

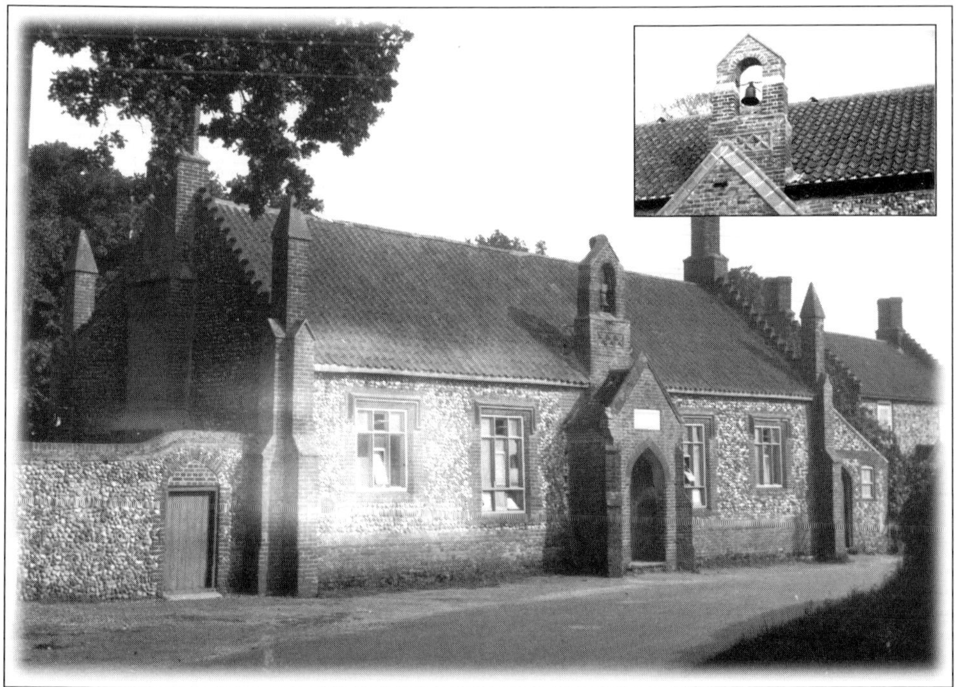

Left: *Sculthorpe Church of England Primary School, August 1939. Only a century earlier it had been the Old Stone Barn.* (Reproduced by kind permission of the Norfolk Rural Life Museum at Gressenhall)

Inset: *The school bell was restored in October 1992. It had last been tolled for the peace celebrations at the end of the Second World War in 1945.*

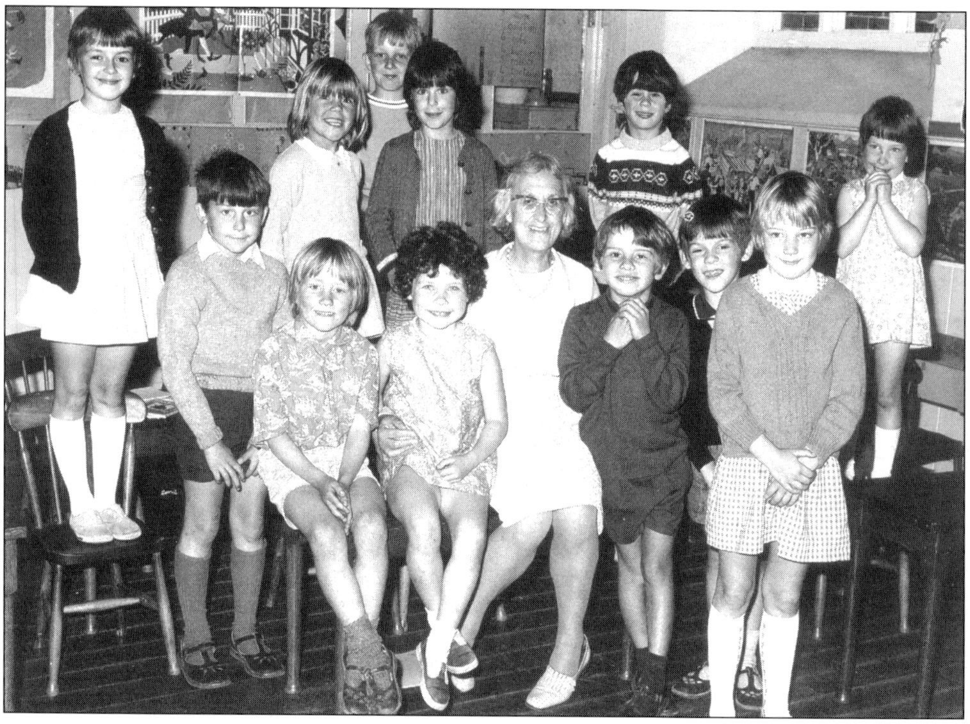

In July 1971 Miss Enid Codlin retired after 22 years as infant teacher at Sculthorpe School. Here she is pictured on her last day at the school with some of her pupils. Left to right, back row: *Theresa Banham, Tracey King, Andrew Betts, Suzette Walters, Melvin Morrison, Debbie Fenn;* front: *Mark Howes, Robert Barrett, Sally Smith, Miss Codlin, Gary Armiger, Gary Windeler, Joanne Palmer.* (Reproduced by kind permission of the *Eastern Daily Press,* Archant Norfolk Ltd)

1945 and the children were given a two-day holiday for the peace celebrations. The post-1945 period involved a rapid series of events including the departure of Mrs Brown and the subsequent appointment of Miss Constance Catlin as headmistress. The demise of the Cranmer Hall estate and the resultant sale of property also saw a final severance of the schoolhouse from the school when this was purchased by Miss Catlin in 1946.

In 1949 Mary Bacon emigrated to America in order to fill a post as priest's housekeeper and teacher at a Roman Catholic boys' school. Her position as infant teacher was filled by Miss Enid Codlin.

In December 1954 Miss Catlin was interviewed by journalist Anthony Brown of the *Daily Mail* for his front-page article on Sculthorpe as the 'Atom Bomb Village'; her response to his question about the problems of low-flying Tornado bombers and Thunderstreak fighters reflected her practical, no-nonsense approach to many situations:

My children have grown up to the noise of planes. So the noise, the screech, whine and scream of jet engines holds no fear for them. I did think it rather extraordinary that the civil defence people wanted to use my schoolroom for a war rest centre – surely Sculthorpe would be one of the first places to be hit!

Miss Catlin's musical talents extended to the Parish Church where she had succeeded Mary Bacon as choirmistress. In later years she would make an annual pilgrimage to Salzburg, the birthplace of Mozart, to attend the musical festival, frequently accompanied by Miss Codlin.

The standard of academic excellence initiated by Miss Catlin and Miss Codlin during the 1950s and '60s laid a solid foundation in scholarly achievement for Sculthorpe Church of England Primary School. Successive teachers have adopted this splendid inheritance and built upon it.

Structurally the interior of the school has been extensively refurbished. The ceilings have been lowered and the Victorian coal fires and ancient stoves, some of the very last to survive in a Norfolk school, have been removed to the Norfolk Rural Life Museum at Gressenhall and replaced with modern gas-fired central heating; a new mobile classroom has also been added in the playground. During December 1994 building work was started on the pre-school nursery wing and indoor toilets at the school. This special occasion was marked by the burial of a time capsule within the foundations of the new block which the pupils had filled with information about the school, the village and life in the 1990s.

Sculthorpe Church of England Primary School is now the oldest surviving Victorian Church school within its original building in the diocese of Norwich and continues to play a vital part in village life. Parents and school governors have established the Friends of Sculthorpe School in an attempt to ensure its long-term survival, their considerable fund-raising activities culminating in annual events such as the splendid summer fêtes, autumn fayres and Victorian evenings.

In May 1989 pupils past and present attended a thanksgiving service in the Parish Church in celebration of the school's 150th anniversary.

Chapter Six

The Parish Church

The earliest documentary evidence for a church in the village of Sculthorpe can be found in the Little Domesday Book of 1086. The entry for the lands of William de Warenne within the manor of 'Sculetorpa' mentions a church and its land or 'glaeba' of 60 acres.

It is rumoured that there are foundations of an earlier church in existence on the northern side of the present churchyard, where there is a slight mound believed to mark the site of an ancient Anglo-Danish church which was subsequently replaced by the church which appears in the Domesday survey.

This early-Norman church appears to have been a substantial stone edifice, a theory verified by a number of discoveries made during the Victorian restoration of the present church in 1860–61. Whilst the Victorian 'galilee' was being built at the western end the foundations of an ancient Norman tower were exposed and broken fragments of Norman masonry were unearthed elsewhere. These included a partially mutilated sheep's head and ornamented pieces of stone pillars. A large boulder flint, a 'hag stone', placed beside the churchyard wall to ward off witches, may also have originated from this building.

It is, however, the ancient Norman font which is the significant surviving link with the eleventh-century church and its historic associations with the Norman house of de Warenne and the Cluniac priories of Lewes and Castle Acre.

The Cluniac Order, adhering to the reformed Benedictine rule, had its mother house at Cluny in

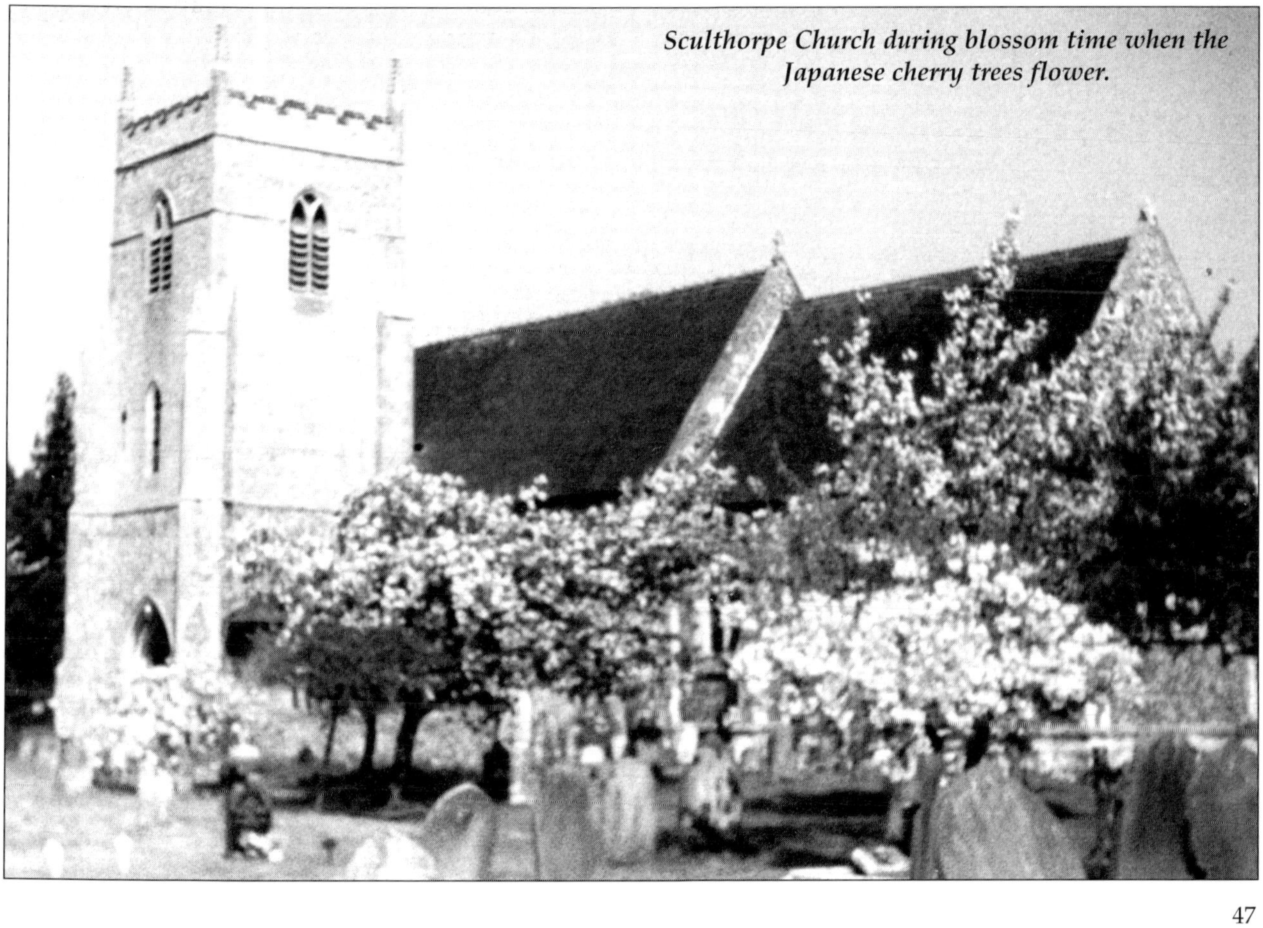

Sculthorpe Church during blossom time when the Japanese cherry trees flower.

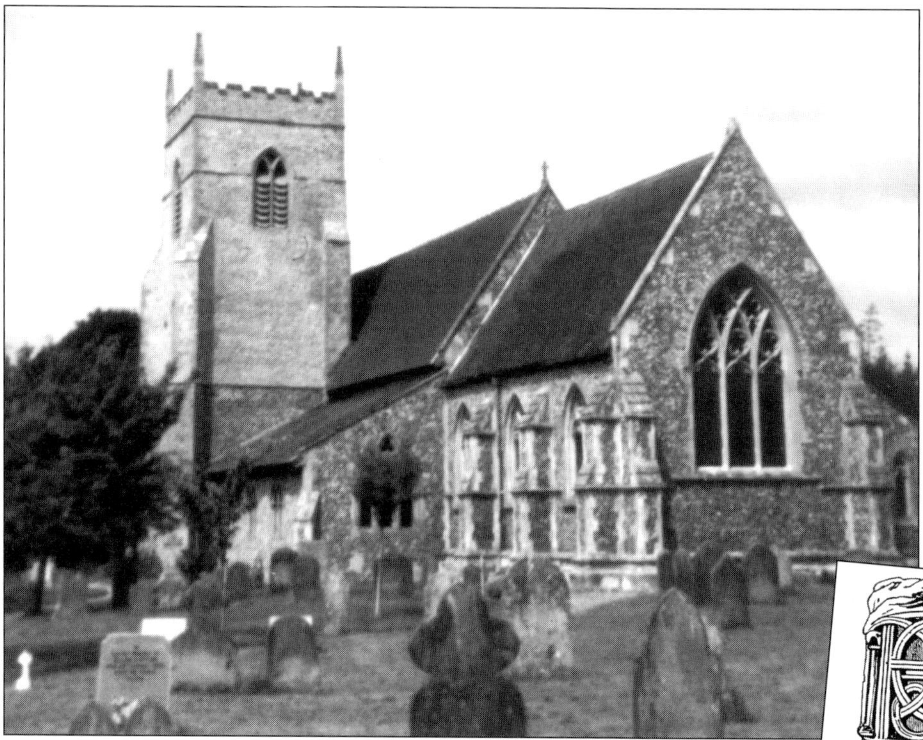

Left: *Sculthorpe Church from the eastern side of the churchyard, July 1978.*

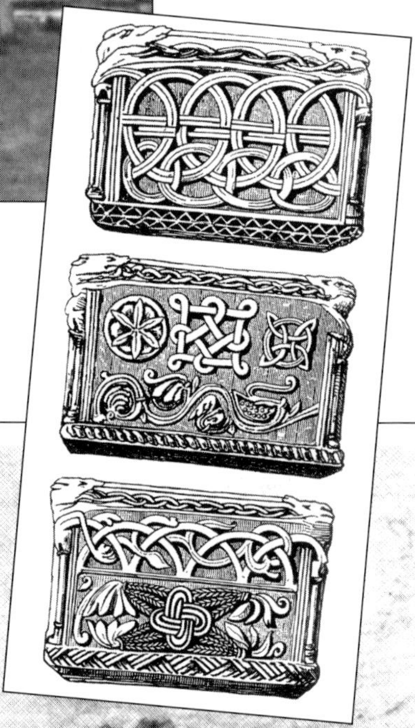

Right: *The ancient Norman font in Sculthorpe Church is believed to date from the early-Norman church mentioned in the Domesday Book. The sketches are taken from* Notes on Sculthorpe Church *by Mrs Herbert Jones, published in 1872.* (Reproduced by kind permission of the Norfolk & Norwich Archaeological Society)

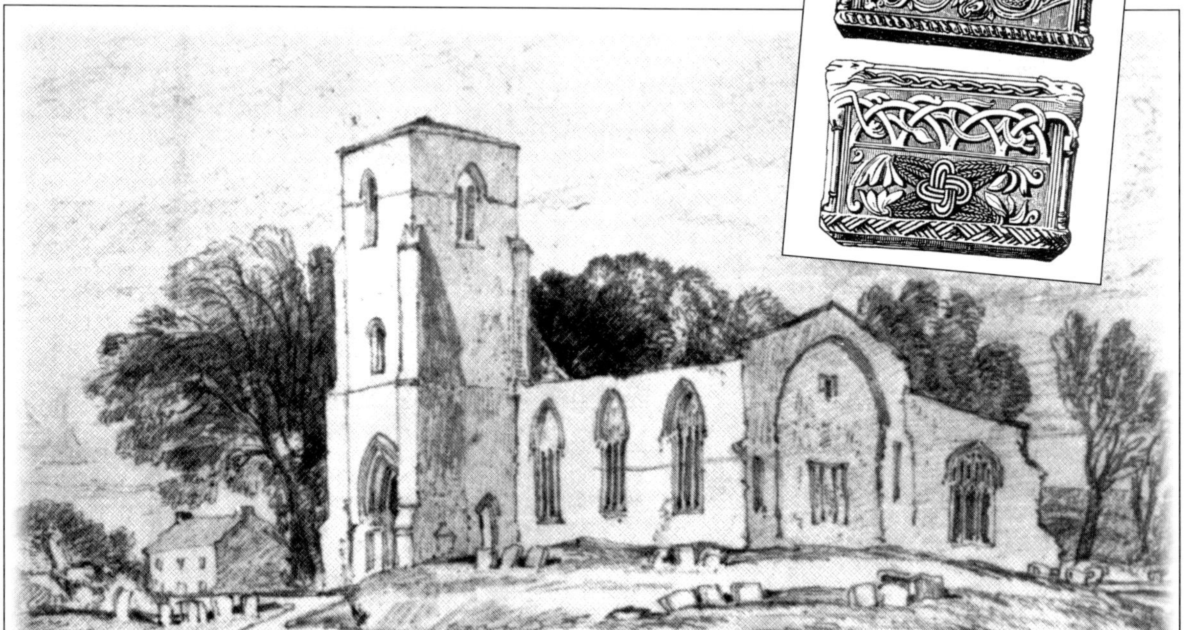

Sculthorpe Church from a sketch by Elizabeth Turner (later Lady Polgrave), 1841. This charming picture with Manor Farmhouse (c.1809) in the background shows how the Parish Church looked before the Victorian restoration. (Copyright: the British Museum. Reproduced by kind permission of the trustees of the British Museum)

Burgundy. This monastic church frequently granted sanctuary to pilgrims and so it was that William de Warenne and his wife Gundrada, a stepdaughter of William the Conqueror, found shelter there whilst on their pilgrimage to Rome. Inspired by what they had seen and experienced at Cluny, William and Gundrada invited Prior Lanzo and some Cluniac monks to settle in England. The Cluniac Priory of St Pancras was founded in 1077 at Lewes in Sussex and by 1090 a daughter house had been established at Castle Acre in Norfolk. Both monasteries were built adjacent to the two principal fortresses of the de Warenne family.

These 'alien' priories, subject to the mother house in Cluny, wielded enormous influence in 'Sculethorp' where the Parish Church was valued at 50 marks. The de Warennes, as lords of the manor and patrons of the living, repeatedly endowed the prior and monks of Lewes with portions of the church tithes of Sculthorpe and this led to lengthy disputes between the Cluniac monks and successive priests of Sculthorpe determined to preserve their living.

The Lewes Cartulary in the British Museum reveals that throughout the twelfth and thirteenth centuries the prior and monks at Lewes became legally adept at defending their portions of the tithes and produced their many deeds and grants bearing the seals of feudal magnates, diocescan bishops and even the Holy Father in Rome as evidence in 1219.

On an earlier occasion the remarkable Pope Innocent III – famous for his patronage of the brotherhood of St Francis of Assisi and for excommunicating King John – had also appointed umpires and issued directives from the Lateran in Rome regarding another legal dispute over the tithes of the settlement of 'Sculethorp'.

The Cluniac Priory at Castle Acre benefited enormously from the de Warenne patronage within the manor of Sculthorpe. In 1257 William de Wauncy, prior of Castle Acre, had a fold course of sheep grazing in Sculthorpe and, in 1262, Earl Warenne granted by deed the manor of Sculthorpe to the monks of Castle Acre to be held by them for one year under a special payment of 242 marks.

The Norman Font

For 900 years the ancient Norman font in Sculthorpe Church has been in continuous use for the celebration of the sacrament of Holy Baptism. *White's Directory and Gazeteer of Norfolk*, published in 1836, describes it as a 'curious Saxon font'.

In 1817 the Norwich School artist John Sell Cotman published many of his etchings in his *Architectural Remains, Vol. I*, including those drawings depicting 'a Saxon font at Sculthorpe Church, Norfolk'.

The majority of modern archaeologists and historians now state that the font dates from the

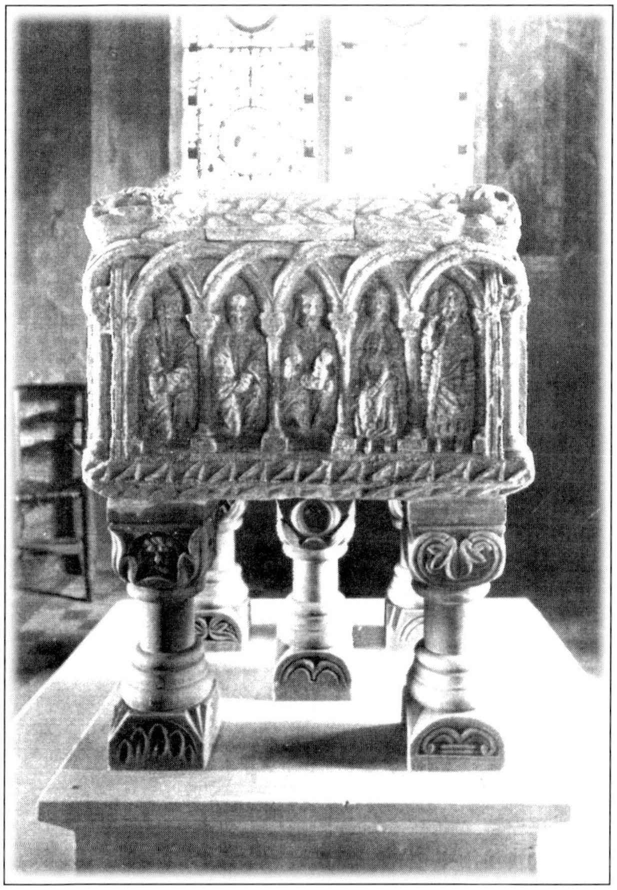

The earliest surviving photograph of the Norman font in Sculthorpe Church, 1870. From An Account of Sculthorpe Church *by Mrs Herbert Jones.*
(Reproduced by kind permission of Father Andrew Thomson, rector of Sculthorpe)

early-Norman period. The massive square bowl, measuring 13½ins deep and 2ft 3ins across, is still lined with its original round lead basin; the base, with its stone columns and steps, dates from the Victorian restoration.

Whilst its origins remain obscure, the very rich geometric carving of the stone has identified the font as the work of a Norman stonemason whose name is not known. It is thought that the same craftsman may also have been responsible for the strikingly similar stone carvings adorning the early-Norman fonts in the churches at Shernborne, South Wootton and Toftrees, in north-west Norfolk.

The link with Toftrees is highly plausible as 'Toffas' appears in the Little Domesday Book as part of William de Warenne's estate valued under 'Sculetorpa'. The fact that both churches retain a Norman font probably carved by the same stonemason points to a possible patronage by the de Warenne family. Many of the interlaced geometric motifs adorning the string course of the early-Norman west font at Castle Acre Priory are also virtually identical to those depicted in the stone carvings of the two fonts at Sculthorpe and Toftrees.

The Sculthorpe font is most famous for a carved

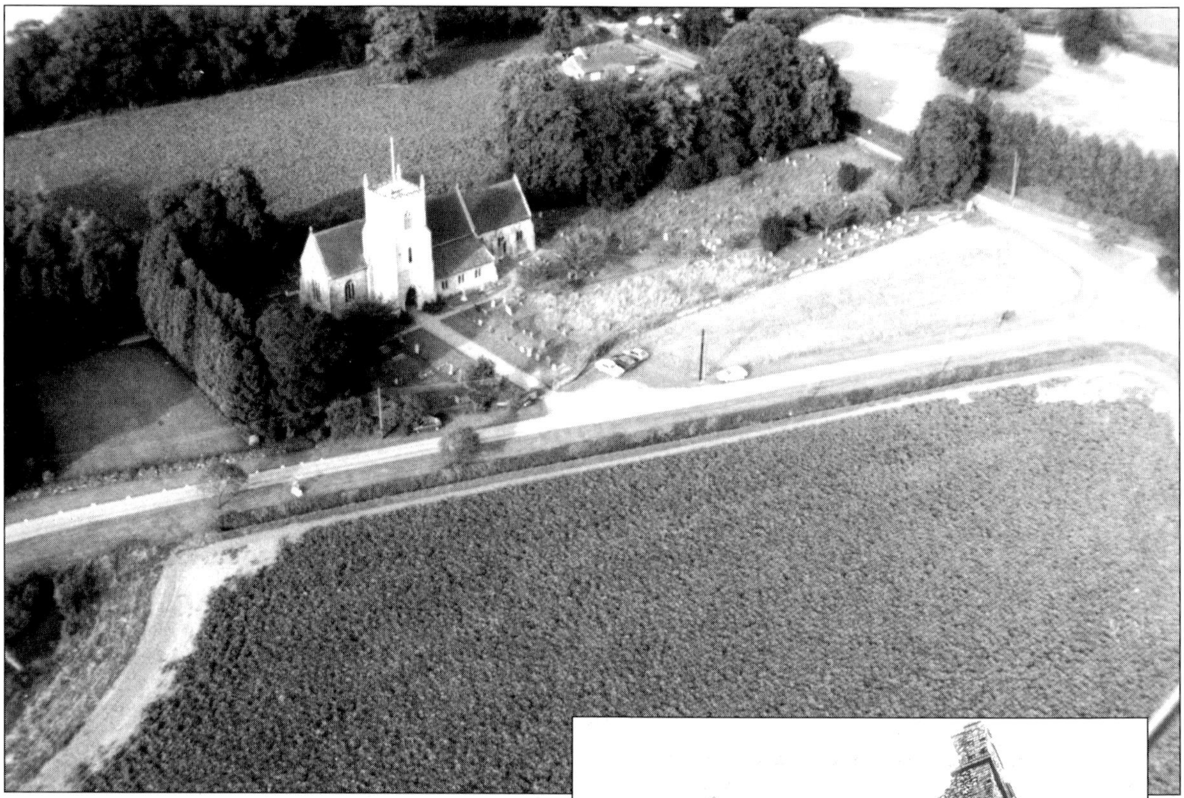

An aerial photograph of the church taken by John Labouchere.

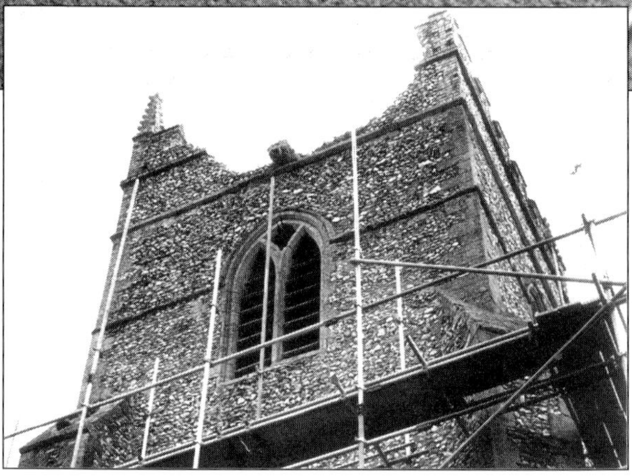

Above: *During the spring of 1972 the Victorian parapet, which had been added to the medieval tower of Sculthorpe Church by Thomas Jekyll at the time of the Victorian restoration in 1860–61, suffered severe damage during a storm. The tower was shored up with scaffolding and the parapet lowered substantially by several feet. The gruesome fourteenth-century gargoyle survived and was incorporated into the new work.* (Reproduced by kind permission of the *Eastern Daily Press*, Archant Norfolk Ltd)

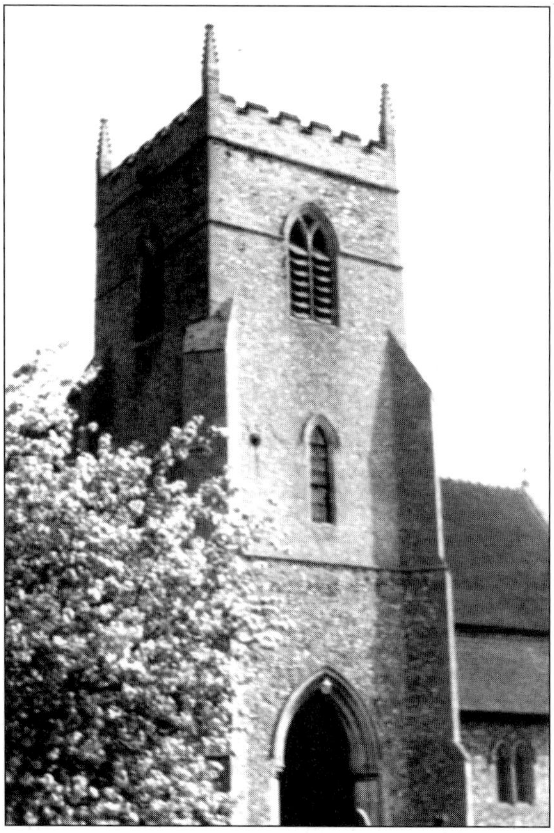

Left: *The early-fourteenth-century south-west tower of Sculthorpe Church has been attributed to the De Norwich family who held the manor here from 1317. Sir Walter De Norwich was Baron of the Exchequer for King Edward II whilst Sir John De Norwich was Admiral of the Northern Fleet at the Battle of Sluys in 1340.*

scene depicting the Adoration of the Magi. The wise men are shown wearing crowns, upholding the tradition established by the Venerable Bede of the three kings, Caspar, Melchior and Balthasar. The figure of Our Lady, enthroned and crowned with the holy infant Jesus seated on her lap, reflects the ancient and traditional imagery depicting the Mother of God as both Queen of Heaven and Seat of Wisdom.

In around 1771 the antiquary Tom Martin of Thetford sketched a ground plan of Sculthorpe Church which is still preserved within his 'Church Notes' in the *Rye Manuscript* at the Norfolk Record Office. This depicts the font standing near one of the fourteenth-century pillars at the north-west side of the nave. The Victorian restoration in 1860–61 saw the removal of the font from the nave to be placed on new columns and a stepped platform at the west end of the north aisle, creating a most attractive baptistry.

Although the Victorians repaired and, in places, re-cut the stonework, much of the original Norman carving survived. In 1236 the Archbishop of Canterbury – St Edmund Rich of Abingdon – ordered that all fonts in English churches should be covered and locked to prevent witches from stealing the Holy Water used at Baptism. The rim of the font bowl at Sculthorpe had been badly damaged, possibly during the Reformation in the sixteenth century, by the breaking of the hinge and staple to remove an ancient cover.

The Tower of Sculthorpe Church and the Green Way to Walsingham

In his 'Church Notes' within the *Rye Manuscript* Tom Martin of Thetford wrote of his visit to the 'Church of Sculthorpe by Ffakenham Market in Norfolk' and described 'a low square steple (with 3 bells) standing at ye south west end of the church and serves instead of a porch.'

The south-west tower of Sculthorpe Church, its base a magnificent porch by which one enters the nave, is thought to date from c.1300 and is in the early-decorated style of the period. A local tradition identifies the family of De Norwich as the driving force behind the construction of this splendid tower. In the year 1317 John de Warenne, Earl of Surrey, presented the manor of Sculthorpe and the patronage of the living to Sir Walter De Norwich and his lady Katherine by a grant of exchange for their estate at Skredington in Lincolnshire. In 1324 Sir Walter exercised his right as patron of the church by presenting the priest, Walter de Thirston, to the living of Sculthorpe. The most celebrated member of this family was Sir John De Norwich of Mettingham Castle in Suffolk, the fourteenth-century admiral responsible for the famous naval victory over the French fleet at Sluys in 1340.

The size of the tower porch reflects its importance during medieval times, the churching of women, acts of penance and a sizeable part of the sacrament of holy matrimony were conducted here.

Robust stone columns, the hood mould and beautifully-carved corbel headstops to the main doorway show that no expense was spared. Above the doorway is a tall fourteenth-century niche, which is empty now but once contained the image of the patron saint, Our Lady, the Mother of Christ.

The patronal dedication of the church has been a common problem for historians; both the Revd Francis Blomefield in his famous eighteenth-century *History of Norfolk* and Hugh Bryant in *Churches of Norfolk: Hundred of Gallow* have suggested either St Mary the Virgin or All Saints but Tom Martin in his 'Church Notes' categorically states that 'the church is dedicated to St Mary.' This would seem the most plausible explanation, especially as the village was situated on the ancient 'green way' to the medieval shrine of Our Lady of Walsingham. The dedication of Sculthorpe Church, and others in the locality, reflects this deep-rooted devotion to the Blessed Virgin Mary.

During the Middle Ages when England was widely known as Our Lady's Dowry, vast numbers of pilgrims, including English kings, passed through Sculthorpe en route to Walsingham. There is an abundance of documentary evidence for the wayside crosses which once stood in Sculthorpe. Bryant's 1826 map of Norfolk depicts 'Cross Green' to the west of the church and Manor Farm, while the Church Terrier of 1613, in the Norfolk Record Office, indicates the presence of the 'High Preaching Cross' on the eastern side of the parish – 'Preaching Cross Field' near Lodge Farm perpetuates the name.

Prior to the Victorian restoration of the church in 1860–61, a beautifully-carved circular stone slab depicting the Crucifixion served as a threshold in the south-west porch entrance. In Tom Martin's sketch, c.1771, it appeared to be the head of a stone cross, possibly taken down and placed here after the Reformation to be sacreligiously trodden underfoot by the parish faithful as a visible protest against 'Popish images'. Was it the head of a medieval churchyard cross or one of the ancient wayside crosses used by the pilgrims as a halting place along the green way to Walsingham? It is to be regretted that it was removed and subsequently lost during the Victorian restoration.

The tiny corkscrew staircase enclosed within the tower porch rises to the ringing chamber above. Since the acquisition of a ring of six bells during the 1930s, campanology, or bell-ringing, has been a popular village pastime. In September 1552, during the Reformation, an Inventory of Church Goods was compiled by the King's commissioners; it included the entry 'Skulthorpe' and mentioned 'one bell weynge 13cwt'.

The King's commissioners, appointed by the

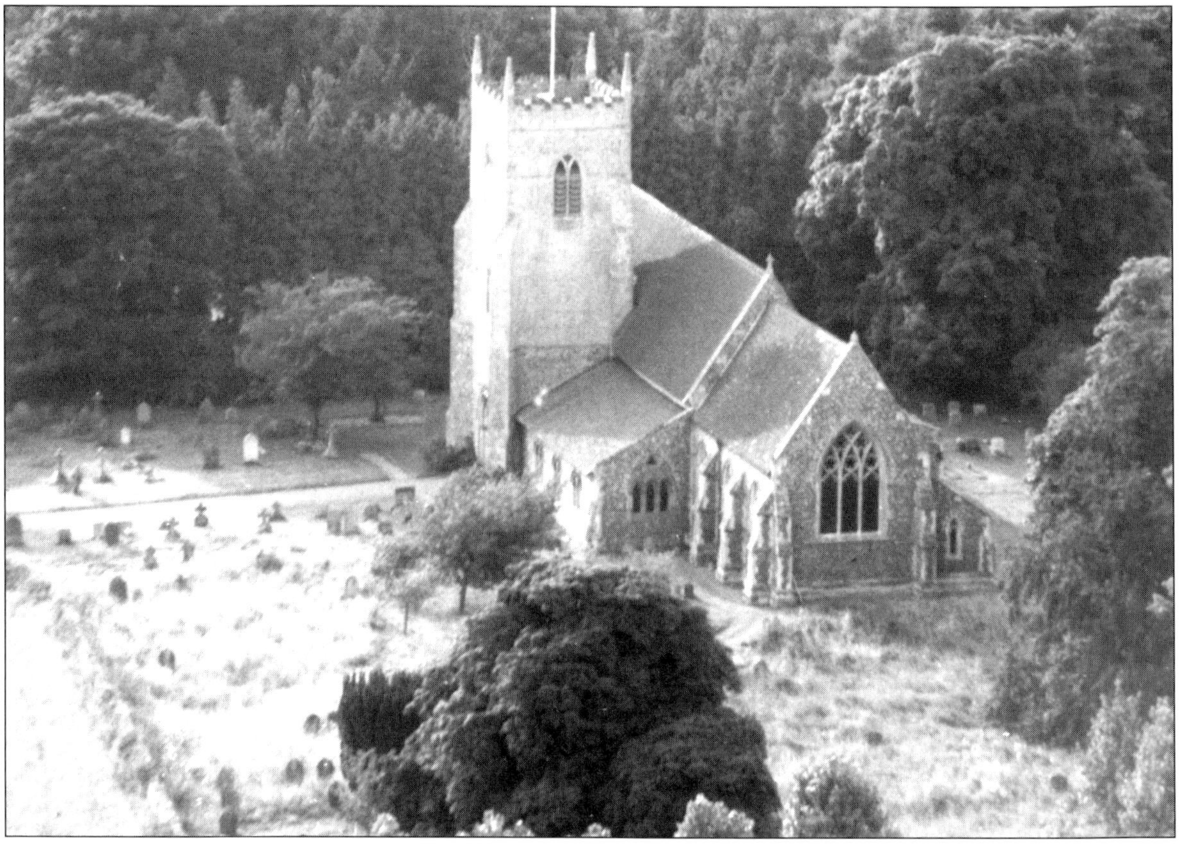

Sculthorpe Church, an aerial view taken by John Labouchere in 1984.

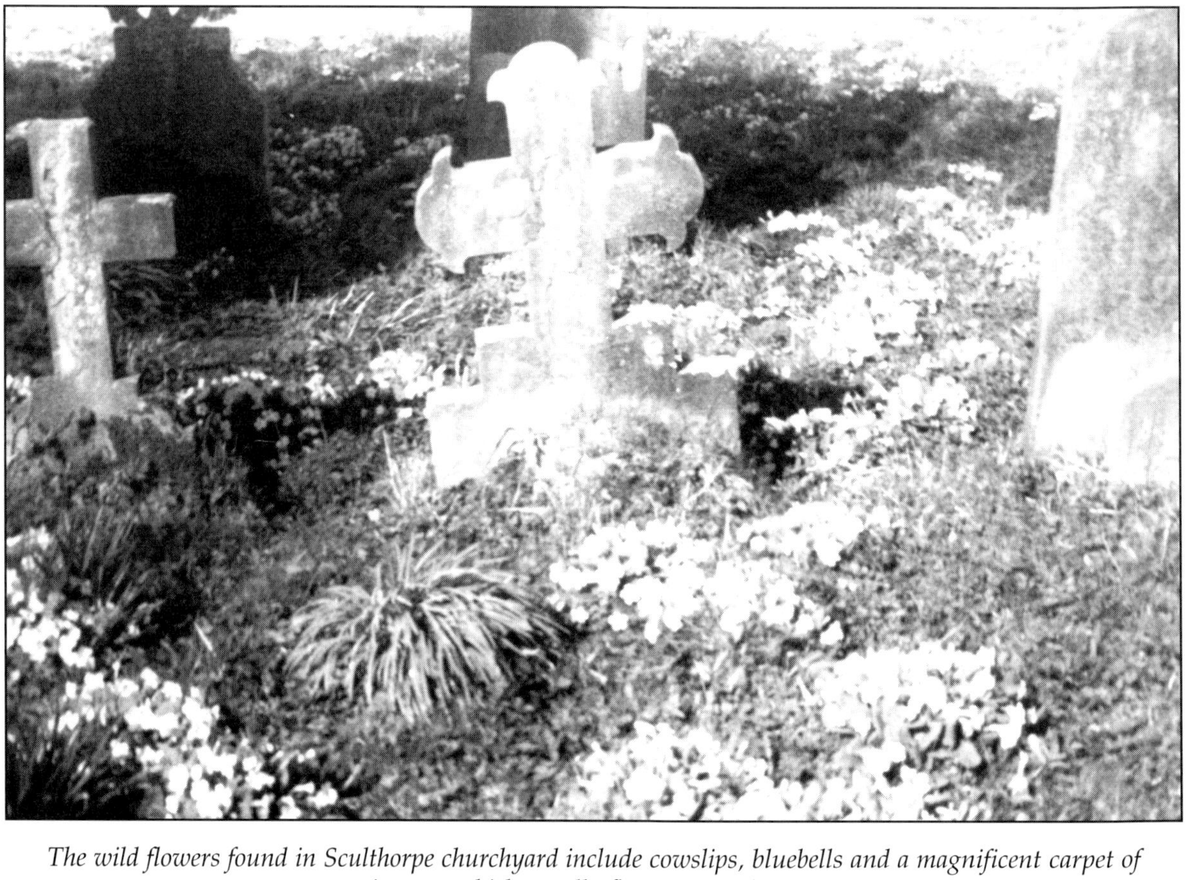

The wild flowers found in Sculthorpe churchyard include cowslips, bluebells and a magnificent carpet of primroses which usually flower around Easter.

Protestant councillors of the boy-king Edward VI in 1552 to seize plate and vestments from the newly-reformed and ritually-cleansed churches, usually spared one bell for each parish and so the great bell 'valewed at 15 shillings the hundred' was left hanging in the belfry of Sculthorpe Church. One of the royal commissioners present here in September 1552 was Sir William Fermour of East Barsham Manor who was both lord of the manor and patron of Sculthorpe Church.

Bell-ringing remained popular, despite the Reformation, and Norfolk in particular was famous for its church bells and its local families associated with the casting of bells in their foundries. During the 1600s Sculthorpe Church acquired three bells.

In 1625 when Dr John Quarles, archdeacon of Northampton, became rector of Sculthorpe a new bell was hung in the church tower. It had been cast by John Draper, the celebrated bell-founder of Thetford, and bore the inscription: 'JOHN DRAPER MADE ME 1625'. John Draper frequently collaborated with local bell foundries including that of John Brend, the famous bell-founder based at All Saint's Green in Norwich. The Brend family had been casting bells in Norwich since 1570.

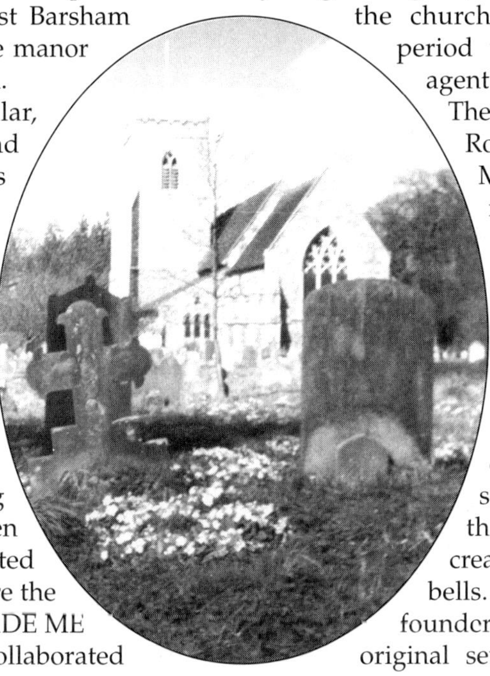
Wild primroses in Sculthorpe churchyard, Easter 1991.

In 1630 a second bell was added to Sculthorpe bearing the inscription 'J.D.J.B. 1630' – proof of the joint partnership of John Draper of Thetford and John Brend of Norwich.

The Puritan Commonwealth saw a reaction against church bells being cast for 'steeple houses' but the restoration of the Stuart monarchy and the Established Church revived the tradition and, in 1675, when the Revd Clement Heigham was rector of Sculthorpe and residing with his wife Susan Skippon at the parsonage house in the village, a third bell was cast and hung in the belfry. It bore the inscription: 'EDWARD TOOKE MADE ME 1675'.

Edward Tooke had continued casting bells at the Norwich foundry after the Brend family ceased to do so in 1670. The churchwarden's account book for 'Skulthorpe', dating from 1729 and held in the Norfolk Record Office, makes occasional reference to the three bells hanging in their frame and the necessary repairs undertaken: in 1766 5s.7½d. was paid to John Nicholls, the blacksmith, for repairs made to the bells and the church gates.

It appears that the bells were rung frequently, especially on occasions such as the Thanksgiving Day which was held on 29 November 1805 in celebration of Lord Nelson's splendid naval victory over the combined French and Spanish fleets at Cape Trafalgar.

During the Victorian restoration in 1860–61 the bells were rehung in a new frame and new floors were added to the tower.

Mrs Marion Howard, Willy Woodhouse's younger daughter, could vividly recall the ringing of the church bells during the Edwardian period when her father became land agent for the Cranmer Hall estate. The Woodhouse family moved to Rose Cottage near the church and Marion Howard particularly remembered the tolling of the 'death knell' for the parish dead, and, in November 1918, at the Armistice, the bells being chimed by the old verger Frank Groom to herald the end of the First World War.

The limitations of having only three bells which were sadly in need of replacement in the church tower led to the creation of the present ring of six bells. In 1929 Alfred Bowell, bell founder at Ipswich, re-cast the three original seventeenth-century bells, wisely retaining their historic inscriptions, and, in 1930, added another three new bells which were inscribed with the names of the three canticles – *Te Deum Laudamus* (We praise thee, O God), *the Venite, Exultemus Domino* (Psalm 95, O Come, let us sing unto the Lord) and the *Magnificat* of Our Lady from St Luke's Gospel.

The art of change-ringing or 'Plain Bob' was initially heard in England when the first full peal of 5,040 changes was rung on the bells of the great civic church of St Peter Mancroft, Norwich, on 2 May 1715.

The re-casting and hanging of the new bells at Sculthorpe Church ensured that Plain Bob became a feature of church life in the village. At Eastertide on 19 April 1931 the first peal of 5,040 changes was rung by the newly-formed band of Sculthorpe bell-ringers. One of its most enthusiastic members was the Captain of the Tower, Bob Lingwood from Rectory Cottage in Creake Road.

During the Second World War the church bells remained silent and were only to be rung in the event of invasion. The post-war period saw revived enthusiasm for bell-ringing in Sculthorpe, encouraged by the Revd John Turney and later by the Revd Fred Gunn. By 1980, when the Revd Jack Pennock was priest-in-charge at Sculthorpe, a new team of bell-ringers had been formed under the expert tutelage of Wilfred Jarvis who had extensive experience of change-ringing in many East Anglian church towers, including the famous bells at the great

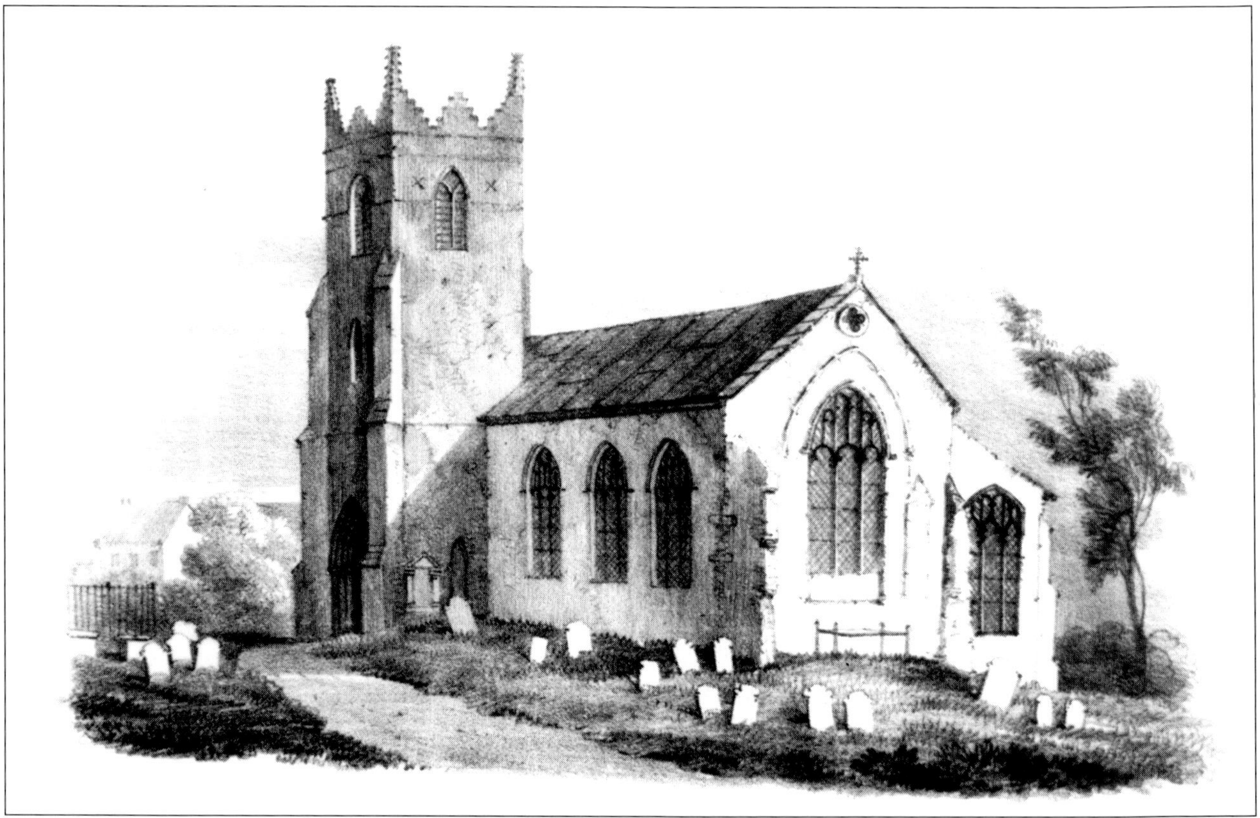

Sculthorpe Church by John Berney Ladbrooke, c.1820. The three late-fourteenth-century Perpendicular windows in the south wall of the nave were removed to make way for the south aisle Lady Chapel in 1860–61. Two were reused in the Victorian 'galilee' and the third was given to Canon Lee Warner of Thorpland Hall who re-erected the window tracery as a folly in his garden where it can still be seen.
(Copyright: Norfolk County Council Library and Information Service)

wool church of Lavenham in neighbouring Suffolk.

A band of handbell-ringers was formed and later the children at Sculthorpe Primary School created their own team of handbell-ringers who regularly performed at school concerts, church garden fêtes and carol services in the Parish Church.

At the time of writing the Captain of the Tower is David Beale, and he and his wife Sue continue to enthusiastically promote the art of campanology in the village.

The passing of time has witnessed changes, repairs and restoration to the south-west tower of Sculthorpe Church. The 1507 will of Emma Barwyke, proved in the Archdeaconry Court at Norwich, contained a bequest made towards the 'reparation of the steeple' at Sculthorpe. The striking lithograph of the church, dated c.1823, by John Berney Ladbrooke of the Norwich School, depicts the church tower with its tall stepped battlements, which appear to have been replaced by a low pyramidal cap in Elizabeth Turner's sketch of the church in the early 1840s.

During the Victorian restoration the architect Thomas Jekyll designed a rather heavy crenellated parapet with crocketted pinnacles and much of the old exterior plaster rendering was scraped away from the tower to expose the medieval flints. A small fourteenth-century window in the tower porch was raised to allow for the doorway into the Victorian south aisle Lady Chapel. Jekyll also designed the doors at the main entrance which are decorated with a beautifully-carved depiction of nightingales flying against a background of hawthorn and apple blossom.

During the spring of 1972 the Victorian parapet was badly damaged in a severe storm, the tower was subsequently shored up with scaffolding and repointed and the parapet skilfully lowered by several feet to its present height. The tower remains in 2003, an enduring statement of faith and continuity in the landscape and a conspicuous landmark within the Wensum valley.

Sir Robert Knollys

Sir Robert Knollys (c.1315–1407) is undoubtedly the most celebrated character in the history of Sculthorpe. He was a veteran commander of the Hundred Years War and a generous benefactor of Sculthorpe Parish Church. He was reputedly born in Cheshire in c.1315, a soldier of fortune and later the brilliant commander of English armies, he was revered by three generations of the Plantaganet royal house. The bold claim of King Edward III to the royal throne of his French ancestors would see the direct involvement of Robert Knollys in many of the key episodes of the Hundred Years War.

From 1346 Robert Knollys was fighting in Brittany, frequently at the side of his great friend Sir Hugh Calverley. Dubbed a Knight in 1351 he became embroiled in the chivalric duel known as the 'Combat of the Thirty' but survived his injuries to gain great notoriety as a mercenary commander and the founder of one of the 'Free Companies'. Sir Robert's band of mercenary soldiers was widely known as the 'Great Company', indulging their lust for blood and glory by conducting widespread campaigns of burning, looting and pillaging across much of northern France. The company would demand huge ransoms by blackmail and terror and accumulated vast reserves of wealth in the process. By 1359 many of these spoils, including the 40 castles captured by Sir Robert in the Loire Valley, had been entrusted to King Edward III as a visible demonstration of Sir Robert's loyalty to the English Crown.

Such victories had a great impact for generations in northern France as people would recall the burnt and blackened gable-ends of their ransacked houses silhouetted against the evening sky – they called them 'Knolles' Mitres' in bitter memory of the devastating raids and murders.

In 1359 Sir Robert Knollys conducted fresh campaigns throughout the duchy of Brittany which led to the defeat and capture of the famous commander Bertrand du Guesclin. Sir Robert gained enormous prestige in doing so and John, Duke of Brittany, subsequently rewarded him for this and other victories by granting him the castle of Derval in 1365. From this fortified citadel Sir Robert was able to continue launching his armed mercenaries into further raids of murderous ransacking.

A wealth of information has been recorded by historians relating to Sir Robert's loyalty to Edward, the Black Prince, eldest son of King Edward III and heir to the English throne. Some authorities even suggest that he was present at the side of the Black Prince at the victorious Battle of Poitiers in 1356. He certainly accepted the personal invitation of the prince to accompany him in 1367 on his famous expedition to Spain. Supported by his numerous fighting comrades, the veterans of the 'Great Company', Sir Robert was able to contribute to the great military victory at the Battle of Najara on 3 April 1367.

In 1369 Sir Robert immediately raised an army to defend his royal master against a French attack within the Black Prince's duchy of Aquitaine. In the pages of the famous *Chronicle* by Jean Froissart it is written that the Black Prince and his beautiful wife Joan the 'Fair Maid of Kent' graciously received Sir Robert Knollys at their residence in Angouleme.

The Black Prince elevated Knollys to the high honour of being 'captain of the knights and squires' within the royal household and gave strict instructions that the famous Knight should be accorded every deference. That such honour should be paid to an upstart such as Sir Robert Knollys must surely have wrankled the nobility serving within the prince's household; pledged to the chivalric code of behaviour they must have regarded Sir Robert's exploits with obvious jealousy and disgust. Their reluctance to serve the mercenary commander would be seen during his campaign of 1370.

Sir Robert was appointed commander of an expeditionary force to France by King Edward at Windsor Castle. He sailed from the port of Dover in July 1370 and with him aboard the ships were 1,500 men-at-arms and 4,000 archers. The historian Derek Pearsall stated that Geoffrey Chaucer, 'the father of English poetry', was present amongst this company, armed with letters of protection from King Edward to undertake a royal mission abroad.

The campaign from Calais to Troyes saw Sir Robert displaying his usual military tactics – burning, plundering and demanding ransoms. He marched his army to the outskirts of Paris in an attempt to goad the French King, Charles V, into battle; the inhabitants of Paris are said to have watched with considerable alarm from the walls of their city as the sky turned black with the smoke from burning towns and villages in the surrounding countryside but the French King prudently resisted the temptation of riding into battle against Sir Robert Knollys.

Members of the nobility travelling with the expeditionary force whispered maliciously about the veteran commander – their favourite insult was to call him the 'old brigand' which led to divisive quarrels and insubordination. The military campaign ended with Sir Robert returning to his favourite castle at Derval in Brittany where he offered his services again to his old friend John, Duke of Brittany.

In 1376 the Black Prince, exhausted following his years of persistent campaigning, died and was buried beneath a splendid recumbent effigy next to the famous shrine of St Thomas à Becket in Canterbury Cathedral. The coat of arms of Sir Robert Knollys appear twice in the vaulted cloister at Canterbury, perhaps a touching heraldic reference to his long friendship with the Black Prince.

In 1377, when the boy-king Richard II, son of the Black Prince, succeeded his grandfather King Edward to the English throne, Sir Robert was still serving the Duke of Brittany and acting as the governor of the castle in Brest. How did Sir Robert Knollys become associated with the village of Sculthorpe? In 1378 the Duke of Brittany exchanged the castle at Brest with young King Richard II for that of Castle Rising in Norfolk and this single act must have effectively introduced Sir Robert as one of the Duke's retainers to this corner of rural England.

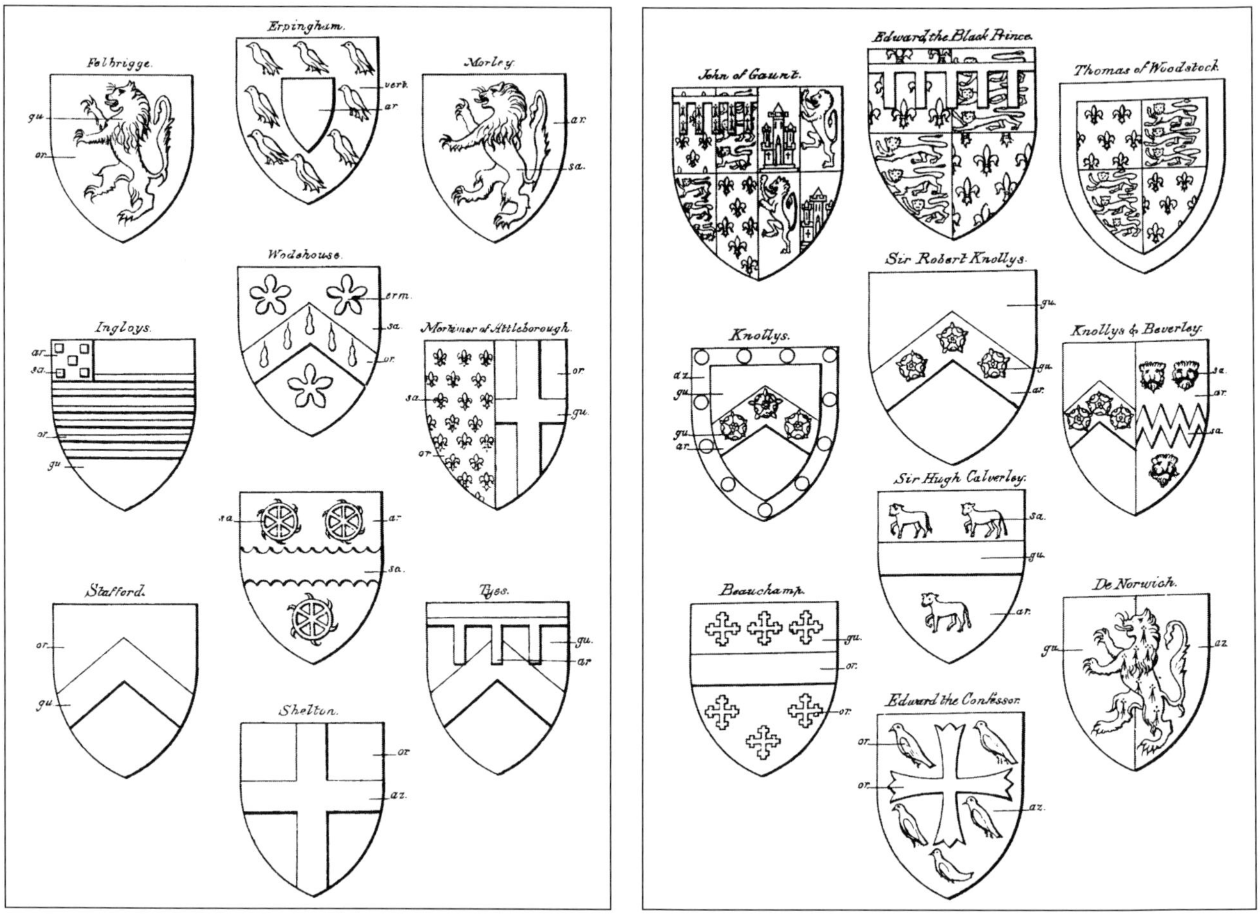

The medieval nave roof of Sculthorpe Church was removed in 1815 but was fortunately recorded by historians from the sixteenth century onwards. It was an angel roof adorned with heraldic shields commemorating the military exploits of Sir Robert Knollys and his fighting comrades during the Hundred Years War with France. From Notes on Sculthorpe Church *by Mrs Herbert Jones, published in 1872.*
(Reproduced by kind permission of the Norfolk & Norwich Archaeological Society)

The magnificent deer park of 'Rising Chace' would have offered excellent opportunities for riding, hunting and hawking and this may have been one of the reasons why Sir Robert continued to be attendant upon the Duke here. Documentary evidence suggests that he visited this part of Norfolk regularly and the chamberlain's accounts for the Guildhall of the Holy Trinity in the port of Lynn reveal that Sir Robert was honourably received and entertained here in 1379 and again in 1380.

In 1379 we find Sir Robert in possession of a royal grant of 'free warren' within the manor of Dunton – a licence from King Richard empowering him to rear and kill beasts and game. The old brigand was keeping a watchful eye on developments in the neighbouring manor of Sculthorpe, which had a sizeable deer chace within the expanse of the Great Common in the Wensum valley.

The absentee lady of the manor of Sculthorpe was then Dame Catherine Brews, the widowed cousin and heiress of the victorious admiral Sir John De Norwich. Dame Catherine had recently been professed a Dominican nun and had entered the Dominican Priory at Dartford in Kent, an austere convent famed for its discipline and learning, where she was undertaking the sale of her estate in Sculthorpe through her trustees.

During June 1381 while Sir Robert was finalising legal transactions in order to acquire the manor of Sculthorpe, the increasingly unstable state of the Kingdom was thrown into turmoil by the rebellion of Wat Tyler, an event known as the Peasant's Revolt. Sir Robert was staying at his London residence in Seething Lane, attended by 120 armed retainers, when news of the rebellion reached him. The wealthy merchants and citizens of London immediately called upon the brave knight to protect them.

Acting in his official capacity as 'Captain of the City Archers and Men-at-arms' Sir Robert was able to mobilise 600 archers and armed soldiers from the Tower of London whilst also ensuring that his own armed retainers kept watch over his house and garden in nearby Seething Lane.

Following Wat Tyler's death at the hands of the Lord Mayor, William Walworth, in Smithfield market, Sir Robert's presence at the side of young King Richard, his cool head and wise words certainly contributed towards the peaceful dispersal of the rebels.

On 27 June 1381 the legal proceedings by which Sir Robert acquired the manorial estate of Sculthorpe were finalised and it was here that he built his fortified manor-house and started a full-scale rebuilding of the Parish Church.

Manor Farmhouse next to Sculthorpe Church is a late-Georgian building dated c.1809; it is called the 'Newhouse' on the Ordnance Survey map of 1838 and stands on the site of 'Ye Antient Manor House' of Sir Robert Knollys which was still partially standing at the time of the compilation of the Sculthorpe Field Book in 1766. The substantial fourteenth-century earthworks surrounding the farmhouse include traces of both the inner and outer moats, which were obviously defensive and prove that Sir Robert was taking no chances when he built his manor-house, especially in the aftermath of the Peasant's Revolt.

The rebuilding of the Parish Church, which spared the ancient Norman font and the early-fourteenth-century tower built by the De Norwich family, included a nave, north aisle and a chancel in the early-Perpendicular style. In 2003 only the core of the nave with its wide chancel arch, the north aisle with its fourteenth-century pillars and the remains of the rood stairwell which once gave access to the medieval rood-loft are all that is left of Sir Robert's work.

The late-fourteenth-century chancel appears to have exceeded the Victorian replacement by 10 feet. Tom Martin's notes and sketch from the *Rye Manuscript*, dated c.1771, mention that 'the chancel (which had a Charnell house under it) is fallen down' and pose a question about 'ye building at ye north east corner of the chancel.' In 1957 Howard Brown, brother-in-law of the rector, the Revd Fred Gunn, carried out a small archaeological dig in the vicinity of the fragmentary remains still left at the north-eastern side of the Victorian chancel, which were identified as part of the fourteenth-century sacristy of the medieval chancel.

The glory of Sculthorpe Church in the late Middle Ages was the magnificent open timber roof of the nave, adorned with winged angels bearing a series of heraldic shields depicting the coat of arms of Sir Robert Knollys and those of his fighting comrades which commemorated their military exploits in the French Wars. It is fortunate that ancient documentary evidence has survived which provides detailed information about the angel roof and its medieval heraldry. Robert Kemp's entry for the church within the *Harleian Manuscript* in the British Library, dated c.1575, mentions the coat of arms 'in the steeple windowes and on the roofe'. Henry Chitting, author of the *Visitation of Norfolk Churches*, dated c.1600–20, also describes 20 shields 'in the roofe of the churche' and the arms of 'Knowles sideth the same coat round about the churche.'

In his *History of Norfolk* the Revd Francis Blomefield included details of the heraldry whilst Tom Martin of Thetford in his 'Church Notes' sketched the arms of Sir Robert Knollys 'on a north window', suggesting that the windows of the church were filled with armorial glass.

Among the characters commemorated by these heraldic devices in Sculthorpe Church were Edward, the Black Prince, and his royal brothers John of Gaunt, Duke of Lancaster, and Thomas of Woodstock, Duke of Gloucester, who had also campaigned with Sir Robert on the Continent. Other shields commemorated local knights such as Sir Peter Tyes of East Barsham, Sir Ralph Shelton of Great Snoring and Sir Simon Felbrigge who was standard-bearer for King Richard II.

The Erpingham shield recalls Sir Robert's link with the illustrious Sir Thomas Erpingham who later fought with King Henry V at the Battle of Agincourt in 1415 and built the splendid Erpingham gateway leading into the Cathedral Close at Norwich. Another shield commemorated Sir Hugh Calverley, perhaps Sir Robert's closest comrade, whose tomb at Bunbury Church in their native county of Cheshire is decorated with both the arms of Knollys and Calverley.

The years spent looting and plundering with the 'Great Company' in France had reaped rich rewards for Sir Robert Knollys. He used his wealth to purchase much landed property in Kent, Yorkshire and the city of London, in addition to his manorial estates in Norfolk. His riches also provided him with the opportunity to instigate a number of charitable and pious good works which he may well have regarded as an act of atonement for his previous behaviour, thus ensuring a swift passage through the cleansing fires of Purgatory at his death. The rebuilding of Sculthorpe Church during the 1380s was one example of this public display of religious piety, another was the rebuilding of the Church of St Lawrence the Martyr at Harpley in West Norfolk. The shields of Sir Robert and his wife Constantia, Lady Knollys, still adorn the medieval rood-screen in Harpley Church and stone shields cut into the battlements of the south aisle also survive. Sir Robert's personal chaplain and confessor was John Drewe, the rector of Harpley from 1389 until 1421, who did much to promote the fame and perpetuate the memory of his patron after Sir Robert's death.

The famous Friary Church of the Carmelite Order – Whitefriars – in Fleet Street, London, was also rebuilt by Sir Robert Knollys. Sir John Hawkwood and Sir Hugh Calverley, two of Sir Robert's old fighting comrades, were involved in his foundation of the Hospice in Rome for the exclusive use by English pilgrims. In August 1389 King Richard II granted his royal licence, permitting Sir Robert to undertake a penitential pilgrimage to Rome, which provided the opportunity for the old knight to personally inspect the English Hospice.

Perhaps Sir Robert's greatest achievements were

the foundation of the College and Hospital of the Holy Trinity and the Blessed Virgin Mary in Pontefract and his involvement in the building of the great stone bridge and chantry chapel at Rochester in Kent.

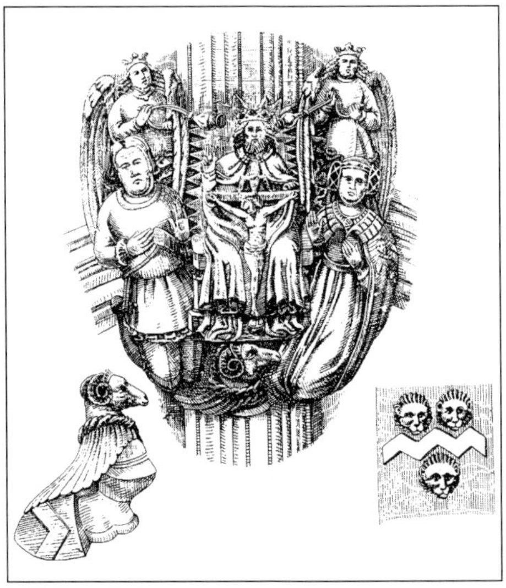

The story of Rochester Bridge is a fascinating tale. In 1387 Sir Robert Knollys and another of his compatriots, Sir John de Cobham, undertook to endow and build a magnificent new stone bridge across the River Medway at Rochester. The Medway town was on the famous road from London to Dover, vitally important for soldiers travelling to fight in France as well as the pilgrims flocking to make their devotions at Becket's Shrine in Canterbury Cathedral.

The work on the bridge is said to have been completed by 1392 and the Bridge Chapel of All Souls by 1397. Here Mass was offered three times a day for both travellers and the Canterbury pilgrims. Most historians now believe it was the King's master mason, Henry Yevele, who was the architect responsible for Rochester Bridge, and his work can be seen in the vast Gothic naves of Westminster Abbey and Canterbury Cathedral.

Another character possibly involved in the construction of this bridge was Geoffrey Chaucer, author of the *Canterbury Tales*, who was both clerk of the King's Works and Knight of the Shire for the county of Kent during this period.

In 1385 King Richard II granted a royal licence to Sir Robert and Constantia to establish a collegiate foundation in Pontefract. This college and hospital, dedicated to the Holy Trinity and the Blessed Virgin Mary, was led by its master, John Stedeman, and six priests and provided for 13 poor people. The master and the priests wore vestments embroidered with the image of the Holy Trinity and the Mystical Rose of Our Lady, a compliment to the three heraldic roses on the chevron of Sir Robert's coat of arms.

According to the sixteenth-century historian John Leland it had been the original intention of Sir Robert to establish this collegiate foundation within the parish of Sculthorpe but Lady Knollys exerted her influence and persuaded him to found the college and hospital in her native town of Pontefract in Yorkshire. Sir Robert would later settle the bulk of his Norfolk estates and the patronage of several Norfolk churches upon the master and chaplains of his college in Yorkshire in order to maintain the poor people housed within its hospital; these included both the manor of Sculthorpe and the patronage of the living of Sculthorpe Church.

Trustees were naturally appointed to maintain this charitable bequest including Sir John de Cobham and Sir Robert's chaplain, John Drewe. Another trustee was Robert de Braybrooke, Lord Bishop of London and a Kinsman of King Richard II, who was appointed Lord Chancellor of England in 1382 and became a fierce opponent of John Wycliffe and his Lollard preachers. The bishop's chaplain, John de Boys, was rector of Sculthorpe from 1380 until 1394 and the de Boys coat of arms, depicting three Catherine wheels, can still be found carved on a number of the fourteenth-century stone corbels in the north aisle of Sculthorpe Church.

Sir Robert Knollys died on 15 August 1407, the Feast of the Assumption of Our Lady, in his fortified manor-house at Sculthorpe, reputedly aged 92 years and widely venerated as a national hero by the people of England. The executor of his will, preserved within Archbishop Arundel's register at Lambeth Palace, was the faithful chaplain John Drewe. Constantia had died in c.1386 and had been buried in the nave of Whitefriars Church in London.

Sir Robert wished to be buried beside his wife and elaborate preparations were made to transport his body to the Friary Church in Fleet Street for his Requiem Mass. Various accounts of his magnificent funeral procession from the manor-house in Sculthorpe to London survive; his body was placed on a splendid litter and taken by night with flaming torches. An inscription *Orate paia Robti Knowles, milit* – pray for the soul of Robert Knollys, soldier – was added to the angel roof within Sculthorpe Church

POSTSCRIPT

Several fourteenth-century stone corbels and the faded painting of an heraldic shield in the north aisle roof are all that is left of the armorial scheme used by Sir Robert Knollys to adorn Sculthorpe Church during the 1380s and yet his legacy has survived.

The famous bridge at Rochester was demolished and replaced in 1856 but the Rochester Bridge Trust, founded by Sir Robert and Sir John de Cobham in 1391, continues to flourish, the Bridge Chapel of All Souls, a ruin for many years, was restored in 1937 and is now the boardroom for the present bridge wardens.

The collegiate foundation in Pontefract was

Above: *Dean Goulburn's nineteenth-century engraving of the cloister boss at Norwich Cathedral, depicting Sir Robert and Constantia, Lady Knollys, worshipping the Holy Trinity.* (Reproduced by kind permission of the Dean and Chapter of Norwich Cathedral)

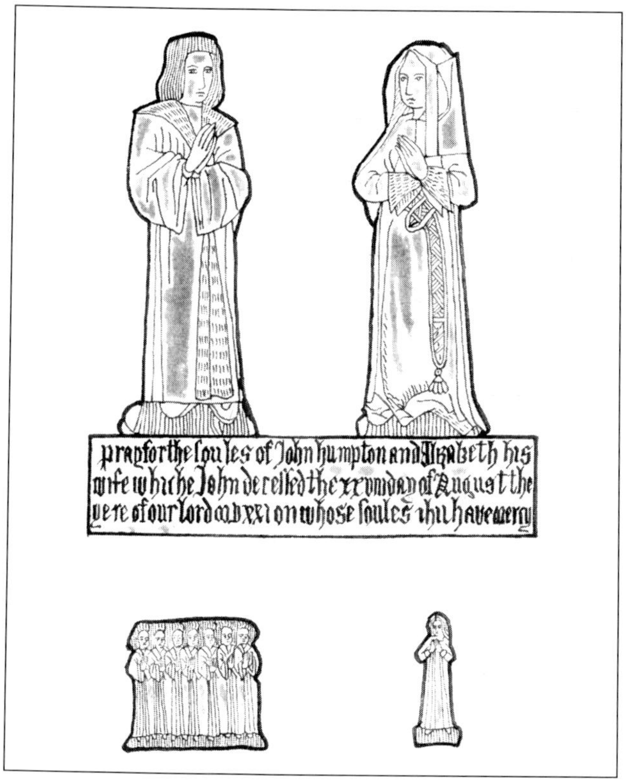

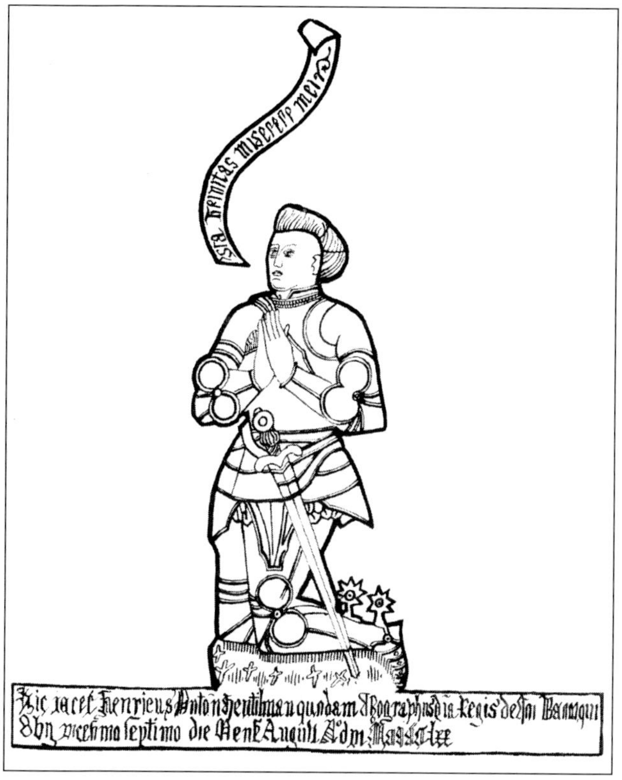

The memorial brasses of John and Elizabeth Humpton and their children, dated 1521 (above left), *and Henry Unton, Receiver of Fines at the Court of Common Pleas, dated 1470* (above right), *from a painting by Mrs Herbert Jones in her manuscript history dated 1870.* (Reproduced by kind permission of Father Andrew Thomson, rector of Sculthorpe)

dissolved in 1549 but partially re-established as the Knollys Almshouse by Queen Elizabeth I in 1563. The arms of Sir Robert Knollys can still be found in many places, most notably as a canted shield with a ram's head crest on the Postern Tower of Bodiam Castle in Sussex, a fortress built by another of Sir Robert's companions, Sir Edward Dalyngrigge.

In the cloister vault at Norwich Cathedral is an early fifteenth-century roof boss depicting Sir Robert and Constantia worshipping the Holy Trinity, this was probably placed here at the instigation of John Drewe who donated £5 to the cathedral in 1421–22 for the soul of his patron.

The Mansion House in London is the annual setting for the ceremony of the Knollys Rose. This commemorates a sentence passed by the Lord Mayor of London upon Sir Robert and Constantia in June 1381. Constantia had committed a daring breach of the civic bylaws by linking her husband's properties in Seething Lane with the construction of a covered footbridge or *haut-pas*. The Lord Mayor, William Walworth, who killed Wat Tyler in the Peasant's Revolt, could not deal too harshly with his old friend on account of his wife's misdemeanour; Sir Robert had just been created a Freeman of the City of London for his part in putting down the rebellion and was greatly respected. The Lord Mayor permitted the offending footbridge to stay in place whilst passing sentence by the imposition of a rose rent. This entailed Sir Robert and Constantia appearing before the Lord Mayor in the Guildhall annually on Midsummer Day to present a red rose from their garden in Seething Lane.

June 1981 marked the 600th anniversary of both the ceremony of the Knollys Rose in London and Sir Robert's acquisition of the manor of Sculthorpe. The present Lord and Lady Knollys visited Sculthorpe Church and planted three rose trees in the churchyard in commemoration of the ancestral link whilst a deputation from Sculthorpe Church later attended the ceremony of the Knollys Rose in the Mansion House and witnessed Lord and Lady Knollys presenting the Knollys Rose to the Lord Mayor of London. A number of tapestry shields worked by the ladies of Sculthorpe have been placed on the piers of the nave in Sculthorpe Church to replace the medieval heraldry lost when the angel roof was removed in 1815.

Nearly 600 years after his death the old brigand's presence continues to be felt in Sculthorpe.

The Memorial Brasses

There are four pre-Reformation memorial brasses in the floor of Sculthorpe Church which were placed at the foot of the chancel steps during the Victorian restoration of 1860–61 and all are extremely popular with brass-rubbing enthusiasts.

The oldest and most beautiful is in memory of Henry Unton who died on 27 August 1470 and was the Receiver of Fines at the Court of the Common Pleas. He is depicted as a martial figure, kneeling at

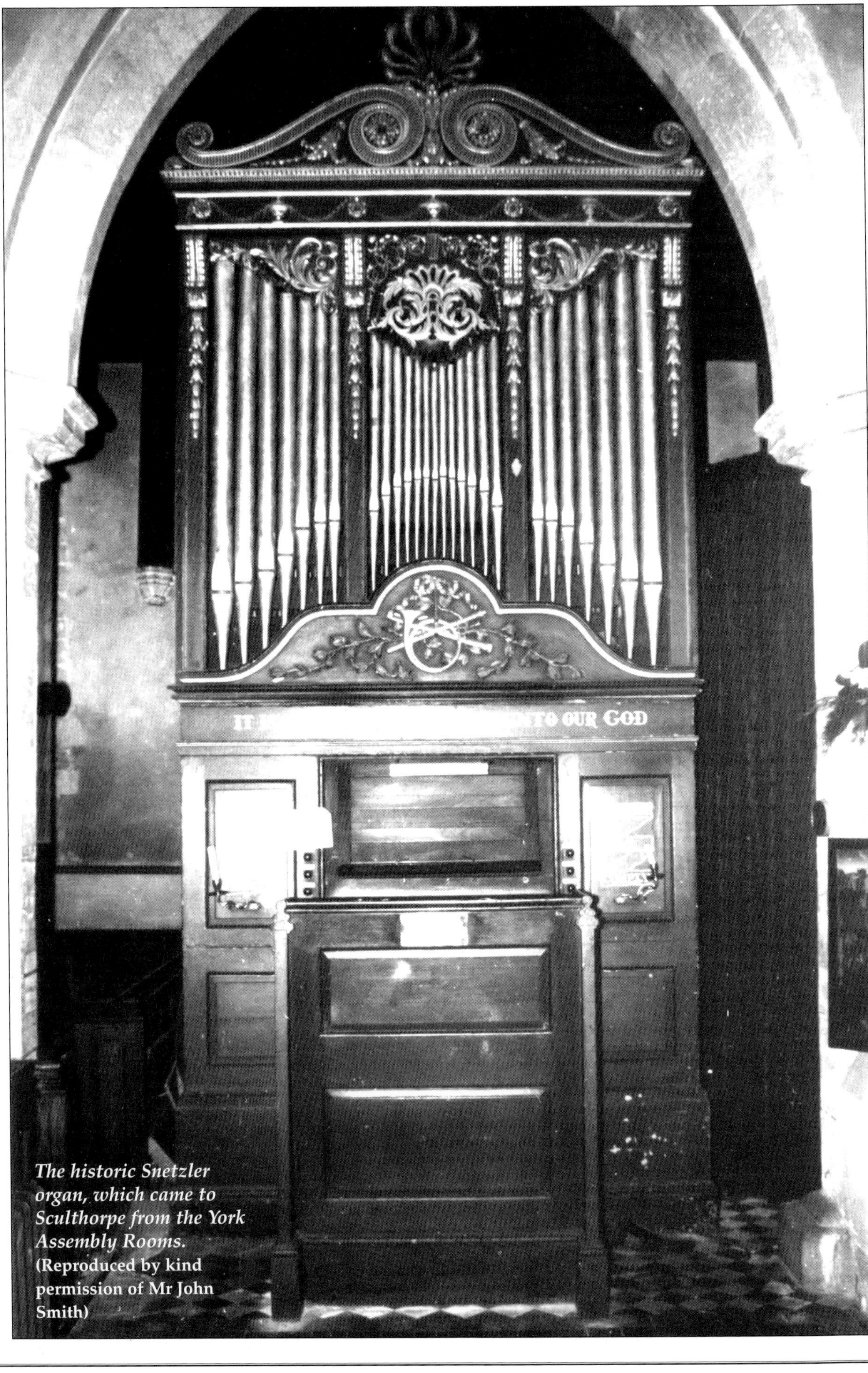

The historic Snetzler organ, which came to Sculthorpe from the York Assembly Rooms. **(Reproduced by kind permission of Mr John Smith)**

prayer, wearing a splendid suit of fifteenth-century armour with sword and spurs. A fluted scroll from his mouth invokes the blessing and mercy of the Holy Trinity. The will of Henry Unton, dated 10 August 1470 and proved within the Prerogative Court at Canterbury, was published in 1841 by the historian John Gough Nichols in *The Unton Inventories*. Although a native of Chorley in Lancashire, Henry Unton appears to have acquired large estates in this part of Norfolk and willed that he might be buried before the 'image of the Holy Trinity' in the church at 'Skulthorpe'; he made a number of bequests to the church: 20d. to the high altar and to the upkeep of the church 6s.8d. He also made ample provision for various Requiem Masses to be offered within the church for the repose of his soul.

According to the Revd Francis Blomefield in his *History of Norfolk* the brass of Henry Unton was originally situated in the floor of the fourteenth-century chancel. Robert Kemp in the *Harleian Manuscript* (c.1575) and John Weever in *Funerall Monuments* (1631) mention the inscription *Orate.p.aia Henrici Unton* – pray for the soul of Henry Unton – which appeared in the glass of a 'chauncell window'.

Indents of four shields and the emblem of the Holy Trinity show that the brass has suffered, possibly at the Reformation. The main inscription, which is in Latin, contains the English word 'Gentilman'.

Henry's brother, Hugh Unton, was the founder of the Unton family established at Wadley in Berkshire; from this line was descended the celebrated diplomat and soldier Sir Henry Unton, appointed English ambassador to the Court of France by Queen Elizabeth I in 1591 and whose life from the cradle to the grave is depicted in the splendid Elizabethan memorial painting at the National Portrait Gallery in London.

The brass of John and Elizabeth Humpton with their seven sons and one daughter is dated 1521. The English inscription requests prayers for the repose of their souls. The figures of John and Elizabeth are depicted in long, fur-trimmed gowns, Elizabeth wearing the gabled English hood popularised by Catherine of Aragon at the English court.

Both John Gough Nichols and Mrs Herbert Jones in her splendid manuscript history of Sculthorpe Church (1870), assert that the surname Humpton is a later derivation of Unton and that John Humpton was possibly the son of Henry Unton. A strong family association has thus been identified with the church. John Gough Nichols mentions Hugh Unton, one of the seven sons of John and Elizabeth depicted in the memorial, who later became a wealthy London merchant and at his death in 1529 bequeathed £10 to the 'church of Scoulthorpe'.

The brass of John and Margaret Stebyrd, a Latin inscription with an heraldic shield, has been dated c.1480 by the British Museum. John Stebyrd came from a long-established Sculthorpe family and appeared in the Manor Court Rolls regarding the deed of the medieval 'Bottemylle' in 1478. His will, originally drafted in 1468, requested that a taper should be lit at the window of his house at the hour of his death and that this and a fresh light should then be burned for his soul in the chancel of Sculthorpe Church. The practice of burning a candle at the window may have been to ward off the Evil Eye. The heraldic shield depicts John Stebyrd's initials flanking a crowned hammer.

The brass inscription – 'Here lyeth Syr George Brown Sometyme parish priest of this town' – has been dated c.1520 by the British Museum. The Revd Francis Blomefield indicated that this memorial was originally placed in the floor of the medieval chancel. 'Syr' was the Catholic title used to address a priest, equivalent to that of reverend or father. Syr George Brown, whose name fails to appear in the official list of the parish clergy, may have been the parish curate who deputised for an absentee rector.

The Snetzler Organ

During March 1974 the Poet Laureate Sir John Betjeman brought a BBC film crew to Sculthorpe Church in order to shoot scenes of the famous Snetzler organ for his documentary film *A Passion for Churches*. This superb eighteenth-century chamber organ situated at the east end of the north aisle was acquired by the church in 1860 and has a long and fascinating history.

The celebrated organ builder John Snetzler was born Johann Schnetzler at Schaffhausen in Switzerland in April 1710, he later settled in England and built his first organ here for George Frederick Handel in 1741. Snetzler's workshop at Oxford Road in London was where he built a number of his most famous instruments including the magnificent organ for St Margaret's Church at King's Lynn in 1754. Dr Charles Burney, father of the eighteenth-century novelist Fanny Burney and friend of the composer Joseph Haydn, was organist at St Margaret's church from 1751–60 and credited Snetzler with the introduction of the organ-stop Dulciana into England at this time.

Snetzler's friendship with Handel, musical director of the Royal Academy and composer to the King's Chapel Royal, appears to have benefited him enormously. Two of Snetzler's instruments were later commissioned for Queen Charlotte's residence at Buckingham House in 1760 and 1763.

The Snetzler organ in Sculthorpe Church was originally built for Lord Burlington's famous Assembly Rooms in York and behind the row of gilt pipes is concealed the Latin inscription *John Snetzler fecit Londini* and the date 1755 whilst the name York appears on the C pipe of the organ stop Open Diapason.

The fashionable citizens of eighteenth-century

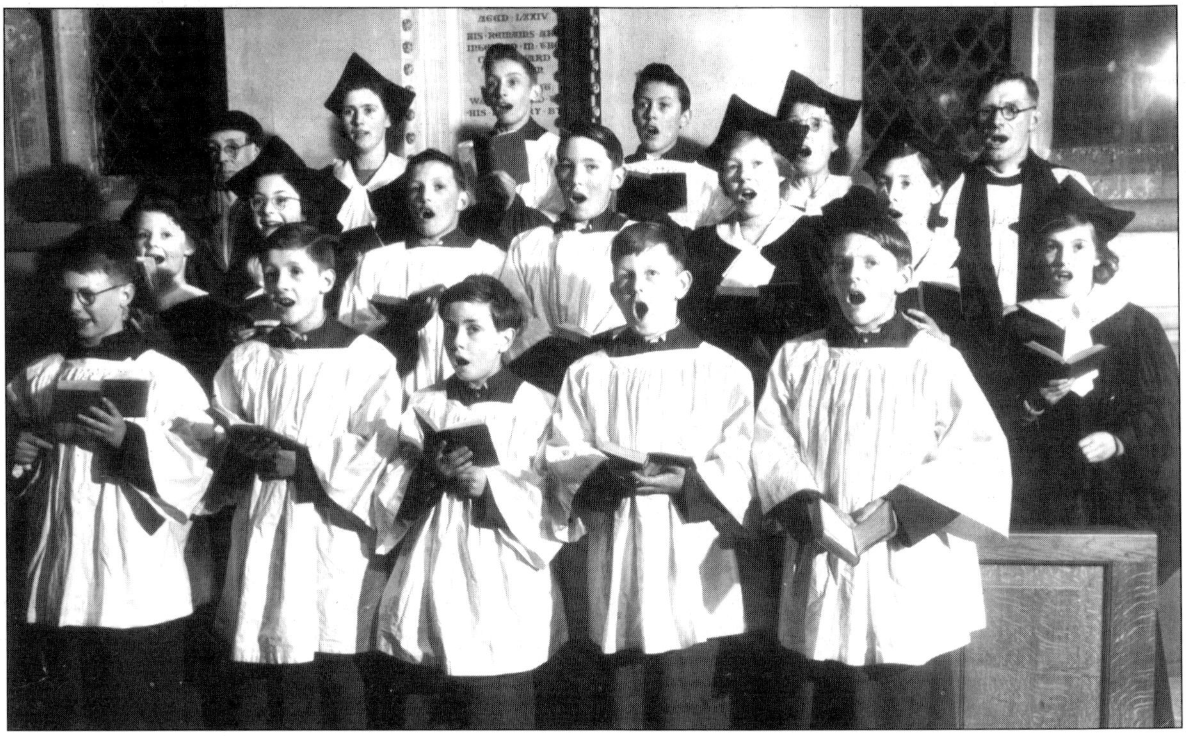

Sculthorpe Church choir, late 1950s. Left to right, back row: *Mrs Minnie Woodhouse (organist), Hettie Hipkin, Edwin Norman, David Playford, Miss Constance Catlin (choirmistress), the Revd Fred Gunn (rector of Sculthorpe, 1955–64)*; middle: *Susan Labouchere, Sonia Hurn, Philip Fuller, Dennis Fuller, Maureen Playford, Miss Clarke, Pam Playford*; front: *John Gunn, Malcolm Hipkin, Stanley Gathercole, John Engledow, Terry Harrison.* (From the collection of the late Mrs May Lingwood. Reproduced by kind permission of the *Dereham & Fakenham Times)*

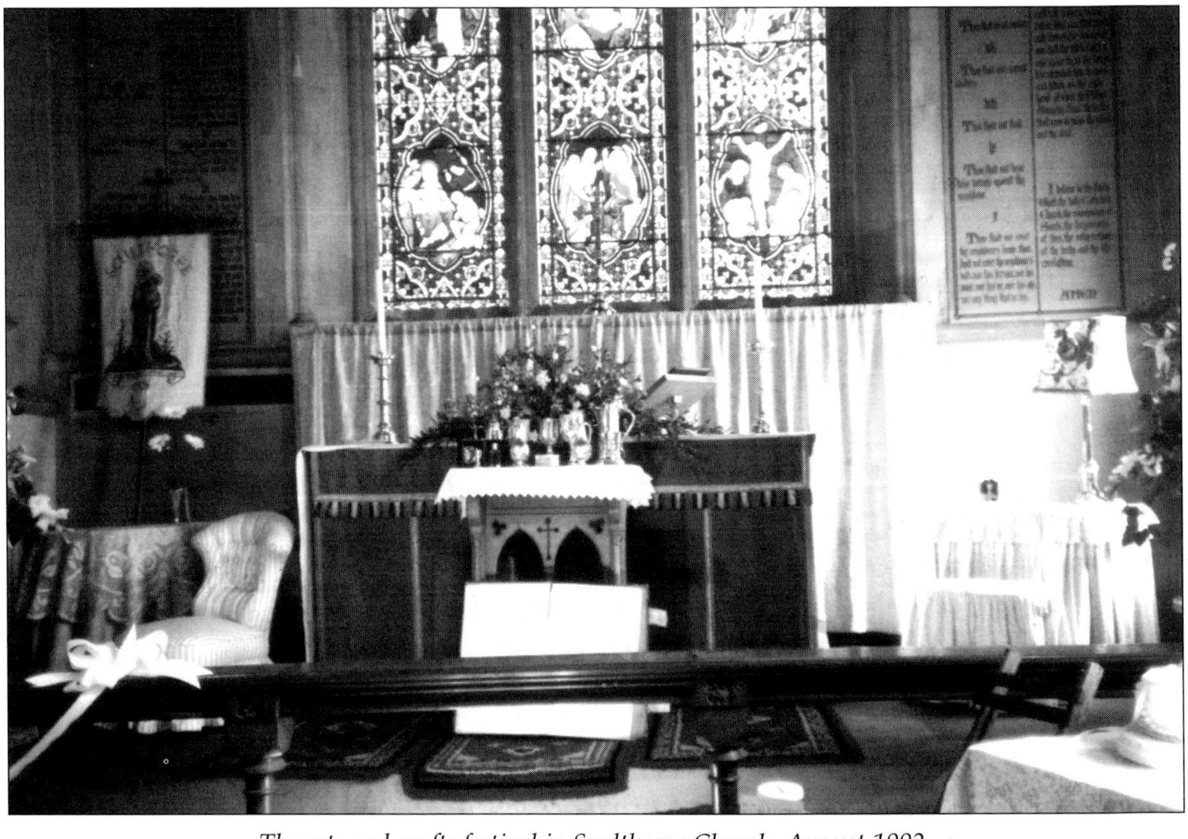

The arts-and-crafts festival in Sculthorpe Church, August 1992.
(Reproduced by kind permission of Mrs Nan Tuck)

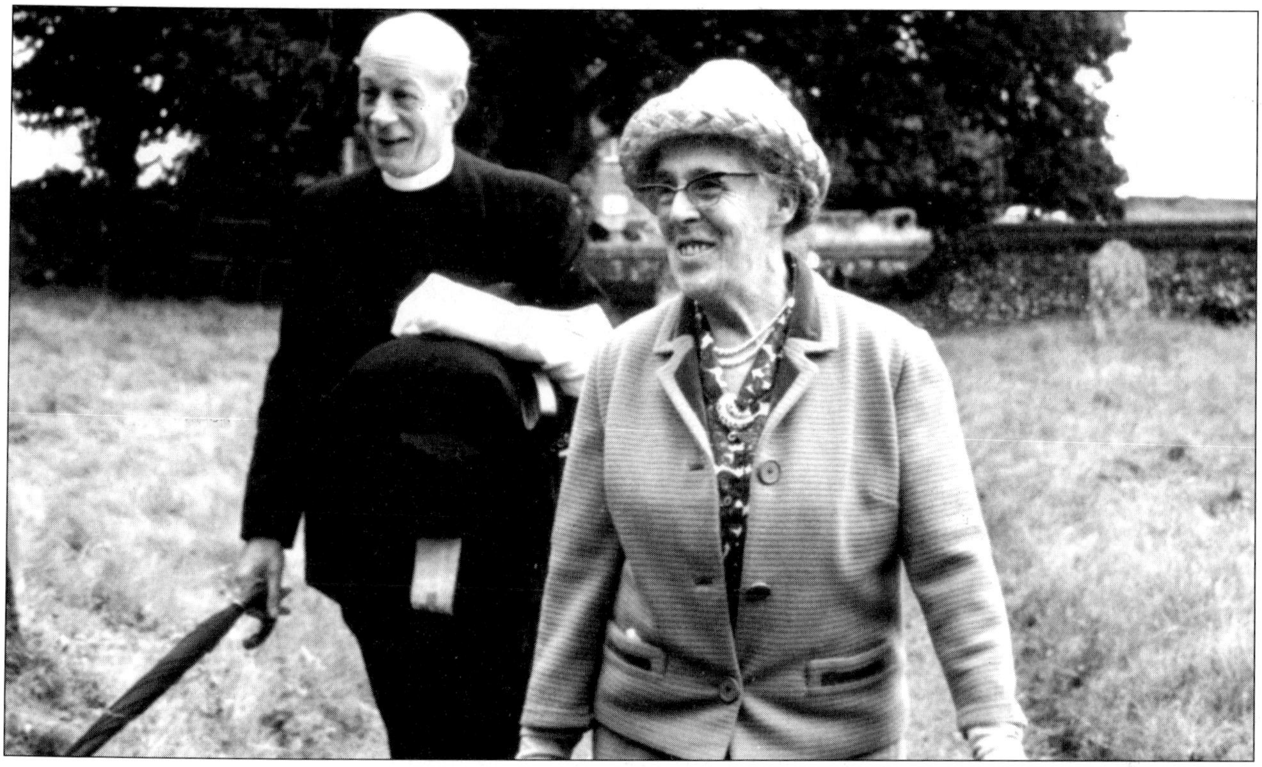

Mrs Minnie Woodhouse was organist at Sculthorpe Church for 63 years. She also played the harmonium at the neighbouring church of St Peter in Dunton-cum-Doughton. She is pictured arriving at Dunton Church to play for Evensong during the late 1960s with the Revd Derrick Woode, incumbent of Sculthorpe with Dunton-cum-Doughton (1965–74). (Reproduced by kind permission of Mr Richard Land)

York and the landed gentry from across the West Riding of Yorkshire flocked to attend the great balls and musical assemblies staged at the Assembly Rooms in Blake Street. The installation of the new organ within the Monday Assembly Room, or Small Ballroom, in 1756 must have been a great occasion; it certainly provided the musical background to the performance of Handel's 'Acis and Galatea' in 1771.

Sir Nikolaus Pevsner in the *Buildings of England* series felt that the ornate decoration of the organ case with its carved and gilded musical trophies might date from a later period. A close inspection of the director's minute-book from the archives of York Assembly Rooms proves this theory to be true – the entry for 6 February 1773 reveals that an order was given for the Monday Assembly Room to be 'ornamented and painted' and the organ to be 'gilt and carved'.

During the refurbishment of the Assembly Rooms in 1860 an instruction was given in the director's minute-book, dated 15 February 1860, for 'the organ in the Small Ball Room (to) be sold', the account ledger for this period also contains an entry, dated 4 June 1860, which says 'received Whitehead for Organ £8.8s.' Mr Whitehead may have been a local dealer in musical instruments and it was probably from him that the Revd Herbert Walsingham Jones, rector of Sculthorpe, acquired the organ for Sculthorpe Church.

Mrs Herbert Jones acted as the organist during her husband's incumbency, entering and leaving the church through a small nineteenth-century door inserted at the eastern end of the north aisle which now gives access to the modern boiler-room.

During the late-nineteenth century and the Edwardian period the organists at the church were the schoolmaster Mr William Fawcett and Miss Page, sister-in-law of Mr Charles Horsley, tenant farmer based at Grove Farm. The organ was then manually pumped by a series of bellows boys including young Jack Lingwood.

Miss Minnie Mallom, later Mrs Jack Woodhouse, was organist at Sculthorpe Church from 1917 until her death in 1980. Mrs Nina Labouchere, wife of the Revd Jack Labouchere, encouraged Minnie to play the organ for the church Sunday school and, when Mr Fawcett left Sculthorpe in 1917, Minnie replaced him as the organist, her first big musical performance being at the Revd Labouchere's funeral in 1920.

Mrs Woodhouse vividly recalled the mishaps caused by a succession of errant bellows boys! At a Harvest Festival thanksgiving service she was about to play the opening for the hymn 'We Plough the Fields and Scatter' when she discovered the bellows boy fast asleep at the side of the organ, and on another occasion, at a village wedding, she was preparing to play Mendelssohn's 'Wedding March' when she found, to her horror, that the bellows boy

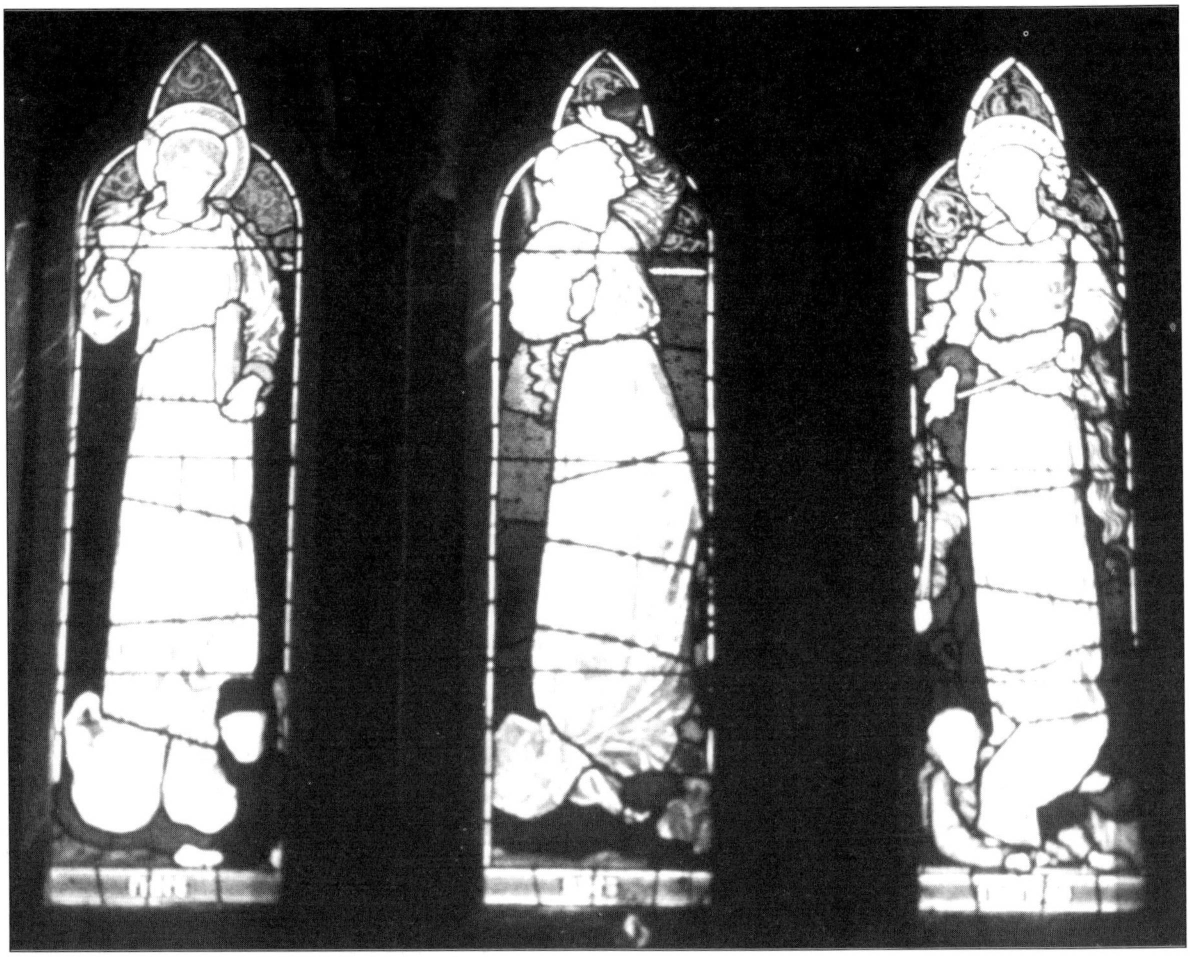

The Burne-Jones window, 'Faith, Hope and Charity', was commissioned from William Morris and Company by Sir Willoughby Jones and shown at the Paris Exhibition in 1867.

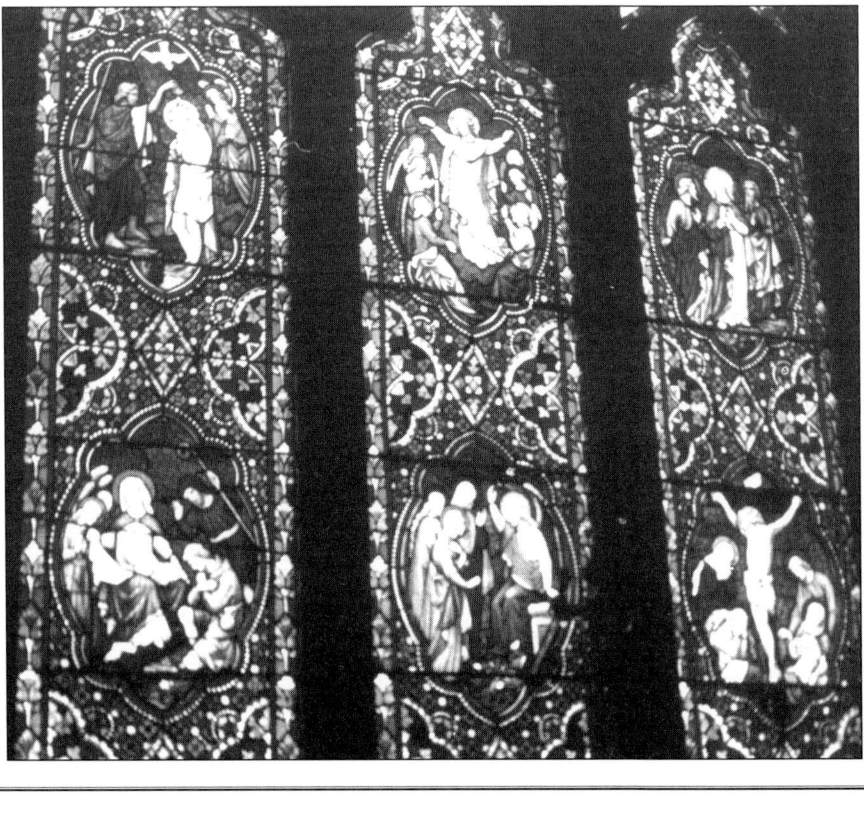

Left: *The Ward and Hughes east window in Sculthorpe Church is the family memorial to Catherine Maria, Lady Jones of Cranmer Hall, who was a native of Long Island, New York, and died in December 1859.*

had been far too preoccupied with watching all the wedding guests arriving and had quite forgotten to pump the bellows.

The organ was thoroughly restored and upgraded with an electric blower in 1951 by Noel Mander, organ builder to St Paul's Cathedral in London.

Mrs Woodhouse was delighted to meet Sir John Betjeman when he visited the church in 1974 and she was deeply touched by the celebrations to mark her 60th year as church organist in 1977. John Labouchere, grandson of the Reverend Jack Labouchere and patron of the living, returned to the village of Sculthorpe to make the formal presentations. A brass plaque on the organist's seat now commemorates Minnie Woodhouse's stalwart 63-year service to the church.

The Snetzler organ is used during Sunday worship at Sculthorpe Church, much to the appreciation of musicians and organists interested in the Baroque tradition of J.S. Bach and George Frederick Handel. It was greatly admired by the Prince of Wales when he visited the church in January 1997.

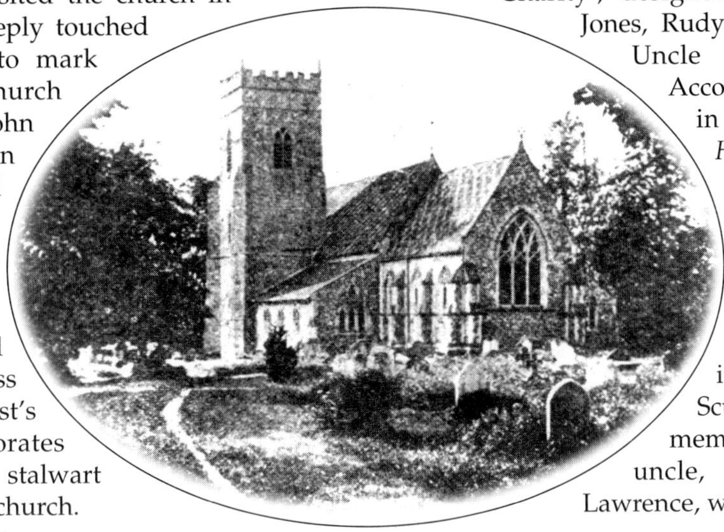

Sculthorpe Church and the churchyard as it looked at the end of Queen Victoria's reign, from a photograph dated c.1896.
(Reproduced by kind permission of Mrs Audrey Jordan, née Armiger)

The Victorian Stained-Glass Windows

The chief glory of Sculthorpe Church is the important collection of Victorian stained-glass windows, two of which represent the work of the firm of Art Workmen established by William Morris and his friends Edward Burne-Jones, Philip Webb, Ford Maddox Brown and Dante Gabriel Rossetti in 1861.

Sir Willoughby Jones of Cranmer Hall, who cultivated close links with the celebrated author and art critic John Ruskin, is thought to have been attracted to the Pre-Raphaelite idiom when he attended the Second International Exhibition staged at the South Kensington Museum in 1862. In the Medieval Court were a number of exhibits – stained glass, painted furniture and tiles – produced by William Morris and Company. These undoubtedly influenced Sir Willoughby and the Herbert Walsingham Joneses in their choice of stained glass to adorn their newly-restored Parish Church at Sculthorpe.

A beautiful window on the south side of the sanctuary in Sculthorpe Church was designed by Ford Maddox Brown for Morris and Company in 1864 and depicts the dramatic biblical stories of the storm on the lake and the rescue of St Peter the Apostle by our Lord walking on the waves. The cliffs and waves remind one of Ford Maddox Brown's famous painting 'The Last of England'.

Another window produced by Morris and Company is the east window of the south aisle Lady Chapel, depicting the three virtues, 'Faith, Hope and Charity', designed by Edward Burne-Jones, Rudyard Kipling's beloved Uncle Ned, in 1865–66. According to Hugh Bryant in *Churches of Norfolk: Hundred of Gallow* Sir Willoughby Jones allowed the Burne-Jones window to be shown at the Paris Exhibition in 1867 prior to its installation in the south aisle of Sculthorpe Church as a memorial to his maternal uncle, Edward Billopp Lawrence, who died in 1861.

In the western 'galilee', designed by Thomas Jekyll, is a famous window depicting the story of Ruth and her descendants, the Royal House of David. This was designed by Robert Turnill Bayne for the stained-glass firm Heaton, Butler and Bayne in 1862 and subsequently shown at the Second International Exhibition.

The east window above the high altar is in a sense two windows. The Revd Edward Marsham in his entry in the church register regarding the chancel, completed in 1848, stated that 'Edward Lawrence Esq, gave the stained glass in the East Window', but inserted above this sentence in the later hand of his successor, the Revd Herbert Walsingham Jones, are the words 'partly at this time, rest in 1861'. It would appear that the top tracery lights depicting the emblem of the Holy Trinity and the Instruments of the Passion, including the sacred monogram, the crown of thorns and the Eucharistic chalice, date from 1848. The three main lights are filled with sumptuous glass by Ward and Hughes of London and date from 1861 in memorial to Catherine Maria, Lady Jones of Cranmer, who was the sister of Edward Billopp Lawrence, the mother of Sir Willoughby and the Revd Herbert Jones and who died at Cranmer Hall in December 1859.

The six picture medallions depict the principal episodes from the life of Christ and are virtually identical to those from the Ward and Hughes glass of 1858 in the north aisle windows of Lincoln Cathedral.

On the north side of the chancel are two windows added by Sir Lawrence John Jones and Evelyn Mary,

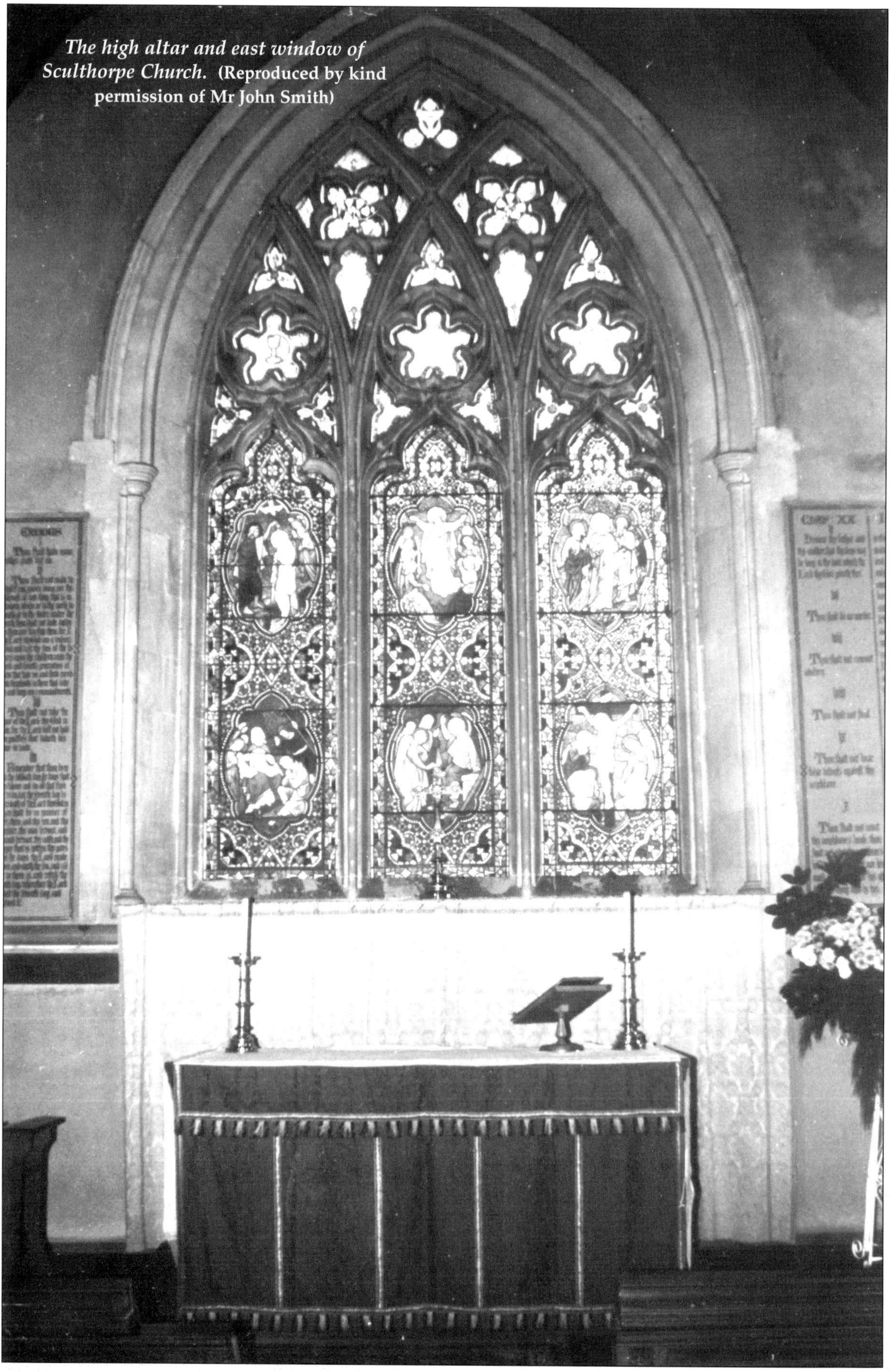

The high altar and east window of Sculthorpe Church. (Reproduced by kind permission of Mr John Smith)

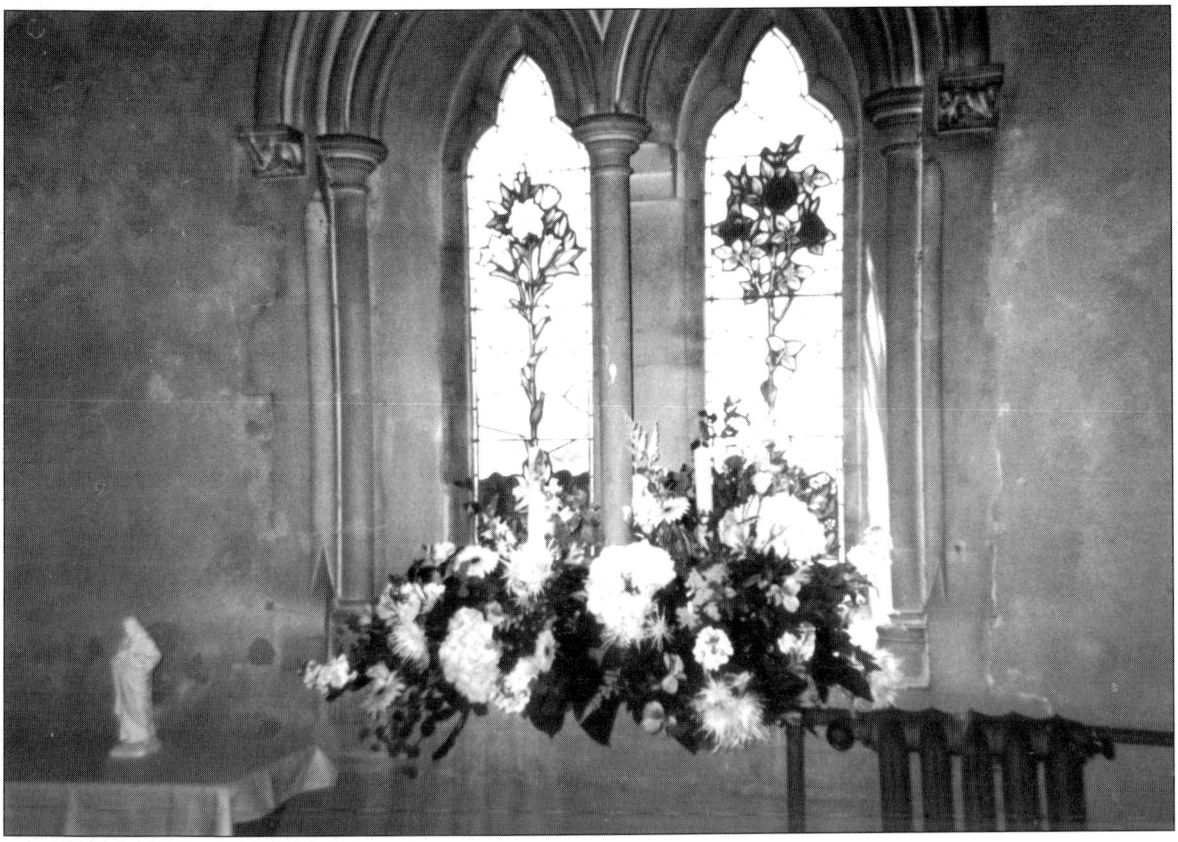

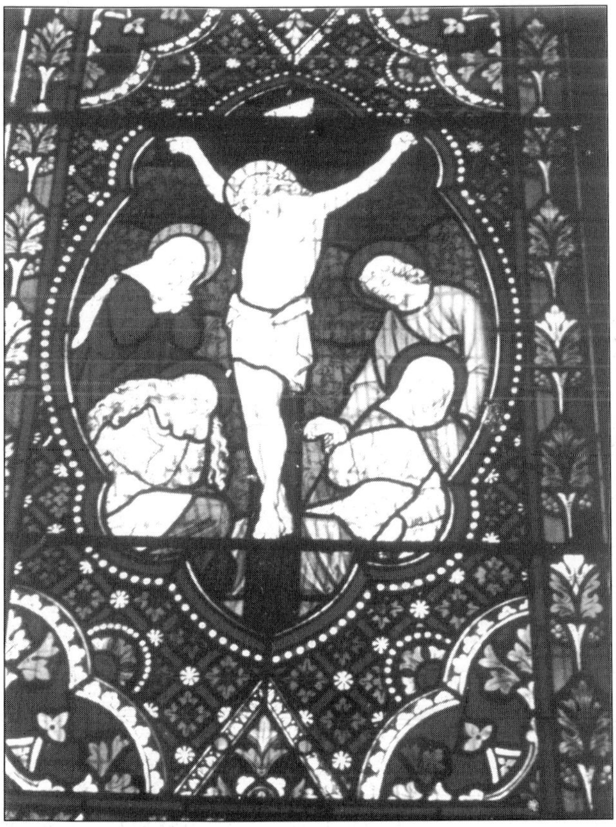

Above: *The stained-glass window in the Lady Chapel commemorates Evelyn Mary, Lady Jones and her three children and was installed in 1921. It depicts the emblems of Our Lady as 'Lily of Israel' and 'Mystical Rose'.*

Below: *A detail of the Nativity of Christ from the east window of Sculthorpe Church.*

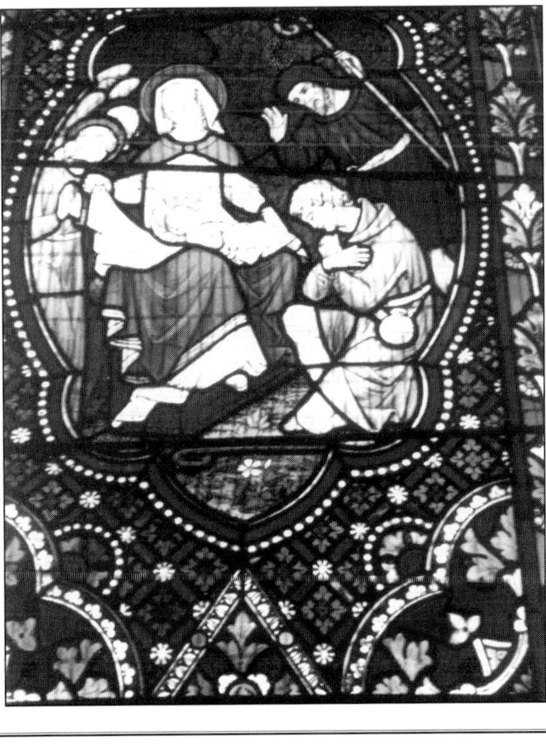

Above: *One of the stained-glass medallions from the Ward and Hughes east window in Sculthorpe Church, depicting the Crucifixion.*

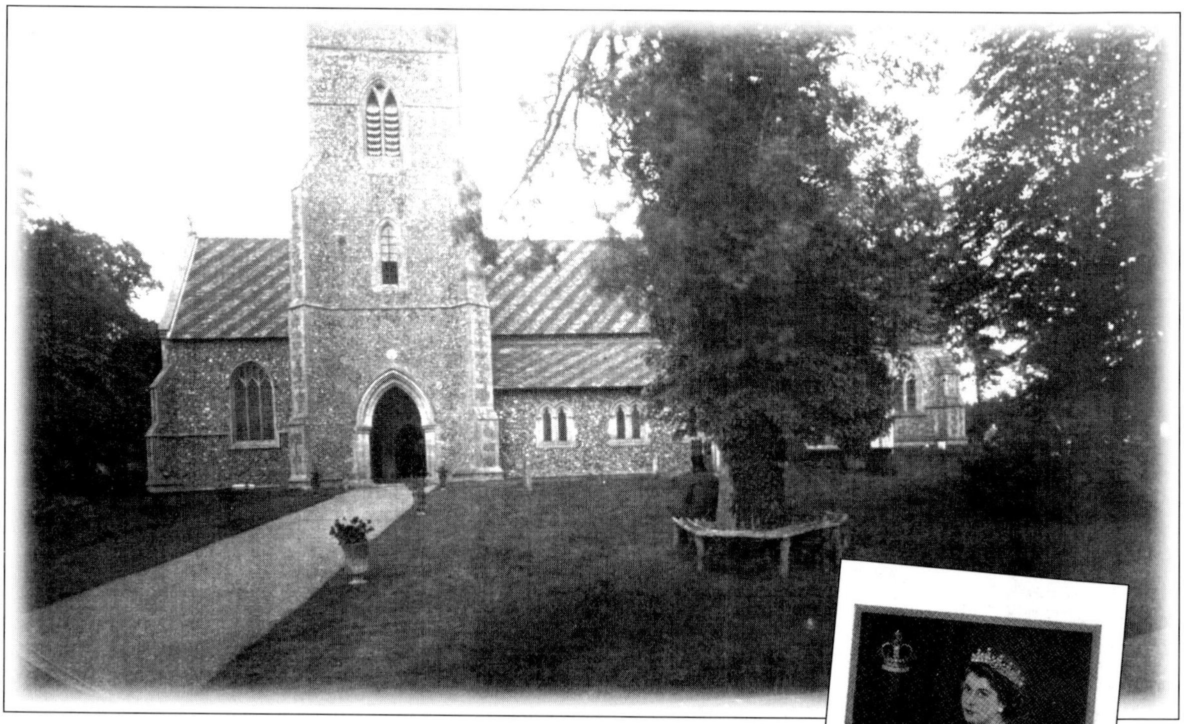

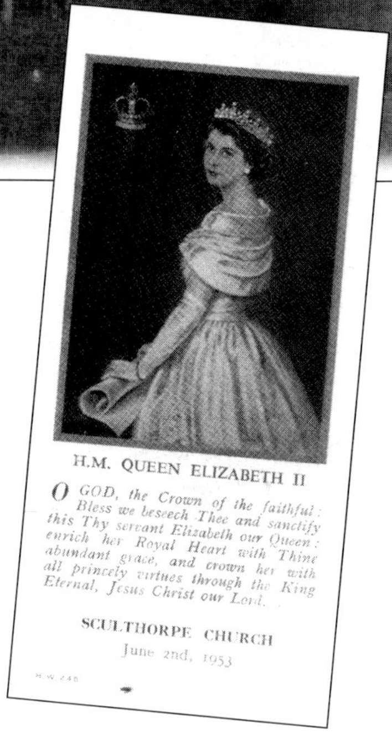

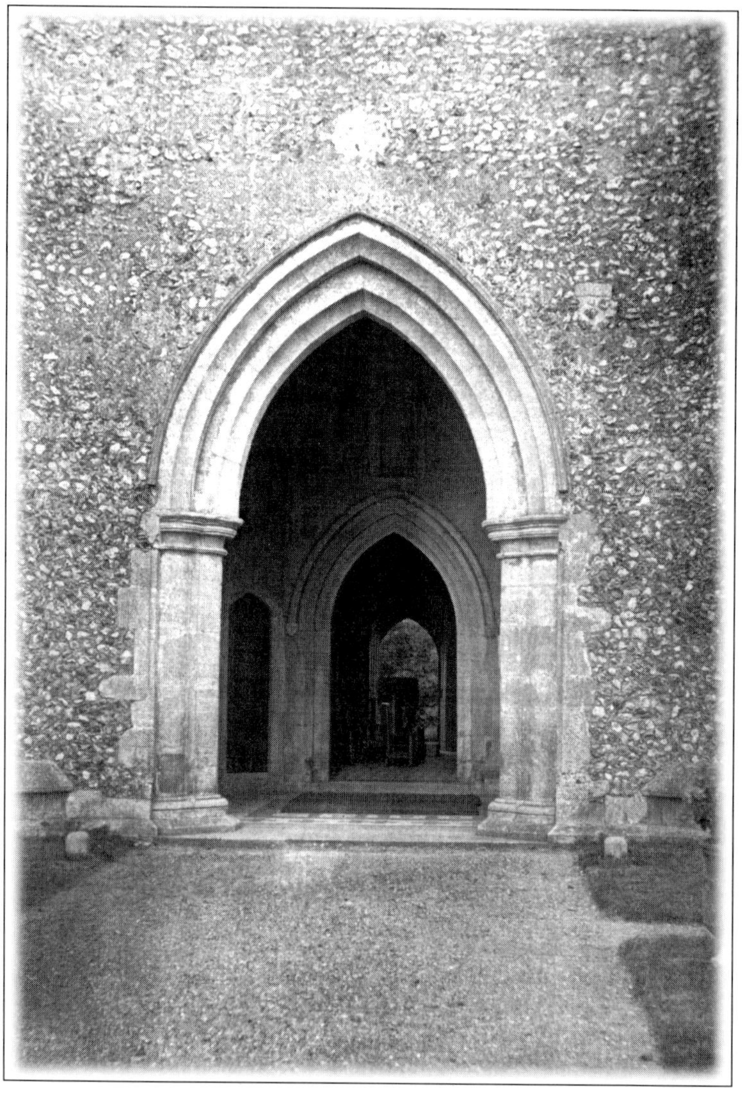

Above: *The Coronation bookmark presented to members of the congregation of Sculthorpe Church in June 1953.* (Reproduced by gracious permission of Her Majesty the Queen)

Top: *Sculthorpe churchyard in 1870.*

Left: *This striking photograph of the south-west tower porch of Sculthorpe Church dates from 1870.* (Both images from *An account of Sculthorpe Church* by Mrs Herbert Jones. Reproduced by kind permission of Father Andrew Thomson, rector of Sculthorpe)

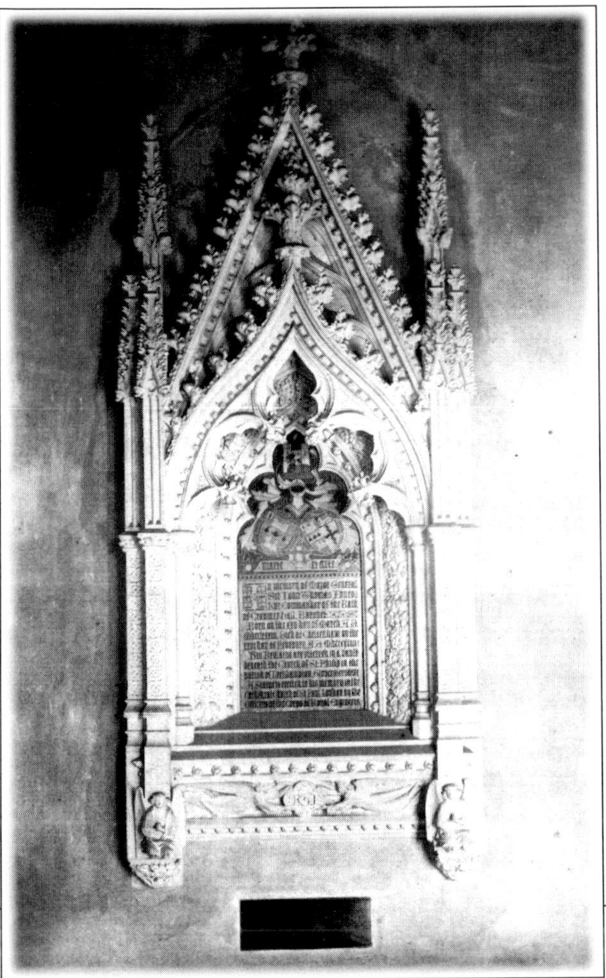

Left: *The ornate Gothic memorial on the north side of the chancel in Sculthorpe Church which commemorates the life of Major-General Sir John Thomas Jones, Knight Commander of the Bath and 1st Baronet of Cranmer. This lavish piece of Victoriana is the work of Myers of Lambeth.* (From *An account of Sculthorpe Church* by Mrs Herbert Jones. Reproduced by kind permission of Father Andrew Thomson, rector of Sculthorpe)

Below: *A view of Sculthorpe Parish Church from the top of Moor Lane. In the foreground is Crockley Pit, an ancient village pond probably dating from the Middle Ages and linked to the fourteenth-century moat surrounding Manor Farm by a ditch and an underground spring.*

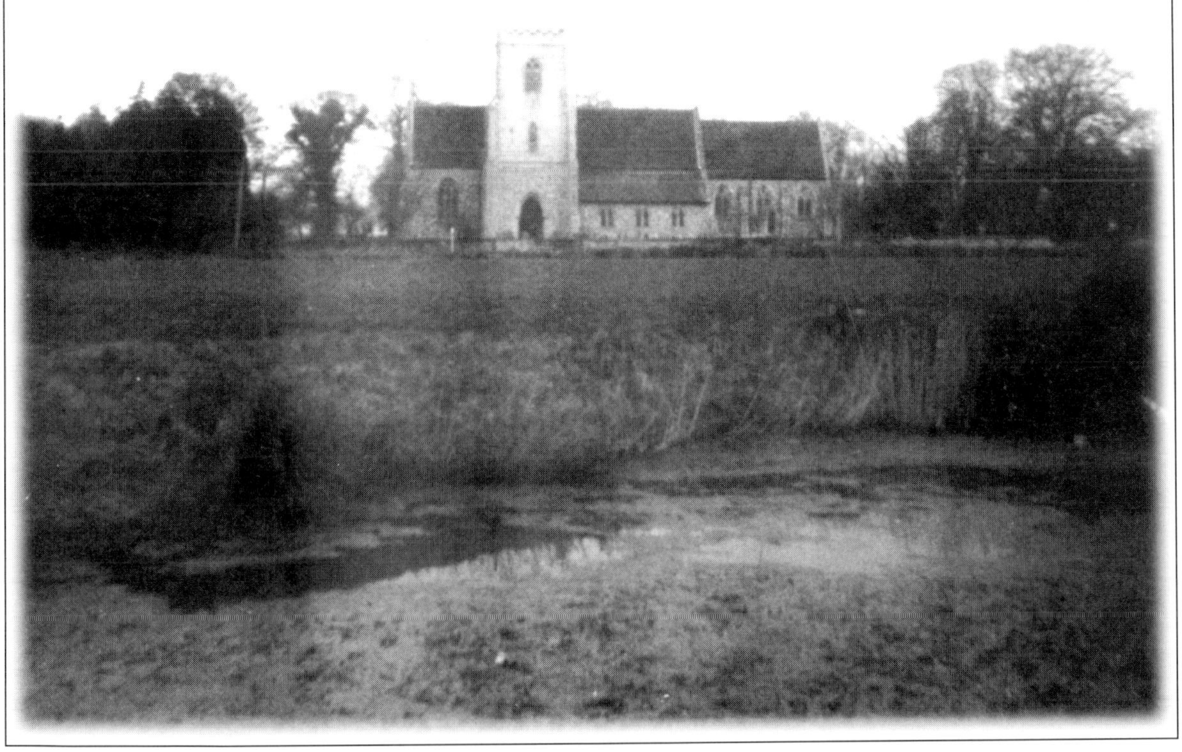

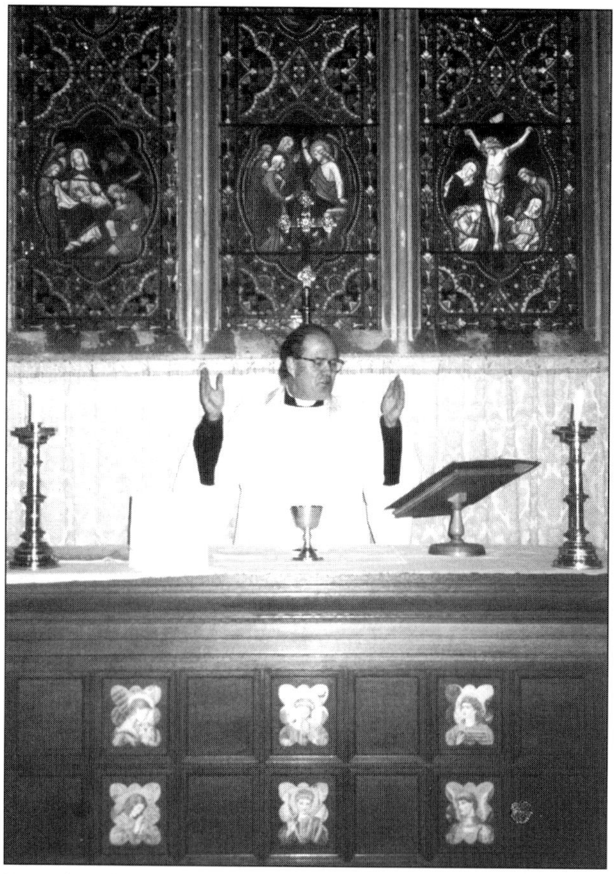

Above: *Father Andrew Thomson, rector of Sculthorpe since 1992, celebrating the Eucharist at the high altar in Sculthorpe Church. Father Thomson came to Sculthorpe from Zimbabwe exactly 100 years after Archdeacon Upcher left the village to become one of the founding fathers of the Anglican Church in Rhodesia. The Cathedral Church of Salisbury, now Harare, takes its patronal dedication of the Blessed Virgin Mary and All Saints from the mother church in Sculthorpe.*
(Reproduced by kind permission of Father Andrew Thomson)

Lady Jones during the early 1890s in memorial of members of the Jones family. The window commemorating two of the children of Sir Willoughby Jones depicts the archangels Michael and Gabriel, whilst the other, depicting Our Lord as the Light of the World and the Good Shepherd, is the family memorial to the Revd Herbert Walsingham Jones who died in 1889. Both windows were designed by Henry Holiday for Powells of Whitefriars.

Above the plain west window is a quatrefoil of an angel harpist, donated by Emily, Lady Jones of Cranmer, in 1861. Two small windows in the south aisle Lady Chapel merit close inspection – a floral trefoil above the Burne-Jones window which is the memorial of Fitzroy Orde, the infant nephew of Mrs Herbert Jones who died in 1859, and a tiny window above the Victorian door leading into the Lady Chapel which shows a Pre-Raphaelite angel sounding the Last Trumpet with the text 'The Trumpet shall sound and the dead shall be raised.'

In 1921 Sir Lawrence John Jones donated the stained glass at the south-east side of the Lady Chapel, which depicts the principal emblems of Our Lady the Blessed Virgin Mary as the Mystical Rose and the Lily of Israel with a red rose tree and a Madonna lily. These commemorate Sir Lawrence's first wife, Evelyn Mary, who died in 1912, and their children, Willoughby John Jones who died at Didlington Hall, the home of Lord Amherst in 1898, the Revd Maurice Herbert Jones who died in 1915 soon after his ordination to the priesthood, and Hester Catherine Jones, a talented artist who died during the Spanish influenza epidemic in 1918.

During 1985 Paul Quail, the distinguished stained-glass artist from Gunthorpe, restored the Ford Maddox Brown window in memory of William Pointer from Manor Farm and also repaired two panels of the Ward and Hughes glass from the east window with money raised for the Church Restoration Fund, which included a donation from Her Majesty Queen Elizabeth the Queen Mother. In 1996 the window depicting the story of Ruth in the 'galilee' underwent a magnificent restoration to commemorate the life of Mark Banham who died tragically in the Sudan during 1993. All of the windows continually receive justifiable recognition by the best authorities on the subject of Victorian stained glass and in January 1997 the Prince of Wales, in his official capacity as Patron of the Norfolk Churches Trust, made a private visit to the church to see for himself the extent of this wonderful inheritance.

Chapter Seven

THE FERMOURS AND THE FLEECE

In 1394, according to the Revd Blomefield's *History of Norfolk*, William Frayermore (Fermour), the vicar of West Barsham, acquired land in the neighbouring parish of 'Sculthorp' from John de Boys, chaplain to the bishop of London, who had relinquished his living in Sculthorpe to become vicar of Faversham in Kent. This is most probably an early reference to the Fermour family who, from the mid-fourteenth century, were involved in the lucrative business of sheep farming at the wool town of Lavenham in Suffolk. During the early-sixteenth century the Fermours' influence in North Norfolk would spread to the parish of Sculthorpe.

In 1520 a legal inquiry was held at the court of the Star Chamber, Westminster, which investigated the unscrupulous conduct of Sir Henry Fermour of East Barsham in Norfolk. Sir Henry had caused alarm amongst the men of Fakenham when he dared to encroach upon their fields and common lands to graze his huge flocks of sheep. He ruthlessly destroyed houses at Thorpland and pastured 800 sheep on a fold course in Sculthorpe where his actual landholdings amounted to a mere five acres, this possibly being the land acquired by William Frayermore in 1394. Sir Henry Fermour was one of the richest men in East Anglia, a prosperous wool merchant and sheep farmer and, by 1523, he held 17,000 head of sheep on 25 fold courses scattered across the county of Norfolk. The evidence for this great wealth made by the 'golden fleece' is reflected in the two magnificent Tudor mansions built by Sir Henry Fermour at Thorpland and East Barsham during the period c.1520–34.

Sir Henry improved his social standing by arranging a series of advantageous marriages for his family. His stepdaughter, Elizabeth Wode, married Sir James Boleyn of Blickling and later became lady-in-waiting to their niece, Queen Anne Boleyn, whom she loathed. His daughter, Ann Fermour, married Sir William Yelverton of Rougham and their fifth son, Launcelot Yelverton, became rector of Sculthorpe from 1564.

The year 1527 saw what was possibly Sir Henry's greatest achievement – the arranged match made between his son, William Fermour, and the mistress Catherine Knyvett, the niece and ward of Thomas Howard, Duke of Norfolk and the cousin of King Henry's second and fifth queens, Anne Boleyn and Katherine Howard. According to Blomefield, Catherine's dowry of £200 – worth some £60,000 in modern times – was settled upon her financially astute father-in-law.

When Sir Henry died in 1534 he left generous bequests to the Orders of Friars in Norwich and Lynn, Little Walsingham, Burnham Norton and Blakeney and also to the Augustinian Priories at Hempton and Coxford. However, England was rapidly changing. King Henry VIII had repudiated his Spanish queen, Catherine of Aragon, for Catherine Fermour's cousin, Anne Boleyn, and, in November 1534, the Act of Royal Supremacy saw the Pope being replaced by the King as the Supreme Head of the English Church.

In Sculthorpe the landholdings were chiefly vested in religious foundations; the manor of Sculthorpe and the patronage of the Parish Church had been settled upon the College and Hospital of the Holy Trinity and the Blessed Virgin Mary, founded by Sir Robert Knollys at Pontefract in 1385, whilst other land in the village had been vested in Hempton Priory by Robert Bernard of Sculthorpe in 1405.

The Dissolution of the Monasteries and the suppression of certain religious chantries and collegiate foundations brought a new landlord to the village, Sir William Fermour and his wife, Catherine, Lady Fermour. In 1545 Sir William's holdings were extended into Sculthorpe Parish when he acquired the former monastic lands which had belonged to the dissolved Augustinian Priory at Hempton. The suppression of the collegiate foundation in Pontefract led to Sir William and Sir Richard Fulmerston, Master of Horse to Lady Fermour's uncle, the Duke of Norfolk, jointly buying the Norfolk estates of 'Pomfret's Manor'. In 1549 the boy-king Edward VI granted the lordship of Sculthorpe and the patronage of the church to both Sir William and Sir Richard.

The advancing trend of land enclosure for sheep farming, a practice continued by Sir William Fermour, increasingly led to social unrest in the Norfolk countryside. In 1549 Kett's Rebellion saw a series of uprisings across the county and Sir William's brother, Thomas Fermour, was brutally murdered by a band of armed rebels in the deer park at Rising Chace.

The Reformation of the English Church was implemented during this period and, in September 1552, Sir William arrived at St Mary's Church in Sculthorpe in his official capacity as one of the royal commissioners appointed by the Government to confiscate Mass vestments and church plate. The Latin Mass had been abolished and replaced with Archbishop Cranmer's Prayer Book and the English rite of Holy Communion.

In 1553 King Edward died and Sir William had to swiftly adjust to and accommodate a new regime under Queen Mary Tudor who restored the Mass. A brisk reprimand from the Privy Council instructed Sir William, as a former royal agent, to return the church items which had been confiscated in 1552. Queen Mary's marriage to her cousin, Philip of Spain, forged a disastrous Anglo-Spanish alliance which eventually led to war with France. In 1557 Sir William Fermour was among those who loaned £100 to Queen Mary in order to aid the war effort. Sir William would surely have had a vested interest in the threatened English port of Calais, prestigious market of the Wool Staple and doorway to Flemish wool markets in the Low Countries.

Sir William died in January 1558, bequeathing 10 shillings to the poor box of each parish in Norfolk where he had a fold course of sheep. His marriage had been childless and his estate devolved upon his nephew Thomas Fermour, the son of his murdered brother. Catherine, Lady Fermour, lived to see her cousin Lady Elizabeth, daughter of Ann Boleyn, exalted as Queen of England.

In 1558 'Catherine Fayremore, widow' exercised her right as patron of Sculthorpe Church to present a new priest, Andrew Cole, to the living. Rumoured to be opposed to the Elizabethan Church Settlement, Cole was replaced in 1564 by Launcelot Yelverton, grandson of Sir Henry Fermour, who was also vicar of Guist. He too must have ministered under something of a cloud of disapproval. His brother, Edward Yelverton, was a devout Roman Catholic who had married Nazareth Bedingfeld of Oxburgh Hall and later harboured the fugitive Jesuit priest, Father Gerard, in his house at Grimston.

Thomas Fermour subsequently sold off much of his late uncle's estate, including 200 acres of land and 147 acres of pasture in Fakenham and Sculthorpe which he sold to Salathiel Kyndersley, rector of Sculthorpe, in 1582. The inclusion of 147 acres of sheep's pasture is evidence indeed of the prosperity of the Fermours and the fleece.

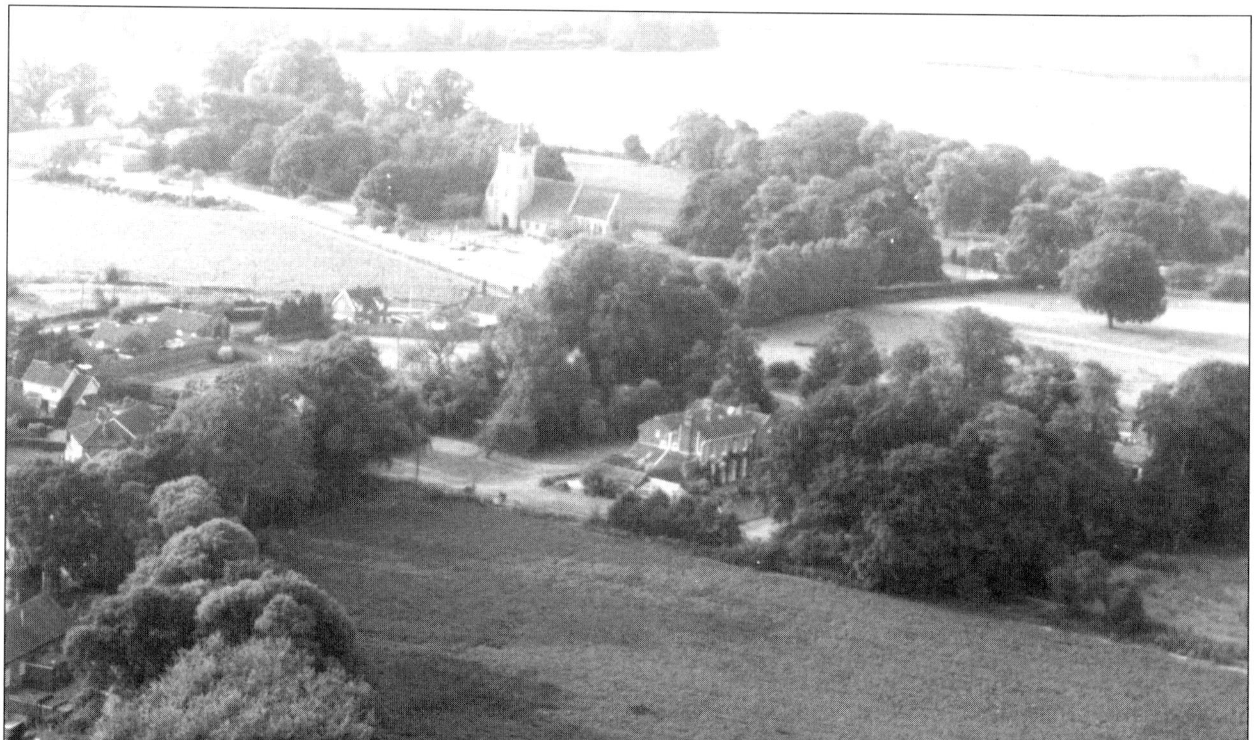

This aerial photograph of Sculthorpe from the south-east shows the Old Rectory, now Sculthorpe House, raised on its ancient moat, an important medieval earthwork. The road just visible in the background is the 'New Road' of 1829, which circles Cranmer Park. (Reproduced by kind permission of John and Henry Labouchere)

Chapter Eight

PARSONAGE TALES

The Old Rectory, or Sculthorpe House, has long been at the centre of village life, its beautifully-kept gardens and tall copper beech trees, the ancient dry moat and climbing roses on the house providing a charming setting for numerous Church garden fêtes, flower shows and the annual strawberry cream tea.

According to the Revd Francis Blomefield, during the thirteenth century the medieval rectors of Sculthorpe had a fortified 'manse' here and it is believed the ancient moat dates from this period. It was originally fed by a natural spring, which can be traced in the Tudor brick cellars beneath the present house. An ancient legend perpetuates the possibility of a tunnel which is traditionally believed to run from the foundations of the house and underneath the croquet lawn in the direction of the Parish Church – one version of this much-worn village tale suggests that the entrance to the tunnel was through a well-head at the rear of the house.

A Church Terrier of glebe lands, held at the Norfolk Record Office, is inscribed in the hand of Salathiel Kyndersley, rector of Sculthorpe: 'in this yarw of the King's Majestyst Reigne Anno Domini 1613' and makes reference to the 'Parsonage of Skulthorpe'. The early-seventeenth-century wing of the present house, with its gables of Jacobean brickwork, stands on an east–west axis and is thought to mark the core of this parsonage house.

John Quarles, Archdeacon of Northampton and a doctor of divinity, was rector at Sculthorpe from 1625 until his death in 1665, a particularly turbulent period in English history which saw the outbreak of the Civil War followed by the austerity of the Puritan Commonwealth. Dr Quarles was a cousin of the Royalist poet Francis Quarles who was cup-bearer at Heidelberg to the 'Winter Queen' Elizabeth of Bohemia, sister of King Charles I and mother of the intrepid Prince Rupert of the Rhine. Unlike his illustrious relation, who was later attendant upon King Charles at his court in Oxford and suffered greatly after having his manuscripts destroyed by the Puritan supporters of Parliament, Dr Quarles managed to keep out of politics and retained his living and raised a family of five children in his parsonage house at Sculthorpe. The death of his wife Mary in November 1642 ensured that the welfare of five young children was invariably more important than becoming embroiled in the struggle between the Crown and Parliament.

The lord of the manor at this time was James Calthorpe of East Barsham whose first wife had been the heiress Mary Fermour, great-great-granddaughter of Sir Henry Fermour. James Calthorpe was Lord High Sheriff of Norfolk in 1643 and a moderate Parliamentarian who, it appears, left Dr Quarles and

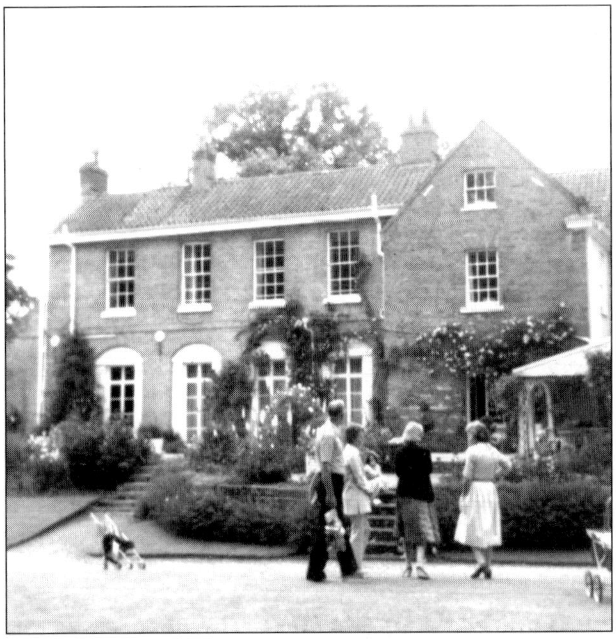

Left: *The Old Rectory, now called Sculthorpe House, is a mixture of architectural styles. The red-brick gabled wing to the right dates from the seventeenth-century parsonage house of the Quarles family. The white-brick Greek revival wing to the left was added in 1812 by the Revd Edward Marsham, rector of Sculthorpe from 1811 until his death in 1859.*

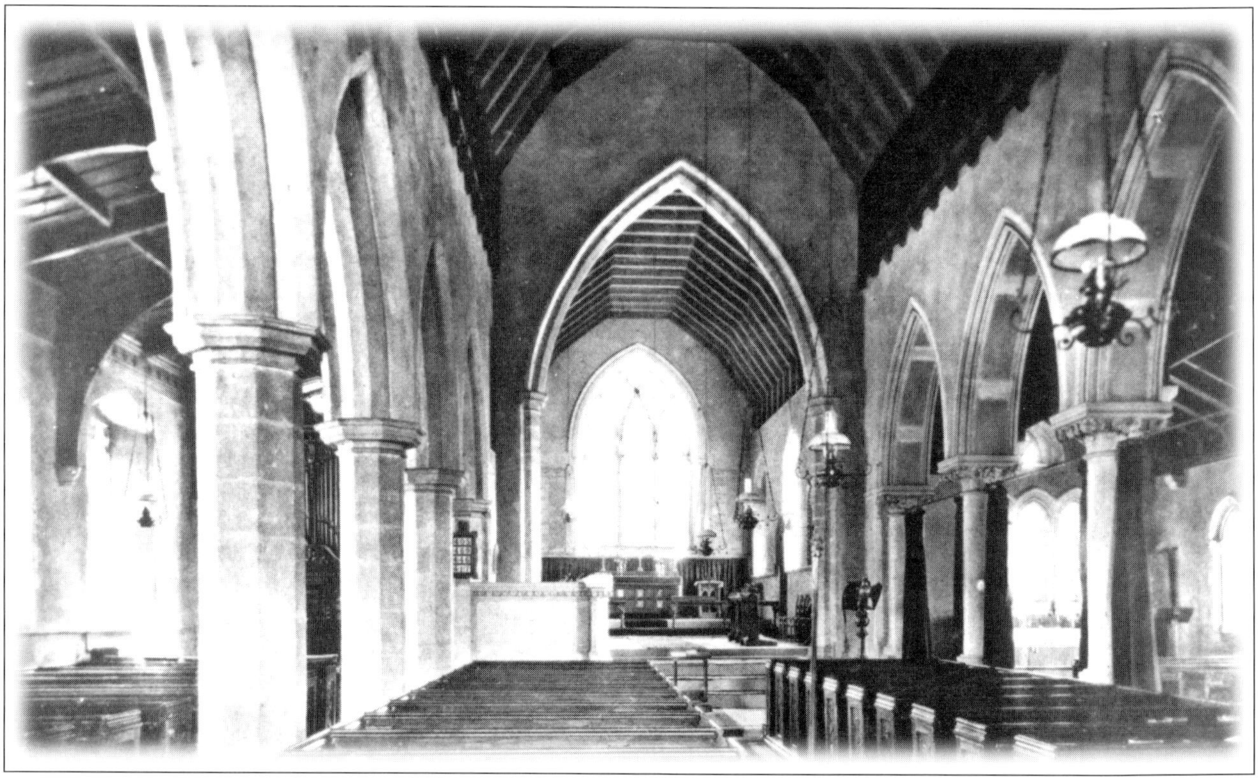

This photograph of Sculthorpe Church dates from the mid-1920s. The hanging oil-lamps with glass mantles survived until the late 1930s. (From the collection of the late William Sewter. Reproduced by kind permission of Mrs Jean Benstead)

his young family undisturbed in their house at Sculthorpe. Both men were doubtless aware of the odious presence of Colonel Oliver Cromwell and his troop-of-horse billeted in Fakenham during March 1643; the mounted Roundhead soldiers must have passed through Sculthorpe on their way to the port of Lynn where rumours of a suspected Royalist rising were already beginning to ferment.

The prohibition of the use of the English Prayer Book seriously affected the celebration of the Anglican sacraments, as indicated by the blank pages of the Sculthorpe Parish Register during this period. Fortunately Dr Quarles weathered the Puritan storm and lived to see the restoration of both the Stuart royal house and the Established Church. In August 1660 he officiated at the Sculthorpe wedding of his daughter Mary Quarles to the Revd Henry Longe, rector of Barrow in Suffolk.

Dr Quarles died in October 1665 and was buried at Sculthorpe, his property in the village was inherited by his eldest son and heir 'Reverend Mr John Quarles in the countye of Northamptonshire, rector of Uffington', who had been born in the parsonage house at Sculthorpe in 1630. This second John Quarles was rector of Sculthorpe for a brief period during 1666 (succeeded by his brother Robert in the same year) and remained patron of the living until his death in 1685. He was buried near his father in the Parish Church but his grave slab was moved during the Victorian restoration and relocated to Jekyll's south aisle Lady Chapel.

In 1667 the Revd Clement Heigham of Barrow, nephew of the Revd Henry Longe who had married the archdeacon's daughter, Mary Quarles, was inducted as rector of Sculthorpe and lived in the parsonage house with his first wife Susan Skippon, niece of the Puritan Major-General Philip Skippon of the New Model Army who had been wounded at the Battle of Naseby in 1645. The Skippon family had long associations with the village of Sculthorpe from c.1600. Clement and Susan's daughter, Elizabeth Heigham of Sculthorpe, married the Revd Francis Wace, rector of Blakeney, and it was their child, Elizabeth Wace, who later married John Jones, a prosperous farmer and merchant from Fakenham and the Collector of Customs at the port of Blakeney. From this union was descended the Jones family of Cranmer Hall in Sculthorpe.

Anne Quarles (1637–1720), widow of the second John Quarles, succeeded her husband as patron of Sculthorpe Church and, in 1687, appointed their son to the living and thus he became the third John Quarles, grandson of the archdeacon, to live in the parsonage house where his father had been born. He is remembered as being one of the victims of a terrible pestilence which swept through the rectory during the Yuletide of December 1693 and January 1694, claiming not only his life but also the lives of two of his infant children. The death of John Quarles on 9 January 1694 ended this remarkable triple dynasty of clerics although the family continued to hold the patronage until c.1700.

Mistress Anne Quarles (1662–1724), sister of the third John Quarles, continued to live with her widowed mother at Sculthorpe and eventually married Robert Donne, attorney of South Creake, who rebuilt Cranmer Hall in 1721. The story of the Donne family can be traced elsewhere in this book.

The Church Terrier of 1784 recorded the substantial rebuilding of the rectory by the Revd Matthew Jones who was also lord of the manor at the end of the eighteenth century, the description mentioned:

> *... one new erected dwelling house, one new erected barn with leantoos, two stables, Granary, carthouse and other outhouses. The Garden, Mote, yards and Inclosure of pasture land adjoining*

A further entry in the flyleaf of the church register also revealed 'January 1st 1779 – The Parsonage Barn blown down between one and two o'clock in the morning. Rebuilt in 1780 by M.J.' The Revd Matthew Jones of Cranmer Hall was rector of Sculthorpe from 1767 and was chiefly responsible for the hedging and enclosure of his glebe lands on the north-east side of the village – the Terrier of 1784 mentions the new hedges of 'white thorn'. The French aristocrat Francois de la Rochefoucauld, in his celebrated book of travel *A Frenchman in England* (1784), described visiting Sculthorpe to see the farm belonging to the Revd Jones which was famous for its improvements and increased rental value. It is thought to have been Glebe Farm in Creake Road which was rebuilt in 1850 by Sir Willoughby Jones. Matthew Jones was also responsible for the rebuilding of the Old Stone Barn, now Sculthorpe School, in 1787.

On 2 September 1791 the Revd Jones married Mrs Anne Astley, widow of the Revd Bernard Astley, the late rector of Little Snoring, in Sculthorpe Church. Anne Astley was born Anne Hase, the third daughter of Edward Hase who built the mansion of Salle Park near Reepham in Norfolk. Her first marriage to the Revd Astley, a younger son of Sir Edward Astley, baronet of Melton Constable Hall, had effectively introduced her to the sphere of her future husband – the Revd Astley had succeeded Matthew Jones as rector of Little Snoring in 1788. When the Revd Jones died in June 1808 his widow assumed the patronage of Sculthorpe Church and lived not only to see two nephews appointed to the living but to also contract a third marriage for herself. Sculthorpe Church was again the setting on 20 February 1810 when Anne Jones, widow, married the Revd Horatio Dowsing, rector of North Barsham and vicar of Hindringham.

A white marble tablet at the west end of Sculthorpe Church, adorned with the quartered arms of the Hase and Dowsing families, commemorates the life of Anne Hase who through her three marriages to Anglican clergymen was in turn Mrs Astley, Mrs Jones and finally Mrs Dowsing. She died in 1828, aged 68, and was survived by her third husband, the Revd Dowsing, who died in 1843 at the grand age of 86.

The Revd Edward Marsham, nephew of Anne Hase, became rector of Sculthorpe in 1811 and succeeded his brother-in-law, the Revd Bartholomew Edwards, to this living. In addition he was also the rector of Wramplingham and his native village of Stratton Strawless in Norfolk. Edward Marsham was descended from the ancient landed family of the Marshams of Stratton Strawless Hall. His paternal grandfather was the eighteenth-century botanist Robert Marsham, patron of the landscape architect Humphry Repton and the influential presence behind the planting of the trees in the Windham's landscape park at Felbrigg. Through his mother, Sophia Hase, Edward was also the grandson of Edward Hase of Salle Park.

An entry from the Sculthorpe baptismal register held at the Norfolk Record Office revealed that 'the Parsonage House began to be repaired in 1812 – by E.M.' The additions made to the house in the 'Greek Revival' style, using white brick, would appear to date from this period. With three comfortable livings the Revd Marsham appears to have lived in the style customary to a landed country gentleman and the refurbished parsonage at Sculthorpe was his principal residence. A closer look at his last will and testament, dated 1858 and kept at the Norwich Court of Probate, provides a fascinating glimpse into his household – we read of his generous bequests to his domestic staff including Martha Bambridge (his cook), William Ellis (his footman), Robert Bassham (his carpenter) and Matthew Seales (his coachman) who conveyed his master around in a close carriage with two carriage horses.

The early-nineteenth century was a period of social and political unrest with the Napoleonic Wars, the rural Swing Riots aimed at landowners, arable mechanisation and the struggle to achieve electoral reform. The Revd Marsham kept a meticulous diary of parish events, in his beautiful copperplate hand, in the flyleaf end papers of the church register, providing a unique record of parish life from this period. The entries include information about the returns from the National Census taken in 1821 and 1831 and the opening of the National School in 1841.

Edward Marsham also recorded details of the many epidemics which spread through the village and these are a painful reminder of Sculthorpe's high mortality rate, especially amongst children and poorer families. There were outbreaks of smallpox in 1816 and 1833, whooping cough in 1814, 1821, 1830, 1841 and 1842, typhus fever in 1838 and 1839, the measles in 1819, in 1827 and 1828 – 'some cases fatal' – and again in 1844, scarletina in 1834 – 'very fatal', scarlet fever in 1844 and influenza in 1833 and again in

February 1837 when the Revd Marsham wrote: 'Influenza prevailed beyond anything I had before witnessed.' The inscriptions upon the graves of the six children of the tenant farmer Peter Smyth-Cole who perished during the period 1834–39 can be found on the north-east side of Sculthorpe churchyard.

In keeping with many landed parsons the Revd Marsham took a keen interest in farming his glebe and immersed himself in the folklore and customs of village life. On 5 December 1812 he recorded the following in Sculthorpe Church register:

> *The boundaries of the parish of Sculthorpe were perambulated. George Thompson, aged 78 years, who had gone the boundaries about 40 years ago, shewed how they were situated. Amongst the persons present were – Edwd Marsham – rector, Mr Dunham Green, Thomas Thurtle, Tuck, Joseph Kendall, Richard Horsley, Thomas Price alias Sapey, George Thompson, John Thompson, Armiger, Crask, Chrisr. Cock, Basham Clerk of Sculthorpe, Mr Diggins of Hempton, Mr Nurse of West Barsham.*

The Inclosure Act of 1829 prompted Edward Marsham to write of his circumstances:

> *In 1829 Sculthorpe Common lands were inclosed and instead of any part being allotted to the rectory, though the claims were allowed – a considerable reduction of the glebe lands took place.*

The churchwarden's account book, held at the Norfolk Record Office, and the historic lithographs by the artists John Berney Ladbrooke and Elizabeth Turner, revealed the increasingly derelict state of the Parish Church. The late-fourteenth-century angel roof in the nave, the legacy of Sir Robert Knollys, was removed and sold by auction during October 1815 for £14.14s.3d. and, in January 1816, the Revd Marsham donated £10 towards the new roof.

The interior of the church, its walls limewashed and whitened, would have presented a very rustic scene with its brick pamments, box pews, decker pulpit and reading desk. The churching pew and Holy Communion table with its purple cloth, the oil lamps hanging from the roof, the north aisle filled with a gallery, the royal coat of arms for King George II carved and painted in 1734 by John Sharwood, and the bier and horsecloth used at parish funerals would have been an impressive sight. During March 1845 the lord of the manor Sir Lawrence Jones donated £40, and the Revd Marsham another £20, to pay for the new barrel organ which was installed in the church. This was replaced by the Snetzler organ from the York Assembly Rooms in 1860.

The influence of both the Victorian Gothic Revival and the Anglo-Catholic movement, with its emphasis on reverent worship and ceremony, were beginning to transform the appearance of English churches and the Revd Marsham recorded in the church register information about the new chancel built at Sculthorpe:

> *1846 – Sir Willoughby Jones, Bart, having constructed a vault for the remains of his brother, Sir Lawrence Jones, Bart, which were brought from Macri in Turkey, where he was murdered – commenced to build at his own expense, a Chancel over the vault – finished in 1848; Edward Lawrence Esq. gave the stained glass in the East window and Dame Lady Jones gave the velvet communion cloth.*

The new chancel, designed by the brother architects Joshua Arthur Brandon and Raphael Brandon, was built in the 'Middle Pointed' decorated-Gothic style, its roof of chequered tiles was a decorative tradition later promoted by Sir Willoughby's great friend John Ruskin in his book *The Seven Lamps of Architecture*, published in 1849.

The entries made by the Revd Marsham in the church register cease after 1858 and in a new hand is the entry: '1859 – February 10th Edward Marsham rector of this parish died after 4 days illness aged 72. April 6th I, Herbert W. Jones read myself in as rector.'

The Revd Herbert Walsingham Jones (1826–89) was the youngest son of Major-General Sir John Thomas Jones and the younger brother of Sir Willoughby Jones, lord of the manor and patron of the living. Like his predecessor, Edward Marsham, Herbert Walsingham Jones, as the younger son of landed gentlefolk, had benefitted from a Cambridge

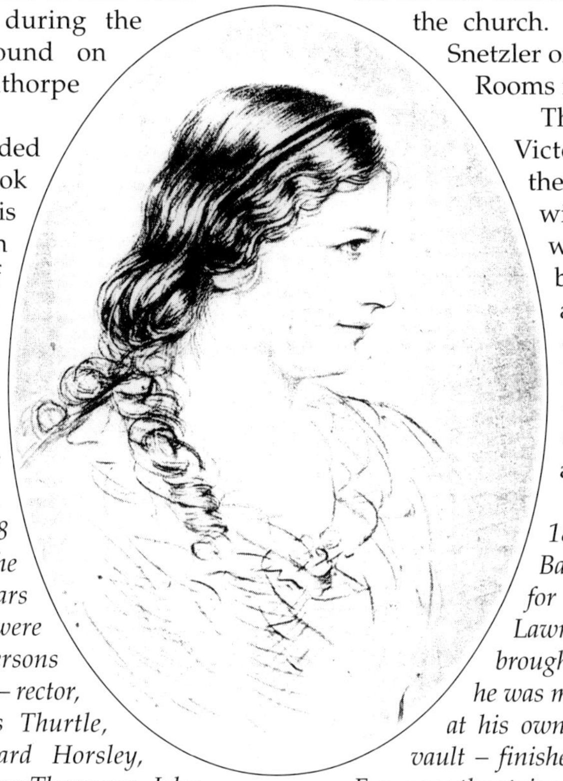

Above: *Mrs Herbert Jones (née Catherine Rachel Gurney) who married the Revd Herbert Walsingham Jones in 1850 and was the niece of the prison reformer Elizabeth Fry. This image is from a portrait dating from her wedding year, 1850.* (Reproduced by kind permission of Lady Harrod, great-great-grandniece of Mrs Herbert Jones)

education and entered the Church, being ordained deacon in 1850 and then priest in 1851. He had served as assistant curate of West Runton prior to his appointment to the rectory of Sculthorpe and in 1850 had married Catherine Rachel Gurney, one of the beautiful daughters of Daniel Gurney of North Runcton Hall and niece of the prison reformer Elizabeth Fry.

The historic setting of the parsonage house, associated with his ancestors Clement Heigham and Susan Skippon who had lived there during the late-seventeenth century, appealed enormously to Herbert Walsingham Jones and his wife and their life here was described in the journals of their niece Laura Troubridge, published as *Life Amongst the Troubridges* by John Murray in 1966. From this exquisite book a wonderful cameo of life at Sculthorpe rectory during the late-nineteenth century can be obtained. Laura described the now-demolished oval drawing-room, which she said was based upon a design from a Russian palace in St Petersburg. The outline of this drawing-room can be traced from the Inclosure Map of 1830 and the foundations survive to this day as the oval herbaceous border overlooking the east lawn.

Mrs Herbert Jones, Laura's beloved 'Aunt Bache', was a talented artist and historian who produced a number of wonderful books including: *Sandringham Past and Present*, dedicated to Albert Edward, Prince of Wales (the future King Edward VII); *Memoirs of Princess Charlotte* and *Some Norfolk Worthies*, in which she writes about her aunt, Elizabeth Fry. Her historical articles appeared frequently in such society periodicals as *The Edinburgh Review* and *The Quarterly Review* and she submitted a transaction *Notes On Sculthorpe Church* to the Norfolk & Norwich Archaeological Society, which was published in 1872. Perhaps her greatest achievement was her manuscript history *An Account of Sculthorpe Church*, compiled in 1870, which contained beautiful examples of her hand-illuminated script and a charming pencil sketch of the village, looking south from the churchyard path with the six-sail Tower Windmill depicted on the skyline.

The Revd Herbert Walsingham Jones and Sir Willoughby Jones were both responsible for the second stage of the Victorian restoration of the Parish Church, undertaken during 1860–61. Herbert Walsingham Jones wrote a most detailed account in the church register, describing the additions of the western 'galilee' and the south aisle Lady Chapel, the re-roofing of the nave, the new pitch-pine pews and stone pulpit. The architect was the fascinating, eccentric Thomas Jekyll who transformed this rustic and rather derelict village church into an ornate and pristine Victorian estate church for the Jones family

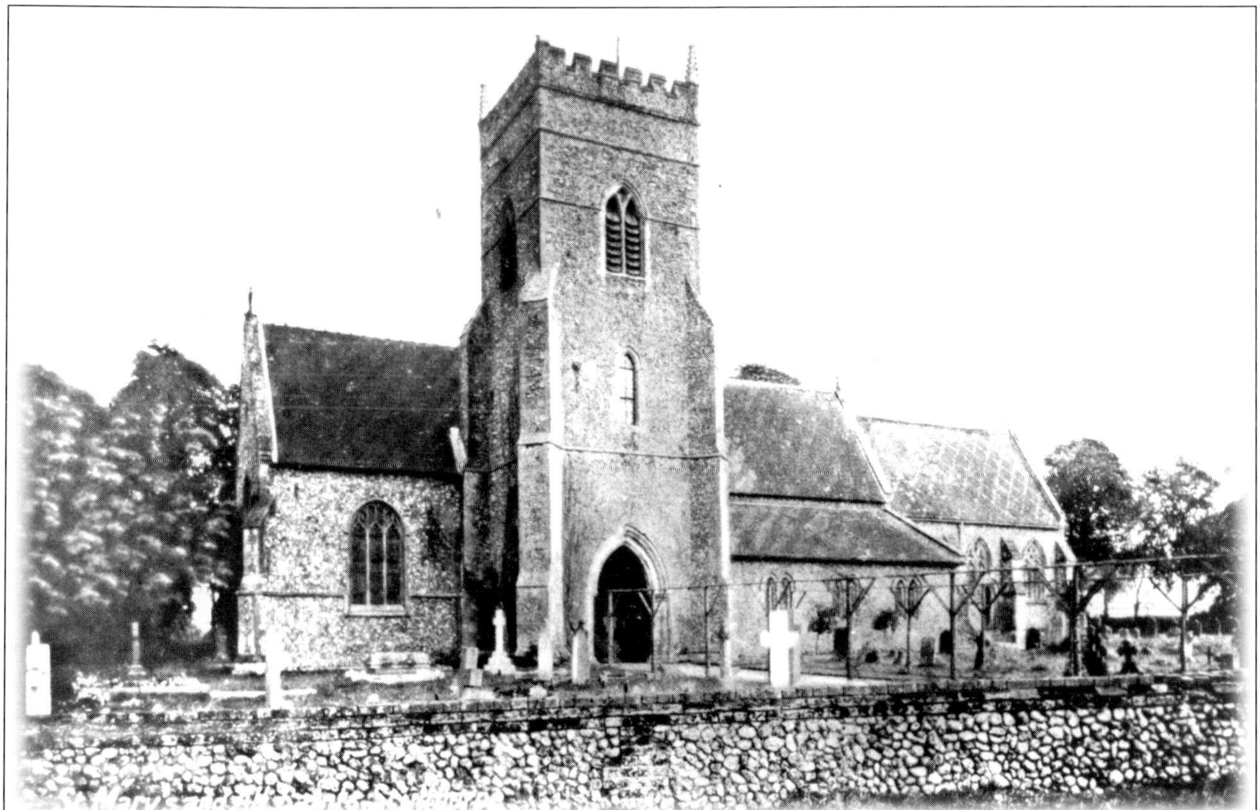

Sculthorpe Church, 1920s. This photograph shows the wooden fretwork of the rose pergola, which once lined the churchyard path, the Victorian western 'galilee', added by Thomas Jekyll in 1860–61 and, in the shadow of the church, the great stone marking the grave of Sir Willoughby Jones who died in 1884. (From the collection of the late William Sewter. Reproduced by kind permission of Mrs Jean Benstead)

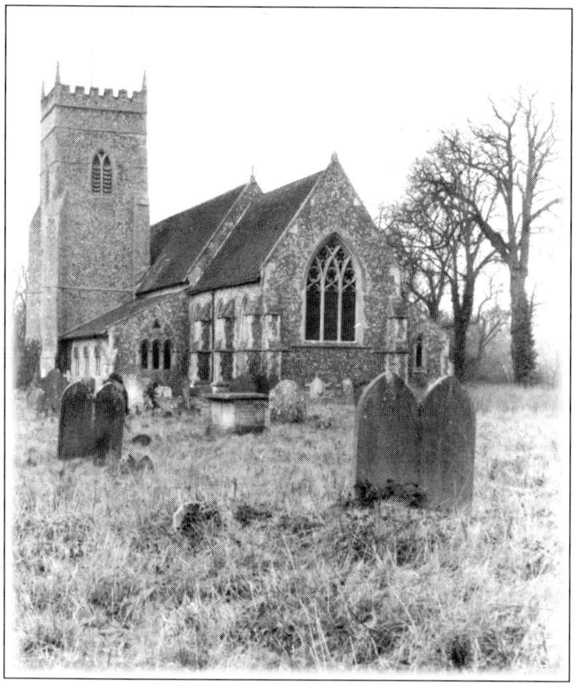

Above: *Sculthorpe Church, late 1940s. This photograph clearly shows the rather heavy Victorian parapet added to the top of the early-fourteenth-century tower.*
(Reproduced by kind permission of Mr Bob Hood)

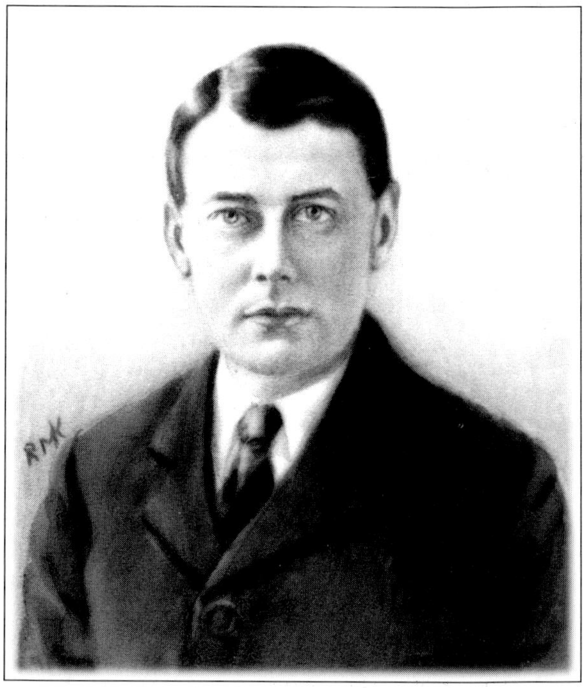

Above: *The Revd John Arthur Labouchere, rector of Sculthorpe 1902–20. From a painting belonging to his grandson, John Labouchere.*

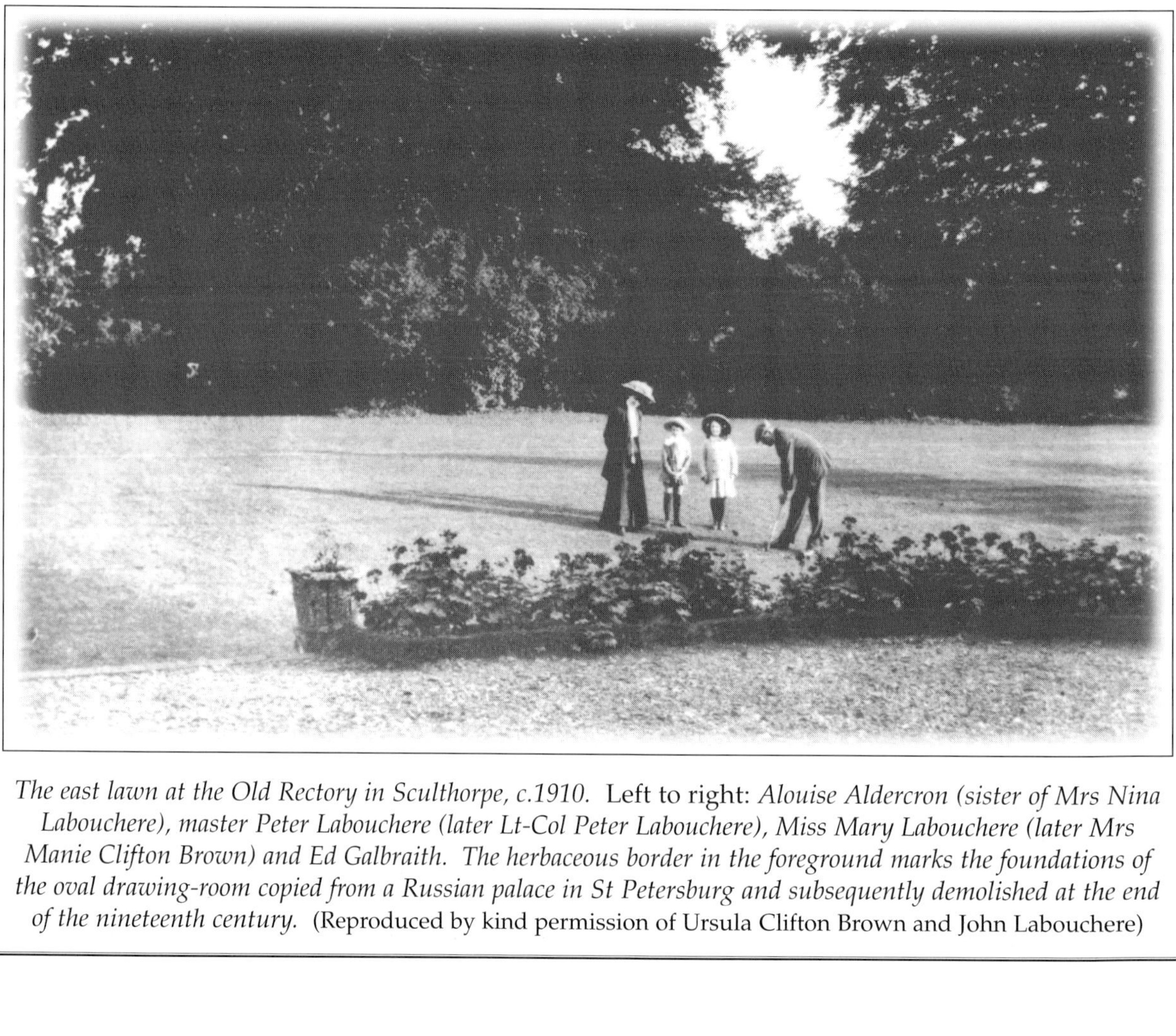

The east lawn at the Old Rectory in Sculthorpe, c.1910. Left to right: *Alouise Aldercron (sister of Mrs Nina Labouchere), master Peter Labouchere (later Lt-Col Peter Labouchere), Miss Mary Labouchere (later Mrs Manie Clifton Brown) and Ed Galbraith. The herbaceous border in the foreground marks the foundations of the oval drawing-room copied from a Russian palace in St Petersburg and subsequently demolished at the end of the nineteenth century.* (Reproduced by kind permission of Ursula Clifton Brown and John Labouchere)

of Cranmer Hall. Jekyll was a much-maligned Victorian architect whose work and designs are now receiving recognition. He was responsible for the ambitious refurbishment of many Norfolk country houses, such as Elsing and Ketteringham Halls, and designed sumptuous wrought-iron work for Barnard, Bishop and Barnard of Norwich. His most celebrated creations were the wrought-iron Norwich Gates at Sandringham House, which were greatly admired at the Second International Exhibition in 1862 held at South Kensington Museum, and the wrought-iron Japanese pagoda which was shown at the Philadelphia Exhibition in 1876 and subsequently adorned Chapelfield Gardens in Norwich.

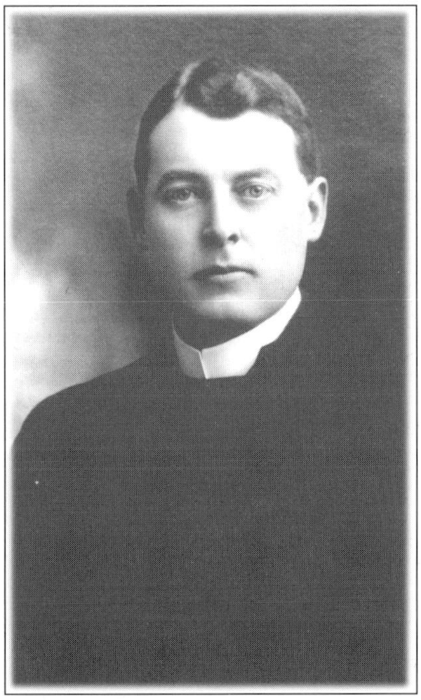

The Revd John Arthur Labouchere, much-loved rector of Sculthorpe from 1902 until his death in 1920.
(Reproduced by kind permission of his grandson, Mr John Labouchere)

Herbert Walsingham Jones would have known Thomas Jekyll through his brother-in-law, the Revd William Gurney, who had married Anna Boileau of Ketteringham Hall, and Jekyll's restoration of the historic interior of Grove House in Tunn Street, Fakenham, during 1860 may have gained him the architectural commission to restore the church in Sculthorpe. The rector's entry in the church register explained that Jekyll employed local craftsmen, stonemasons and estate carpenters to create his designs – the head carpenter was Robert Bassham of Sculthorpe. Mrs Crane and Mrs Howard often recalled how their paternal grandfather, Samuel Woodhouse, one of the estate carpenters who made the village coffins in his cart shed at April Cottage in Moor Lane, had also been involved in the Victorian restoration of the Parish Church. The work was completed by May 1861 and the church register recorded that 'Dr Pelham, Bishop of Norwich, preached the opening sermon on Whit Monday afternoon 1861.'

The Reverend and Mrs Herbert Jones lost their only child, a son, Bertram, in 1868, but they became the devoted guardians of their orphaned nephews and nieces, the children of Lady Troubridge, sister of Mrs Herbert Jones.

Life Amongst the Troubridges recorded the delightful tales of Laura Troubridge and her brothers and sisters staging theatricals at the rectory and attending dances hosted by Sir Willoughby Jones and his family at Cranmer Hall.

Herbert Walsingham Jones died in February 1889 after nearly 30 years as rector of Sculthorpe; he is commemorated by a stained-glass window on the north side of the chancel in Sculthorpe Church which depicts Our Lord as the Light of the World and the Good Shepherd from the design by the Pre-Raphaelite artist Henry Holiday for the glaziers Powells of Whitefriars. Mrs Herbert Jones, now a much-celebrated historical authoress, spent her final years at No.32 Albert Hall Mansions in London where she died in December 1895. Her coffin was brought back to Norfolk and laid to rest at the side of her husband and their only child in the churchyard at Sculthorpe.

The new rector, the Revd James Hay Upcher, was responsible for the demolition of the oval drawing-room at the rectory. He was greatly loved in the parish but, after only three years, he left Sculthorpe in 1892 to join Bishop Knight-Bruce in Rhodesia and became Archdeacon Upcher in the Anglican Diocese of Mashonaland. One of the last babies to be baptised in Sculthorpe by the Revd Upcher was Eleanor Manning Woodhouse (later Mrs Eleanor Crane) in September 1891. Archdeacon Upcher became one of the founding fathers of the Anglican Church in Rhodesia and built a small brick church in Salisbury which he dedicated to the Blessed Virgin Mary and All Saints, being the patronal dedication of his former church in Sculthorpe. The cathedral in modern-day Harare marks the site and perpetuates this patronal dedication. During the Boer War Archdeacon Upcher served as an Army chaplain and witnessed the Relief of Mafeking in May 1900 where Colonel Robert Baden-Powell, founder of the Boy Scout movement, had bravely defended the besieged British forces. The Archdeacon's final years were spent working with the Epiphany Mission in Rusape.

The Revd John Arthur Labouchere became rector of Sculthorpe in 1902 shortly before his marriage to Nina Dorothea Adlercron. Mrs Crane and Mrs Howard recalled their first meeting with the new parson when he walked up the garden path to their home at Rose Cottage near the church and asked to speak with their father, Willy Woodhouse, who was land agent for the Cranmer Hall estate. The rectory was being redecorated for its new incumbent and arrangements were made for the Revd Labouchere to stay with the Woodhouse family at Rose Cottage.

The Revd Labouchere was descended from a French Huguenot family of cloth merchants who lived in the town of Orthez and had suffered religious persecution for their Protestant faith following the Revocation of the Edict of Nantes by King Louis XIV in 1685. The reverend's great-uncle was the radical Liberal politician Henry Labouchere, a

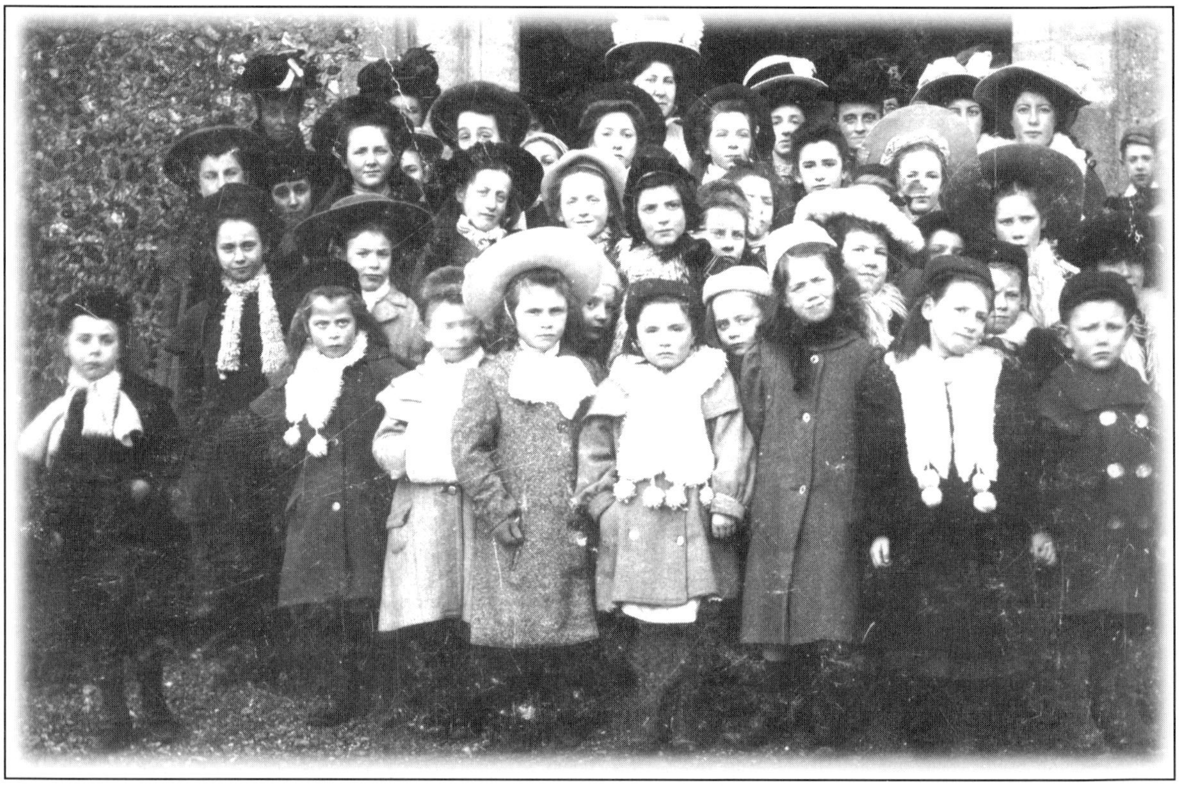

Sculthorpe Church Mission, February 1909. Back row, centre: *Ellen Winn;* back row, first and second from the right: *Marion and Eleanor Woodhouse;* next row down, fifth and seventh from the left: *Minnie Mallom and Ivy Sands;* front row, second from the left: *Daisy Lingwood;* front row, third from the right: *May Gathercole and behind her May Calcutt (later Mrs May Wright).*

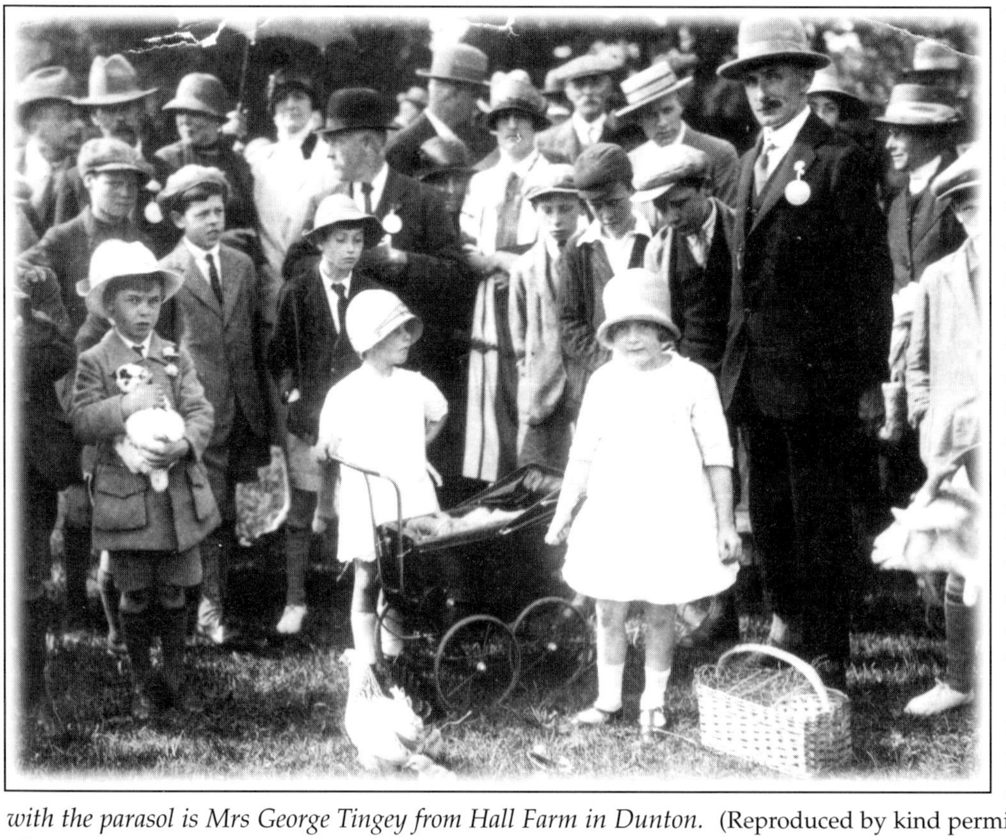

Left: *Pet's corner at the annual flower show held on the Rectory Glebe, 1920s. The tall figure on the right of the photograph is Billy Crane and the two little girls in the front are his two elder daughters, Edna and Gwen Crane, with their pet hen and baby chick, which won first prize. To the left of the photograph the impressive-looking lady with the parasol is Mrs George Tingey from Hall Farm in Dunton.* (Reproduced by kind permission of Mr Richard Land)

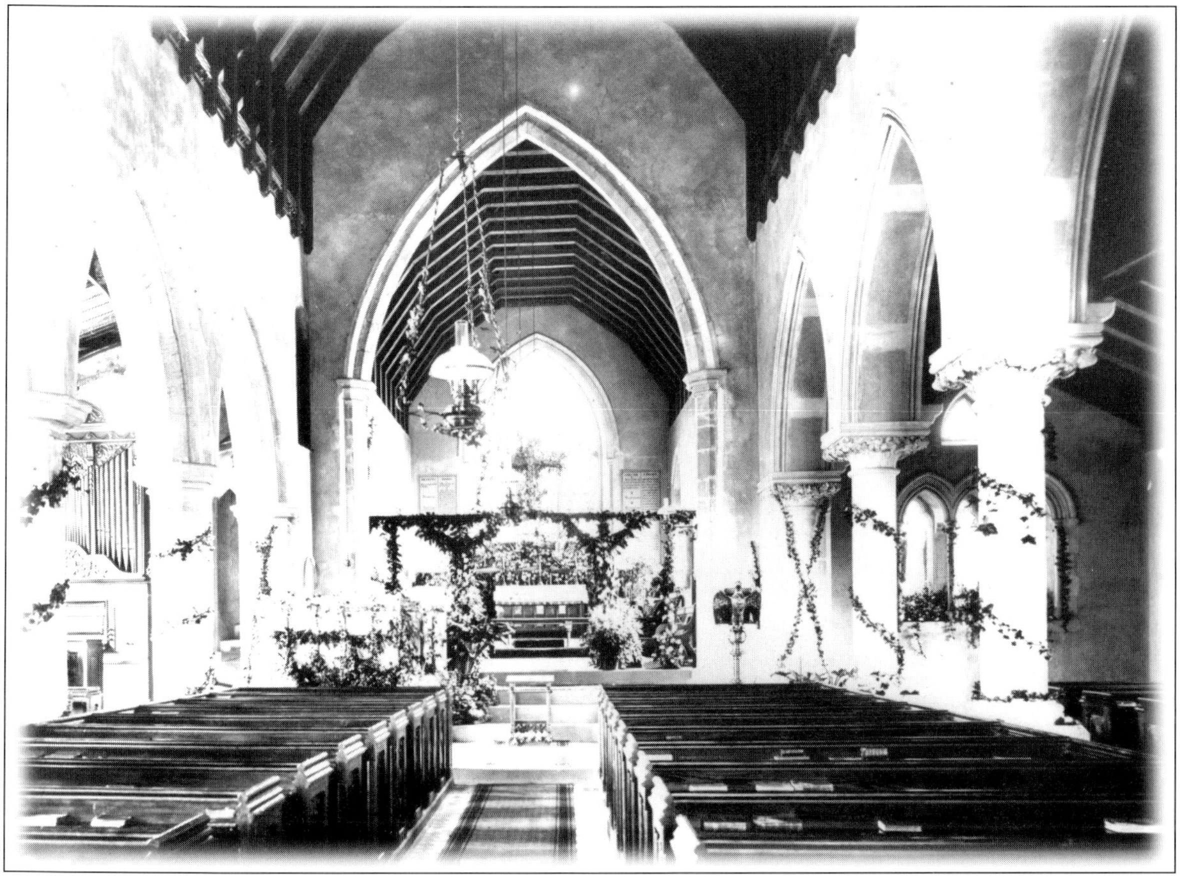

The interior of Sculthorpe Church, c.1905. The portable rood-screen was decorated with spring flowers every Easter by Mrs Ellen Woodhouse and her daughters Eleanor and Marion. (Reproduced by kind permission of Father Andrew Thomson, rector of Sculthorpe Church)

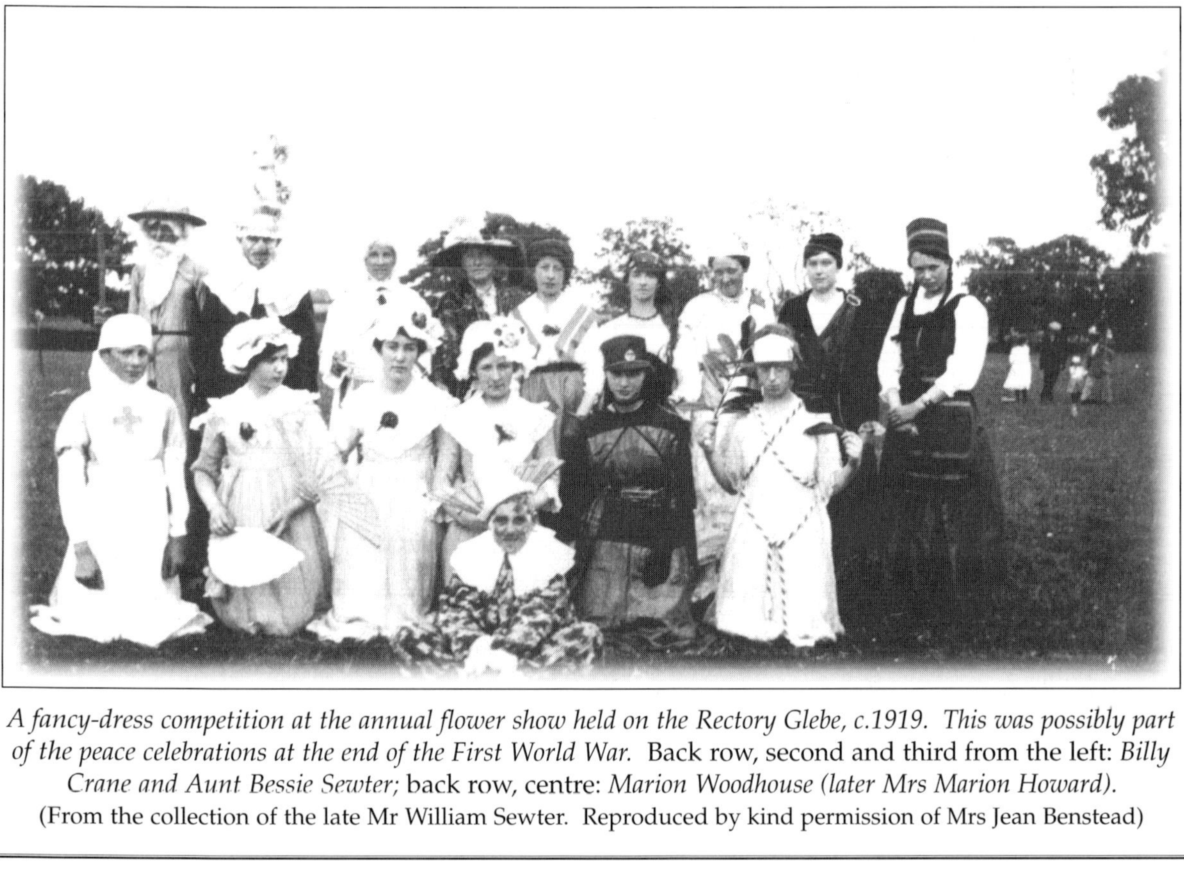

A fancy-dress competition at the annual flower show held on the Rectory Glebe, c.1919. This was possibly part of the peace celebrations at the end of the First World War. Back row, second and third from the left: *Billy Crane and Aunt Bessie Sewter;* back row, centre: *Marion Woodhouse (later Mrs Marion Howard).* (From the collection of the late Mr William Sewter. Reproduced by kind permission of Mrs Jean Benstead)

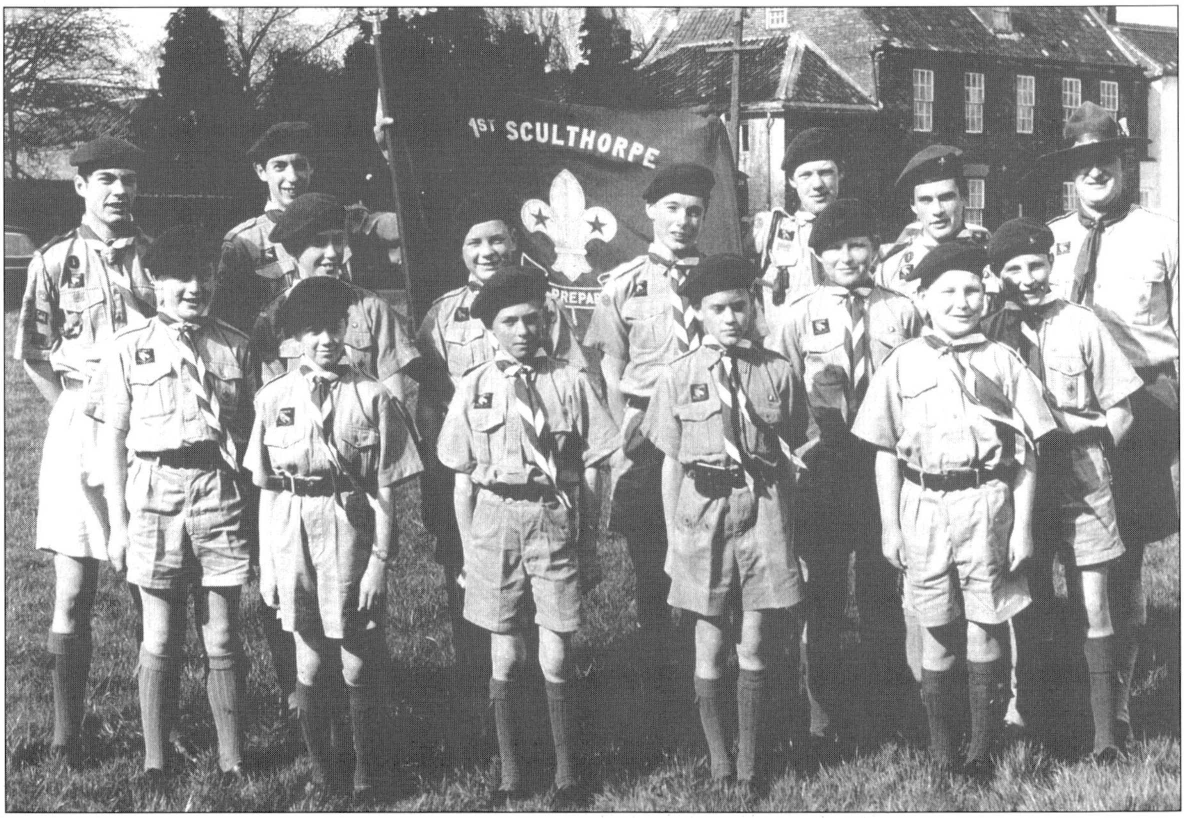

The 1st Sculthorpe Boy Scouts was originally founded by the Revd Christopher Chitty in 1936. During the incumbency of the Revd Fred Gunn (1955–64) there was a considerable revival in the Scout movement. Here the Scouts are pictured during the early 1960s. In the back row with the Scout flag are: *Melvin Vertigans, Ray Norman, Maurice Vertigans, Colin Lingwood and Bernard Edge ('Skip'). Melvin Vertigans and Colin Lingwood were decorated as Queen's Scouts during this period.* (From the collection of Mrs Jean Edge. Reproduced by kind permission of the *Lynn News*)

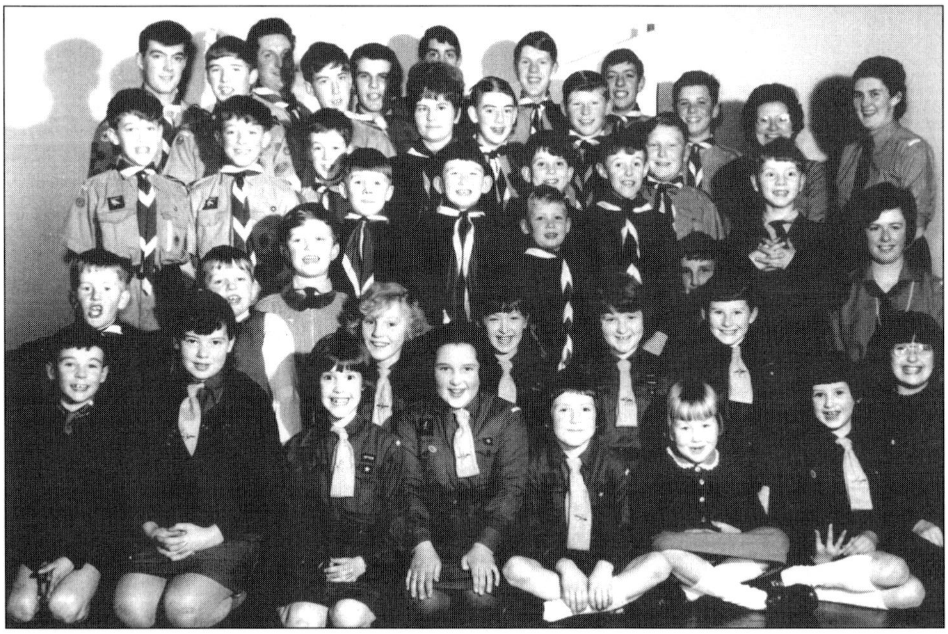

Left: *Sculthorpe Boy Scouts, Cubs, Girl Guides and Brownies, c.1966.* Back row, third from the left: *Bernard Edge ('Skip') with some of the young Scout leaders including Melvin Vertigans and Ray Norman;* back row, second from the right: *Jean Edge (Bernard's wife) who was 'Brown Owl' for many years;* middle row, far right: *Pat Williamson who was 'Tawny Owl'.* In the centre of the photograph is: *Ann Armiger who helped with the Cubs.* Among the young faces are: *Desmond Mackay, Angela and Sheila Pawley, Diane and Carol Matless, Peter and Valerie Futter, Rita Pratt, Margaret Playford, David Gibson, Karen Manning, Bruce and Graham Webster.* (From the collection of Mrs Jean Edge. Reproduced by kind permission of the *Lynn News*)

friend of Mr Gladstone and critic of Queen Victoria.

The new parson and his young wife became extremely popular, like the Revd and Mrs Jones before them, taking a very keen interest in every aspect of parish life. The Revd Labouchere initially visited the cottages on horseback and later in his Daimler motor car which he had bought from Mr Lockhart-Ross, the tenant of Cranmer Hall. Mrs Labouchere was involved with both the church Sunday school and the Mothers' Union, and she visited the elderly inhabitants of the Beckham Almshouses in Moor Lane, bringing gifts of warm blankets, hot soup and beef tea. Mrs Crane and Mrs Howard remembered the wonderful parties held in the parish room at the rectory when the Revd Labouchere staged his magic lantern shows or produced a white rabbit out of his conjurer's top hat!

The Revd Labouchere enjoyed attending shooting parties and was an excellent shot, perfecting his skills at Sculthorpe Rifle Club. During the shooting season he never conducted a wedding before 3 o'clock on Saturdays because he was always keen to spend his mornings out with his gun. His reputation as a 'shooting parson' once prompted his young son Peter to make an amusing reference to his father's passion for shooting. Bishop Bowers of Thetford, the rector of North Creake, affectionately known as the 'Bishop of the Great Eastern' because of his passion for the railways, frequently descended upon Sculthorpe Rectory in his horse-drawn Episcopal coach to visit the Labouchere family. On one occasion he playfully hoisted young Peter Labouchere up onto his shoulders and asked him 'Now what would you like to be when you grow up, Master Peter?' 'I suppose to be just like my Daddy,' came the instant reply. 'To go shooting all the days of the week and preach to the people on Sundays!'

Mrs Crane and Mrs Howard remembered helping their mother, Mrs Ellen Woodhouse, with the floral decoration of the church at Easter. The Revd Labouchere installed a portable fretwork rood-screen which spanned the chancel arch and was adorned with daffodils, narcissi and arum lilies. During February 1909 the Revd Labouchere, assisted by the Reverends Henry and Philip Clarke, held a parish mission in Sculthorpe Church. The south aisle was refurnished as a Lady Chapel and Dr Mercer from Newport in the United States presented the high altar with its Pre-Raphaelite paintings.

During 1914–15 A-Division of the Berkshire Yeomanry were billeted at the rectory and presented an inscribed copy of the Bible to the Laboucheres' cook, Jessie Winn, on the eve of her wedding to the gardener, Bob Lingwood. Rectory Cottage on the glebe was completed in 1916 and became home for the newlyweds.

In 1920 the Revd Labouchere died and a final pastoral letter to his parishioners from his sickbed conveyed his deep affection for the people of Sculthorpe and 'a high regard for the Norfolk character'. Mrs Labouchere retired to her new home at Burnham Thorpe Lodge near Nelson's church but this was not the end of the Labouchere link with Sculthorpe.

The annual church garden fêtes and the flower shows held in the rectory gardens and on the glebe meadow were wonderful occasions with tents and marquees, fancy-dress competitions and a pet's corner. During the 1920s the whole village turned out for these summer events with the local gentry arriving in their motor cars. Scrumptious teas were served, prizes given and sideshows and stalls raised funds for the Parish Church. The flower show ran an annual competition for the village children to produce the best-decorated eggcup. Doris, Leslie, Joyce and Ronnie Lingwood remembered the wild-flower competition in which the children were encouraged to gather wild flowers on the Turf Moor, such as marsh orchids and ragged Robin and to fill their jam jars to take up to the rectory.

In 1935 the Revd Christopher Chitty became rector. A product of Balliol College, Oxford, and Cuddesdon Theological College, he had been ordained a priest in Canterbury Cathedral and from 1930–34 had been part of the Jerusalem Mission, acting as chaplain to the Anglican bishop in Egypt and

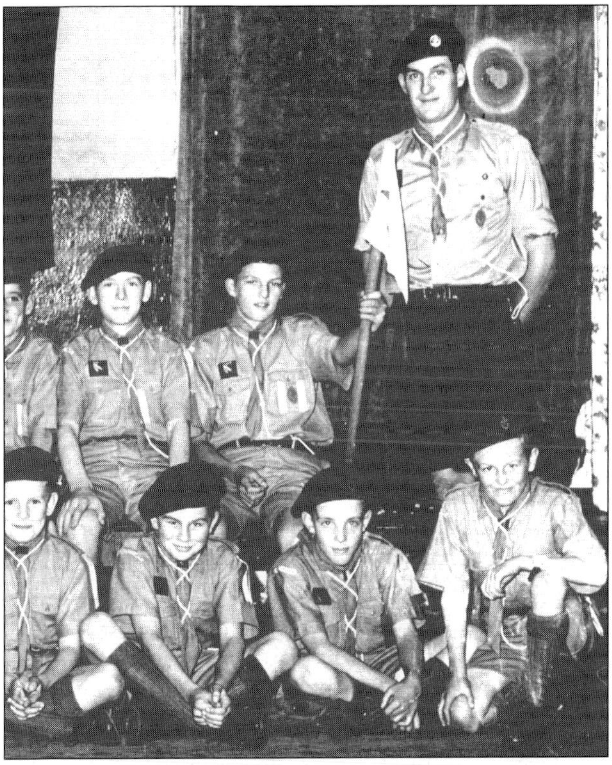

Bernard Edge was 'Skip' for many years. This photograph, dating from the late 1950s, shows Bernard with some of the Boy Scouts from the time, including: Terry Harrison, Philip Fuller, David Lingwood, Buster Futter and John Engledow. (From the collection of Mrs Jean Edge. Reproduced by kind permission of the *Lynn News*)

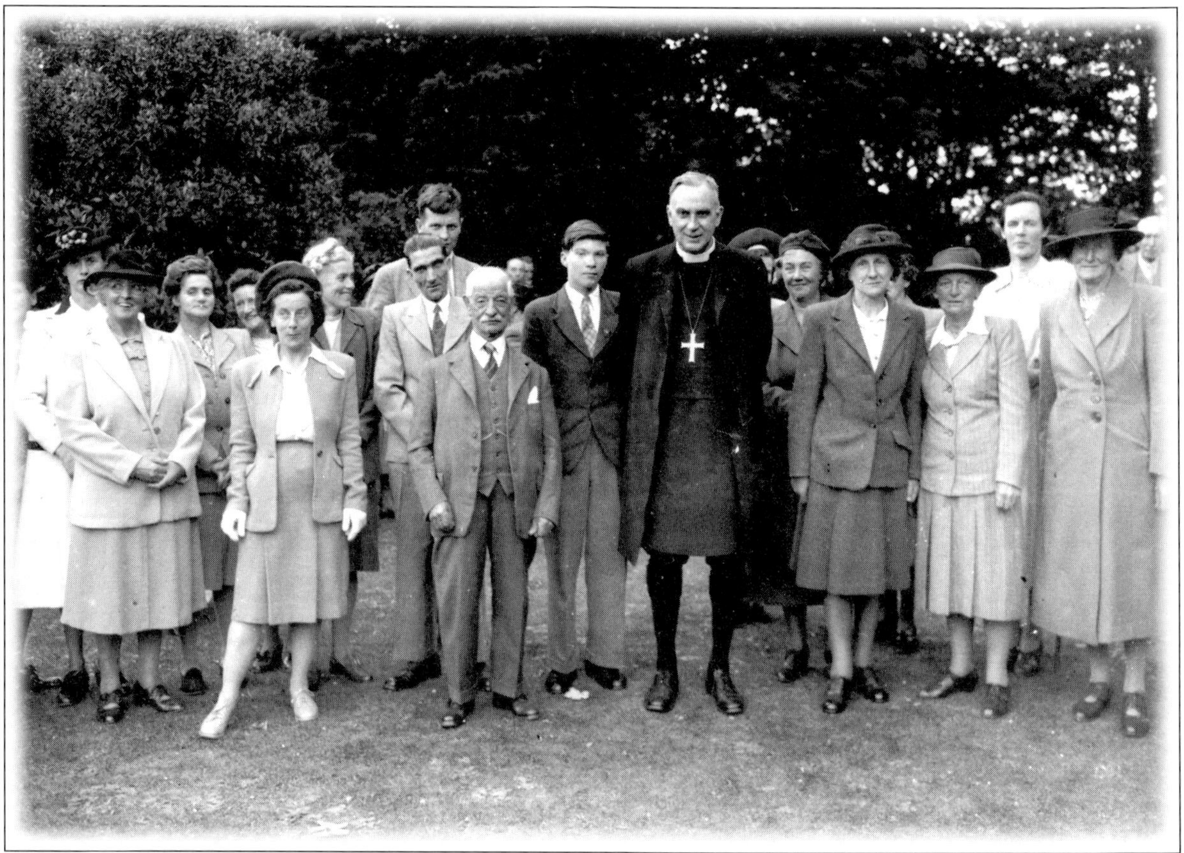

Above: *The service of dedication and thanksgiving for the new church rugs was held at Sculthorpe Church on Wednesday 6 July 1949. This was followed by a reception at the Old Rectory by kind invitation of Colonel Labouchere and his wife Peg. Pictured here are some of those involved in making the rugs.* Left to right, the photograph includes: *Mrs Hettie Hipkin, Mrs Eleanor Crane, Mrs Norah Armiger, Mrs Violet Skippon, Mrs Howes, Mr and Mrs George Wright, Colin Labouchere* (behind), *Willy Woodhouse, Brian Wright, the Bishop of Thetford, Mrs Piggott, Mrs Hood, Mrs Jessie Lingwood and Mrs Peg Labouchere.* (Reproduced by kind permission of the Norfolk Rural Life Museum at Gressenhall)

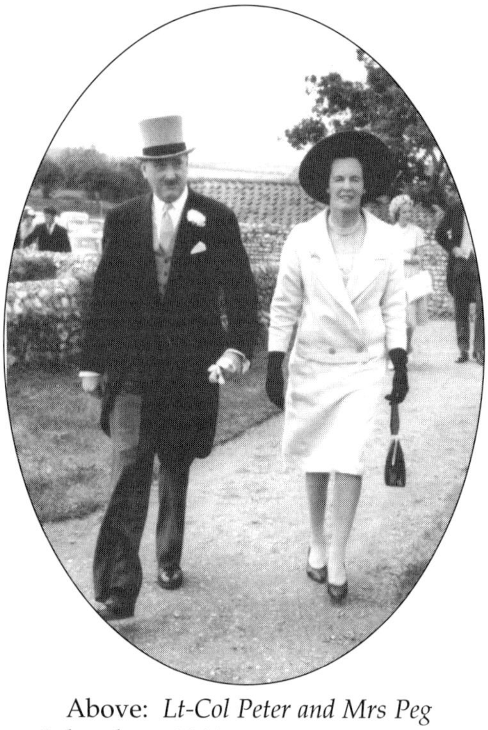

Above: *Lt-Col Peter and Mrs Peg Labouchere, 1961.* (Reproduced by kind permission of Colin Labouchere)

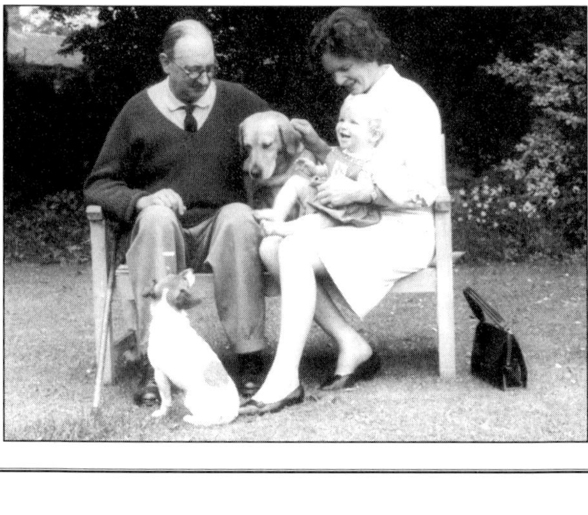

Right: *Lt-Col Peter and Mrs Peg Labouchere with their first grandson, Peter Colin Labouchere, in the garden at the Old Rectory, Sculthorpe, 1963.* (Reproduced by kind permission of Colin Labouchere)

assistant chaplain at St Mary's Anglican Cathedral in Cairo.

The Revd Chitty is best remembered for starting the Sculthorpe Boy Scouts in 1936. The Scout Room was situated at the rectory with the Revd Chitty acting as Scoutmaster and Arthur Playford as his assistant. The boys who participated were mainly drawn from church-going families – the Playford boys, Bob Hood, Harold Lingwood and his cousin Ronnie Lingwood and Austin Cornwall who still has his original Boy Scout uniform from the late 1930s. Arthur Playford received the Boy Scouts' bravery award for his heroic attempt in trying to rescue poor old Mr Panks, tragically caught and crushed in machinery at Oliver Rix's foundry in Creake Road. The Boy Scouts frequently attended church parade, particularly on St George's Day, 23 April, and pitched their tents on the rectory meadow for week-end camp during the Easter holidays. Ronnie Lingwood remembered one Easter Sunday when the Boy Scouts emerged shivering with cold from their tents to attend church parade, only to find the meadow grass covered with an inch or two of snow, which had fallen during the night.

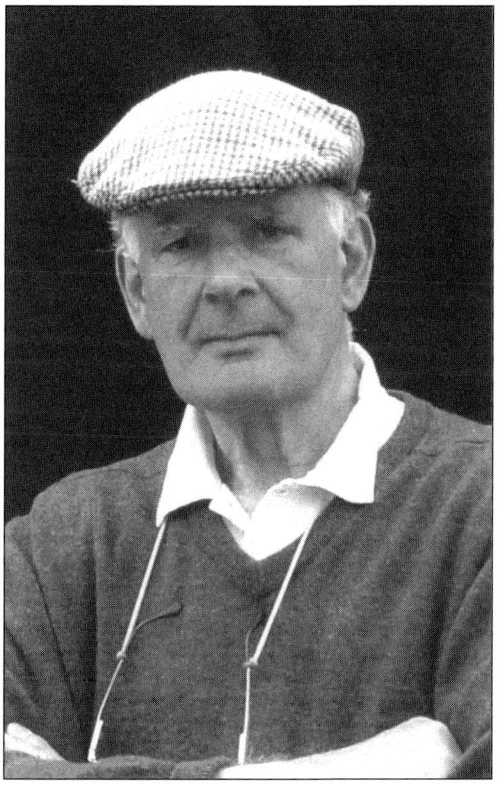

John Labouchere (above) *maintains strong links with the village of Sculthorpe and is patron of Sculthorpe Parish Church.*

With the departure of the Revd Claude Cotter in 1948 the church commissioners sold the rectory house and the bulk of the glebe lands, thus effectively severing the centuries-old link between the parsonage and the Parish Church. A smart new rectory was built near the crossroads of the Creake–Fakenham turning and this continued to serve successive parish priests until it was finally sold by the church commissioners in 1982.

Lieutenant-Colonel Peter Labouchere and his sister 'Manie' Clifton Brown cherished fond memories of their Edwardian childhood at the Old Rectory in Sculthorpe and as Master Peter and Miss Mary Labouchere, the children of the Revd and Mrs Jack Labouchere, they had continued to visit their native village and call in upon old friends. Mrs Clifton Brown admitted she particularly enjoyed sampling a glass or two of the highly potent homemade cowslip wine, for which this village was famous!

In 1948 Lt-Col Labouchere retired from Army life and the sale of the Old Rectory in Sculthorpe enabled him to acquire his birthplace; Peter and his wife Peg were able to make this a very happy home for their expanding family of four children – John, Colin, Henry and Susan. Peter took great interest in the life of the Parish Church; in 1949 the Jones family conveyed the patronage of the living to him and this continues to be held by his eldest son, John Labouchere. The Lt-Col and his sister jointly presented their father's family Bible to Sculthorpe Church – a beautiful crimson-morocco-bound Baskerville Bible of 1773, with silver clasps and adorned with the family coat of arms.

During the Second World War thieves stole a series of rugs from the chancel and the Lady Chapel in the Parish Church. They had been made during 1909 in the drawing-room at the Old Rectory by members of the congregation under the direction of the Revd and Mrs Labouchere.

In March 1949 history effectively repeated itself with the creation of 18 new rugs as replacements for those made 40 years earlier. Some of the original rug makers from the Edwardian period were involved: Willy Woodhouse and his daughter Eleanor Crane, Jessie Lingwood and 'Aunt Bessie' Sewter from the village shop, who were joined by other members of the congregation. The venue was again the Old Rectory and in the same drawing-room. Lt-Col Labouchere and his sister, who remembered the original rugs being made during their childhood, also enthusiastically supported the venture. The project received widespread newspaper coverage and a letter of support from Queen Mary.

Peter Labouchere's wife Peg had been born Helen Margaret Coles of an old Scottish family and is affectionately remembered in the village for her passion for horse riding and rearing bloodstock. She rode with the West Norfolk Foxhounds and was highly successful in breeding ponies and training gun dogs. Her sparkling spirit of adventure had ensured her participation as a driver in the Monte Carlo rally and her possession of an aircraft pilot's licence, she was also a talented artist, in both watercolours and oils, and a keen botanist and gardener. Many of the climbing roses which cover the east side of the Old Rectory were planted by Peg Labouchere.

Both Colonel and Mrs Labouchere were Parish Councillors and District Councillors, serving on the old Walsingham Rural District Council. They

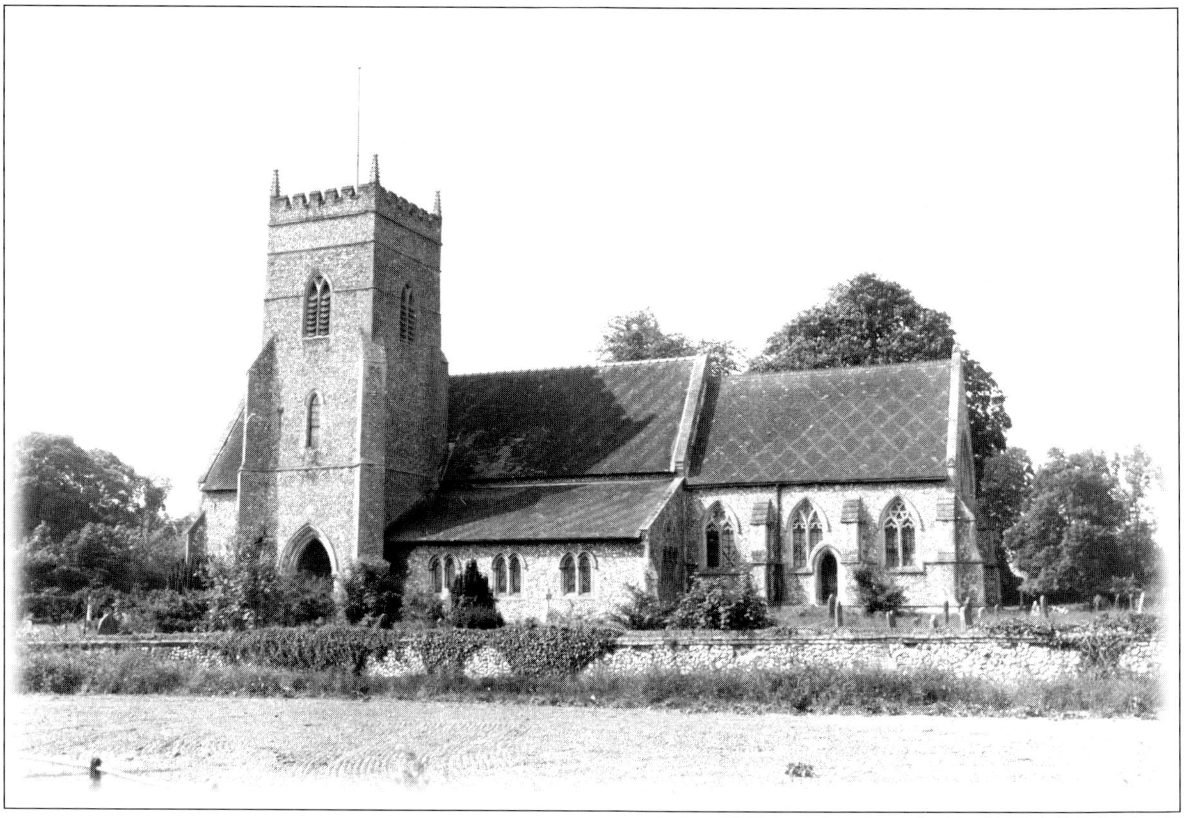

Sculthorpe Church, 1930s. (Reproduced by kind permission of the Norfolk Rural Life Museum at Gressenhall)

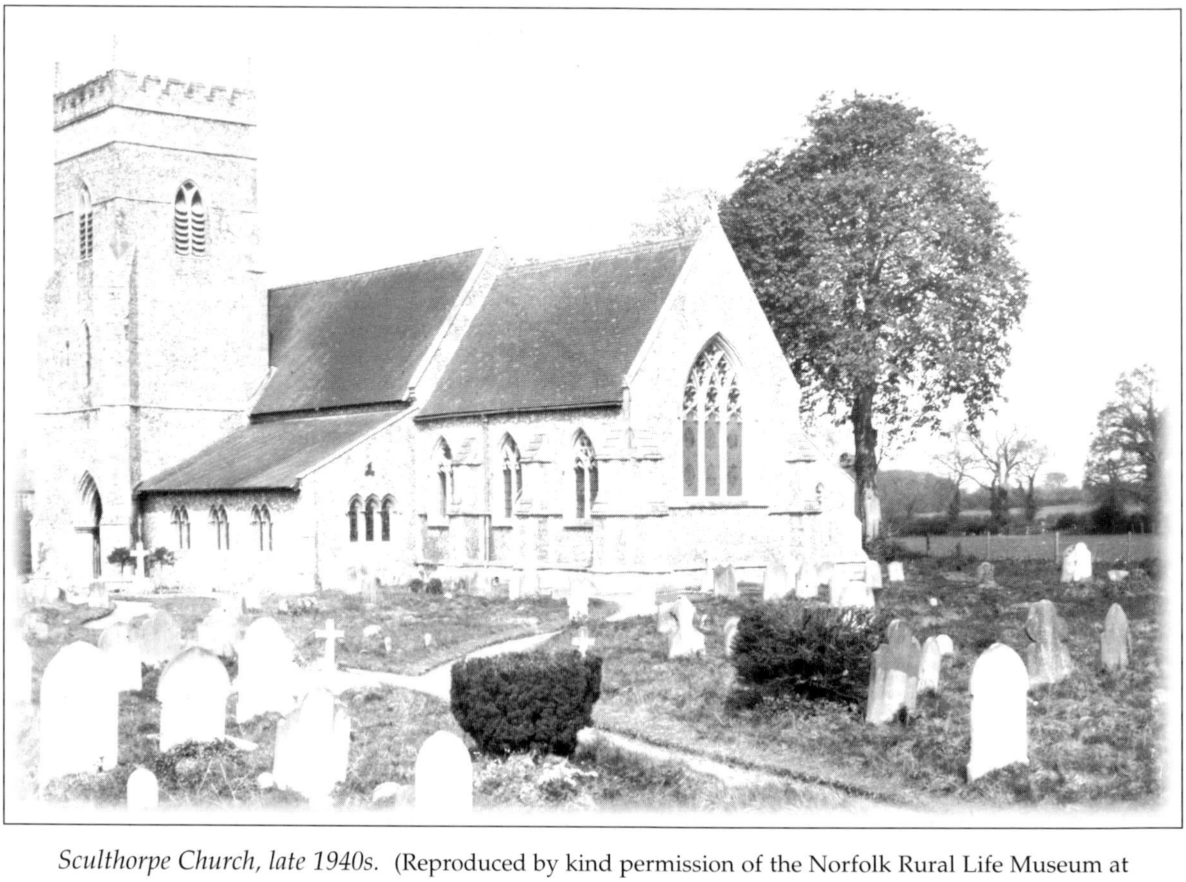

Sculthorpe Church, late 1940s. (Reproduced by kind permission of the Norfolk Rural Life Museum at Gressenhall)

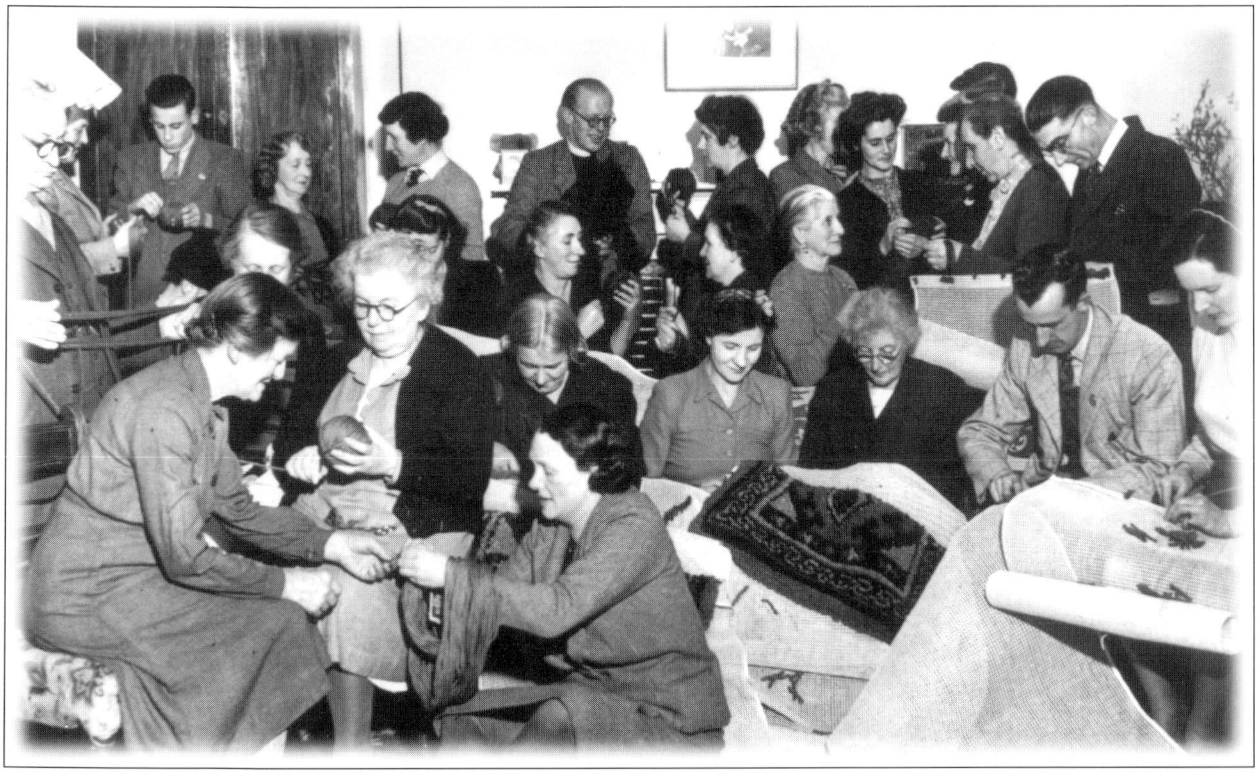

The Old Rectory, 1949. In this photograph the congregation and friends of Sculthorpe Parish Church are busily engaged working on a set of new woollen rugs to replace those made 40 years earlier and subsequently stolen from the church during the Second World War. Left to right, back row: *Colonel Peter Labouchere, Colin Mack, Miss Ethel Filby, Miss Catlin, the Revd and Mrs John Turney, Mrs George Wright, Mrs Nora Armiger, Mrs Violet Skippon, Granny Spalding, Mr George Wright;* middle: *Mrs Rose Applegate, Mrs Jarvis and Aunt Bessie Sewter;* front: *Willy Woodhouse, Mrs Jessie Lingwood, Mrs Hood* (behind), *Aunt Millie Woodhouse, Mrs Piggott, Mrs Manie Clifton Brown, Miss Kathleen Andrews, Mrs Eleanor Crane, Mr Ray Hipkin, Mrs Peg Labouchere.* (Reproduced by kind permission of the *Dereham & Fakenham Times*)

actively supported both the Red Cross and the Royal British Legion and Colonel Labouchere was involved with the committee and the fund-raising activities for the new village hall, which was being planned for Sculthorpe. During January 1964 Colonel Labouchere died at the Old Rectory in the same bedroom in which he had been born in 1905. He was buried in Sculthorpe churchyard, next to his parents' grave outside the south aisle Lady Chapel. Peg Labouchere remained with her children at the Old Rectory until she sold the property in 1966 to Philip Maitland Gore Anley and his wife Claire. The Laboucheres moved to Willersey in Gloucestershire where Peg Labouchere continued her riding and bloodstock interests. On New Year's Eve 1975 Peg was tragically killed in a hunting accident, riding to hounds with the North Cotswold Hunt. Her remarkable life was celebrated with a memorial service at Sculthorpe Church in January 1976.

The Labouchere family maintain their close link with the village of Sculthorpe and the Parish Church. John Labouchere continued the family love for horses and bloodstock and, inspired by the writings of Aim Felix Tschiffely, undertook a hair-raising 5,000-mile journey with three horses across the Andes in South America, which lasted a year from December 1990 to December 1991. His autobiographical book *High Horses: An Andean Adventure* was published in 1992 and his fascinating lectures illustrated with many photographic slides have provoked great interest, especially in Sculthorpe.

John's younger brother, Henry Labouchere, is an aircraft pilot and engineer engaged in the rebuilding and selling of vintage aircraft. During 1984, as part of the celebrations to mark the 50th anniversary of the Great Air Race, Henry flew in a 1932 De Havilland Puss Moth on an eight-week journey from England to Melbourne in Australia. At the time of writing he has continued to participate in numerous air rallies and is an enthusiastic member of the De Havilland Moth Club.

The arrival of the Anleys at the Old Rectory caused the house to be renamed Sculthorpe House. Philip Anley died in 1968 but his widow Claire, the daughter of Major Ralli of Barwick House, continued to live here until 1982. Her extremely successful smallholding, with fields of strawberries and blackberries, provided much-needed employment for the village.

The owners in 2003, Mr and Mrs John Bruce, have reverted to using the fields for the grazing of horses and have maintained the outstanding beauty and character of this ancient parsonage house and its historic gardens.

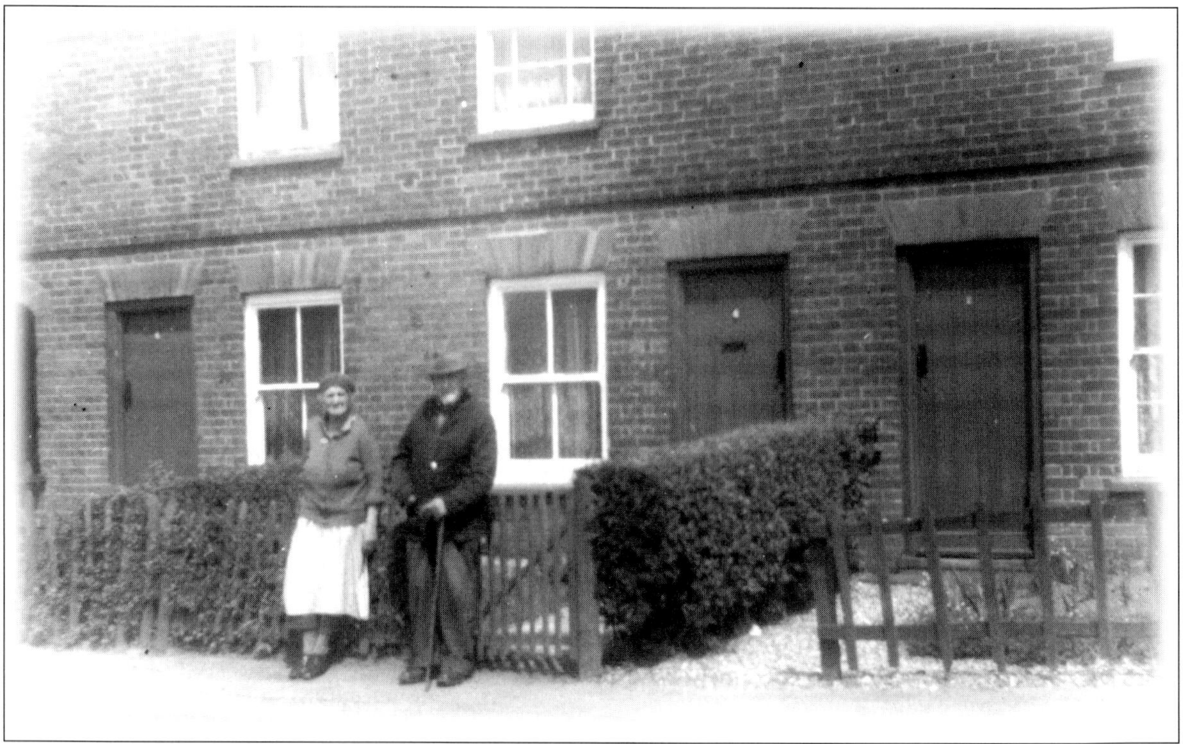

Nos 2, 4 and 6 The Street, Sculthorpe, late 1940s. Mr and Mrs White are outside their home at No.4.
(Reproduced by kind permission of Mrs Joyce Lingwood)

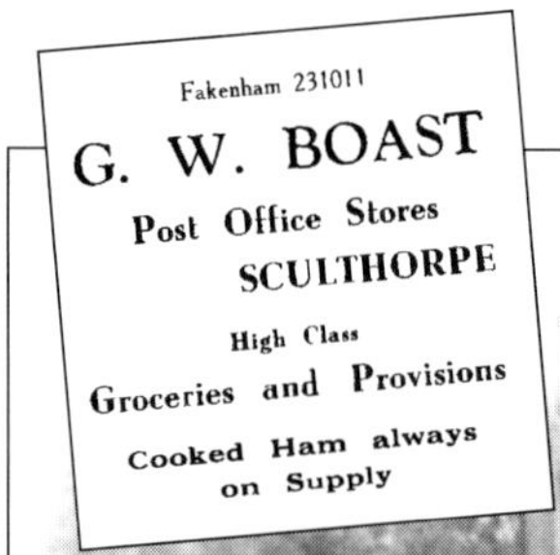

Left: *An advertisement for George Boast's Post Office Stores.*

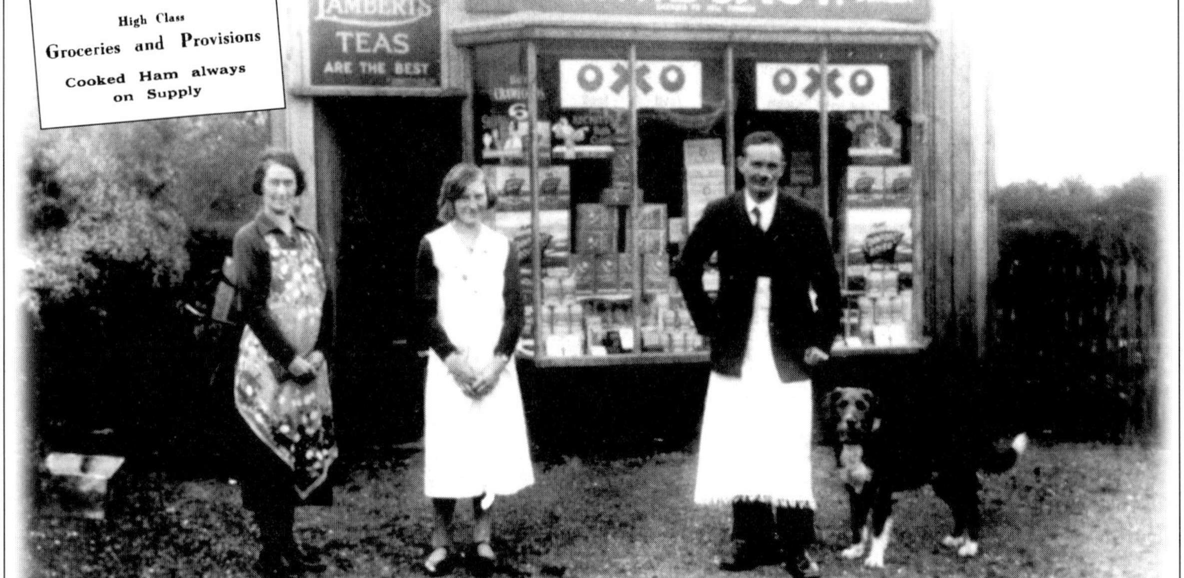

George Boast's grocery shop during the late 1930s. Left to right: *Mrs Winifred Boast, Miss Vera Short and Mr George Boast, with Jeff the dog. Mr Boast also provided a grocery provisions service, cycling around the neighbouring hamlets of Dunton-cum-Doughton, Shereford and Toftrees with his wares in a huge basket attached to his bicycle. In 1946 Aunt Bessie Sewter resigned from her position as village sub-postmistress and George Boast became the new sub-postmaster.*
(Reproduced by kind permission of Mr Kenneth Boast, George's son)

THE HORSLEY FAMILY

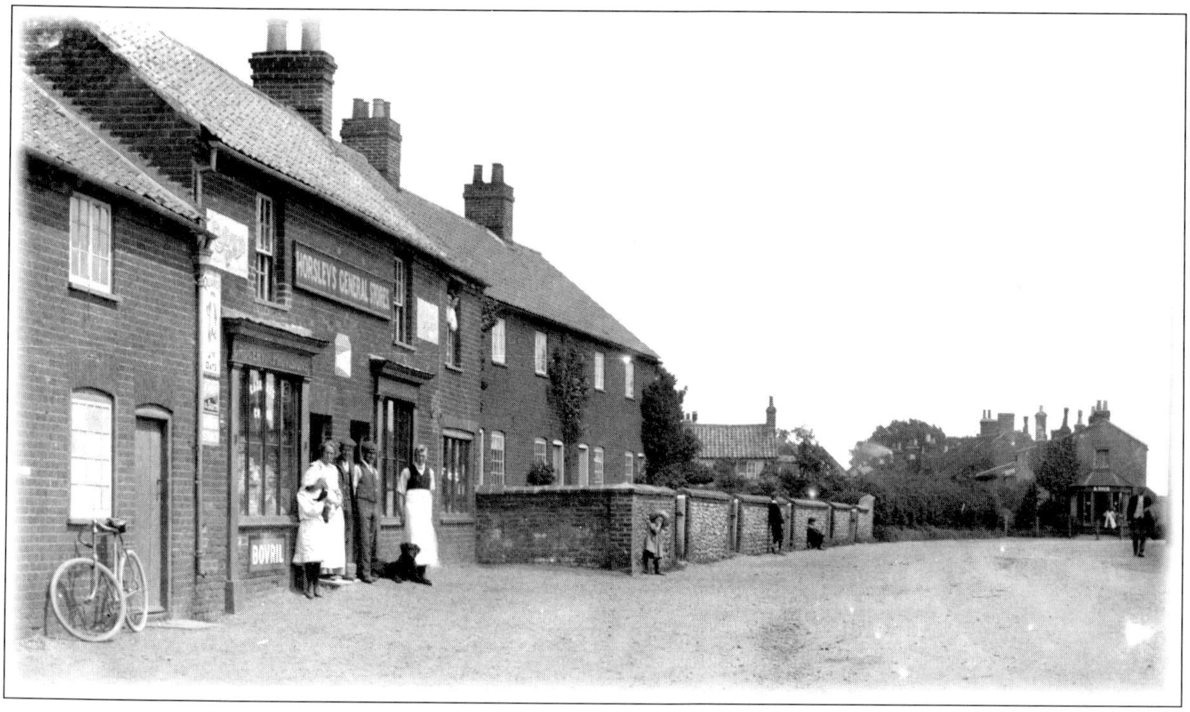

The Street, Sculthorpe, c.1910. It was then the main Lynn Road or Front Street. The Horsley family are standing outside Horsley's General Stores; the young man in a grocer's apron is their assistant Mr George Boast. In the distance are the Drift Cottages in Chapel Lane and Tuck's Bakery. This delightful picture was purchased by the author for £10 from Stamp Corner on Elm Hill in Norwich!

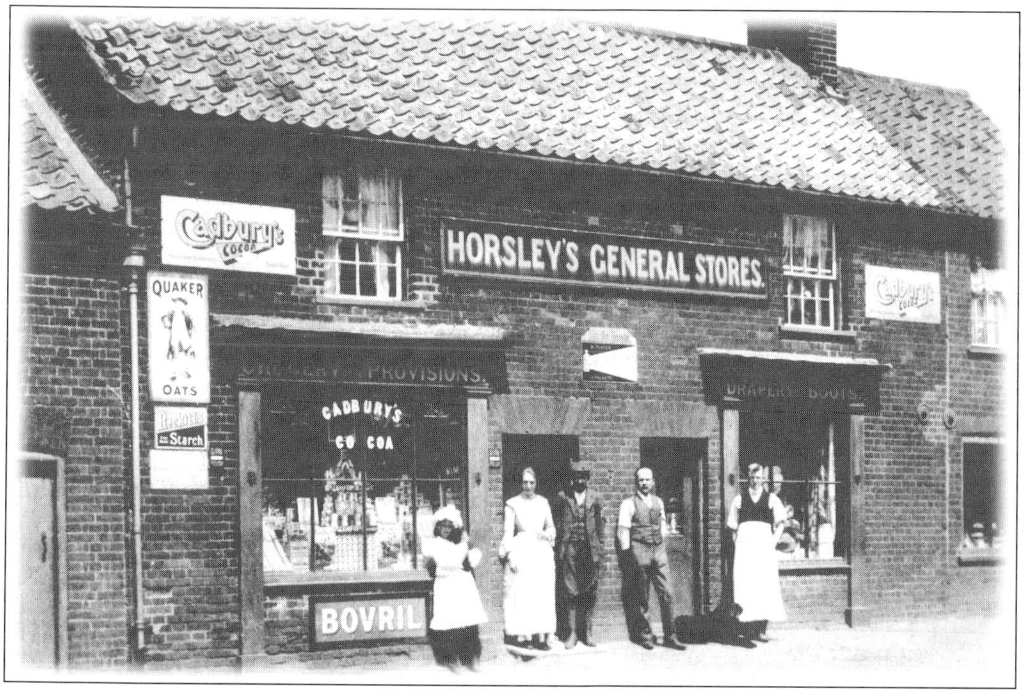

Horsley's General Stores, The Street, Sculthorpe, c.1910. Mrs Lucy Horsley and family are outside the shop and the young shop assistant, George Boast, stands to the right. Mrs Crane and Mrs Howard remembered their visits to Horsley's General Stores during the Edwardian period – they particularly enjoyed buying a quarter of pear-drops and bootlace liquorice. The shop provided groceries, drapery and boots. During the opening year of the First World War it burnt to the ground and remained a ruin for many years. A new cottage now stands on the site and only the old vinegar shed with a chimney pot survives to the rear.

(Reproduced by kind permission of Mr Kenneth Boast)

THE TUCK FAMILY

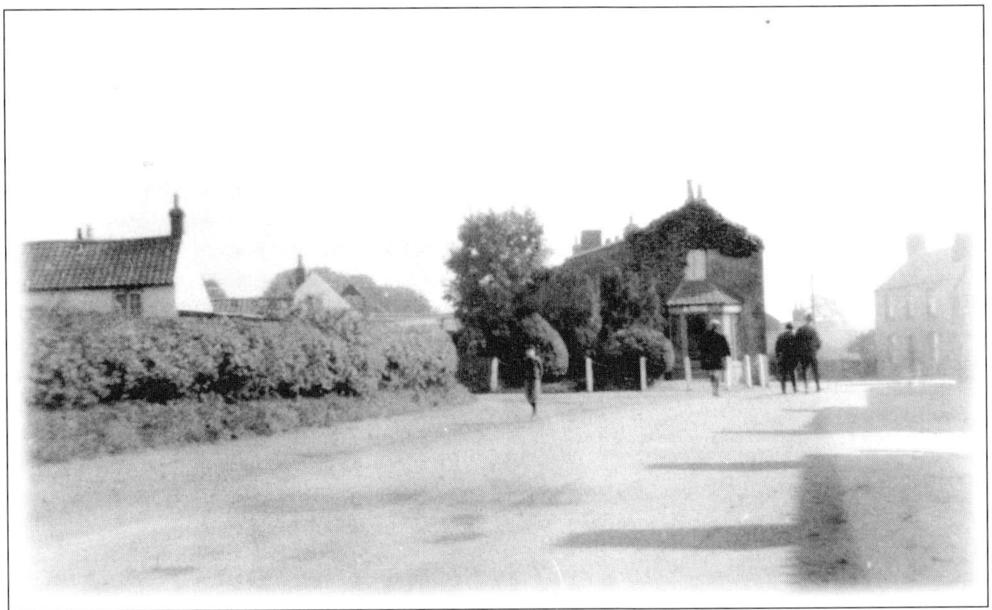

Left: *A view of Bay House, Robert Tuck's shop, and the Drift Cottages in Chapel Lane, c.1910.* (Reproduced by kind permission of Mr Kenneth Boast)

Right: *Bay House, Robert Tuck's Bakery, in The Street, c.1910. Among the members of the Tuck family pictured here are* (left to right)*: Detective Inspector Willy Tuck of Scotland Yard, Robert Tuck and Charles Tuck. The lady in the big picture hat is Winifred Tuck (later Mrs George Boast).* (Reproduced by kind permission of Joe and Nan Tuck)

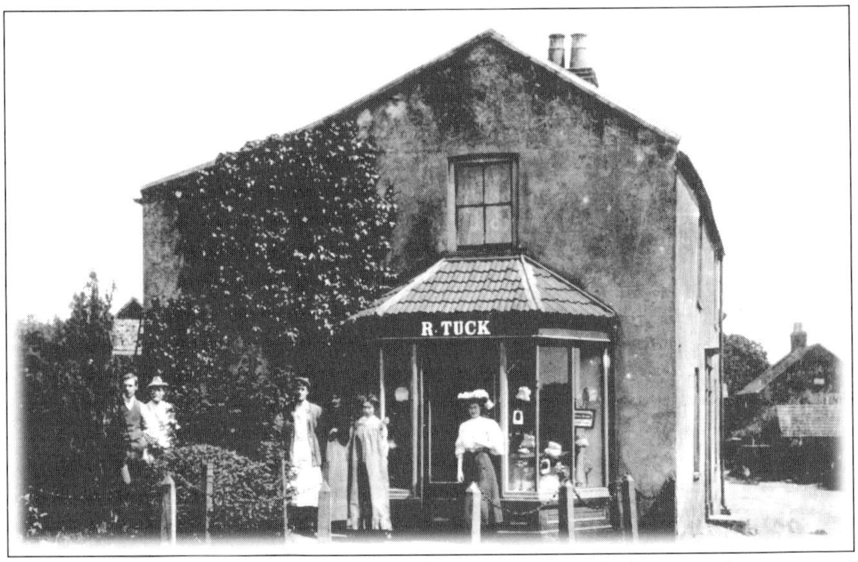

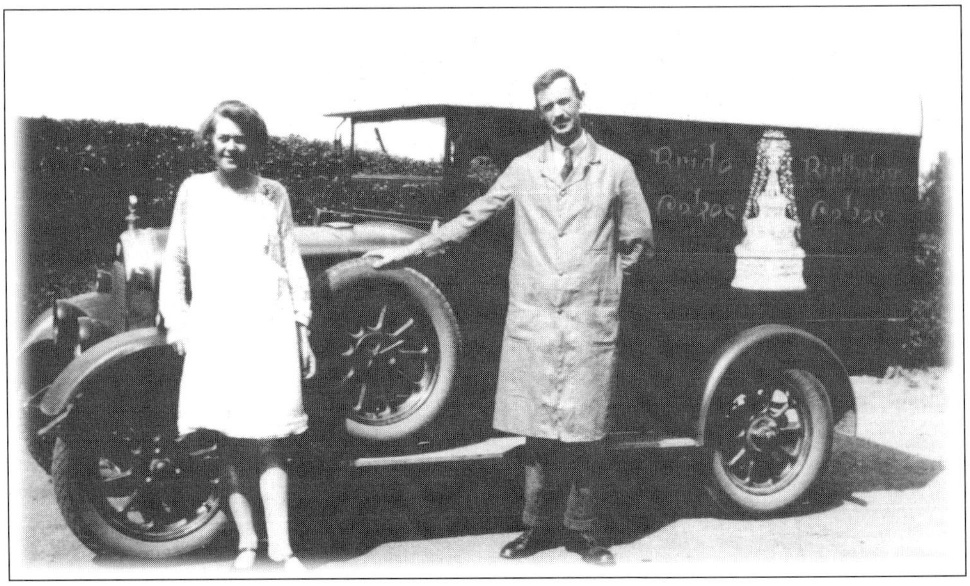

Left: *Charles Tuck with his daughter Cherri and the bakery van in Sculthorpe, 1930s.* (Reproduced by kind permission of Mr Kenneth Boast)

The Sewter Family

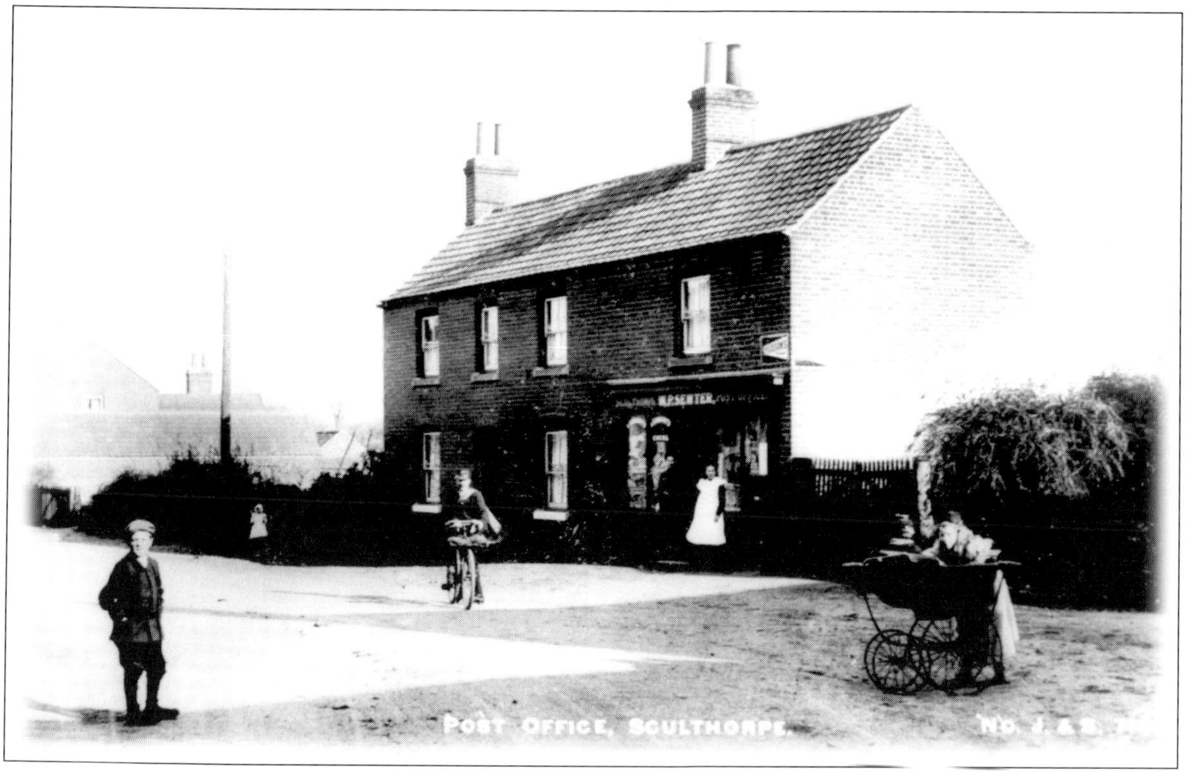

W.P. Sewter's Post Office and General Stores, The Street, Sculthorpe, c.1910. At the door of the shop is Mrs W.P. Sewter with her daughter Hannah Bessie Sewter, later known affectionately as 'Aunt Bessie'. The little boy to the left of the picture is Jimmy Lingwood. (From the collection of Mrs Doris Mitchell. Reproduced by kind permission of the Norfolk Rural Life Museum at Gressenhall)

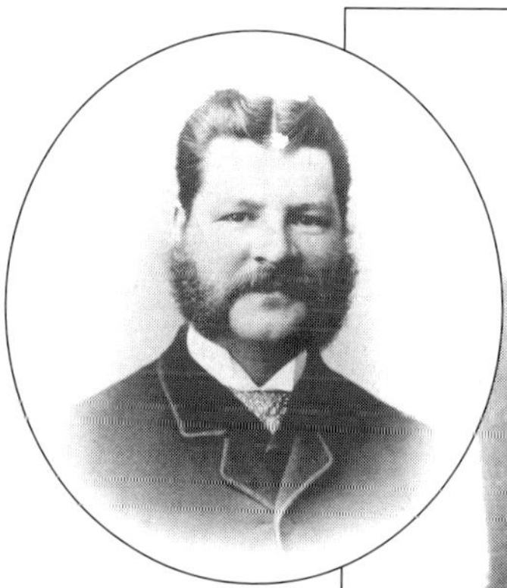

This Edwardian photograph is of Mr William Parke Sewter of The Street, Sculthorpe, who founded the family fortunes with his Post Office and General Stores. (From the collection of the late Mr William Sewter. By kind permission of Mrs Jean Benstead)

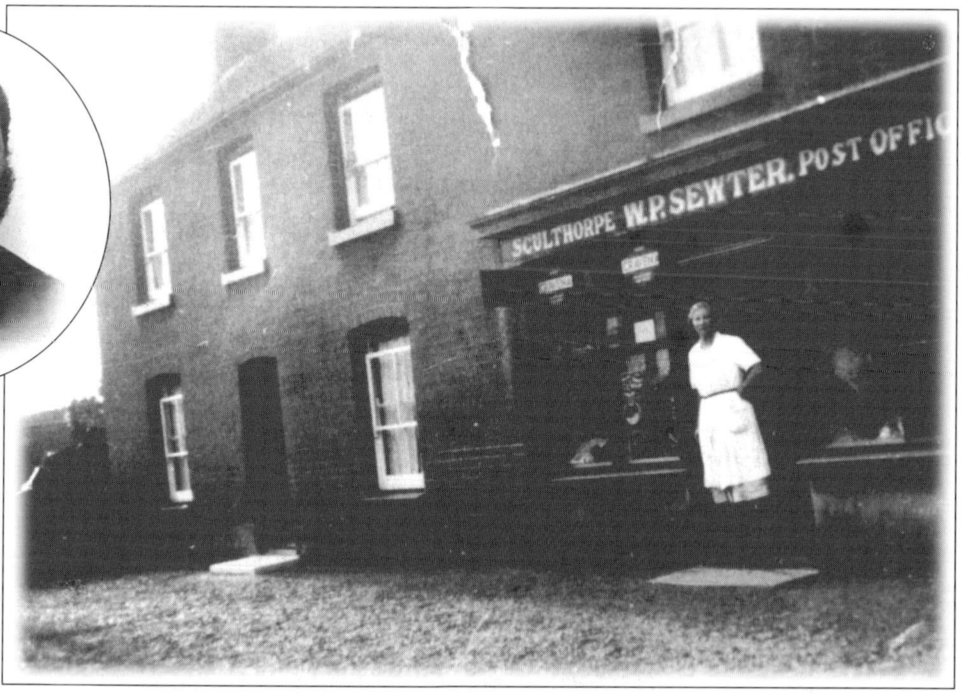

Miss Hannah Bessie Sewter, affectionately known as Aunt Bessie, stands in the doorway of Sewter's shop during the 1920s. The daughter of William Parke Sewter, she ran the village stores and acted as sub-postmistress with the help of her sister, Aunt Sally, and later her nephew, William Sewter. Their wonderful brand of baking lard, 'Aunt Bessie's lard', remained a closely guarded family secret! (From the collection of the late Mr William Sewter. Reproduced by kind permission of Mrs Jean Benstead)

THE SEWTER FAMILY

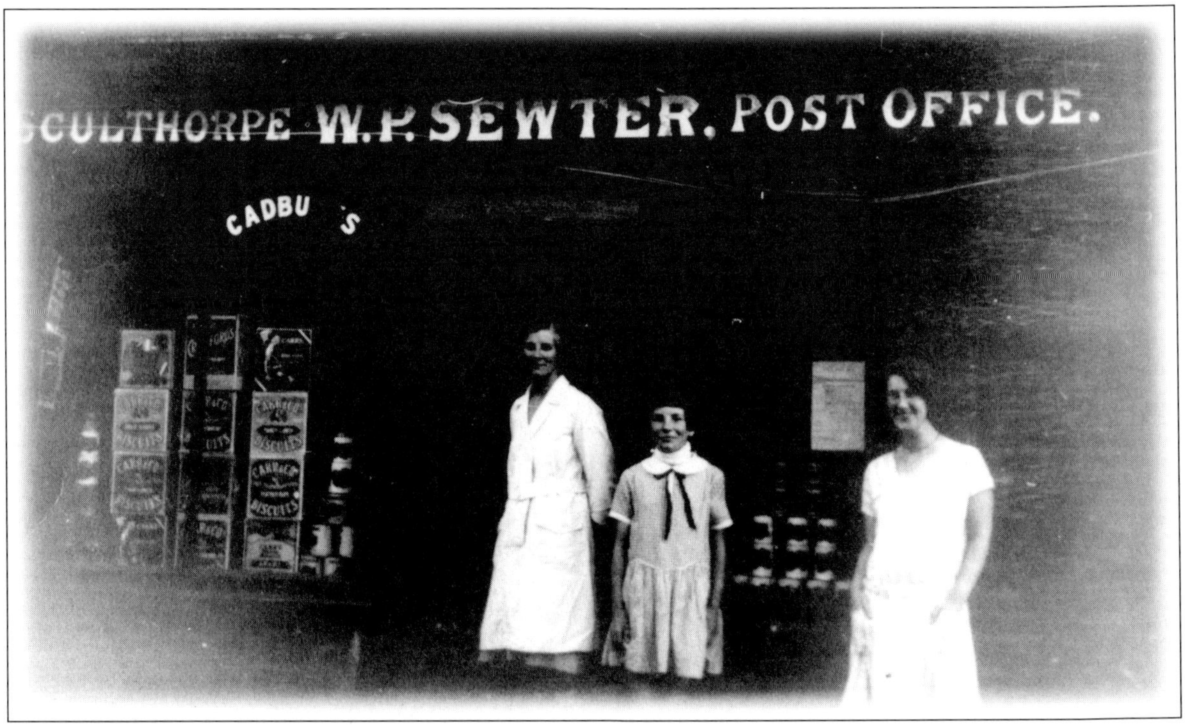

Aunt Bessie Sewter with young Molly Armiger at the door of Sewter's shop, 1920s. (From the collection of the late Mr William Sewter. Reproduced by kind permission of Mrs Jean Benstead)

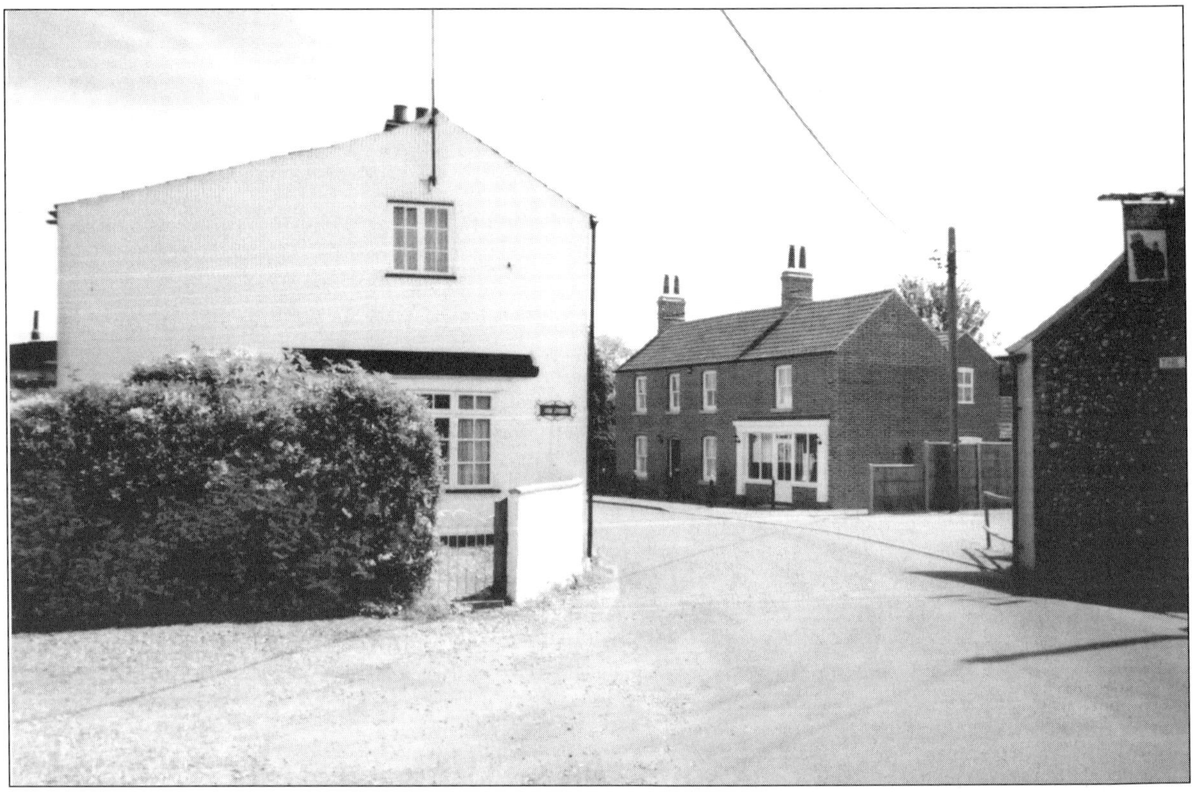

A modern view of Bay House (left), *Sewter's shop* (centre) *and the Horse & Groom public house* (right), *The Street, Sculthorpe, 2002. Sewter's shop is now a private house but has been carefully restored and the shop front retained.*

THE ARMIGER FAMILY

Left: *Ivy Cottage in the old Fakenham Road near Falgate Farm, 1930s. This was the home of George Armiger junr who succeeded his father as the village chimney sweep. His wife, Daisy, also ran an extremely successful market garden and is shown here at the gate.* (Reproduced by kind permission of Mrs Audrey Jordan (née Armiger), niece of Mr and Mrs George Armiger)

Below: *Members of the Armiger family at Bankhurst in the old Fakenham Road near Falgate Farm, late 1880s. This was the home of Mr George Armiger senr, the village chimney sweep.* (Reproduced by kind permission of Mrs Audrey Jordan (née Armiger), his granddaughter)

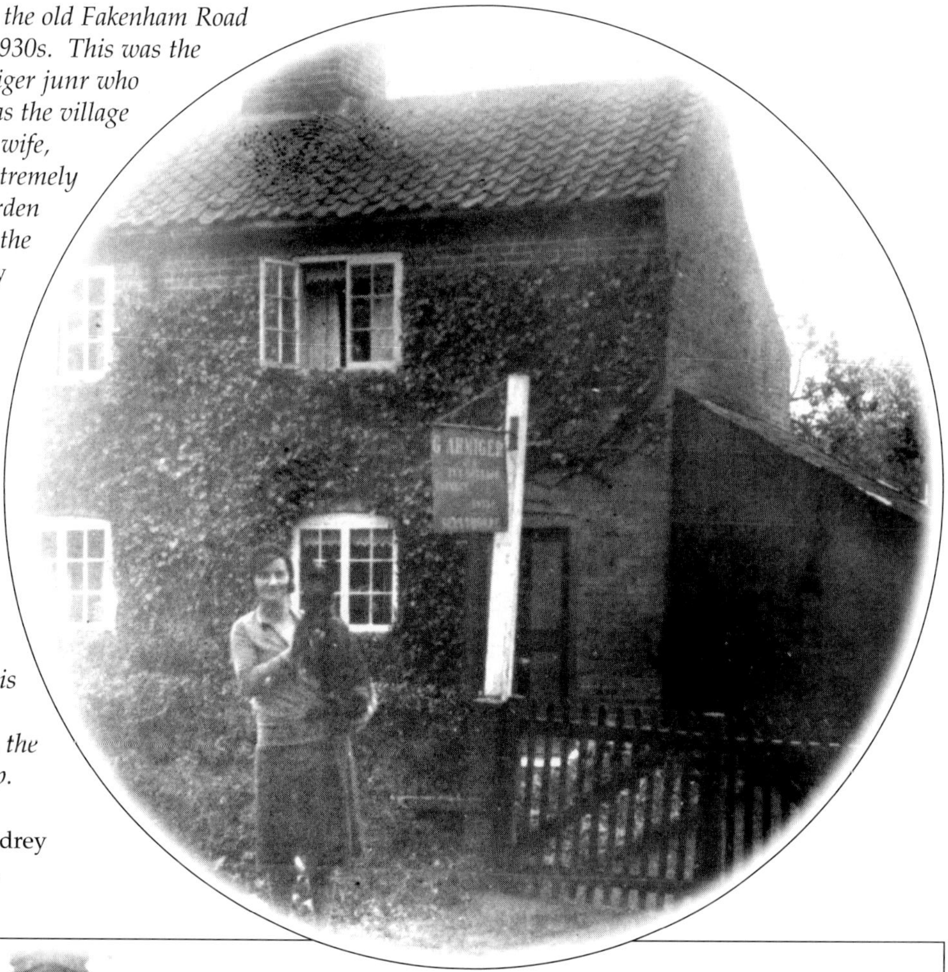

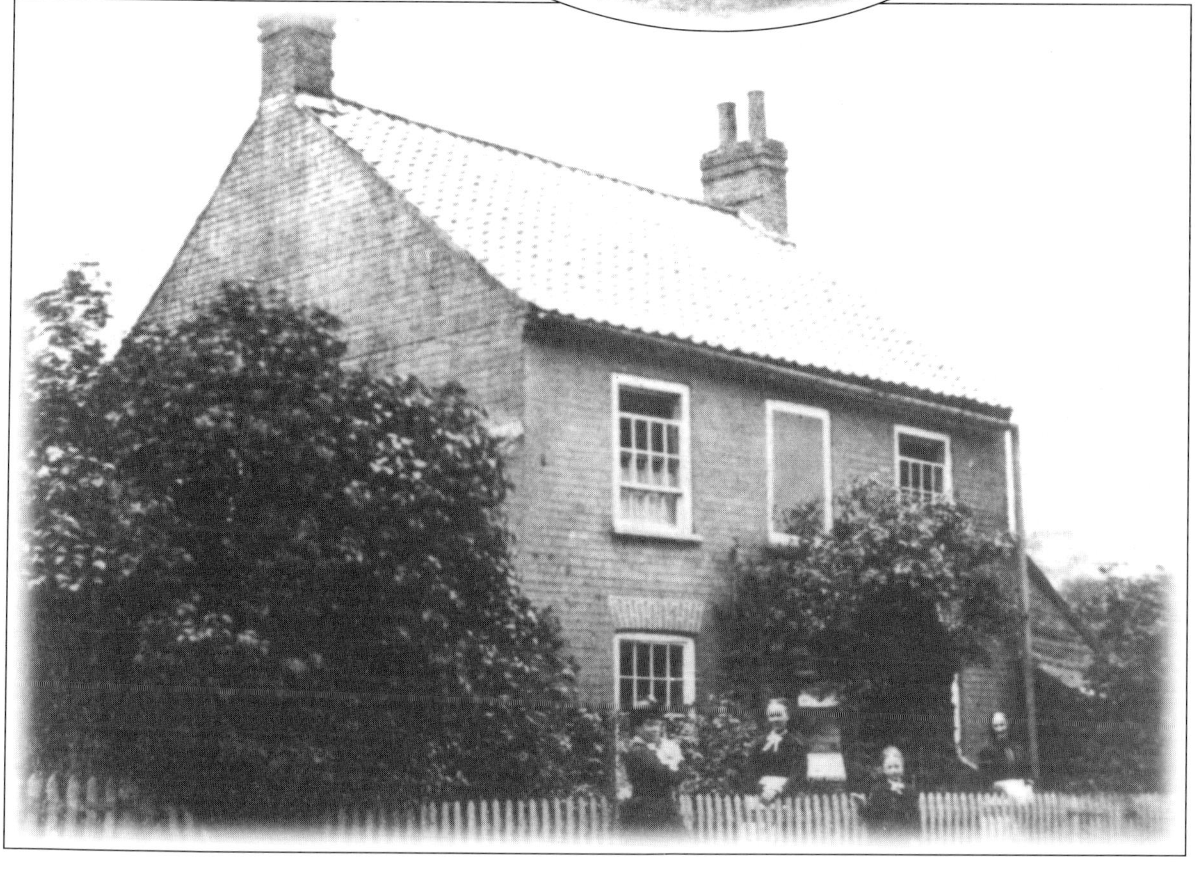

THE ARMIGER FAMILY

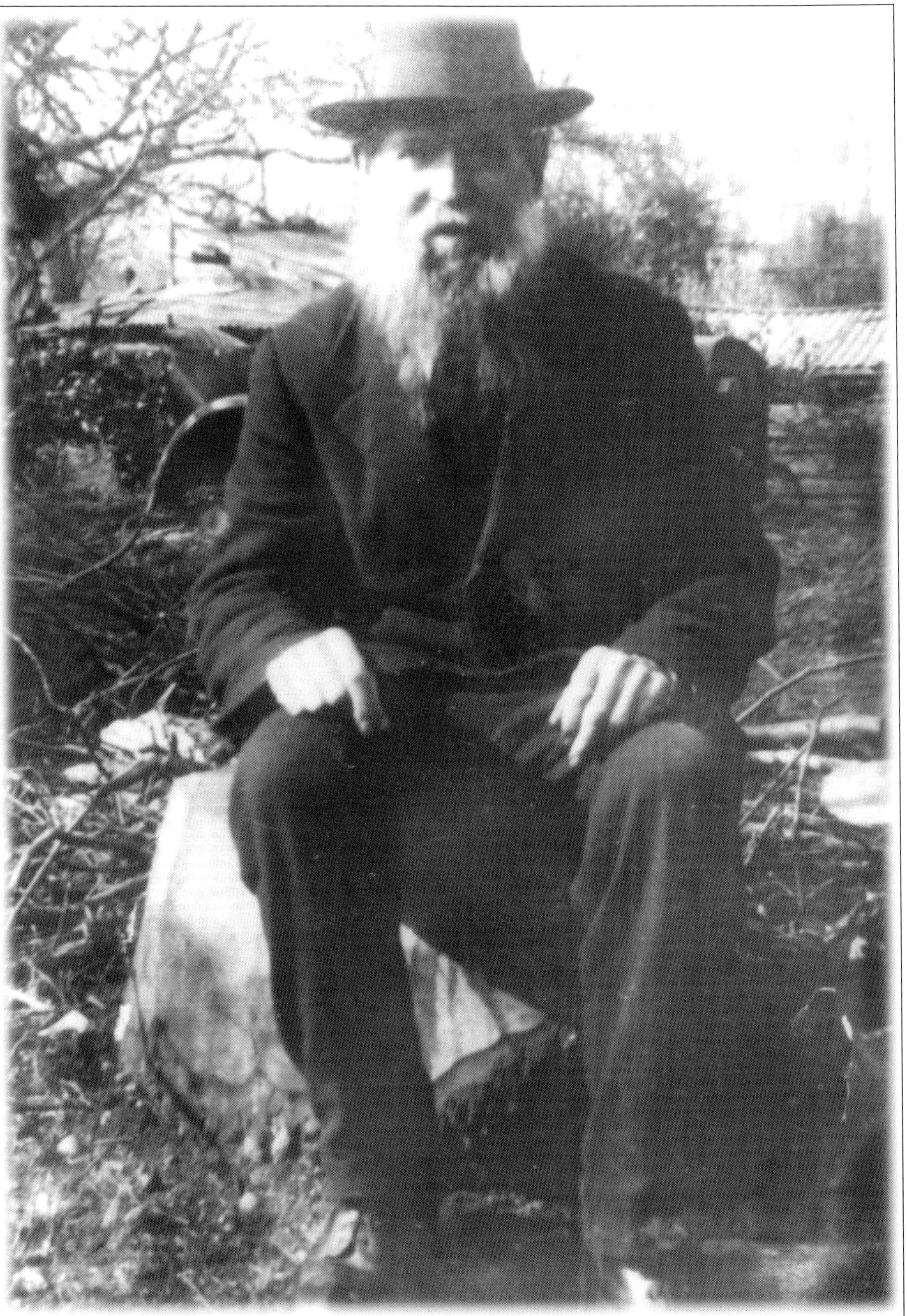

The village chimney sweep, Mr George Armiger senr, during the 1920s. He was affectionately known as 'Sweep Armiger'. (Reproduced by kind permission of Mrs Audrey Jordan (née Armiger), his granddaughter)

THE LINGWOOD FAMILY

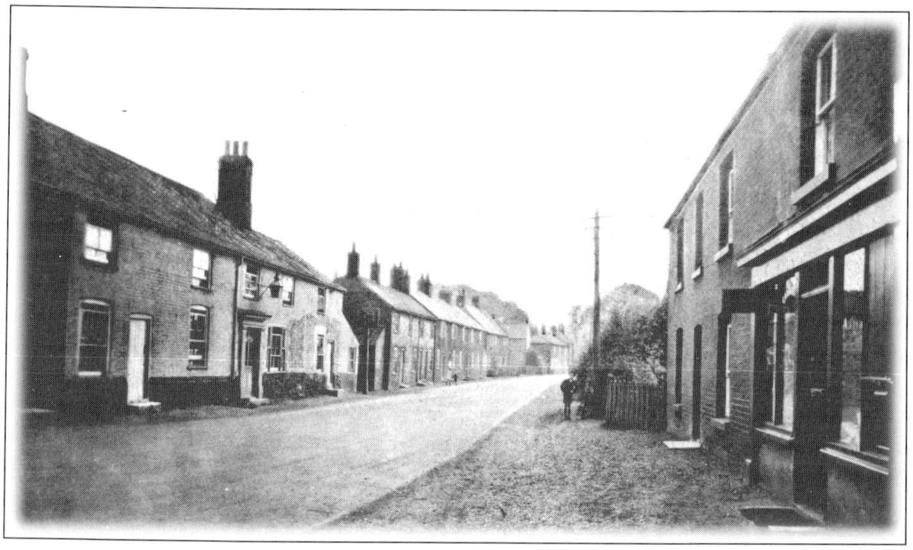

Left: *The Street, Sculthorpe, c.1923. The little boys standing by the telegraph pole are Albert and Leslie Lingwood. In the distance are their sisters, Doris and Joyce, and their mother, May Lingwood, standing at the door of No.22 The Street. Prior to the 1968 bypass this was the main Fakenham to King's Lynn road, improved by the Turnpike Trust of 1826. During the 1920s and '30s Queen Mary frequently passed through the village in her chauffeur-driven Daimler Brougham, with her sister-in-law, Queen Maud of Norway, and her daughter, the Princess Royal, on their shopping expeditions to Fakenham.* (Reproduced by kind permission of Mr Bob Hood)

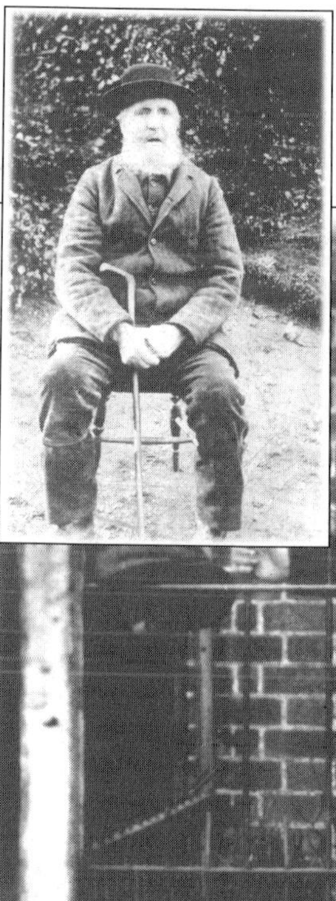

Left: *Robert Lingwood (1828–1909) who lived in one of the cottages adjacent to the Greyhound public house from 1856 until 1881 when he returned to live with his family in his native hamlet of Dunton-cum-Doughton.*

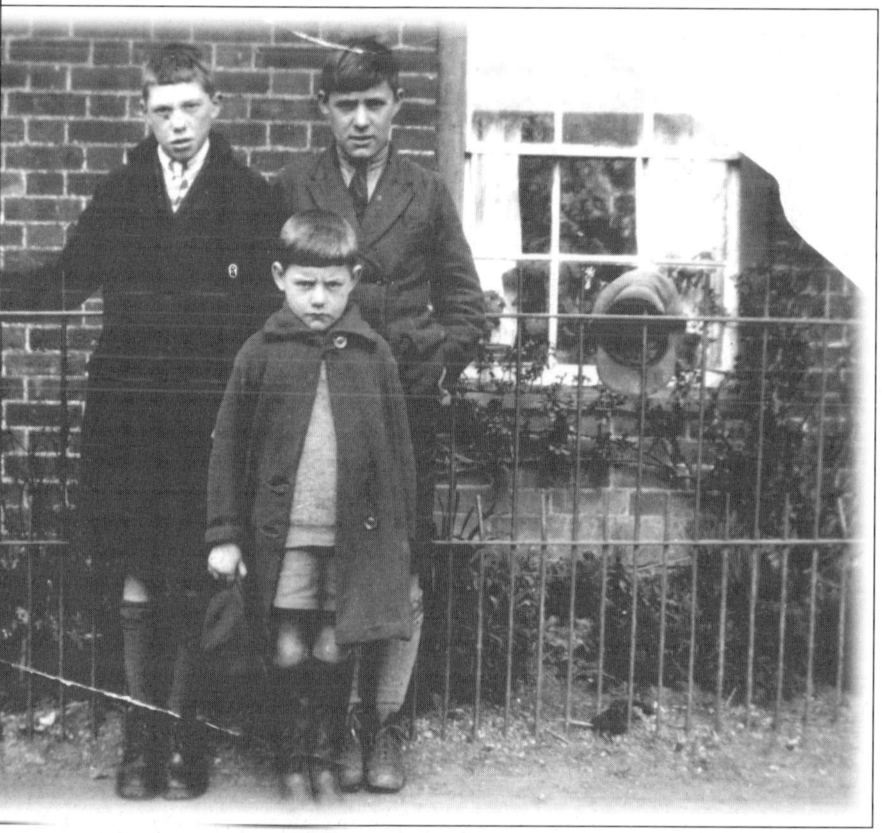

These village lads were certainly no angels! Arthur Vertigans, Leslie Lingwood and Ronny Lingwood standing outside Rose Cottage in The Street, Sculthorpe, during the 1930s. Their favourite prank was to cut a square of turf and place it over the top of the chimney pot on the little cobbler's shop standing in Pound Yard off Moor Lane. They usually succeeded in smoking out the village cobbler!

THE LINGWOOD FAMILY

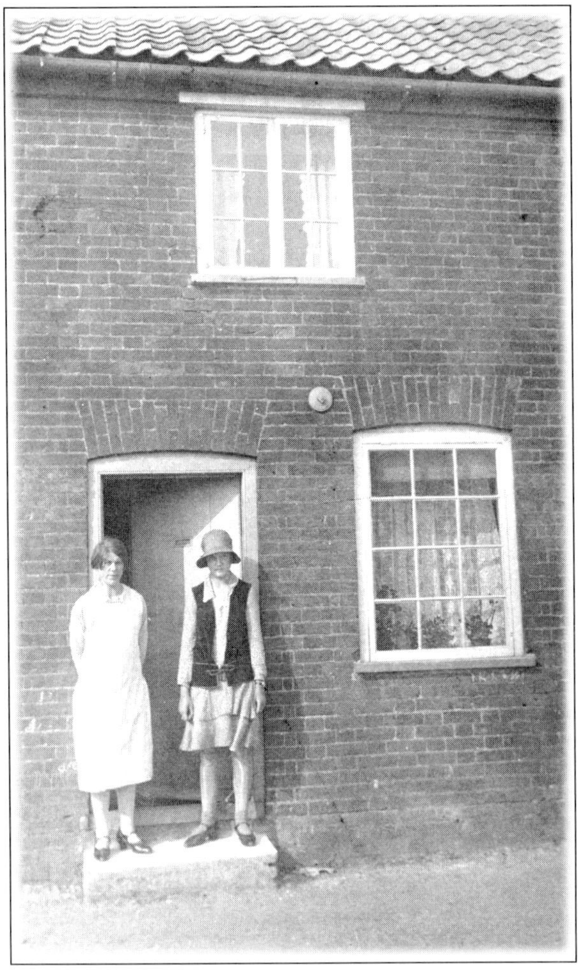

Left: *No.22 The Street, Sculthorpe, late 1920s. May Lingwood stands at the cottage door with her eldest daughter Doris who was then employed as kitchen maid at Bagthorpe Hall. This row of cottages was built in 1860 and 1863. The weekly rent during the late 1920s was 3s.6d.*

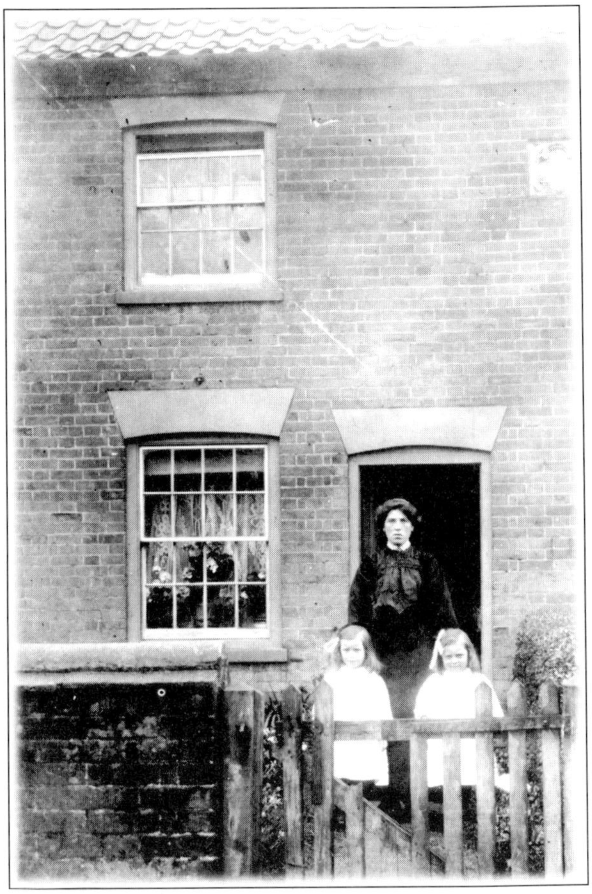

Above: *Mrs Sarah French (née Lingwood) with daughters May and Margaret at their cottage in The Street, originally built by the Revd Sir Edward Repps Jodrell of Salle Park in 1865.*

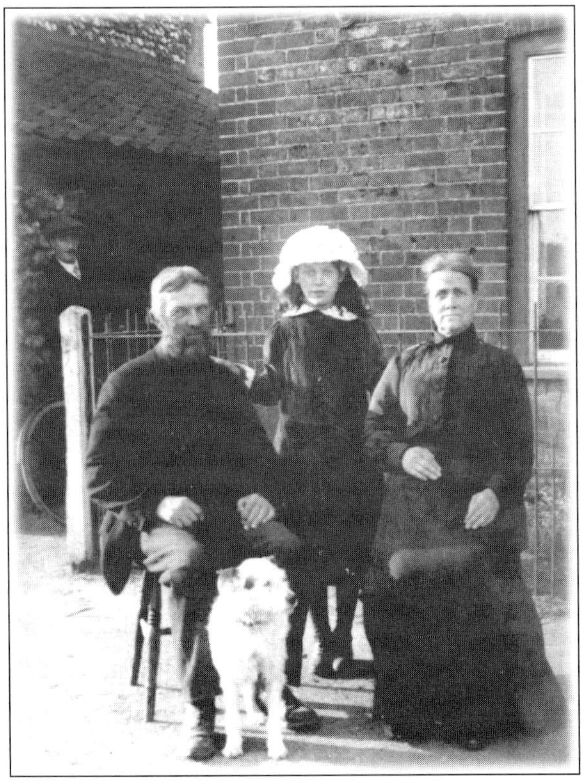

Left: *John and Evelina Lingwood with Daisy Lingwood outside Rose Cottage, The Street, Sculthorpe, 1915. John Lingwood had a smallholding on the north side of the parish and kept horses, pigs and chickens. Barsham Road is still called John Lingwood's Lane by the older members of the community.*

THE LINGWOOD FAMILY

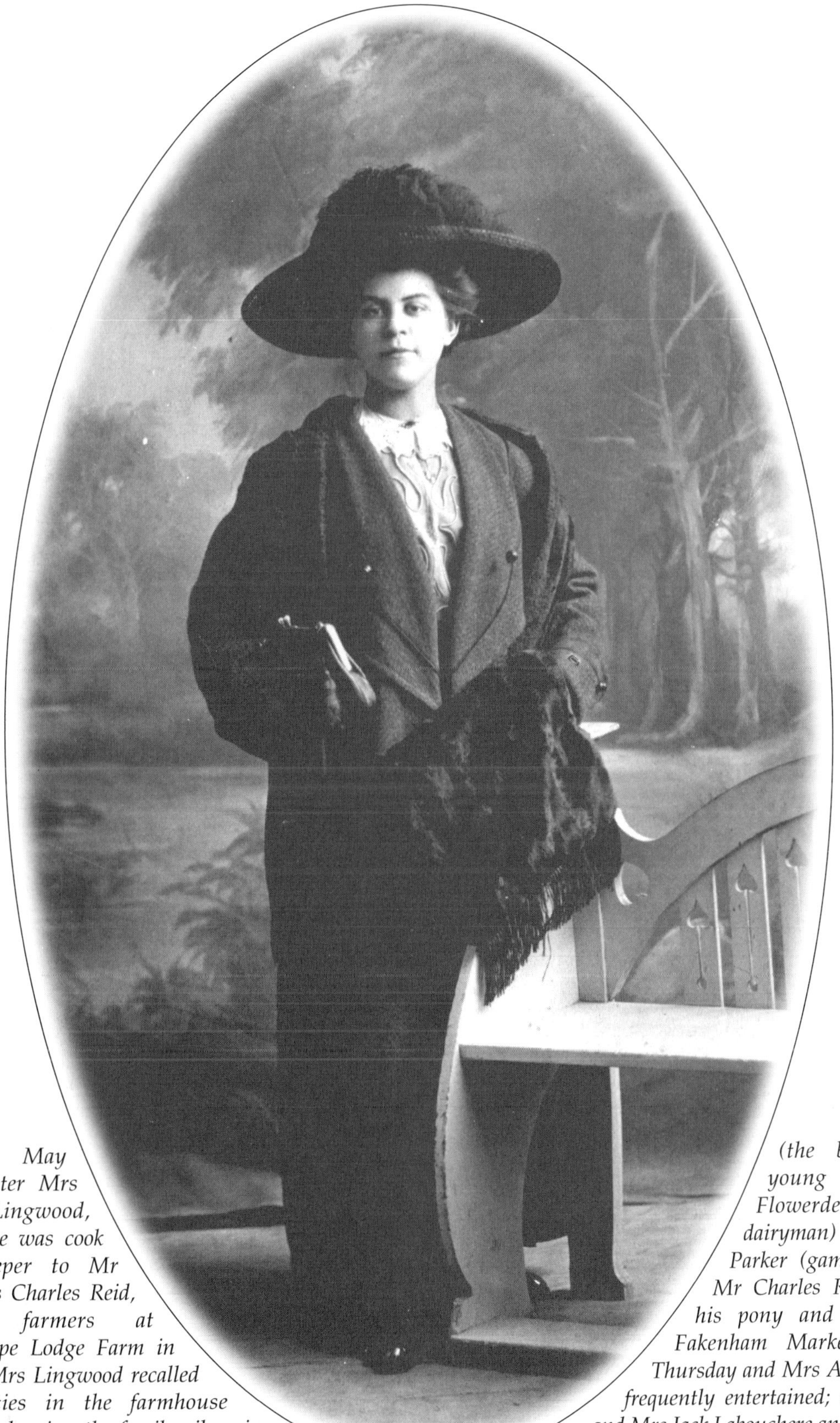

Beatrice May Tyler, later Mrs Jack Lingwood, when she was cook housekeeper to Mr and Mrs Charles Reid, tenant farmers at Sculthorpe Lodge Farm in 1910. Mrs Lingwood recalled her duties in the farmhouse such as cleaning the family silver in the housekeeper's pantry. Other members of staff included Gladys Glasspoole (under-house parlour maid), Reggie Groom the verger's son (the bootboy), young Bertie Flowerdew (the dairyman) and Mr Parker (gamekeeper). Mr Charles Reid took his pony and trap to Fakenham Market every Thursday and Mrs Anne Reid frequently entertained; the Revd and Mrs Jack Labouchere and Mr and Mrs Ernest Syder were often guests at her dinner parties. (Reproduced by kind permission of Mrs Gwen Windeler (née Lingwood))

Leslie Lingwood celebrated his return to Sculthorpe from German prison camps with a 'burn-up' on a Norton 500cc motorcycle which belonged to Geoffrey Minns! This view of Moor Lane and the church was taken in the summer of 1945. (Reproduced by kind permission of Mrs Gwen Windeler, née Lingwood)

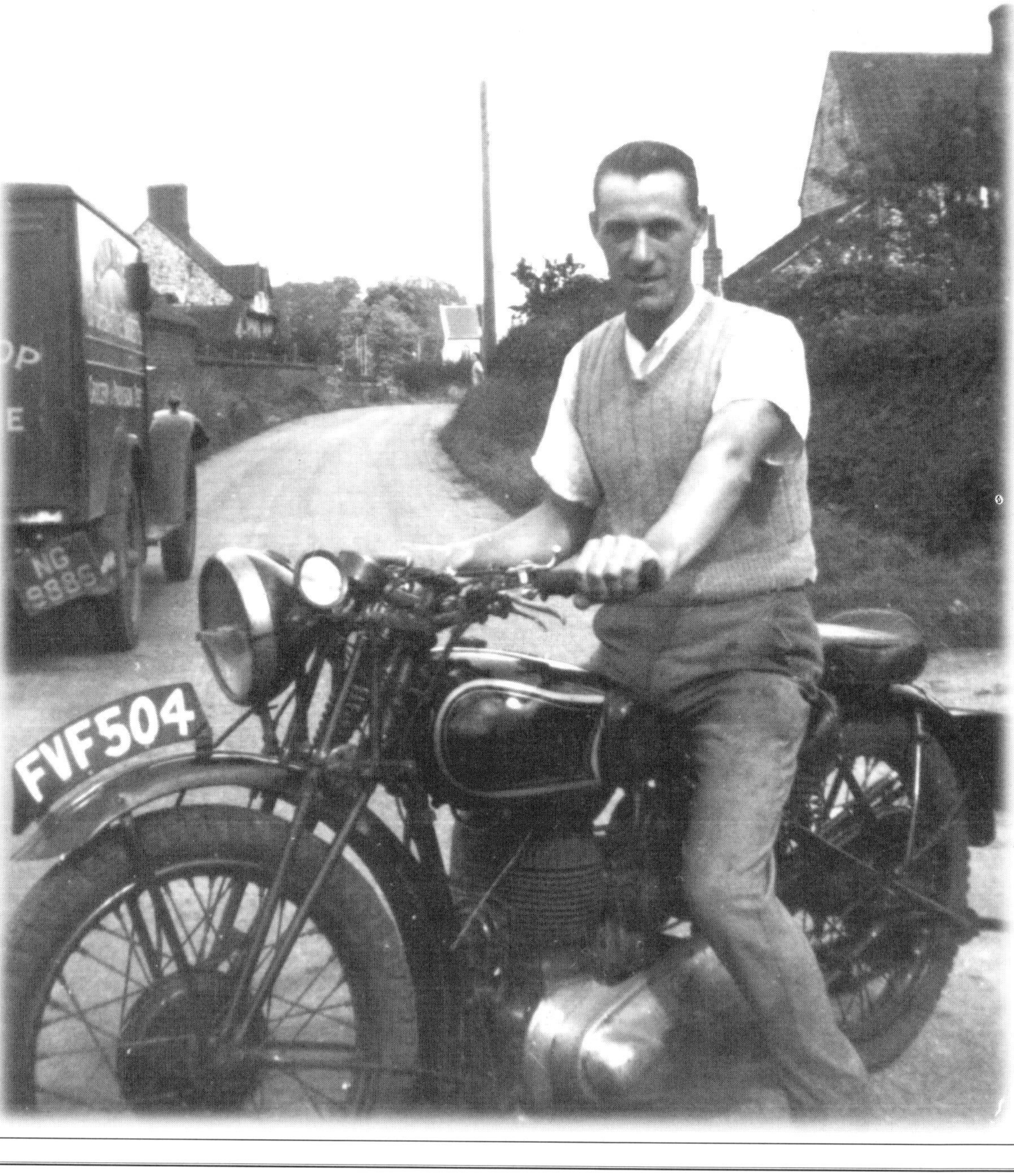

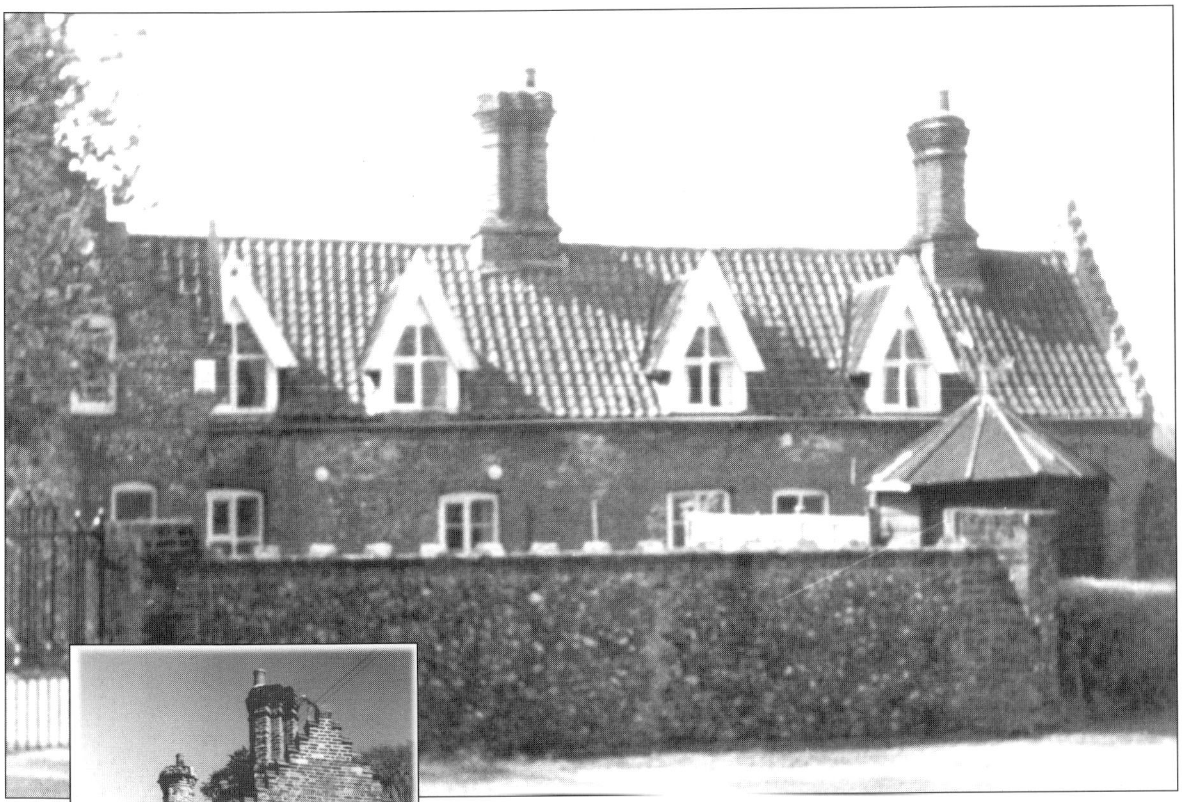

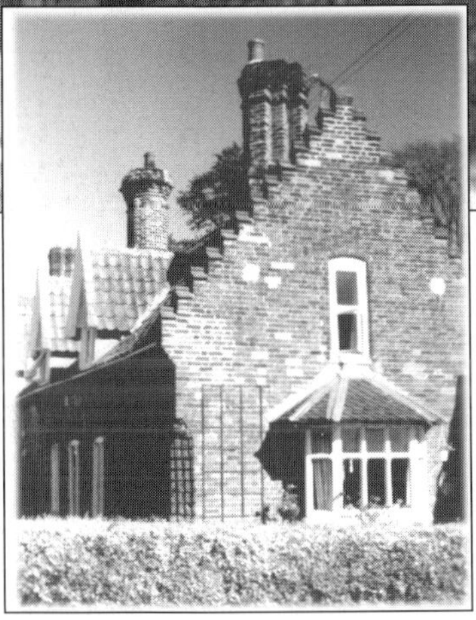

Above: *Rose and Ivy Cottages near the church, Sculthorpe.*

Left: *Ivy Cottage with its Dutch crow-stepped gable dating from the late-sixteenth century. The cottages were restored and a neighbouring cottage added by the Revd Herbert Walsingham Jones in 1859.*

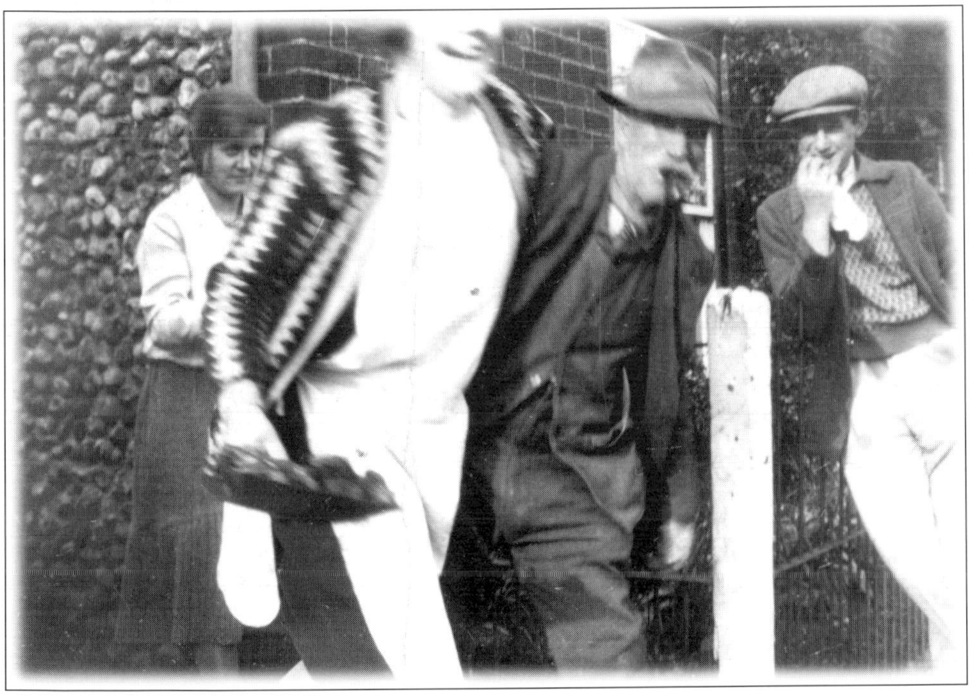

Left: *Fun and laughter in The Street outside Rose Cottage, 1930s.* Left to right: *Doris Lingwood, May Wright, Grandad Greeves, Albert Lingwood. The strong community spirit which existed in the rows of Victorian estate cottages is vividly recalled by former inhabitants.*

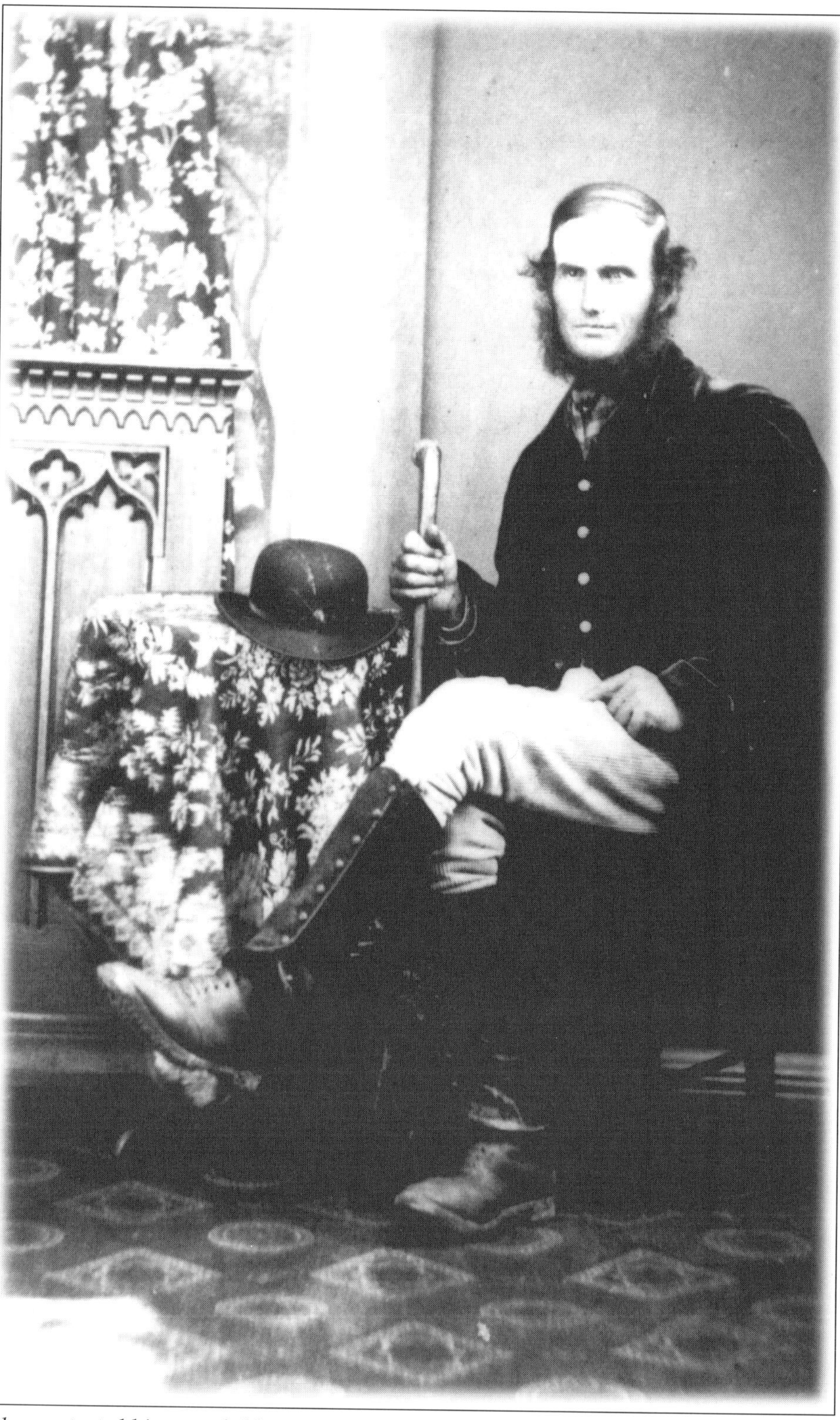

Lawrence Harper, the landlord of the Red Lion, c.1860. Lawrence Harper (1833–96) was landlord of the Red Lion in Sculthorpe during the 1860s. Originally a groom at Cranmer Hall, Lawrence met and fell in love with Jane Gilder, the daughter of Benjamin Gilder who was coachman to Sir Willoughby Jones. Lawrence and Jane were married at Sculthorpe in 1860 by the Revd Herbert Walsingham Jones and settled as landlord and landlady at the Red Lion in The Street.

Lawrence was an extremely successful horse dealer and compiled a book about horse remedies and cures. He displayed strange powers over the control and handling of horses. These skills were traditionally believed to be possessed by grooms and horse dealers, known long ago in Norfolk as 'Toadmen'. On one occasion in the Red Lion Lawrence became embroiled in an argument with a rival horse dealer over who could handle horses better. Lawrence demonstrated his remarkable powers as a Toadman by going outside to The Street where his rival's horses were harnessed to a wagon. He cast a spell over them and they absolutely refused to budge until Lawrence had given the word and broken the spell! This story was subsequently related in the local area and remains a part of village folklore. Lawrence Harper was later landlord of the Black Swan at South Creake and then the Buck in Syderstone whilst he continued with his horse dealing and bloodstock interests. His sister Hannah married Robert Lingwood of Sculthorpe and Dunton-cum-Doughton and the Lingwoods of Sculthorpe are descended from this union. (Reproduced by kind permission of Mr John Harper of New Zealand)

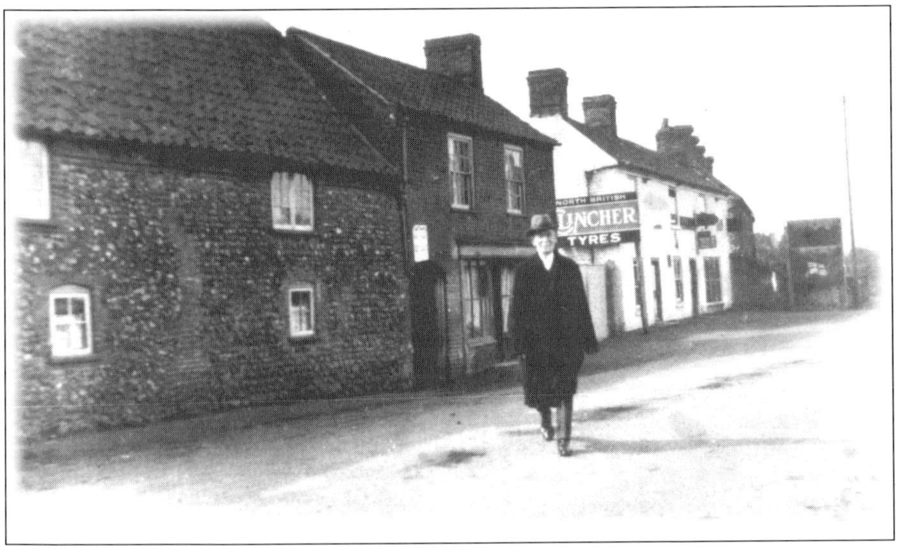

Left: *The Red Lion in The Street at Sculthorpe when it had become Ernest Hannant's garage. This photograph, showing Mr Robert Tuck the village baker, dates from the late 1920s. The Red Lion, which had belonged to the Revd Horatio Dowsing, rector of North Barsham in 1819, was a Bullards public house during the late-nineteenth century. It finally ceased trading in 1915 and has been a garage for many years.* (Reproduced by kind permission of Mr Kenneth Boast, grandson of Mr Robert Tuck)

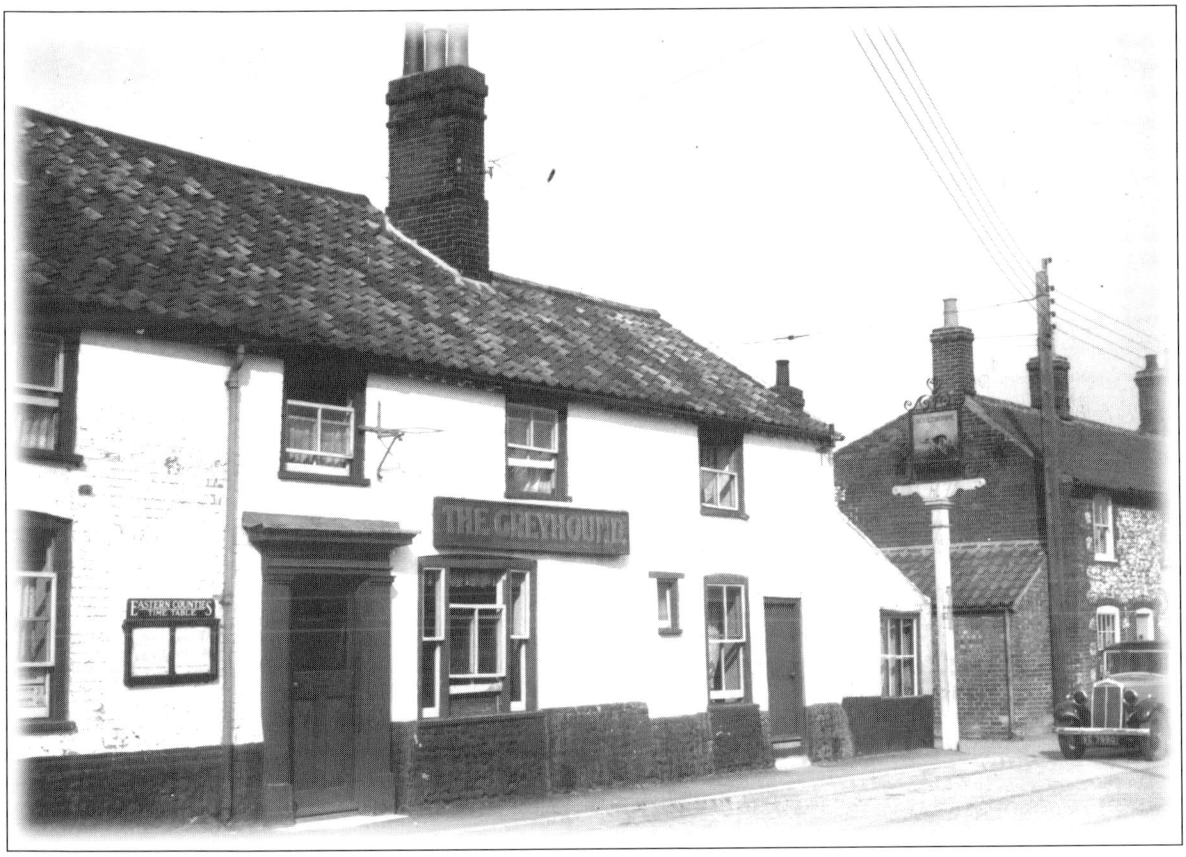

The Greyhound in The Street, Sculthorpe, 1939. The deeds of this ancient village beerhouse date back to 1703 and in 1819 it was 'known by the name and sign of the Greyhound.' There are still many ancient beams dating from the seventeenth century and original period features, and the rear trapdoor and beer cellar, which was used as an air-raid shelter during the Second World War, also survive. This photograph shows the adjacent cottage and the little outbuilding – originally a blacksmith's and butcher's shop – which have since been demolished. Steward and Patterson's brewery, based in Norwich, acquired the pub in 1880. From c.1903–58 the licensees were the Armiger family. The pub ceased trading in 1964 and is now the home of Mrs Doris Mitchell who has done a great deal to preserve almost all of the former pub's original character.
(Reproduced by kind permission of the Norfolk Rural Life Museum at Gressenhall)

Oliver Rix Ltd

Eagle Iron Works, the iron and brass foundry and agricultural implements works in Creake Road, was founded in 1862 by James Blackett, a wagon builder and iron and brass founder, assisted by William Blackett, wheelwright and blacksmith. The original site is now occupied by the modern Foundry Close housing estate and the pond nearby still perpetuates the founder's name: Blackett's Pit. Oliver Rix served his apprenticeship under James Blackett and eventually became the manager of Eagle Iron Works. When James Blackett died in 1891 Oliver Rix acquired the firm from the executors and it became Oliver Rix Ltd.

Among the farming implements and machinery patented by the firm were the 'King Elevator', first used on the royal estate at Sandringham, and the 'Norfolk Muck Spreader', created in 1911. Mr Archie Filby, nephew of Oliver Rix, joined the company in 1921 and was later promoted to become manager. After Oliver Rix died in 1933 Mr Filby took over the firm. The first combine harvester in Great Britain appeared at Bluestone Farm in neighbouring South Creake in 1931 and Oliver Rix Ltd later became an agent for the new Massey-Harris combine harvesters. In June 1950 Mr Filby was presented to King George VI and Queen Elizabeth at the Royal Norfolk Show; by this time Oliver Rix Ltd had received the prestigious accolade 'By Royal Appointment' and frequently supplied farm machinery for the Sandringham estate. In 1952 Commander Peter Tunbridge, RN, joined the firm and was later appointed a director of Oliver Rix Ltd.

The company employed many villagers; in earlier times it had also offered a much-respected funeral service. Mr George Patfield often walked at the head of the funeral cortèges in the village, having made a number of the oak coffins at Oliver Rix's carpentry shop. In 1960 Oliver Rix Ltd was restructured as a public company – Archie Filby remained chairman and Mr John Riches was appointed managing director. The firm retained its name, even after Mr Filby's death in 1965, but in 1973 it was purchased by John Riches and was renamed John Riches Agricultural Ltd. Since John Riches sold the business to Cargill's in 1979 it has changed hands several times, to Cowies Eastern Tractors, Boston Tractors and now Norfolk Farm Machinery Ltd. It remains a flourishing and highly successful business in repairing and supplying farm machinery in a productive rural area.

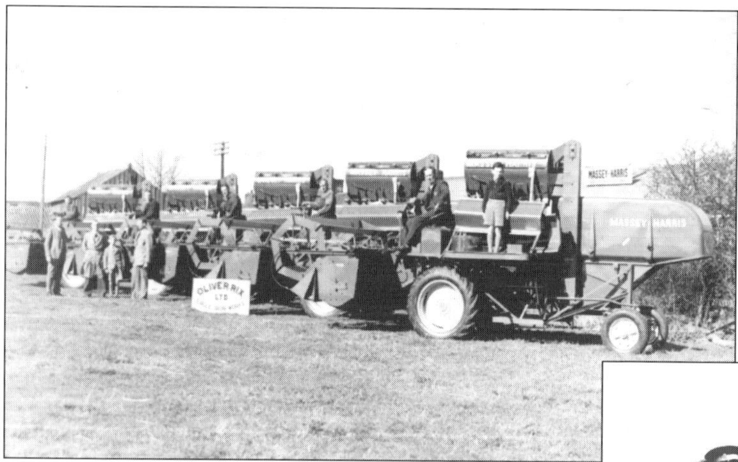

Left: *Oliver Rix Ltd, 1950s. Among those pictured are Mr Archie Filby and, on the Massey-Harris combine harvesters, Dick Yallop, Jack Playford and Michael Sturman. The firm expanded into flourishing outlets, trading under the Oliver Rix Group name at Norwich, Melton Constable, Wrentham and Peterborough.*

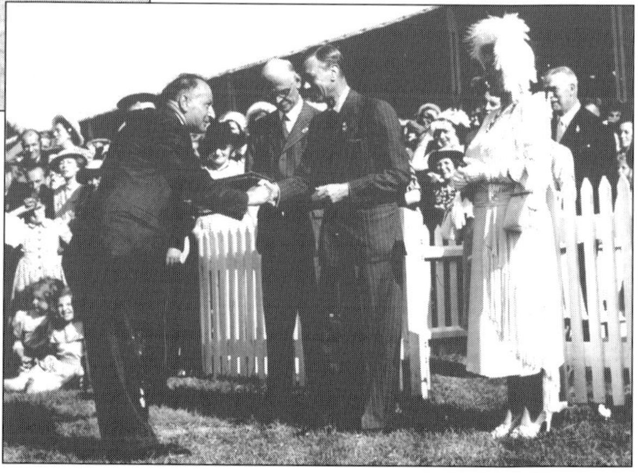

Right: *Mr Archie Filby is presented to King George VI and Queen Elizabeth at the Royal Norfolk Show in June 1950. The show took place at Anmer on the Sandringham estate. Oliver Rix Ltd supplied farm machinery to the royal estate on a regular basis.* (Reproduced by kind permission of the *Lynn News*)

Chapter Nine

CRANMER HALL AND ITS FAMILIES

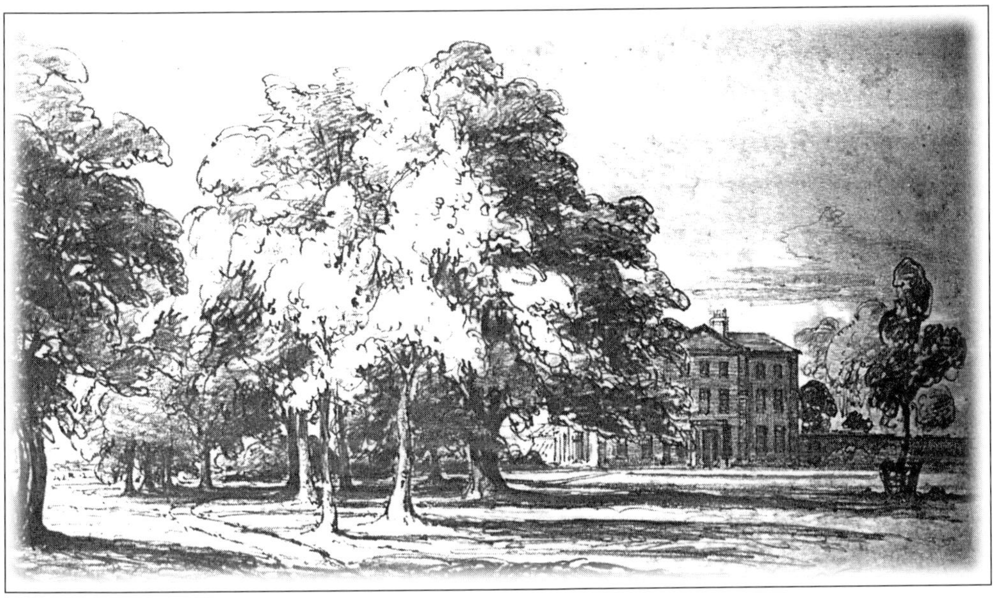

Prior to the Second World War eighteenth-century Cranmer Hall, situated in richly-wooded parkland, was the centre of a flourishing Norfolk country estate. During springtime the picturesque qualities of Cranmer Park were enhanced by a sea of wild daffodils, primroses and bluebells and, at the time of writing, the hall, shorn of its top storey and standing separately from its former park, remains an important family home and the key to a fascinating chapter in the history of Sculthorpe.

The name Cranmer is thought to be derived from the 'Crane Mere' or heron marsh, a sizeable stretch of water together with wetland north-east of the hall, the environs of which yield evidence of Bronze-Age and Romano-British habitation and, during the Middle Ages, were possibly developed as a heronry. One of the earliest recorded references to the name appeared in the Sculthorpe Church Terrier of 1613 where it was written: 'in the west field of Skulthorpe and in this sheeps pasture lying is Cranmor Furlong.' There was also mention of the 'close of William Yelverton called Cranmor Close which abutteth on the common way leading to Siderston (Syderstone).' The Yelvertons of Rougham owned considerable property in the parish during the late-sixteenth and early-seventeenth centuries. Lancelot Yelverton was rector of Sculthorpe (1564–70) and his elder brother, Henry Yelverton, the patron of the living. Lancelot and Henry were the cousins of the lord of the manor, Thomas Fermour of East Barsham.

The 'Cranmor Knapp Furlong in the west Ffield' featured again in the Terrier of 1709 and in the later 1784 Terrier the 'Cranmer Foldcourse in the estate of Mr Daniel Jones, Gent' was mentioned, the folding and rearing of sheep being centred on this side of the village.

The present Cranmer Hall was not the first house by this name to stand on the site; it was preceded by a sixteenth-century mansion, a knapped flint and brick building, the substantial foundations of which were exposed during repairs to the house in 1965.

Above: *Cranmer Hall and its parkland in 1849, during the first period of alterations initiated by Sir Willoughby Jones.* (Reproduced by kind permission of Mrs Louise Hurst)

This charming photograph of Cranmer Hall dates from the late 1860s. The tiny gravel path in the foreground stretched across Cranmer Park to Sculthorpe Church and formed the 'sermon walk', much used by the Jones family and their household when they attended divine service at the church every Sunday. (Copyright: Norfolk County Council Library and Information Service)

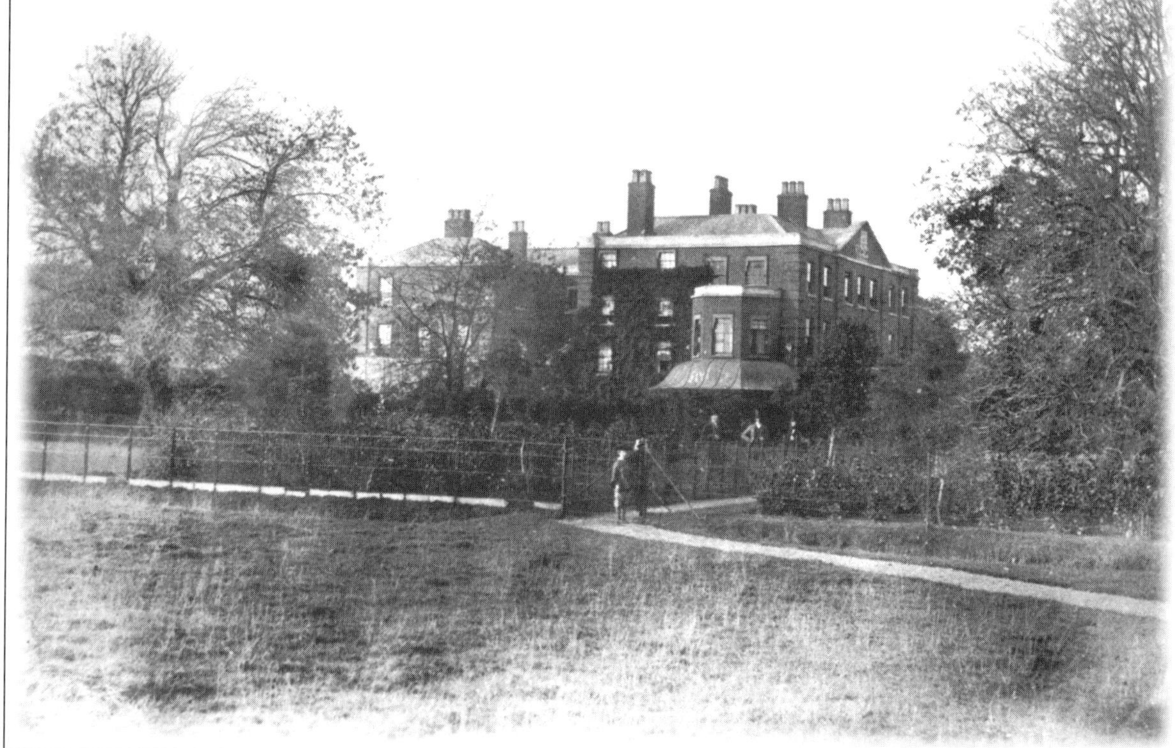

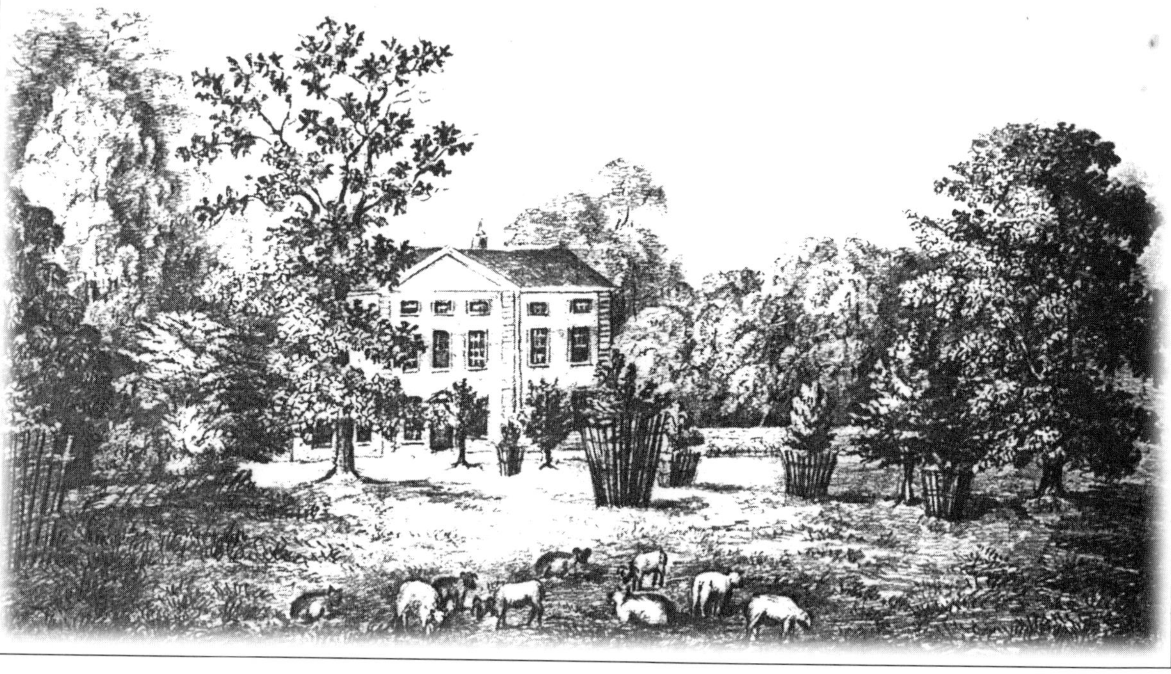

Cranmer Hall as it looked in 1842. New trees have been planted alongside the driveway and in the foreground are a flock of Norfolk Horn sheep. This drawing was given by Sir Lawrence Evelyn Jones, 5th Baronet of Cranmer, to the late Mr John Hurst who restored the hall in 1965.
(Reproduced by kind permission of Mrs Louise Hurst)

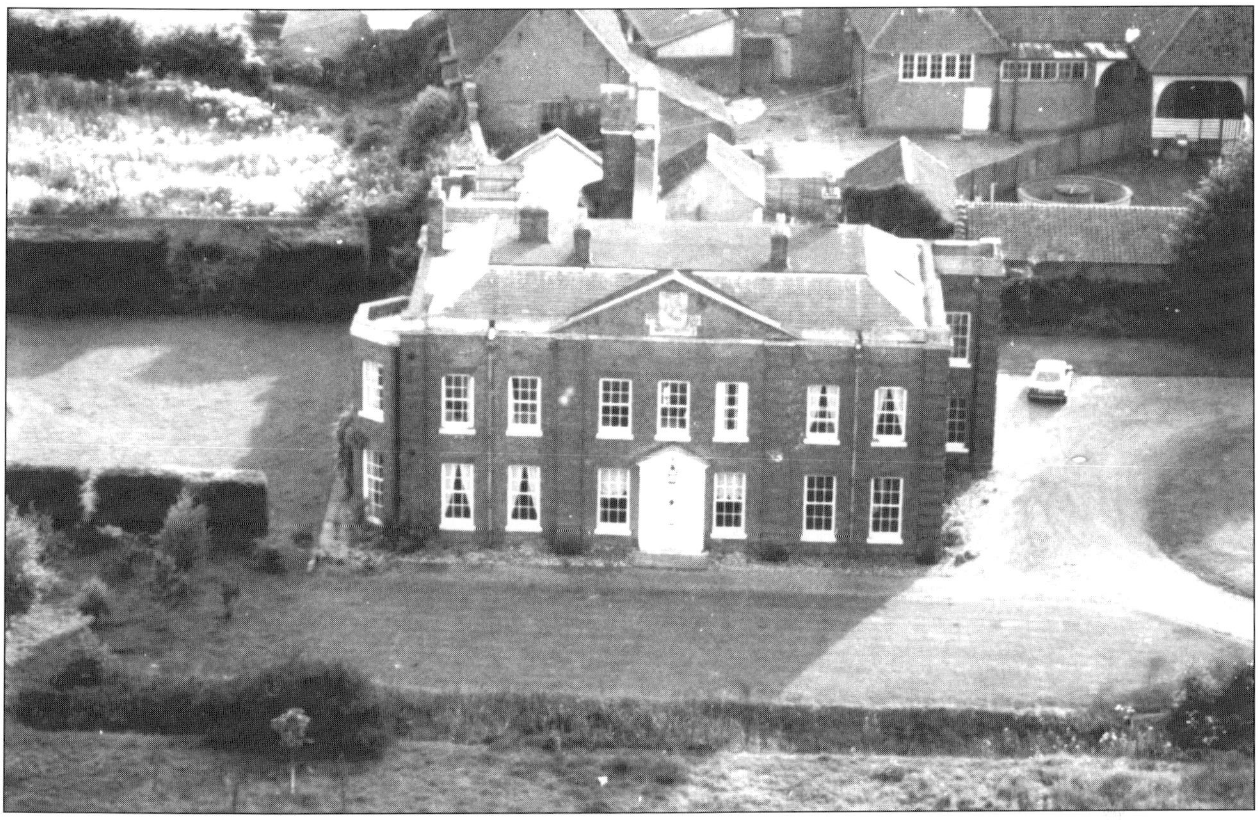

Cranmer Hall from the air. This photograph shows the eighteenth-century ditch or 'ha-ha' which would have kept sheep and cattle out of the hall gardens. (Reproduced by kind permission of John and Henry Labouchere)

Recently more sixteenth-century brickwork has been identified in the cellars. The residence was supposedly built by the Yelverton family and later became the property of the Quarles family, who held the living of Sculthorpe Church for much of the seventeenth century.

The house was strategically positioned at a major crossroads with, from the north, Greengate Way, the ancient Roman road which stretches inland from the coast at Holkham Bay and through Waterden to Cranmer, which can still be traced south of Cranmer Park down to the Roman ford at Sculthorpe Mill. This remained until 1829 when the park was circled by the New Road, the important Holkham to Raynham route which was often used by the horse-drawn carriages of the landed gentry as a direct route between the home of the Coke family at Holkham Hall and that of the Townshends at Raynham Hall. This was crossed on a west to north-east axis by the Lynn Way or Through Gate, later known as Rudham Road Gate, a major route running from the Augustinian Priory at Coxford, through Tattersett and past the early-nineteenth-century Brazen Hall to Cranmer and then through North Barsham to Houghton St Giles and Little Walsingham, possibly another pilgrim route to the medieval shrine of Our Lady. This road is still represented in part by the present driveway down to Cranmer Hall and, beyond, into the Rudham Road Gate Plantation, a route now truncated by the perimeter of RAF Sculthorpe. Faden's 1797 map of Norfolk, Bryant's 1826 map and the mid-eighteenth-century Cranmer estate maps, now held in the Norfolk Record Office, reveal the original importance of these two roads.

The northern Roman road is the most famous; in 1985 the distinguished broadcaster and historian Magnus Magnusson discussed the stretch of road running through Sculthorpe in an Anglia Television archaeological documentary, 'Look What We've Found', and suggested the plausible theory that it was a *Via Militare*, a Roman military road, dating from the first century AD and constructed through Iceni territory. The construction would have taken place following the bloodshed of the Boudicca Revolt in AD61, in a bid to establish a swift route for Roman soldiers in their attempt to pacify the native Iceni population. Sir Nikolaus Pevsner in the *Buildings of England* series felt that this road linked Roman settlements at Sculthorpe and Toftrees. Certainly most historians now believe the road was an important link from the coast to the major Roman settlement established at Beacon Hill near Pudding Norton and Toftrees, an important defensive site which has yielded hoards of Roman coins and substantial fragments of tiles and pottery artefacts.

During the year 1881, a rubbish pit was unearthed in Cranmer Park, about 250 yards north-east of the hall. The pit contained broken fragments

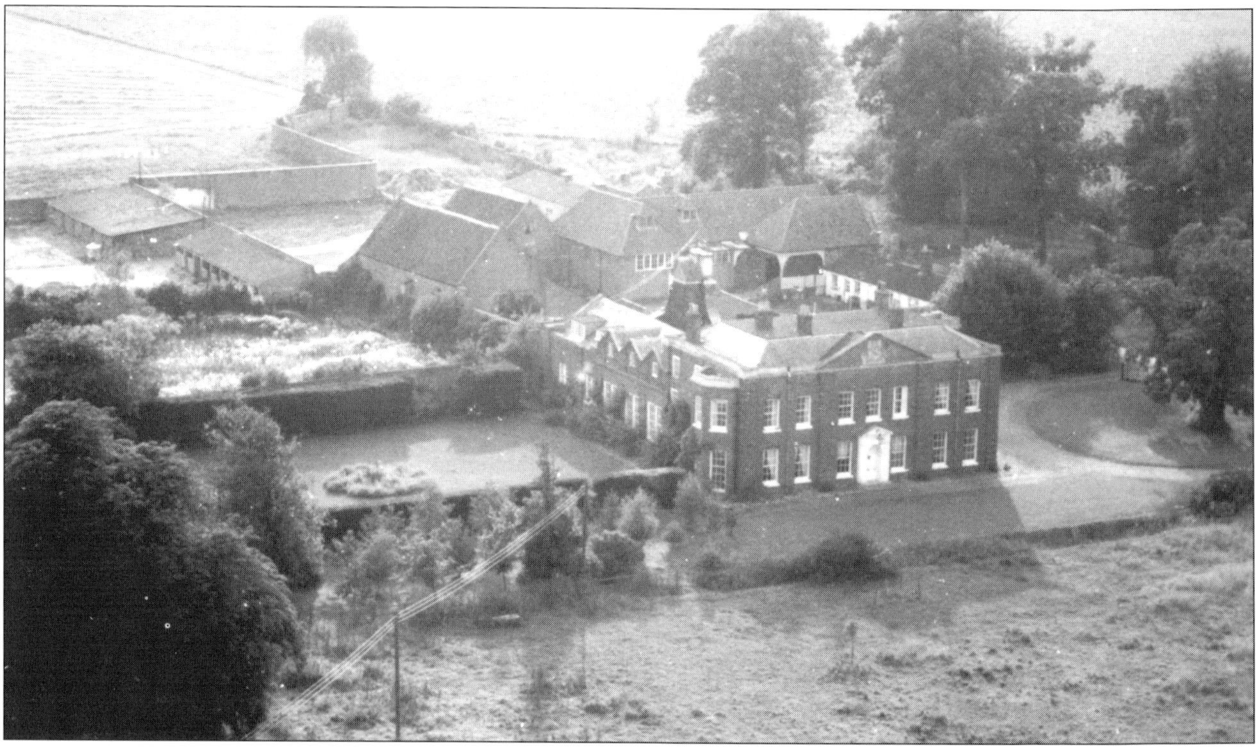

Cranmer Hall, 1984. (Reproduced by kind permission of John and Henry Labouchere)

of red-glazed pottery dating from the second century known as Samian ware, which was produced in Roman Gaul and marked with the name of the potter IANVARIVS or *Januarius*. Fragments of native pottery, a cremation urn and animal bones were also found. The artefacts, listed in the *Archaeological Journal*, were deposited at the Ashmolean Museum in Oxford. Sir Lawrence John Jones later informed the authors of the *Victoria County History of Norfolk* that a Roman smother-kiln and Roman pottery had been discovered. Was this evidence of the Roman settlement discussed by Pevsner or of a Romano-British 'villa' or farmstead, which may have existed either on or near the site of the present Cranmer Hall? It is an attractive theory but remains very much in the realm of conjecture.

The present hall is intimately associated with the Donne family who acquired the Cranmer estate through marriage into the Quarles family. According to the church register of Holt, the Norfolk Donnes, of Welsh origin, were resident in the county from the late-sixteenth century when new weavers were being encouraged to settle in East Anglia. Robert Donne of South Creake (1656–1723), attorney and builder of the present Cranmer Hall, was the youngest son of 'Thomas Donne of Holt Markett, Dornix Weaver' and the brother of William Donne of the Old Hall in Letheringsett. This branch of the family may have been distantly related to the poet John Donne, Dean of St Paul's, though some historians remain sceptical.

Certainly by the late-seventeenth century Robert Donne owned property in South Creake. The churchwarden's account book from South Creake stated that he provided 'white thorns' for the churchyard fence in 1690 and in 1704 he signed himself as 'Captain of the Train Band', a reference to his command of the local militia during the period of the War of the Spanish Succession with France.

Robert's second marriage to the heiress Anne Quarles of Sculthorpe (1662–1724) brought him into possession of her family inheritance and the patronage of the living of Sculthorpe Church, although it was only after the death of her elderly mother in November 1720, in her 83rd year, that Robert Donne undertook to demolish his wife's ancestral home at Cranmer and build a new and fashionable Palladian manor-house on the same site. The bricks for this residence are traditionally believed to have been 'fired' in the park, Claypit Clump and the Brickyard Plantation apparently marking the site of these early-eighteenth-century claypits and brick kilns. The seven-bay central block of the hall, pedimented with rusticated brick quoins and internally retaining much of its original Georgian panelling and plasterwork, is dated c.1721 and has strong local affinities with much of the early-Palladian architecture of the period to be found in this part of Norfolk.

The lead downpipes on the façade of Cranmer Hall are gilded with the Donne family crest of the 'Wolf salient'. This also appeared on Robert Donne's grave slab (1723) in Sculthorpe Church and that of his brother William (1684) in St Andrew's Church, Letheringsett. The poet John Donne had previously used this same wolf-headed crest on the title page of his first folio-volume of poems. Mary Barham-Johnson, distinguished historian, genealogist and descendant of the Donnes, felt this to be strong evidence for suggesting kinship with the poet.

In 1705 Robert Donne, as patron of the living, presented his son by his first marriage, the Revd Thomas Donne (1679–1739), as rector of Sculthorpe. By 1710 Robert had also been able to secure for his son the cure of vicar of South Creake and both offices were held by Thomas until his death. The Revd Thomas Donne maintained a particularly close link with the family of his paternal uncle, William Donne of Letheringsett. His first cousin, Roger Donne of Wacton (1678–1722), was, in 1700, a tanner by trade and the tenant farmer of John Mallom of Wacton Hall in Norfolk. John Mallom's youngest daughter, Audrey Mallom (1677–1758), appeared to have become acquainted with the Cranmer Donnes through Roger and eventually married the Revd Thomas Donne and came to live in the parsonage house in Sculthorpe.

It was also during this period that Roger Donne won the hand of Katherine Clench of Sculthorpe (1675–1733). On the side of her father, Bruin Clench, Katherine appeared to have been related to the Quarles family and, on the side of her mother, Katherine Hippesley, claimed descent through the female line from Mary Boleyn, aunt of Queen Elizabeth I. Mary Boleyn had preceded her unfortunate sister Anne as the mistress of King Henry VIII and it is now believed by many authorities that her offspring, Katherine and Henry Carey, were actually the King's children. Katherine Clench could, therefore, claim the royal blood of the Tudors as well as that of the Boleyns and the Howard Dukes of Norfolk as part of her heritage.

On 27 February 1700 'Roger Donne, tanner, and Katherine Clench' were married in Sculthorpe Church. This marriage was important because Roger and Katherine were the grandparents of the famous eighteenth-century poet and hymn writer, William Cowper (1731–1800). Cowper prided his supposed descent from John Donne 'our venerable ancestor, the Dean of St Paul's' and it is to be hoped that he was also aware of the more distinguished lineage of his maternal grandmother.

Roger and Katherine Donne settled at his farm in Wacton but by 1702 Roger was the tenant of Ludham Hall, the seventeenth-century farmhouse which had replaced the monastic grange of the Abbots of St Benet's Abbey, and it was here that Cowper's mother was born. Both must have occasionally returned to visit their respective families in Sculthorpe and Katherine, in her widowhood, may have known the newly-built Cranmer Hall where the Revd Thomas Donne and his wife Audrey lived following the death of his father, Robert, in 1723.

An entry from the church register dated 7 June 1739 revealed that 'The Reverend Mr Thomas Donne, of Cranmer House in the Parish of Sculthorpe, and both patron and Rector of the same Church, was buryed', two days after his death on 5 June at the age of 60 years. The Revd Robert Donne (1708–67), the son and heir of Thomas and Audrey, succeeded his father as rector of Sculthorpe and lived at Cranmer Hall. He remains a rather shadowy personality and his only son, also named Robert, received a good education at Caius College in Cambridge but died young.

The widowed Audrey Donne (née Mallom) lived to the age of 81 years, surviving her immediate contemporaries and witnessing the sale of the Cranmer estate by her son Robert to Daniel Jones, attorney of Fakenham, during February 1750. In 1758 she was buried beside her husband, close to other members of the Mallom family, in the north aisle of Sculthorpe Church. Their grave slab, carved with the arms of Donne impaling Mallom, is now partially obscured by the Snetzler organ.

The purchase of the Cranmer Hall estate by Daniel Jones opens another chapter in the story of the house. The Jones family, like the Donnes, originated from Wales and had lived for many years at Sunny Hill, Glanbranie, in Carmarthenshire. David Jones (1678–1759), an apothecary, came to Norfolk and founded the family fortunes through his advantageous marriage, in 1702, to Mary Sheldrake. Mary was the wealthy heiress of an important Fakenham family who owned considerable property in the town – the Sheldrake Charity Cottage in Oak Street, Fakenham, perpetuates the family name to this day. Much of this estate eventually passed to David and Mary's two sons, John Jones (1705–69), the prosperous Fakenham merchant who married Elizabeth Wace, granddaughter of the Revd Clement Heigham, rector of Sculthorpe, and Daniel Jones (1708–83), the influential attorney and landowner who acquired the Cranmer estate.

In 1963, during repairs to the tower of Fakenham Church, a series of splendidly-carved eighteenth-century timbers were exposed, one of which, dating from 1745, was found bearing the name of Daniel Jones as churchwarden. In the detailed correspondence of the Revd Patrick St Clair, rector of Sustead in Norfolk during the 1730s–'40s, Daniel emerged as a prominent citizen in Fakenham. Following the great fire in the town on 4 August 1738 when 26 thatched and timber-framed shops and houses were destroyed in the Old Market Place, Daniel Jones played a decisive role in attempting to gain financial relief for victims by petitioning the local gentry. Thomas Coke, Earl of Leicester and the creator of Holkham Hall, was often badly in need of money to fund his unfinished Palladian mansion and, during the 1740s, borrowed increasingly large amounts of money from Daniel for this purpose. The attorney appears to have borne the often slow repayments made by his distinguished client with somewhat patient resignation!

Daniel's acquisition of Cranmer, finalised on 14

February 1750, marked his rising status as a country gentlemen. He already owned some property in the parish of Sculthorpe and had purchased from the Donne family the patronage of the living of Sculthorpe Church. Old estate maps from this period, surveyed and drawn by John Aram and now kept at the Norfolk Record Office, as well as Faden's map of Norfolk (1797) and Bryant's map (1826), show the smaller eighteenth-century park at Cranmer prior to the Inclosure Act of 1829 and the construction of the New Road in the same year which substantially extended it. The original Fakenham to Creake and Burnham Market road, Creake Gate Way, curved south of the present 1829 cut, skirting the park and the ice-house through what is now the Lodge Plantation and is still partly traceable as a minor footpath. The Avenues, described in the Sculthorpe Field Book of 1766, were then long, rather formally regimented vistas of trees with a 'small shrubbery' to the south.

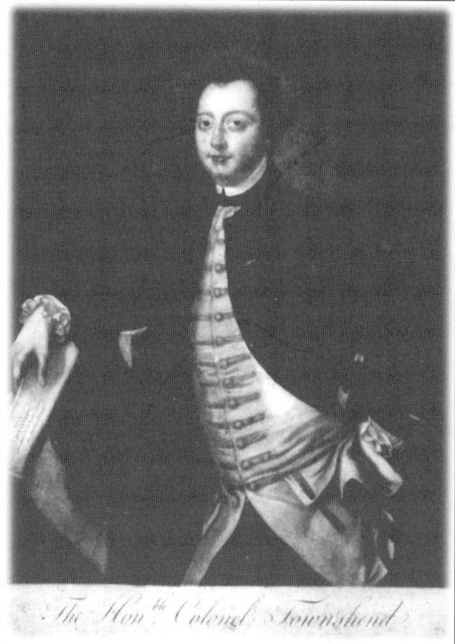

The Hon. Colonel George Townshend (later 4th Viscount and 1st Marquess Townshend) from a portrait by Thomas Hudson. During the 1750s George Townshend rented Cranmer Hall from the elder Daniel Jones and made it his country seat with his first wife, Lady Charlotte. Here he pursued his love of horse riding and fox-hunting, framed his controversial Militia Bill and finally prepared to join General Wolfe on the expedition against Quebec. (Reproduced by kind permission of the present Marquess Townshend)

Daniel's legal practice in Fakenham, where his elderly parents still resided, prevented him from being able to live at Cranmer Hall for much of the 1750s although significant improvements were made to the hall during this period. The Sculthorpe Field Book mentions the adjoining 'Ffarm House, Barns, Stables, Coachhouse, Yardes and Gardens to the same belonging.' A notable structure surviving from the mid-eighteenth century is the fine brick and pantiled barn, built to the rear of the hall in what was then the stackyard. The initials and date 'D.J. 1752', for Daniel Jones, can still be detected, fashioned in contemporary ironwork, on the barn's gable-end. Much of this work was apparently funded by Daniel's tenant, Colonel George Townshend of Raynham, who rented the hall during this period. Armstrong's eighteenth-century *History of Norfolk* stated that Townshend was the individual who 'greatly improved and ornamented the house and buildings.'

George Townshend (1724–1807), later 4th Viscount and 1st Marquis Townshend of Raynham, has emerged as the most fascinating and controversial character in the history of Cranmer Hall. Letters addressed to 'Colonel the Hon. George Townshend' whilst at Cranmer, which have been discovered in the library and attics at Raynham Hall, reveal an energetic, spontaneous and often explosive young aristocrat indulging his passion for horse riding, fox-hunting and rearing bloodstock, 'leaping and hounds', which frequently brought him into conflict with neighbouring landowners. Grandson of the famous 2nd Viscount Charles 'Turnip Townshend', George had served in the Army under 'Butcher Cumberland', most notably at the Battle of Culloden in 1746 when the Jacobite forces of the 'Young Pretender', Bonnie Prince Charlie, had been finally routed. The young soldier had then become the Duke of Cumberland's aide-de-camp and appointed Lieutenant-Colonel to the 1st Regiment of Foot Guards but caused a considerable scandal by making a series of personal attacks upon his unpopular royal patron, primarily achieved by the art of sketching a series of satirical caricatures. These cruelly accurate political cartoons speedily ensured his fall from the Duke of Cumberland's favour.

During the early 1750s, Cranmer Hall provided a haven for Colonel Townshend, especially at a time of personal and political estrangement from his father, the 3rd Viscount Townshend. He had made his fortune by contracting a lucrative marriage with the Lady Charlotte Compton, Baroness Ferrers of Chartley and heiress of the 5th Earl of Northampton, which also proved to be an enduring love-match. Townshend was the Whig Member of Parliament for Norfolk and at Cranmer he was able to devote his energies to pressing political matters, particularly the framing of his controversial Militia Bill, besides enjoying the sporting pursuits of a country estate. The acquisition of certain properties in the parish of Sculthorpe included the rebuilding of the ancient water-mill on the River Wensum in 1757.

Much has been made of George Townshend's celebrated quarrel with Thomas Coke, Earl of Leicester, over the matter of both the Militia Bill and Townshend's love of fox-hunting. R.W. Ketton-Cremer in his book *Norfolk Assembly* charted the angry exchange of letters despatched between Holkham Hall and Cranmer Hall but categorically stated that the elderly Earl of Leicester wisely resisted Townshend's reckless demand for satisfaction by a duel!

In February 1759, the Year of Victories, George Townshend accepted his appointment as

Brigadier-General to serve under Major-General James Wolfe in his famous campaign against the Marquis de Montcalm at Quebec. He left Cranmer Hall to join the ship *The Neptune* which embarked from Spithead on a nine-week sea voyage to Canada. General Wolfe's death at the culmination of the British victory over Montcalm on the Heights of Abraham resulted in Brigadier-General Townshend's unexpected command of the British Forces, which ensured that he formally received the French surrender of the city of Quebec to the British Crown.

After the glory of the Quebec campaign General Townshend returned to Norfolk and continued to live at Cranmer Hall with his wife Lady Charlotte. In 1761 his country residence as Member of Parliament for Norfolk was given as the 'Hon. General George Townshend, Cranmer Hall', but following the death of his father in 1764 George Townshend inherited the family title and estate and subsequently returned to the Townshend seat at Raynham Hall.

Daniel Jones appears to have spent his final years at Cranmer, having secured the living of Sculthorpe Church for his eldest son, the Revd Matthew Jones in 1767. By 1780 his principal address was 'Daniel Jones Esq., of Cranmore, Sculthorpe.' The church register recorded the burial of 'Daniel Jones, Esquire, late of Cranmer House in this Parish' in October 1783.

Among the estate and family papers deposited by the Major (later Sir Lawrence Evelyn Jones) at the Norfolk Record Office in 1946 was a splendid inventory of the personal effects of 'the late Daniel Jones, Gent., at his late dwelling house Cranmer Hall, Norfolk' which was compiled after his death in 1783. This remarkable document literally takes the reader on a ramble around the interior of Cranmer Hall, listing and describing the individual contents in their rooms with the monetary value; thus one can visualise the servant's quarters, the housekeeper's room with its 'Japan tea urn' and 'copper coffee and chocolate pots', and the dairy with its 'barrel churn, milk pail and stool'. Cranmer, like other eighteenth-century houses, brewed its own beer and there are detailed descriptions of the brew-house, brew-house chamber and the beer cellar.

The inventory also listed the principal apartments: the hall; the best parlour; the evidence room; the dining-room; the keeping parlour; the crimson room; the tent bedroom with its 'tent bedstead'; and the best bedroom containing 'a bedstead with mahogany fluted posts'. Much of the furniture appeared to have been either in apple wood, walnut or mahogany, traditionally first imported into England from Jamaica in c.1720. Quality items were encountered, such as 'a pair of handsome oval pier glasses in gilt and carv'd frames', a 'table for backgammon', a 'chamber clock', a 'capital mahogany bookcase with a Chinese glaz'd front' and a 'pair of globes (by Adams)' besides more mundane objects such as 'the mahogany stand' for the 'pot de chambre' and the obligatory 'warming Pan'! A glimpse was provided into the coach-house containing a 'post chaise and harness', valued at £15.

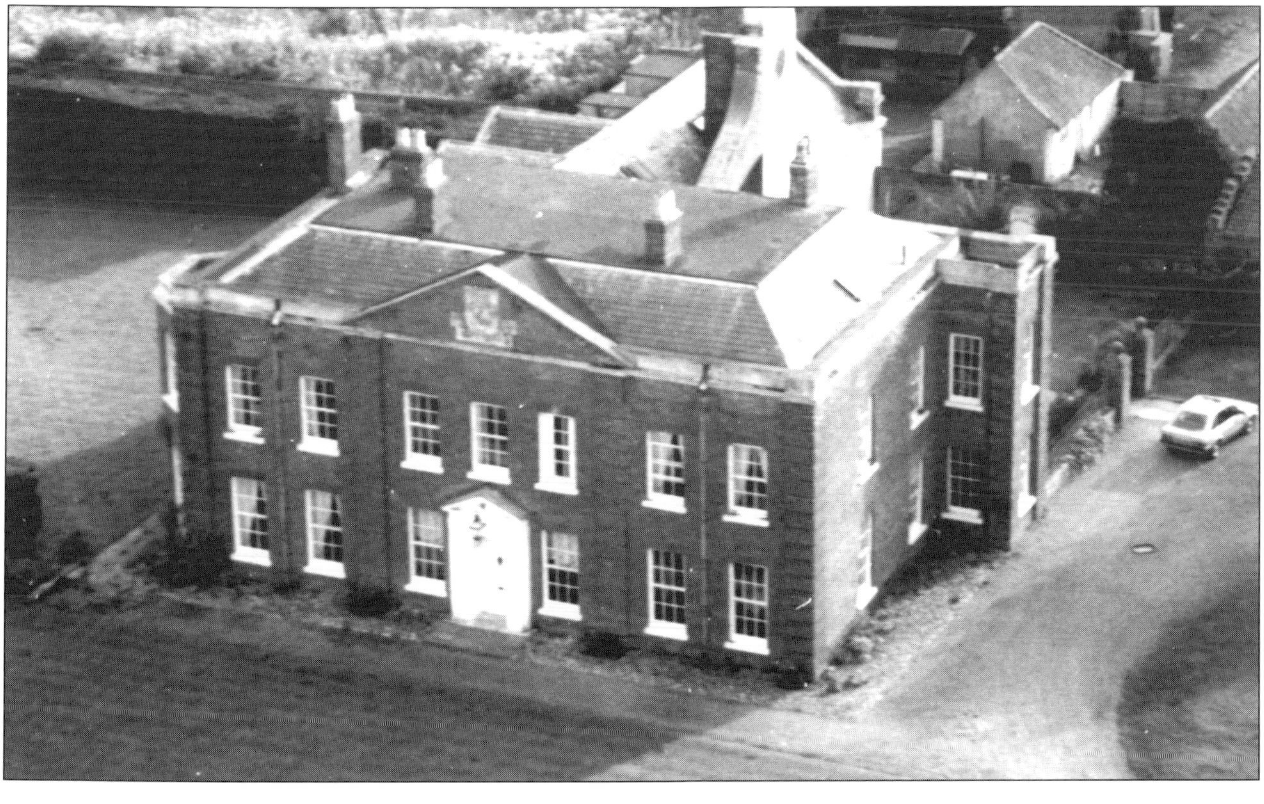

Cranmer Hall, 1984. The hall is the country seat of Dr and Mrs Edward de Bono. (Reproduced by kind permission of John and Henry Labouchere)

Daniel Jones was survived by his two sons, the Revd Matthew Jones (1742–1808), who was both rector and lord of the manor of Sculthorpe, and Daniel Jones of Fakenham (1746–1820). This younger Daniel was also an attorney and acted as agent for both the Astleys at Melton Constable Hall and Coke of Norfolk at Holkham. His dealings in both land stewardship and the legal profession made him a very rich man and, following the death of his elder brother in 1808, he inherited the bulk of the Cranmer estate. According to Bazil Cozens-Hardy in his transaction *Norfolk Lawyers*, published by the Norfolk & Norwich Archaeological Society in 1964, Daniel Jones junr was fêted by Sir Jacob Astley of Melton Constable Hall who commissioned the fashionable society painter, Sir Thomas Lawrence, to paint the attorney's portrait in a calculated bid to gain a handsome bequest in Daniel's will. When Daniel died in 1820, aged 74 years, the estate was bequeathed to his cousin, Major-General Sir John Thomas Jones, and Sir Jacob Astley received nothing! Lawrence's portrait was duly despatched from Melton Constable Hall by the disgruntled baronet and remained at Cranmer Hall until the Jones family finally sold the estate in 1946.

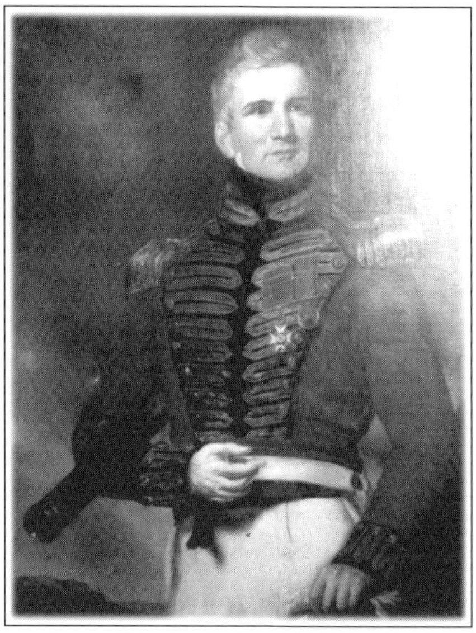

Major-General Sir John Thomas Jones, 1st Baronet of Cranmer, Knight Commander of the Bath (1783–1843). (Copyright: Institution of Royal Engineers. Reproduced by kind permission of the Institution of Royal Engineers)

It appeared that Daniel Jones junr was concerned for the material welfare of his former sister-in-law, the enigmatic Anne Hase, who had now married her third husband, the Revd Horatio Dowsing. Although his cousin inherited the estate in 1820, Daniel had made ample provision for Mrs Dowsing to remain as the tenant of Cranmer Hall where she had once presided as Mrs Matthew Jones. The claims for the Inclosure Award, 1829, revealed that Major-General Sir John Thomas Jones only became 'entitled in possession' after Anne Dowsing had died in 1828.

Sir John Thomas Jones (1783–1843) of the Royal Engineers earned a glowing reputation as a military engineer at many of the celebrated sieges during the Peninsular War. He undertook the lines of defence constructed at Torres Vedras and Badajoz and won the mutual admiration and respect of his great friend, the 'Iron Duke' of Wellington, victor of Waterloo. Born at Languard Fort near Felixstowe, John Thomas Jones was grandson of the merchant John Jones and great-nephew of the elder Daniel Jones of Cranmer Hall, which eventually made him the heir of his cousin, the younger Daniel.

At the siege of Burgos in Spain during 1812 Lieutenant-Colonel Jones was waving his hat in the air as the signal to the Duke of Wellington that a breach in the enemy defences was about to be made when he was shot through the ankle by a French bullet. This caused him to suffer years of increasing ill health yet he continued to serve Wellington, inspecting the Allied defences in the Low Countries and reputedly walking across the battlefield at Waterloo with the Duke in 1815.

Despite inheriting the Cranmer estate in 1820, the Major-General only visited Norfolk occasionally. Ill health and public duties prevented him from enjoying much time in the county but improvements were initiated, Cranmer Park being extended and enclosed with new plantations of trees following the construction of the New Road in 1829. The Duke of Wellington had introduced his friend to the fashionable society resort of Cheltenham Spa in Gloucestershire and the Major-General subsequently acquired a mansion on the Pittville estate, which enabled him to take the spa waters in the Pittville pump room.

John Thomas Jones received numerous accolades for his services to the nation during the Napoleonic Wars, largely at the instigation of his patron, the Duke of Wellington. He served as aide-de-camp to King George IV, King William IV and, after 1837, to the young Queen Victoria. It was through the Duke's influence that he was created a baronet in September 1831 and dubbed Knight Commander of the Bath. His published work *Journals of the Sieges Undertaken by the Allies in Spain* was widely acclaimed.

The family reputation was reflected in the distinguished careers of the Major-General's brothers including Captain George Jones, Royal Navy, who served under Lord Nelson and Captain Sir William Hoste on his flagship *HMS Amphion,* and Sir Harry David Jones, the governor of Sandhurst who served in the Peninsular War and, in 1855, was commanding engineer of British Forces at Sebastopol during the Crimean War.

The Major-General had married Catherine Maria Lawrence of Long Island, New York, in 1816 and the family name was increasingly referred to as 'Lawrence-Jones of Cranmer Hall'. In 1843 Sir John Thomas Jones died at his house on the Pittville estate in Cheltenham and was buried in the Church of SS Philip & James at nearby Leckhampton. He is commemorated in an ostentatious memorial of Victorian-Gothic pinnacles by Myers of Lambeth in the chancel of Sculthorpe Church and in the south

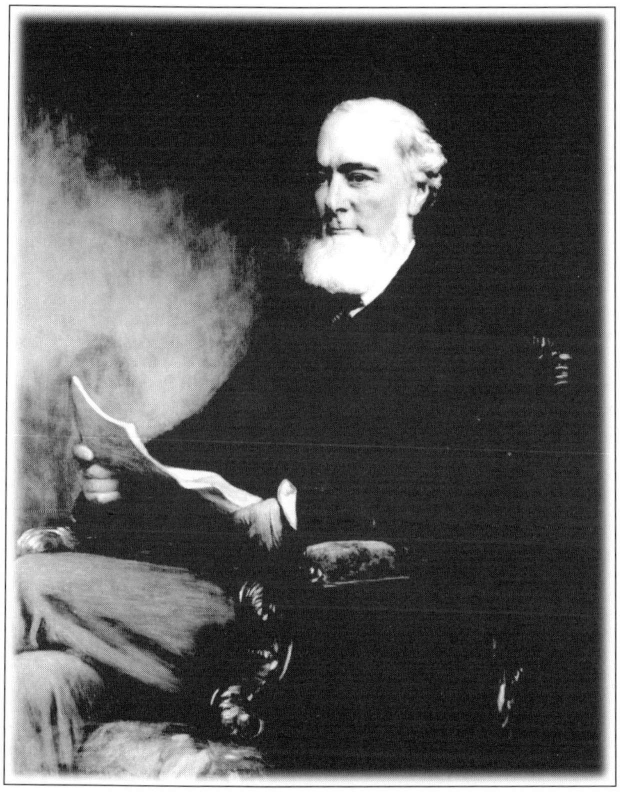

A portrait of Sir Willoughby Jones, 3rd Baronet of Cranmer Hall, by the artist H.T. Wells, which used to hang in the Shirehall at Norwich. Sir Willoughby, who cultivated the friendship of John Ruskin and commissioned the Burne-Jones window of 'Faith, Hope and Charity' from William Morris and Company, which can be found inside Sculthorpe Church, was a much-loved squire and generous patron of the church.
(Reproduced by kind permission of Norwich Castle Museum and Art Gallery)

transept of St Paul's Cathedral in London there is a magnificent white-marble statue by the sculptor Behnes which was commissioned by his brother officers of the Royal Engineers.

Sir John's eldest son, Sir Lawrence Jones (1817–45), 2nd Baronet, was tragically murdered by Turkish bandits and the family estate passed to the Major-General's second son, Sir Willoughby Jones (1820–84), 3rd Baronet, who eventually abandoned a promising legal and political career to become a much-loved country squire on his Norfolk estate.

From 1847 until 1848 Sir Willoughby was Tory Member of Parliament for Cheltenham Spa but the responsibilities of the family inheritance encouraged him to settle at Cranmer Hall and make it his country seat. His involvement with the restoration of the Parish Church in Sculthorpe and the chancel covering the vault which contains the coffin of his murdered brother is recorded elsewhere in this book. Sir Willoughby appears to have been suitably impressed by the work undertaken by his chosen architect Raphael Brandon, based at 11 Beaufort Buildings in the Strand, and in 1849 commissioned him to design the gates and gatehouse lodge at the entrance to the newly-landscaped Cranmer Park. Raphael Brandon's letter of 1849, which contained his plans and suggestions, can be found within the manuscript history of Sculthorpe Church, compiled by Mrs Herbert Jones in 1870. The finished results were a set of wrought-iron gates with piers of brick and stone and a picturesque lodge fashioned in the thatched and rustic cottage ornée style.

The building of Cranmer Lodge and the park gates initiated the start of many improvements to the hall and gardens during this period. A walled kitchen garden, greenhouses filled with hothouse fruits such as peaches, nectarines, figs and grapes, and a thatched summer-house were added. The top storey of the original Georgian hall was heightened and the pediment adorned with the family coat of arms and motto *Marte et arte*, 'by war and art'. A bay window with a cast-iron canopy was built on the south side and a new wing of three storeys built on the north side of the house in 1853. Sir Willoughby also undertook substantial improvements to the estate farms which included the rebuilding of Glebe Farm in Creake Road in 1850 and the building of the Home Farm at Cranmer in 1855.

Sir Willoughby cultivated the arts, especially the friendship of the author and critic John Ruskin who frequently despatched letters to Cranmer Hall from his retreat in the Lake District. The Pre-Raphaelite stained glass adorning Sculthorpe Church is further evidence of Sir Willoughby's artistic tastes. In 1875 Sir Willougby commissioned the architect Philip Webb, who had designed the Red House as a 'palace of art' for his friend William Morris at Bexleyheath in Kent, to add a two-storied south wing at Cranmer Hall which included a neo-Jacobean drawing-room with panelling and plaster-barrel ceiling and a carved oak stairwell. The south wing was completed with a tall buttressed chimney which served as a clock tower; its twin-dial chiming clock was designed by Dents who had made the clock at Big Ben for the Houses of Parliament at Westminster. Philip Webb also designed the coach-house, carriage arch and groom's quarters to the rear of the hall next to the Stackyard Barn of 1752.

Sir Willoughby took his responsibilities as squire and churchman very seriously. Every Sunday the time-honoured ritual of a walk across the park to attend morning service at the Parish Church was undertaken. Sir Willoughby, his wife Emily, Lady Jones and their children were followed by the household servants, the grooms, the gardeners and the estate workers. The tiny gravelled pathway stretched from Cranmer Hall across the park and over a small brick bridge, which had been built to the rear of the medieval moat at Manor Farm, to the west side of Sculthorpe churchyard – parts of this Victorian 'sermon-walk' still survive.

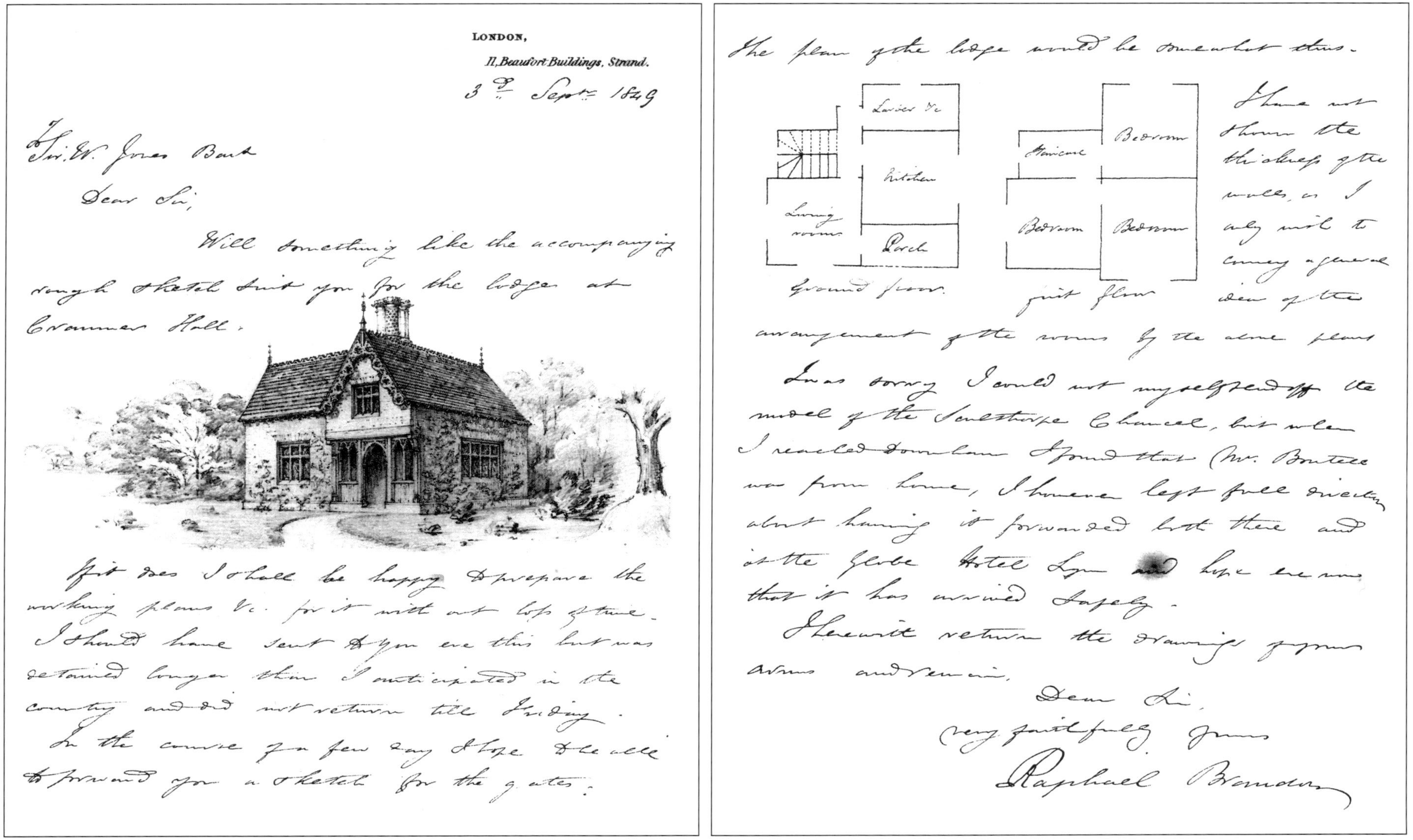
LONDON,
11, Beaufort Buildings, Strand.
3rd Septr. 1849

To Sir W. Jones Bart
Dear Sir,
Will something like the accompanying rough sketch suit you for the lodges at Cranmer Hall.

If it does I shall be happy to prepare the working plans &c. for it without loss of time. I should have sent to you ere this but was detained longer than I anticipated in the country and did not return till Friday.
In the course of a few days I hope to be able to forward you a sketch for the gates.

The plan of the lodge would be somewhat thus.

Larder &c
Kitchen
Living room
Porch
Ground floor.
Staircase
Bedroom
Bedroom
Bedroom
first floor

I have not shown the thickness of the walls, as I only wish to convey a general idea of the arrangement of the rooms by the above plans.

I was sorry I could not myself send off the model of the Sculthorpe Chancel, but when I reached Downham I found that Mr. Bouteel was from home, I however left full directions about having it forwarded both there and to the Globe Hotel Lynn and hope ere now that it has arrived safely.
I herewith return the drawings of your Arms and remain,
Dear Sir,
very faithfully yours
Raphael Brandon

Raphael Brandon's letter to Sir Willoughby Jones with proposals for the planned lodge at Cranmer, 1849.
(Reproduced by kind permission of Father Andrew Thomson, rector of Sculthorpe)

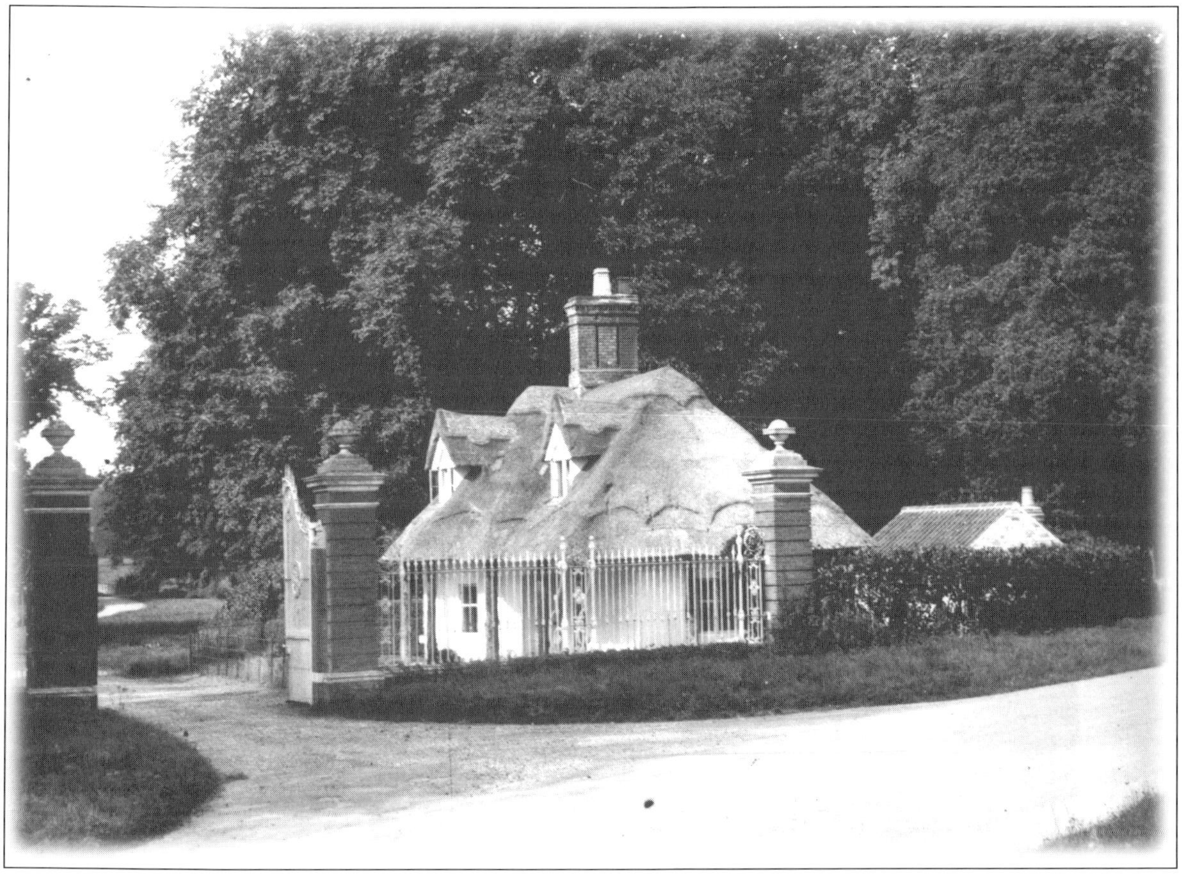

Cranmer Lodge, late 1930s. The building was designed as a thatched cottage ornée by Raphael Brandon for Sir Willoughby Jones in 1849. The wrought-iron gates, also designed by Brandon, were requisitioned for scrap metal during the Second World War and have since been replaced with new ones.
(Reproduced by kind permission of the Norfolk Rural Life Museum at Gressenhall)

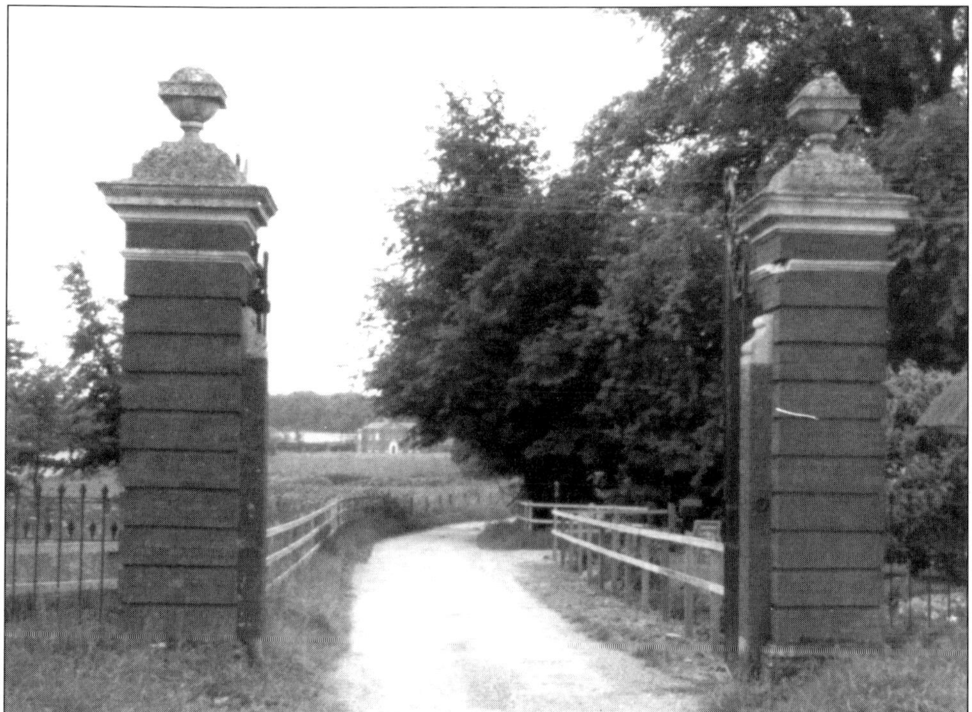

Left: *Cranmer Lodge gates, 1978. The driveway to Cranmer Hall was originally an important road from East Rudham and Coxford Priory to Little Walsingham and may have been used by medieval pilgrims travelling to and from the famous shrine of Our Lady.*

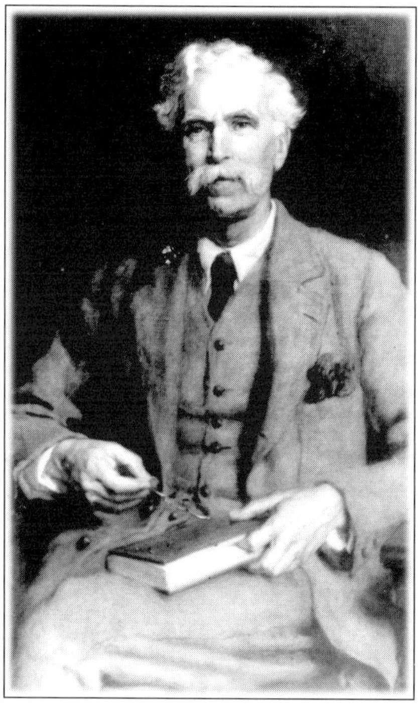

Left: *A portrait of Sir Lawrence John Jones which now hangs in the Council Chamber of Fakenham Town Council. Sir Lawrence was born in the heyday of the Cranmer Hall estate and lived to see its demise. In 1919 he presented the evergreen oaks at Bale and the ancient woodland of Bulfer Grove near Gunthorpe to the National Trust.* (Reproduced by kind permission of Fakenham Town Council)

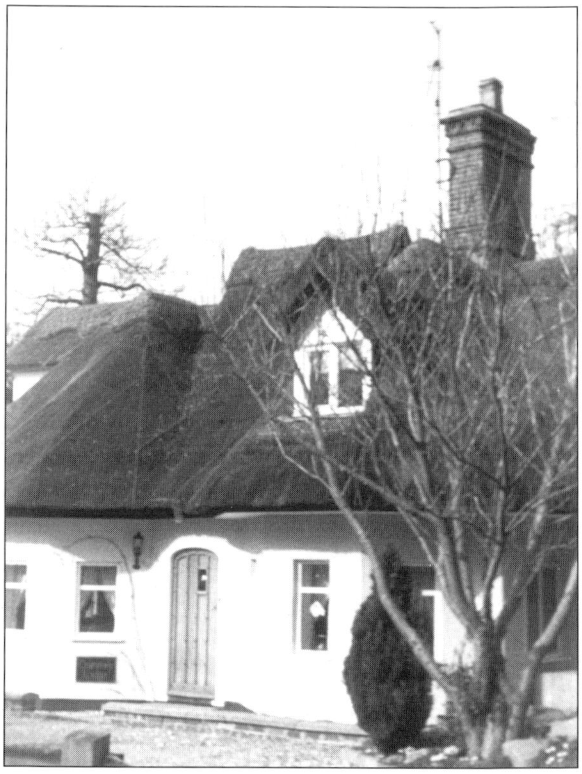

Cranmer Lodge as it appears at the time of writing.

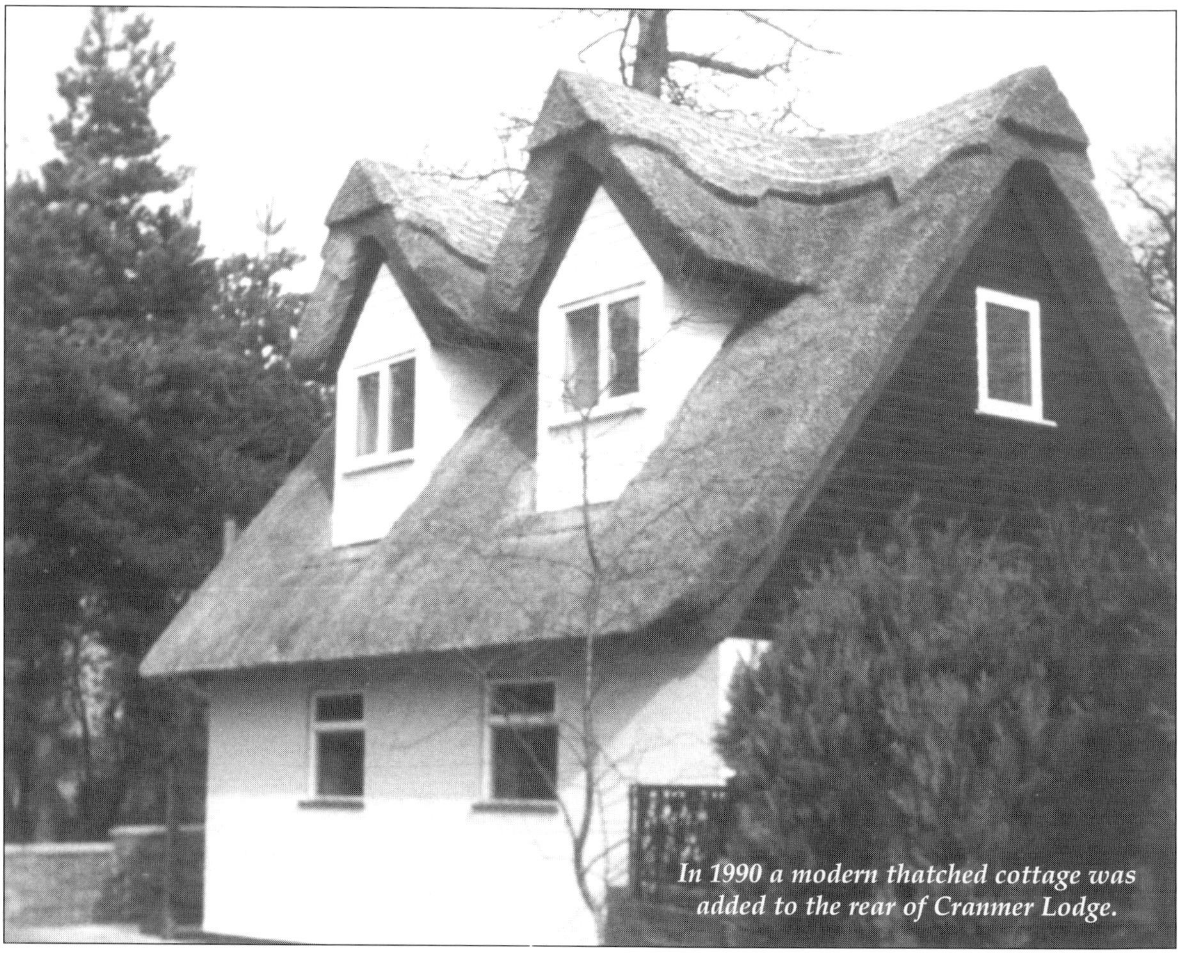

In 1990 a modern thatched cottage was added to the rear of Cranmer Lodge.

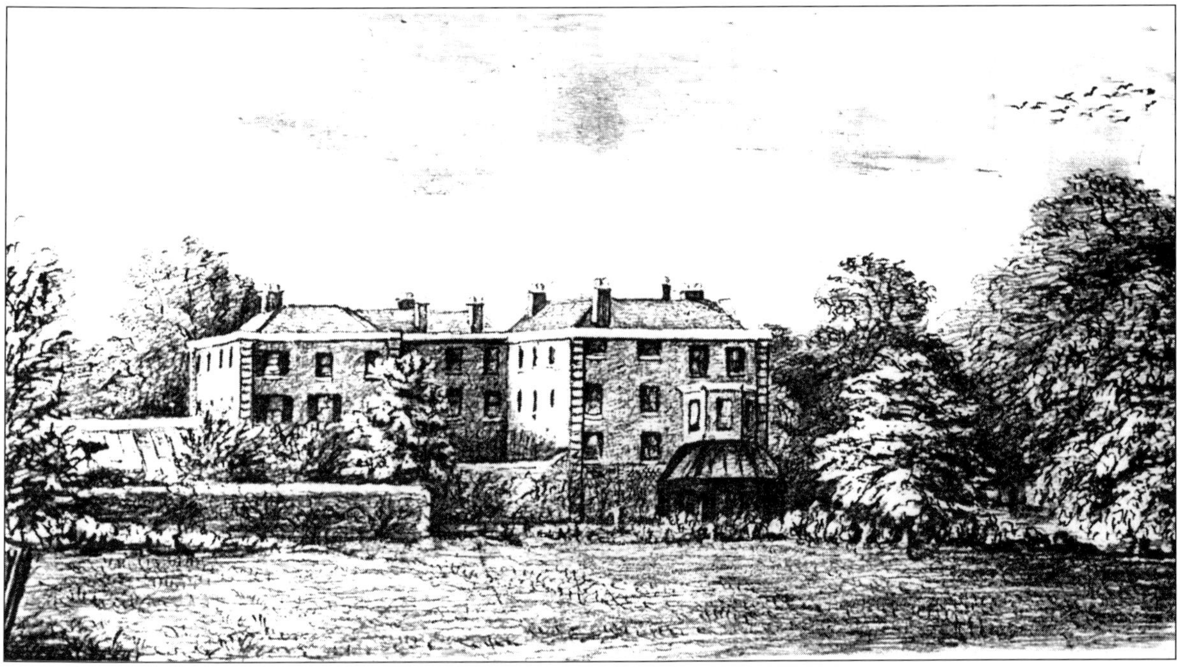

The south garden front of Cranmer Hall, 1854. The bay window, cast-iron canopied verandah and the rear block, completed in 1853, show the first period of additions made by Sir Willoughby Jones. (Reproduced by kind permission of Mrs Louise Hurst)

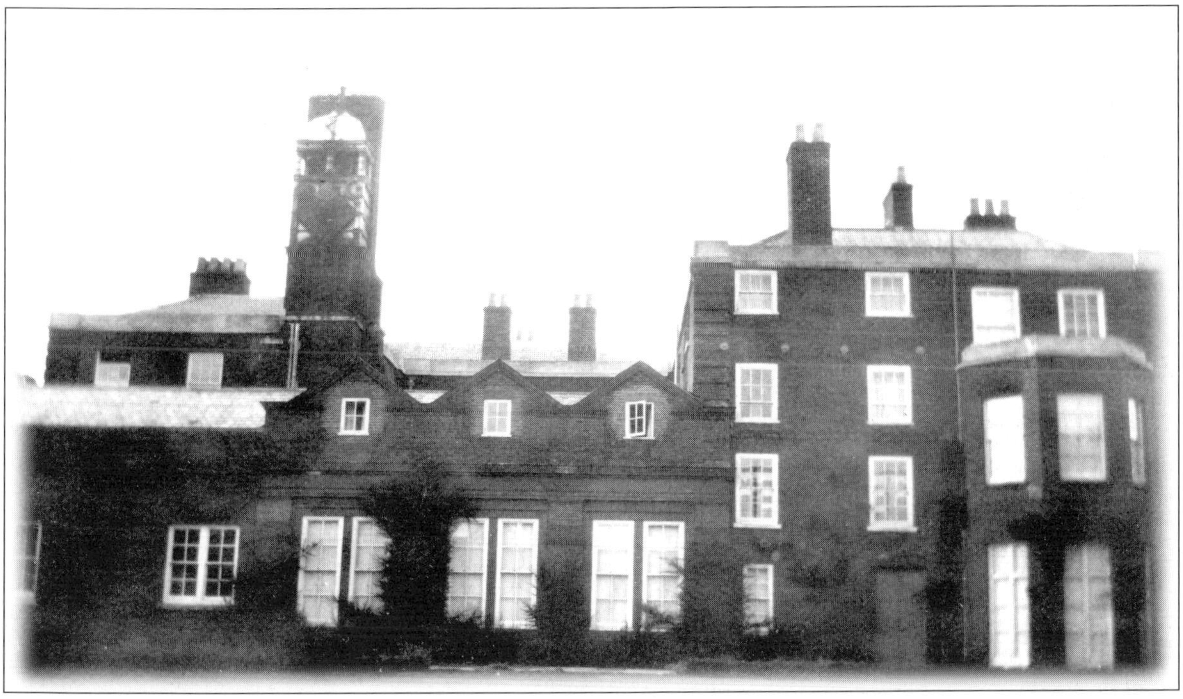

Cranmer Hall, the south-facing garden front, early 1930s. This photograph was taken after Major Jones had made a number of improvements to the house. The original Georgian Hall, built in 1721 by Robert Donne, is represented by the main block to the right. The tall chimney with its twin-dial clock and the neo-Jacobean drawing-room with three gables were added in 1875, designed by the architect Philip Webb. (From the collection of the late Willy Woodhouse. Reproduced by kind permission of Mr Richard Land)

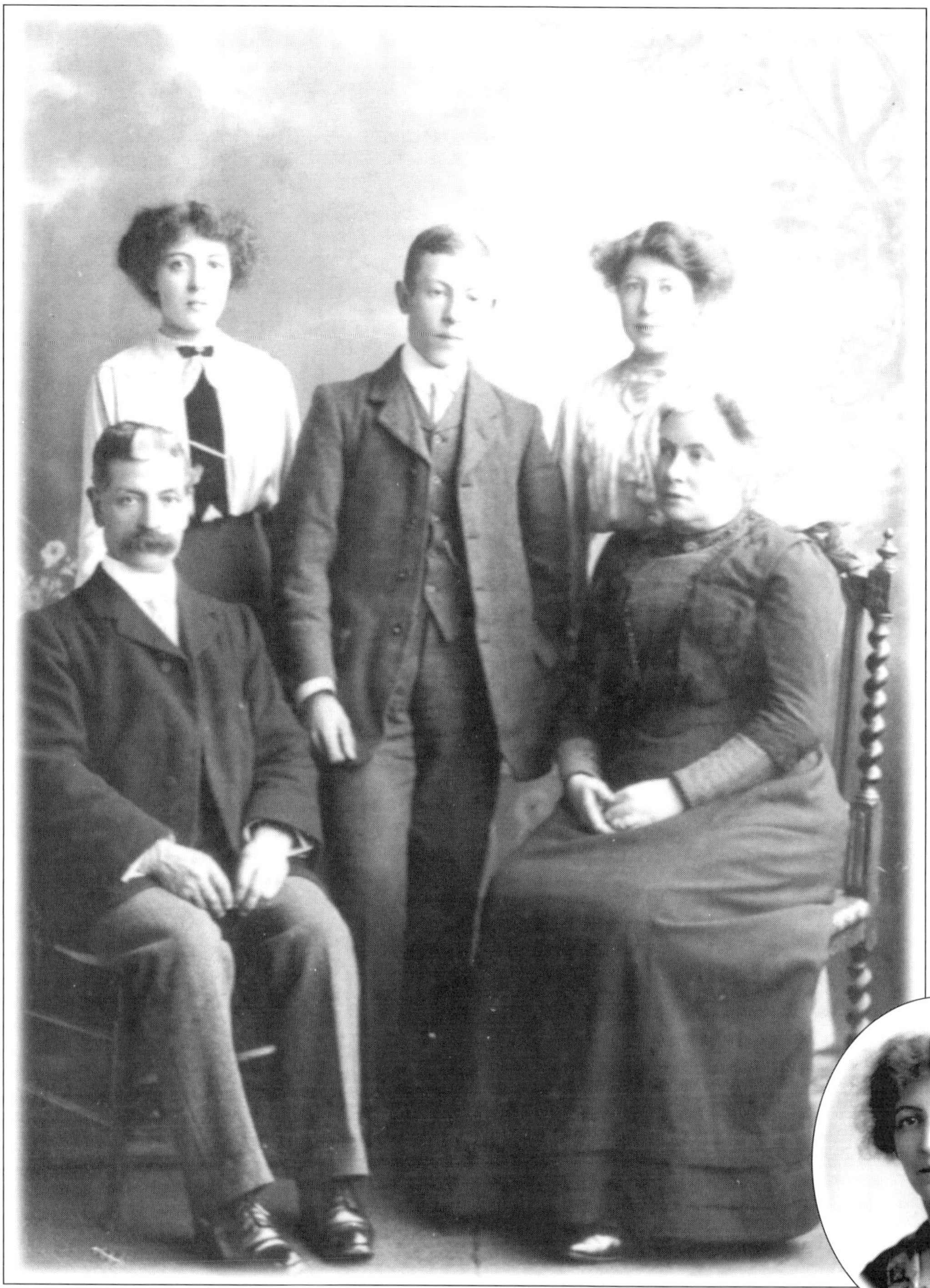

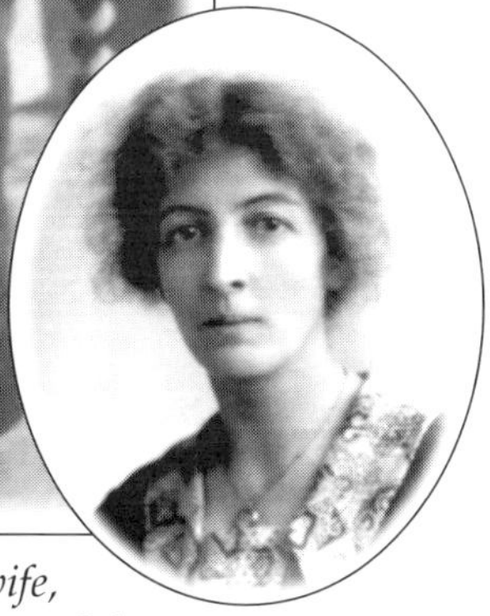

Above: *The Woodhouse family, c.1914.* Seated: *Willy Woodhouse and his first wife, Ellen, who died in 1919.* Standing, their three children, from left to right: *Eleanor, John and Marion. The family moved from Cranmer Lodge to Rose Cottage near the Parish Church in 1900. Willy rendered 60 years' loyal service to the Jones family on the Cranmer Hall estate. For much of that time he was the estate agent and Rose Cottage was the estate office.* (Reproduced by kind permission of Willy Woodhouse's great-grandson Mr Richard Land)

Inset: *Miss Eleanor Woodhouse (later Mrs Eleanor Crane), 1891–1985, a much-loved native of Sculthorpe who was born at Cranmer Lodge and had vivid memories of life on the Cranmer Hall estate. She particularly remembered how the village was a haven for the red squirrel, especially in the woods at Cranmer Park and in Moor Lane with its tall elm trees. 'My sister Marion and I kept a red squirrel as a pet,' she recalled. 'He lived in a hollow of an elm tree in the garden at Cranmer Lodge and we both fed him on a daily basis.'* (Reproduced by kind permission of Mr Richard Land)

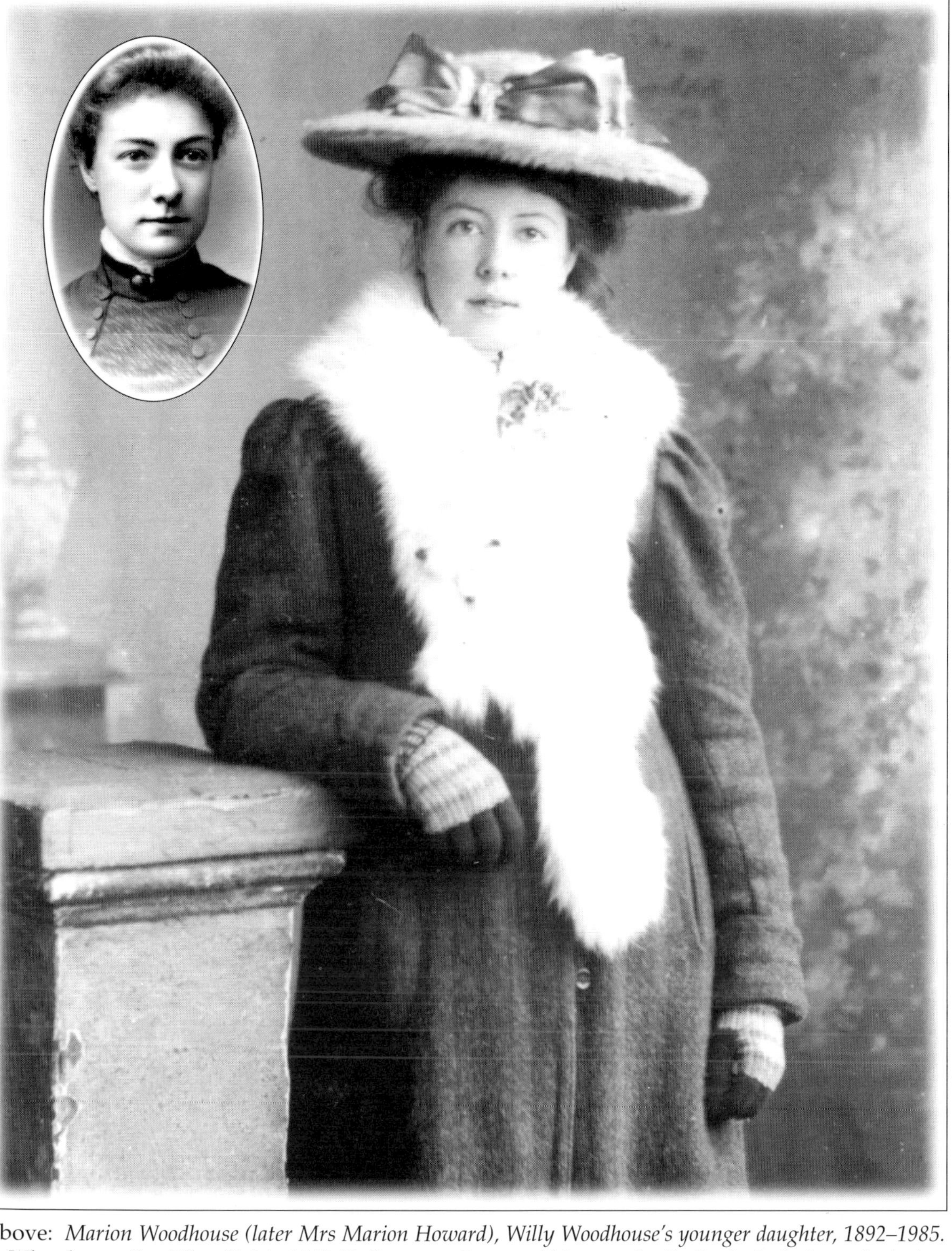

Above: *Marion Woodhouse (later Mrs Marion Howard), Willy Woodhouse's younger daughter, 1892–1985. When her mother Ellen died in 1919 Sir Lawrence Jones and his second wife, Paula, Lady Jones, invited Marion to spend some time with them at their town house at Harrington Gardens, London. Mrs Howard recalled: 'They were terribly kind and the servants very attentive, although some of the staff had expected 'young Miss Marion' to be a very little girl, not a grown-up young lady of 27 years old!'* (Reproduced by kind permission of Mr Richard Land)

Inset: *Mrs Ellen Woodhouse (née Manning), originally lady's maid to Evelyn Mary, Lady Jones, the first wife of Sir Lawrence John Jones. When the Jones family moved to a villa near St-Raphael in France in 1896 the Woodhouse family acted as caretakers at Cranmer Hall. Mrs Woodhouse was responsible for the curtains, chintzes and furniture.* (Reproduced by kind permission of Mrs Woodhouse's great-grandson, Mr Richard Land)

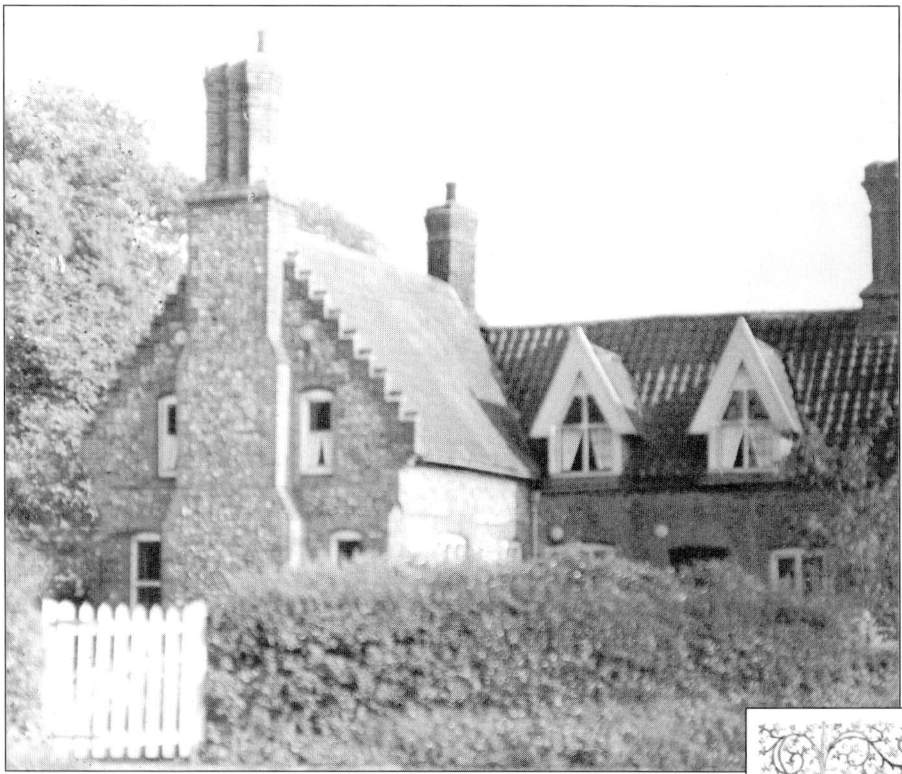

Left: *Rose Cottage in the days when it was the estate office for the Cranmer Hall estate and the home of Mr Willy Woodhouse and family.* (Reproduced by kind permission of Mr Richard Land)

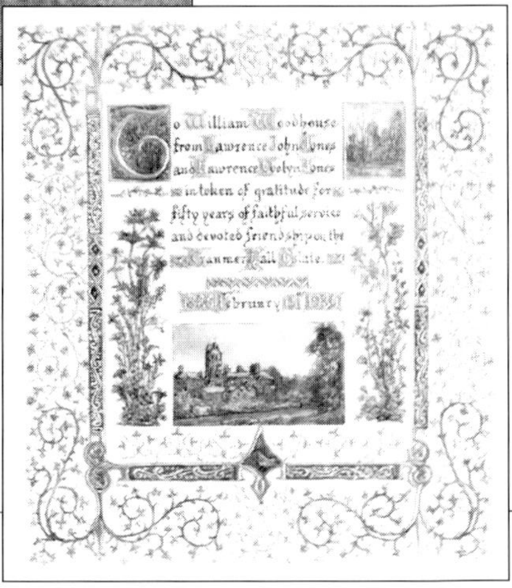

Right: *A hand-illuminated picture commemorating Willy Woodhouse's 50 years' loyal service on the Cranmer Hall estate, 1936. This is the work of Paula, Lady Jones, who was a distinguished artist and illuminator and also painted the illuminated list of rectors in the Parish Church. Willy Woodhouse received a motor car from Sir Lawrence and the Major but unfortunately he was unable to drive; his sole attempt saw him running the vehicle into the churchyard wall!* (From the collection of the late Willy Woodhouse. Reproduced by kind permission of Mr Richard Land)

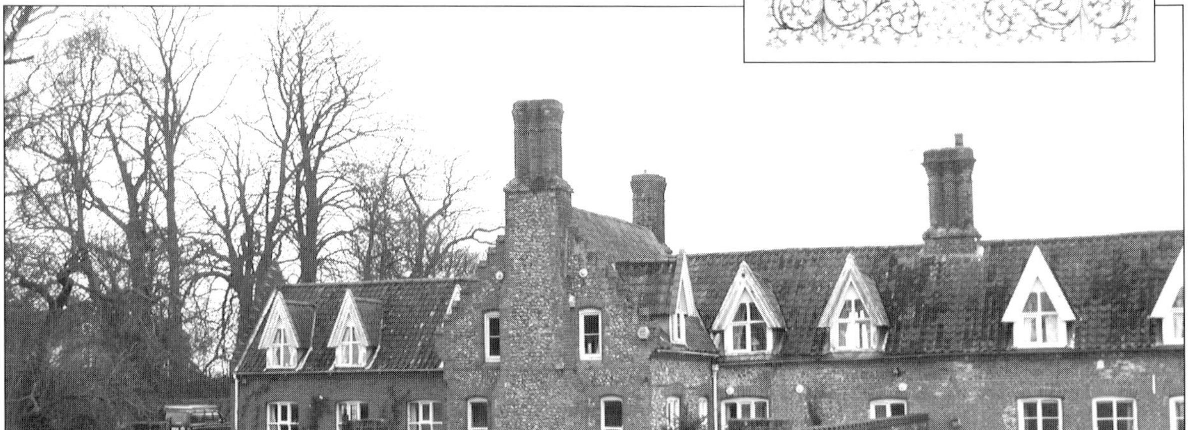

Rose Cottage and Ivy Cottage, 2002.
(Photograph by Mr Richard Land)

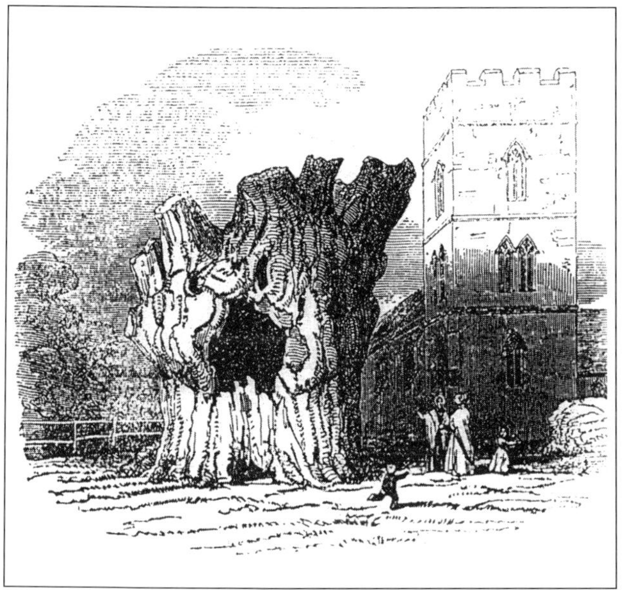

The Great Oak at Bale on the Cranmer Hall estate, from an engraving from the May 1845 edition of the Illustrated London News. *By 1860 this gigantic tree had become unsafe and Sir Willoughby Jones ordered that it be cut down and carted off to the woodyard at Cranmer Hall.* (Reproduced by kind permission of the *Illustrated London News* picture library)

In March 1863 Albert Edward, Prince of Wales (later King Edward VII), married Princess Alexandra of Denmark and the event was marked by widespread celebrations. In Sculthorpe Sir Willoughby Jones provided his tenants with 70 stones of beef and his brother, the Revd Herbert Walsingham Jones, produced a most remarkable round wedding cake, 10 feet across and weighing some two-hundredweight. The Prince and Princess of Wales established themselves with considerable style at their new country seat of Sandringham House and, during the 1870s, Sir Willoughby and Emily, Lady Jones, were among the local gentry invited to attend the balls and dances staged within the Great Saloon.

Sir Willoughby's legal and political brains were suitably employed by his involvement in local politics and the dispensation of local justice. In 1851 he was Lord High Sheriff of Norfolk and, for many years, presided as Justice of the Peace and chairman of the Norfolk Court of Quarter Sessions in the little Georgian courthouse at Walsingham which is now a splendid museum. At the 1865 election he embraced the Liberal cause and campaigned as the Liberal candidate for West Norfolk. Education was another great passion and he was chairman of the Norwich centre of the Cambridge Local Examinations, taking a very keen interest in all kinds of schools from Greshams School in Holt to the Church school in Sculthorpe, which his father had helped to establish. The schoolchildren in Sculthorpe were often invited to attend a picnic in Cranmer Park, especially in the spring when they were encouraged to gather wild primroses in baskets.

During the nineteenth century the Cranmer estate extended beyond Sculthorpe and Fakenham into several surrounding villages such as Alethorpe, Pensthorpe, Kettlestone and Bale. The village of Bale was famous for a huge, ancient tree, the Great Oak of Bale, which featured in the May 1845 edition of the *Illustrated London News*. During 1860 the hollow trunk of this celebrated oak was cut down by the order of Sir Willoughby Jones and taken by farm wagons, decorated with flags, to the woodyard at Cranmer Hall. Such a curious spectacle drew large crowds in Fakenham and from across the estate. Sam Woodhouse from April Cottage in Sculthorpe was one of the estate carpenters involved in cutting down the tree.

In August 1884 Sir Willoughby died and the estate was inherited by his eldest son, Sir Lawrence John Jones (1857–1954), 4th Baronet. Sir Willoughby's second son, the Rt Revd Herbert Edward Jones, doctor of divinity, was Suffragan Bishop of Lewes and has an imposing memorial in Chichester Cathedral.

Sir Lawrence married Evelyn Mary Bevan of Northgate House, Bury St Edmunds, in 1882. Their wedding was rather a grand society affair at St Margaret's Church, Westminster. The new bride arrived at Cranmer Hall accompanied by her personal maid, Miss Ellen Manning. Sam Woodhouse, the estate carpenter, and his young son, Willy Woodhouse, were employed in the woodyard and saw-pit at Cranmer which was how Willy met the lady's maid. In time Willy and Ellen were married and settled at Cranmer Lodge, and it was here that they raised their three children: Eleanor, Marion and John Woodhouse.

In later years Eleanor and Marion recalled their happy childhood at Cranmer during the last years of Queen Victoria's reign. They were allowed to play with Sir Lawrence's youngest child Miss Rachel Jones and remembered the games of hide-and-seek at the hall and taking afternoon tea up on the roof of the house! A parlour maid brought up the tea tray as a special treat. During the summer there were picnics in the Old Square Wood by the Roman road or an outing with their father in the pony and trap to see the outlying estate farms at Kettlestone and Bale. In 1896 Sir Lawrence John Jones and his family moved to a villa at Valescure near St-Raphael on the Cote d'Azur, and the Woodhouses remained at Cranmer, acting as caretakers until a tenant was found. Willy Woodhouse was now land agent for the Cranmer estate and dealt with the tenant farmers, the rents, leases and estate accounts.

In 1897 the village celebrations for Queen Victoria's Diamond Jubilee were centred in Cranmer Park. Mrs Harriet Rix decorated straw hats with blue cornflowers, there were flags and bunting, games and an abundance of sweets and nuts distributed to

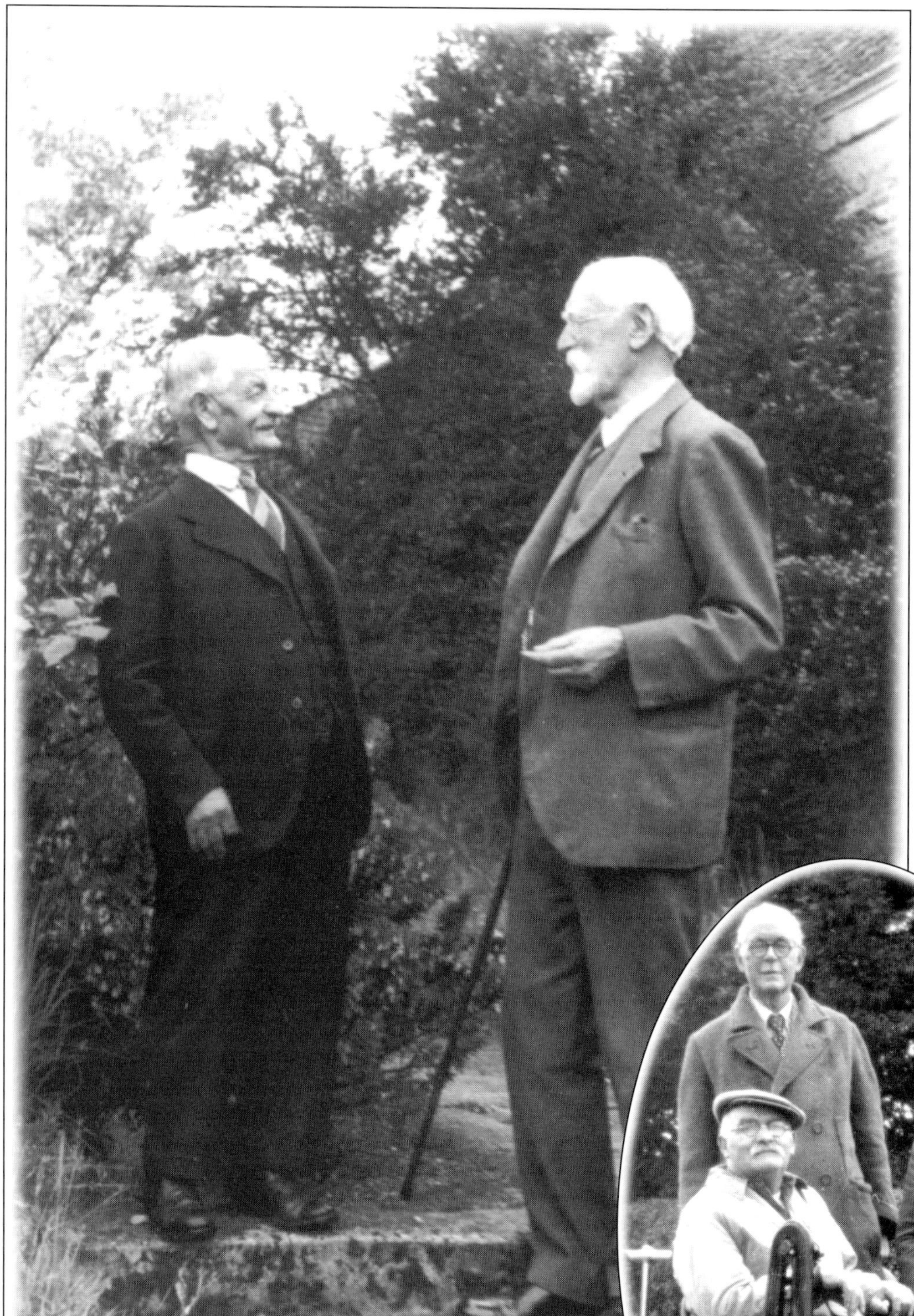

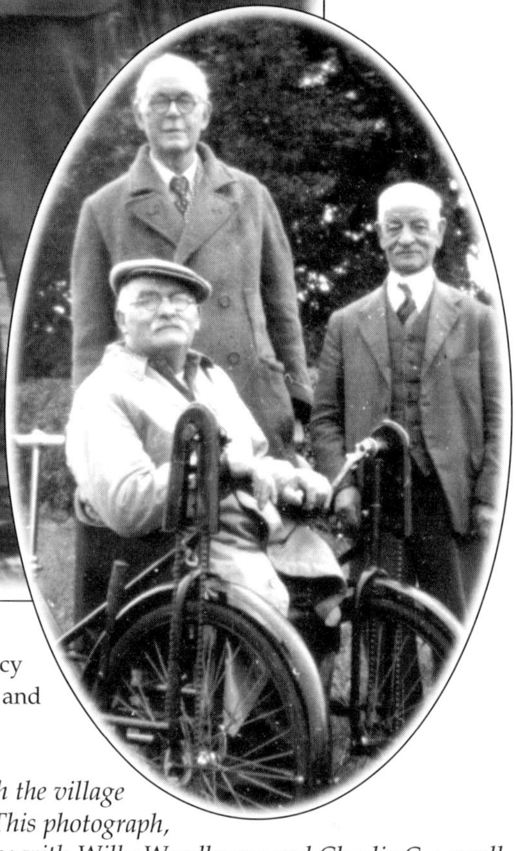

Above: *Willy Woodhouse with Sir Lawrence John Jones at Cranmer Hall, June 1945.* (From the collection of the late Nancy Morse. Reproduced by kind permission of Mrs Vivien Asquith and Mrs Lavinia Monaco)

Right: *Sir Lawrence Evelyn Jones maintained close links with the village of Sculthorpe after his family left Cranmer Hall. This photograph, dating from the mid-1950s, shows Sir Lawrence with Willy Woodhouse and Charlie Cornwall.* (Reproduced by kind permission of Mr Richard Land and Mr Austin Cornwall)

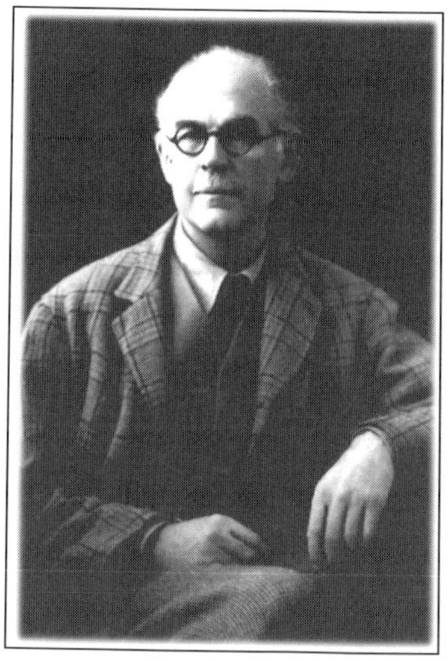

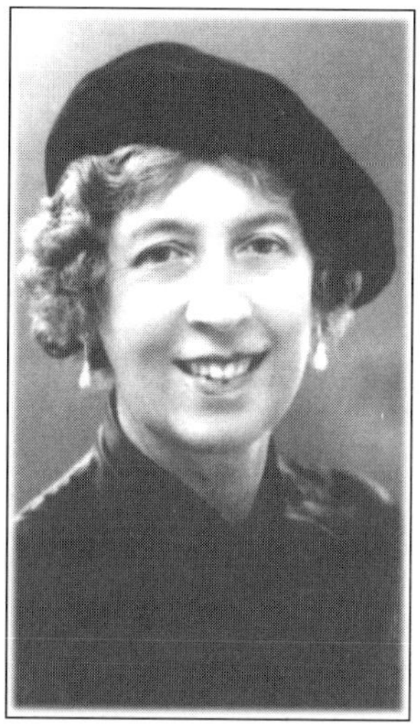

In 1929 Major (later Sir) Lawrence Evelyn Jones (left) *assumed responsibility for the Cranmer Hall estate from his father. His memories of life at Cranmer can be read in his autobiographical books* A Victorian Boyhood, An Edwardian Youth *and* Georgian Afternoon. *Lady Evelyn Jones* (right) *was the much-loved lady of the manor and the driving force behind Sculthorpe Women's Institute and the Red Cross convalescent hospital which she established at Cranmer during the Second World War.* (Left: from the collection of the late Stanley Gathercole; right: from the collection of Mr Bob Hood whose father was butler to the Major and Lady Evelyn during the 1930s and '40s. Both images reproduced by kind permission of Mrs Vivien Asquith and Mrs Lavinia Monaco, daughters of the Joneses)

the children. A huge tea party was held for the estate workers and their families.

Eleanor and Marion remembered the outbreak of the Boer War in 1899 when the young under-gardener Owen Pleasants, 'Lad', was called up to fight in South Africa, much to the sadness of his father, James Winn, 'Master', who was the head gardener at Cranmer. Owen Pleasants survived the South African war and subsequently settled in the Cape.

In 1900 the Woodhouse family moved to Rose Cottage near the Parish Church, a pretty gabled cottage built in 1859 by the Revd Herbert Walsingham Jones for his gardener. This became the estate office where Willy Woodhouse worked into the early hours, laboriously pouring over the estate accounts by the light of an oil lamp. It was here that Eleanor and Marion remembered hearing the news of the death of Queen Victoria in January 1901.

Sir Lawrence John Jones and Evelyn Mary, Lady Jones, frequently returned to England, primarily to visit their sons who were being educated at Eton. They also visited Sculthorpe, descending upon the Woodhouse family at Rose Cottage. On one notable occasion, during the summer of 1904, they brought a very distinguished royal guest to luncheon, His Highness Prince Frederick Duleep Singh, the younger son of the Maharajah Duleep Singh of Elveden, the former ruler of the Punjab who had surrendered the famous Koh-i-noor diamond to Queen Victoria. Prince Freddy was a distinguished local historian who collected miniatures, china and numerous *objets d'art*, besides being a connoisseur of English country houses. He had expressed a desire to visit Cranmer Hall to see the famous pictures by Lawrence and Napier, the letters written by the Duke of Wellington to Sir John Thomas Jones, the lock of the Emperor Napoleon's hair and the Philip Webb drawing-room.

Mrs Ellen Woodhouse attempted to prepare a splendid luncheon worthy of the occasion and was suitably rewarded with a royal compliment; Prince Freddy thoroughly enjoyed his lunch and asked Lady Jones that he might congratulate 'Your Ladyship's excellent chef.' 'My Chef?' Lady Jones exclaimed, 'Your Highness must surely mean my old maid Ellen!'

The Edwardian period saw the arrival of Mr George Grant Lockhart Ross as the tenant of Cranmer Hall. Mr Lockhart Ross is chiefly remembered as the founder president of Sculthorpe Rifle Club, which proved to be enormously popular in the village. He lived a rather solitary life at the hall, attended by his housekeeper Miss Harris and his butler Keeble, and was the first person in the parish to own a motor car, a chauffeur-driven Daimler. His first chauffeur, Mr Schofield, was sacked, but his replacement, Mr William Crane, proved to be more enduring. Billy Crane, who had married Eleanor Woodhouse, remained as chauffeur until Mr Lockhart Ross vacated Cranmer Hall in 1929. Billy and Eleanor then moved from Ivy Cottage near the church to the Old Forge on the corner of Moor Lane and The Street. Here Billy established a flourishing filling station, with motorcycles, a bicycle shop and taxi-hire facilities. His motorised weddings became a speciality and Crane's Corner is remembered with great affection.

In 1929 Sir Lawrence John Jones, now residing at 39 Harrington Gardens in London with his second wife Paula, Lady Jones, passed the Cranmer estate over to his son, Major Lawrence Evelyn Jones (1885–1969). Major Jones, who had been wounded and taken prisoner during the First World War, was employed in London by the merchant banker Herbert Wagg and now turned his attentions to making Cranmer Hall his country residence and family home. In this venture he was supported by his charming wife, Lady Evelyn Jones (1886–1971).

Lady Evelyn was the daughter of Albert, 4th Earl Grey of Howick, who had been administrator of Rhodesia and later governor-general of Canada for King Edward VII. Her great-grandfather Charles, 2nd Earl Grey, had been the famous Whig Prime Minister responsible for the Great Reform Act of 1832 and the introduction from China of the delicious

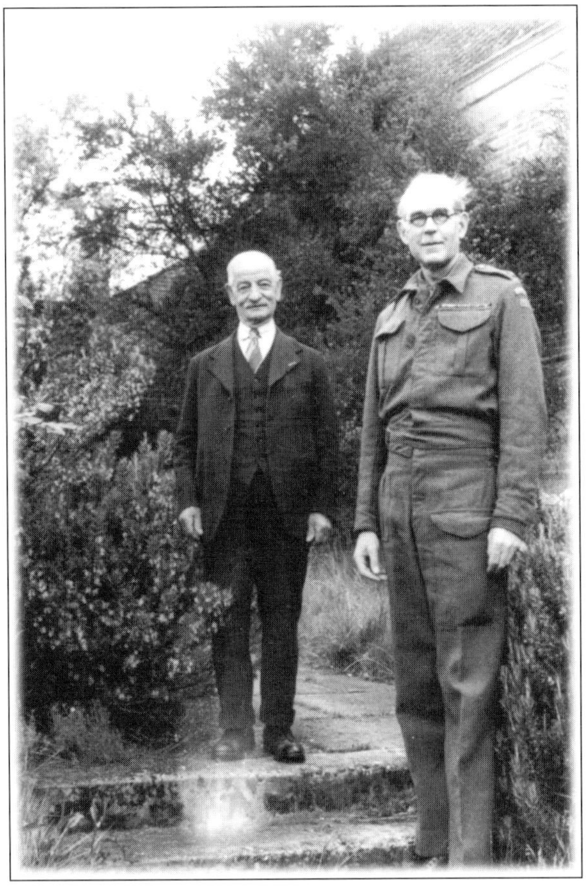

Above: *Willy Woodhouse with Major Jones in uniform as the local Home Guard Commander, Cranmer Hall, June 1945.* (From the collection of the late Hon. Nancy Morse. Reproduced by kind permission of Mrs Vivien Asquith and Mrs Lavinia Monaco)

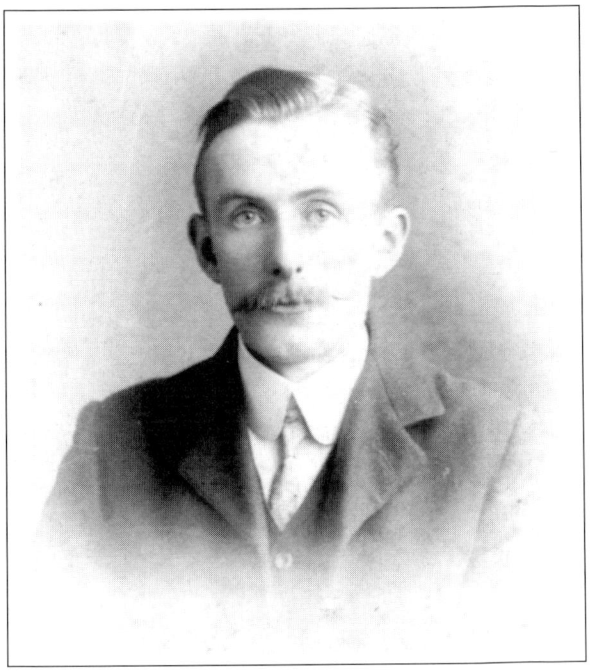

Above: *William 'Billy' Crane (1885–1963). Originally chauffeur to Mr George Lockhart Ross, Billy Crane opened his filling station, including a bicycle and sweet shop, taxi-hire service, motorised weddings and motorcycle agency, at the Old Forge in 1929. 'Crane's Corner' was a flourishing business on the junction of Moor Lane and The Street during the period 1929–55.*

Below: *Billy Crane pictured with his second wife, Eleanor Woodhouse.* (Both images reproduced by kind permission of their grandson, Mr Richard Land)

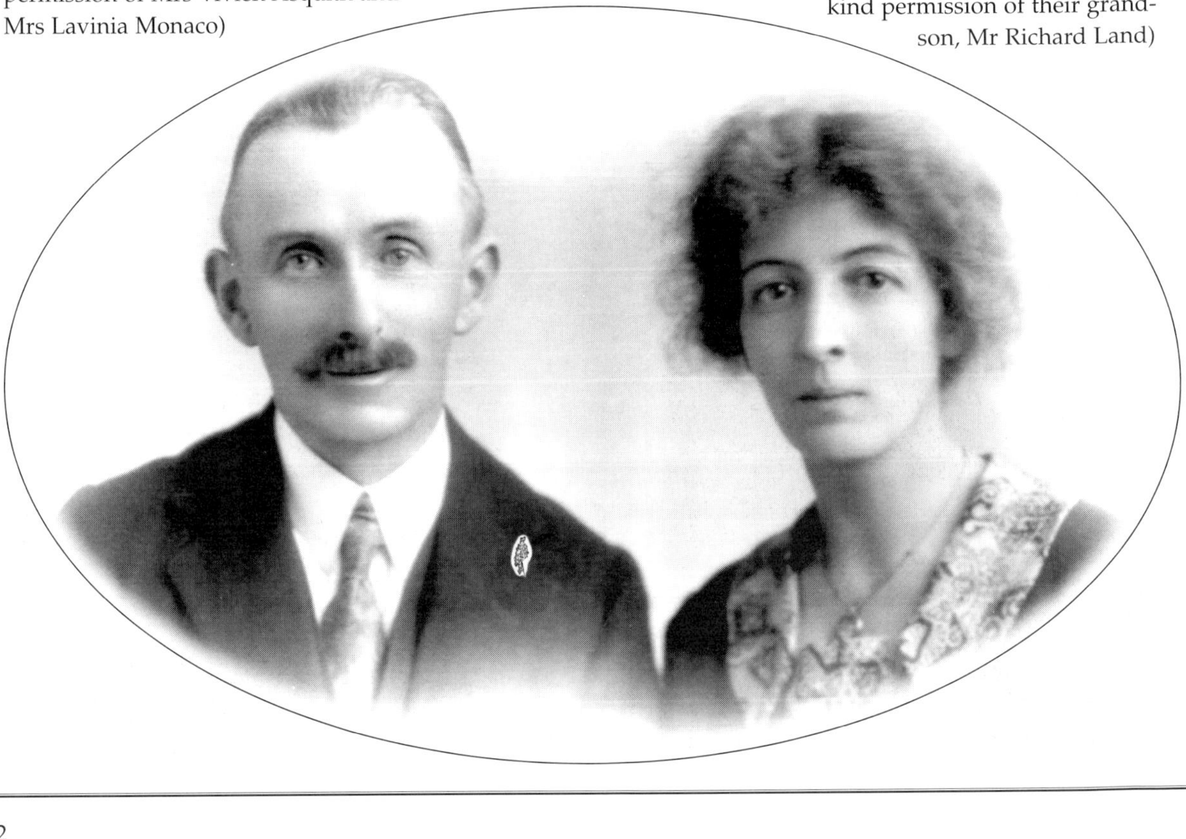

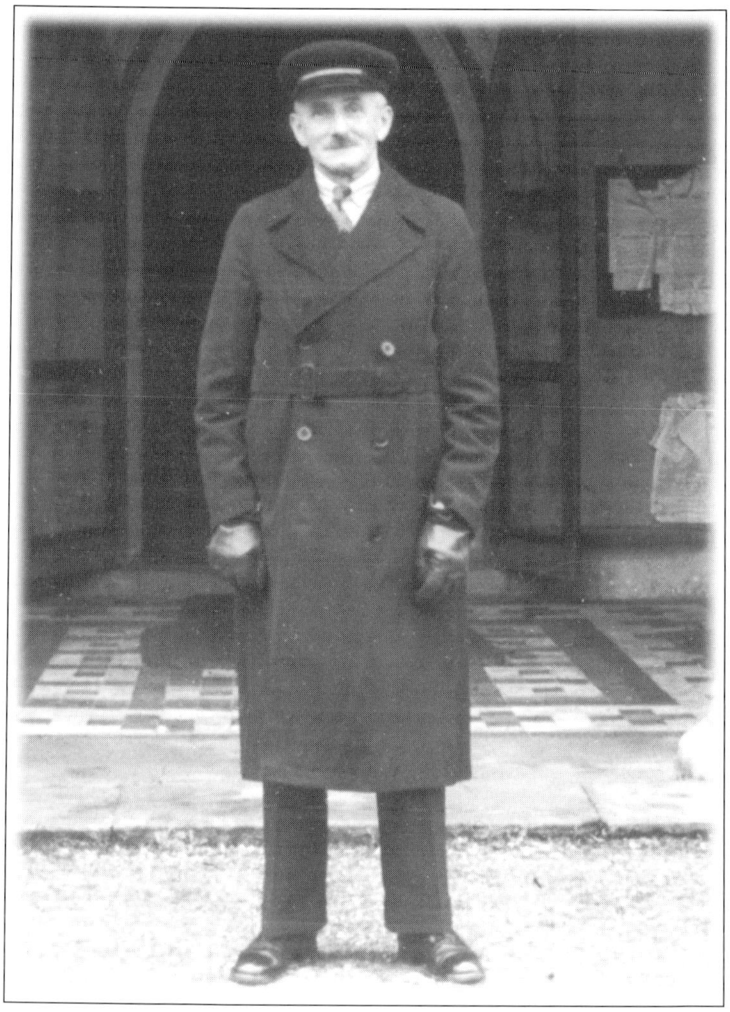

Left: *Billy Crane in chauffeur's uniform at a wedding outside Sculthorpe Church during the 1940s.* (Reproduced by kind permission of Mr Richard Land)

Below: *Billy Crane's motorised weddings were a feature of village life from 1929 until 1955. Here he is with his wedding car at Sculthorpe Church in December 1951 at the wedding of Miss Gwen Lingwood.* Left to right: *Billy Crane, Gwen Lingwood and her father, Jack Lingwood.* (Reproduced by kind permission of Mrs Gwen Windeler (née Lingwood))

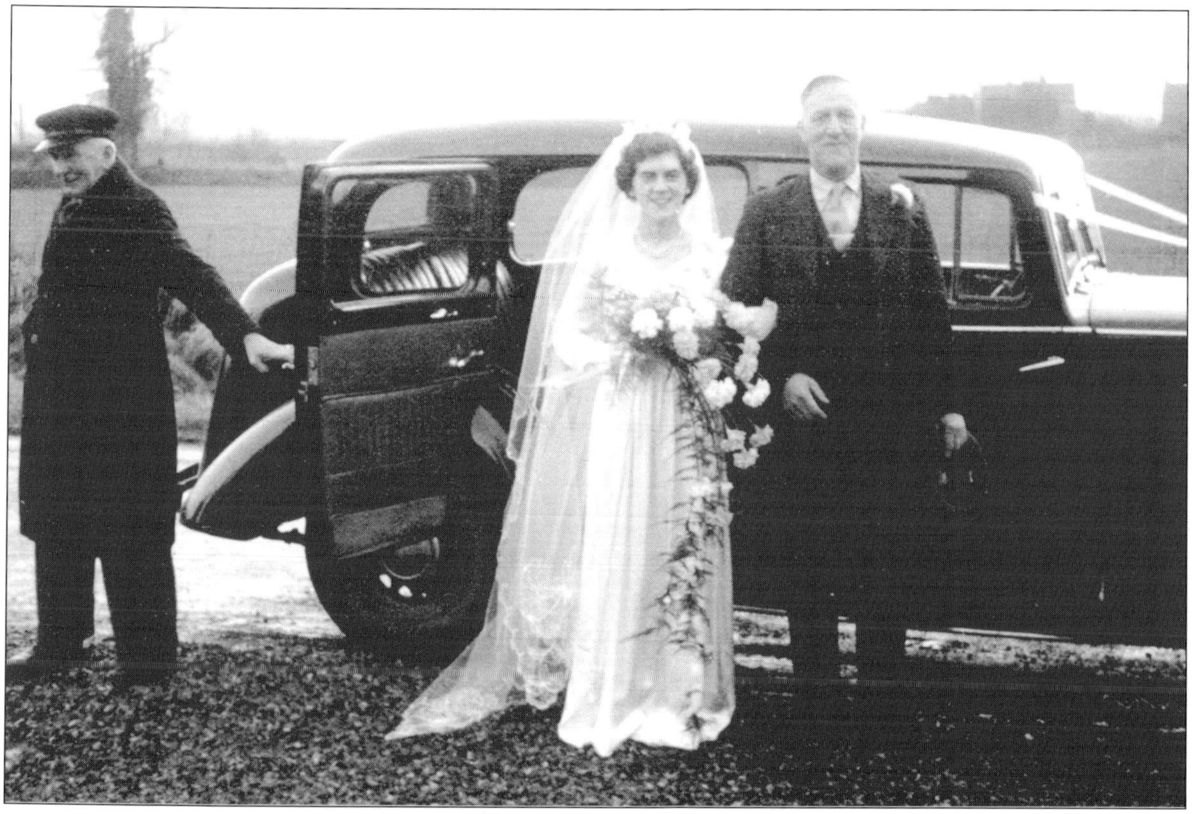

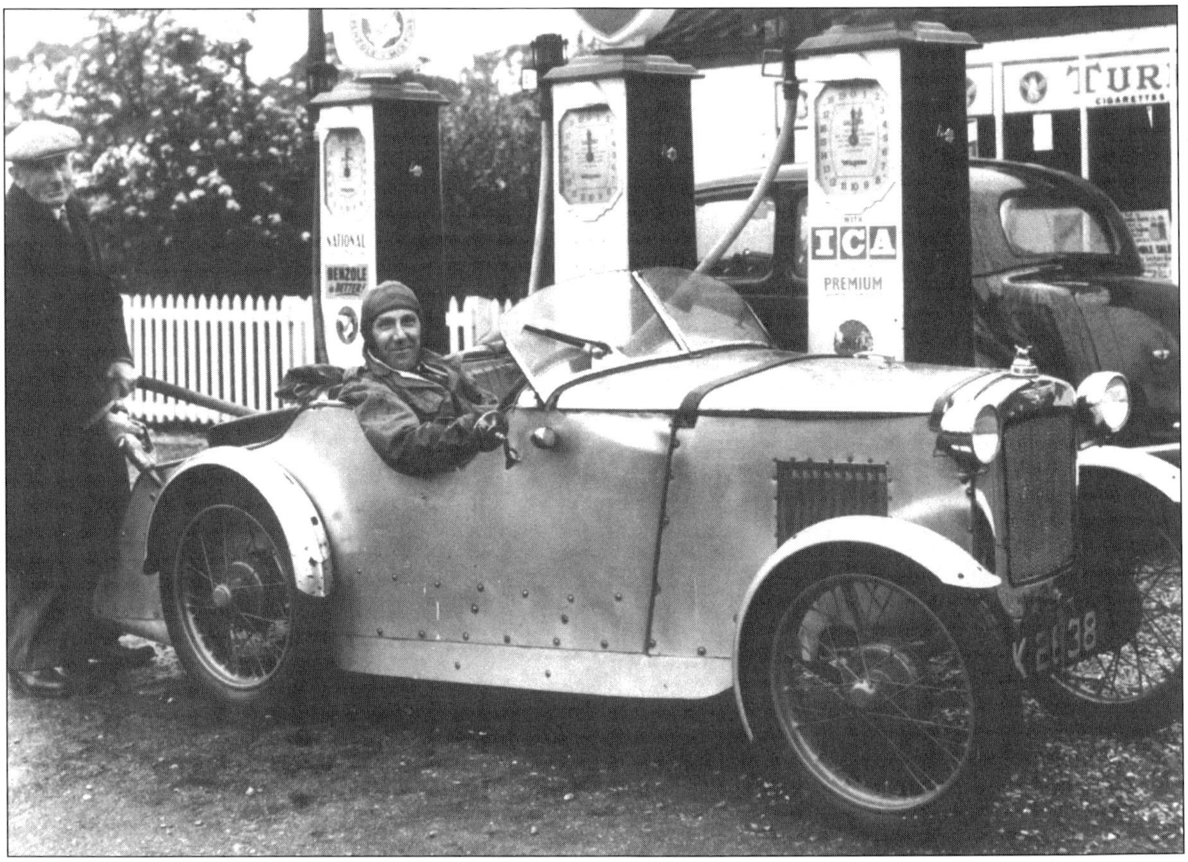

Crane's Corner, 1954. Billy Crane is pictured with Stanley Gathercole in the driving seat of his handmade Austin 7! (From the collection of Mrs Evelyn Gibson, Stanley's daughter. Reproduced by kind permission of the *Eastern Daily Press* and the *Dereham & Fakenham Times*)

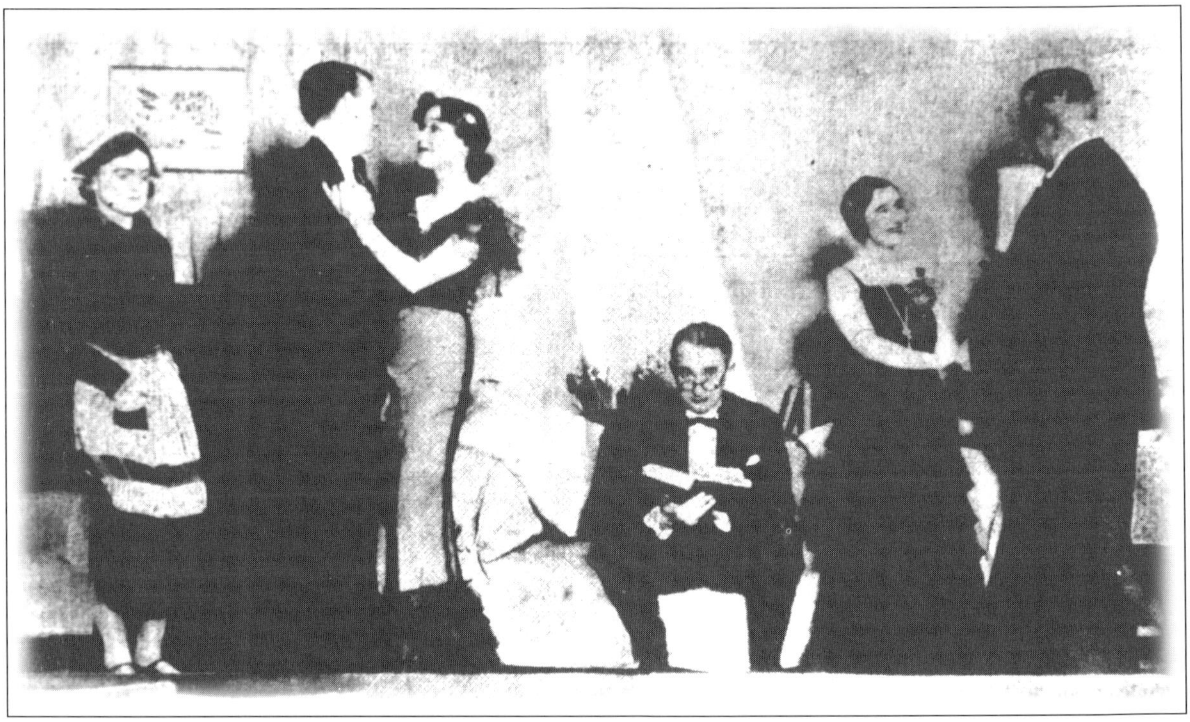

A performance of A.A. Milne's play Belinda *was staged in the lecture room at Sculthorpe during January 1937. Nancy Jones of Cranmer Hall* (third from the left) *starred. The performances helped to raise funds for Nurse Green, the village nurse, and for a new village hall, which was not realised until 1966.*
(Reproduced by kind permission of the *Dereham & Fakenham Times*)

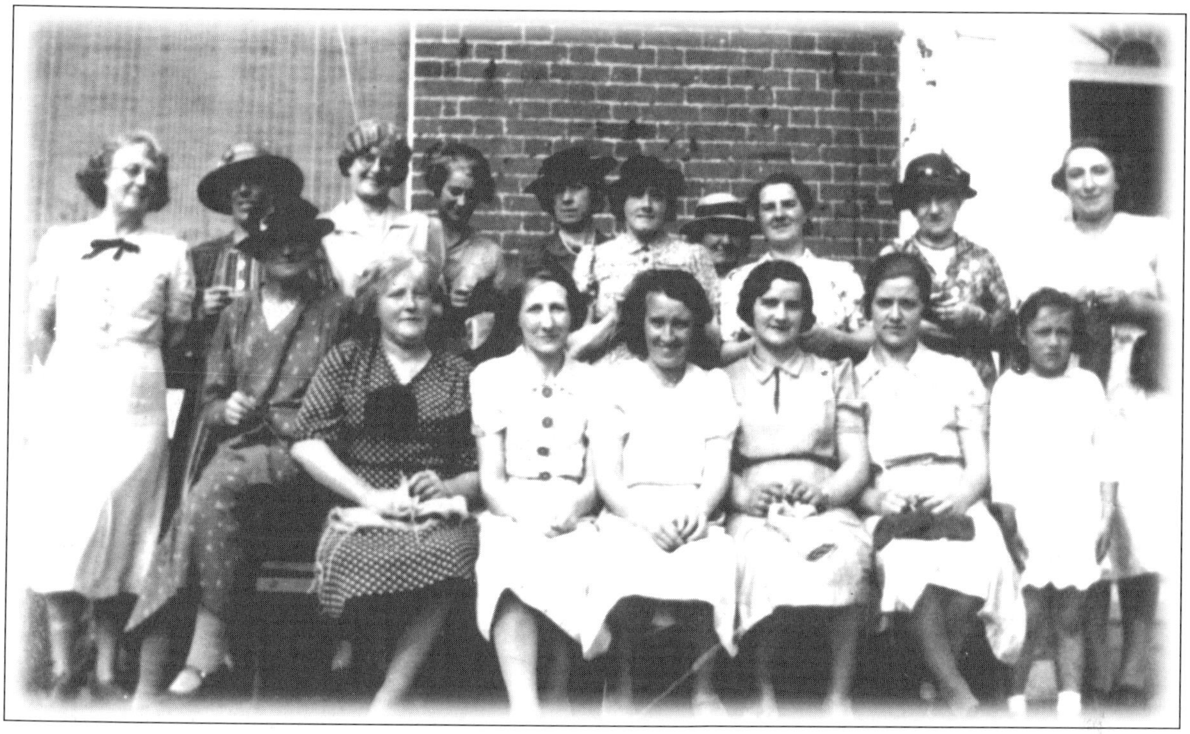

Sculthorpe Women's Institute organised a working party during the summer of 1940, knitting 'comforts' for the troops. This wartime photograph was taken at Manor Farm in Sculthorpe. Left to right, standing: *Miss Sawyer, Mrs Minnie Woodhouse, Mrs Dodman, Mrs Cook, Lady Evelyn Jones, Mrs Ella Williamson, Nanny Fox, Mrs Lowe, Miss Reinhardt (lady's maid), Mrs Rose Applegate;* seated: *Mrs Jessie Lingwood, Mrs Harriet Short, Mrs Hood, Mrs Beets, Mrs Daisy Armiger, Mrs Doris Greeves. The little girl was Mrs Cook's daughter. Mrs Rose Applegate remembered how this little girl was quite unable to pronounce her surname, calling her 'Mrs Appleblossom' instead!* (Reproduced by kind permission of the *Eastern Daily Press* and the *Dereham & Fakenham Times*)

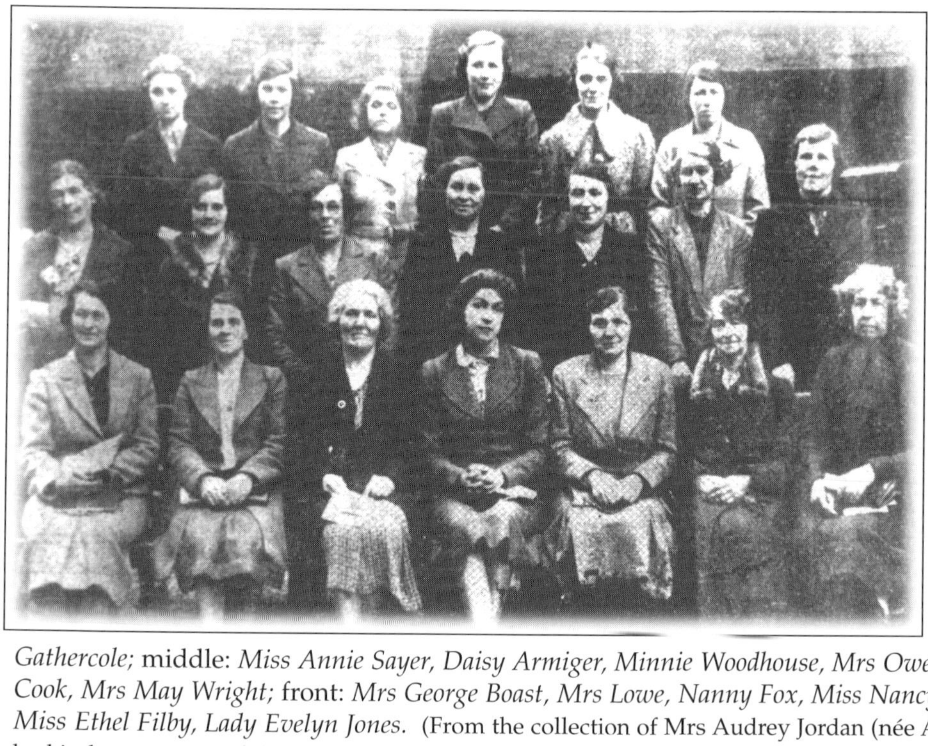

Left: *Sculthorpe Women's Institute Choir, 1939. This society was founded and trained under the talented musical direction of the Hon. Nancy Jones of Cranmer Hall. It competed successfully in numerous choral concerts and musical recitals in St Andrew's Hall, Norwich, and gained distinguished awards.* Left to right, back row: *Phyllis Lowe, Phyllis Wright, Susie Fox, Miss Hood, Joyce Lingwood, Edna Gathercole;* middle: *Miss Annie Sayer, Daisy Armiger, Minnie Woodhouse, Mrs Owen, Mrs Applegate, Mrs Cook, Mrs May Wright;* front: *Mrs George Boast, Mrs Lowe, Nanny Fox, Miss Nancy Jones, Mrs Jarvis, Miss Ethel Filby, Lady Evelyn Jones.* (From the collection of Mrs Audrey Jordan (née Armiger). Reproduced by kind permission of the *Eastern Daily Press* and the *Dereham & Fakenham Times*)

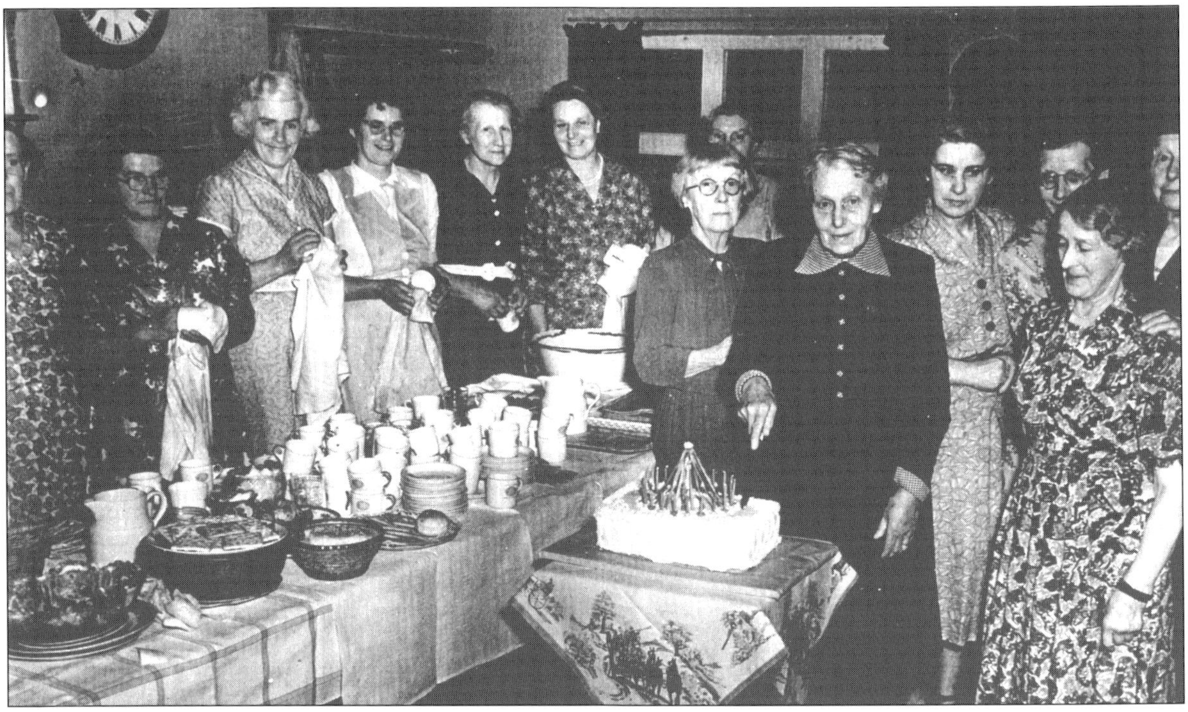

Sculthorpe Women's Institute was launched by Lady Evelyn Jones and the ladies of Sculthorpe during the early 1930s and continued until the early 1960s. This photograph was taken during the early 1950s at a Women's Institute birthday party – Mrs Darby Greeves, the oldest member, cuts the birthday cake. Among those pictured here are: *Mrs Minnie Woodhouse, Mrs Barnes, Mrs George Wright, Mrs Peggy Marshall, Mrs Hood, Mrs Dorrie Pearson, Mrs Mabel Boyce, Miss Sawyer, Mrs Darby Greeves, Mrs Turney, Mrs Cornwall and Miss Ethel Filby.* (From the collection of Mrs Jean Allison. Reproduced by kind permission of the *Dereham & Fakenham Times*)

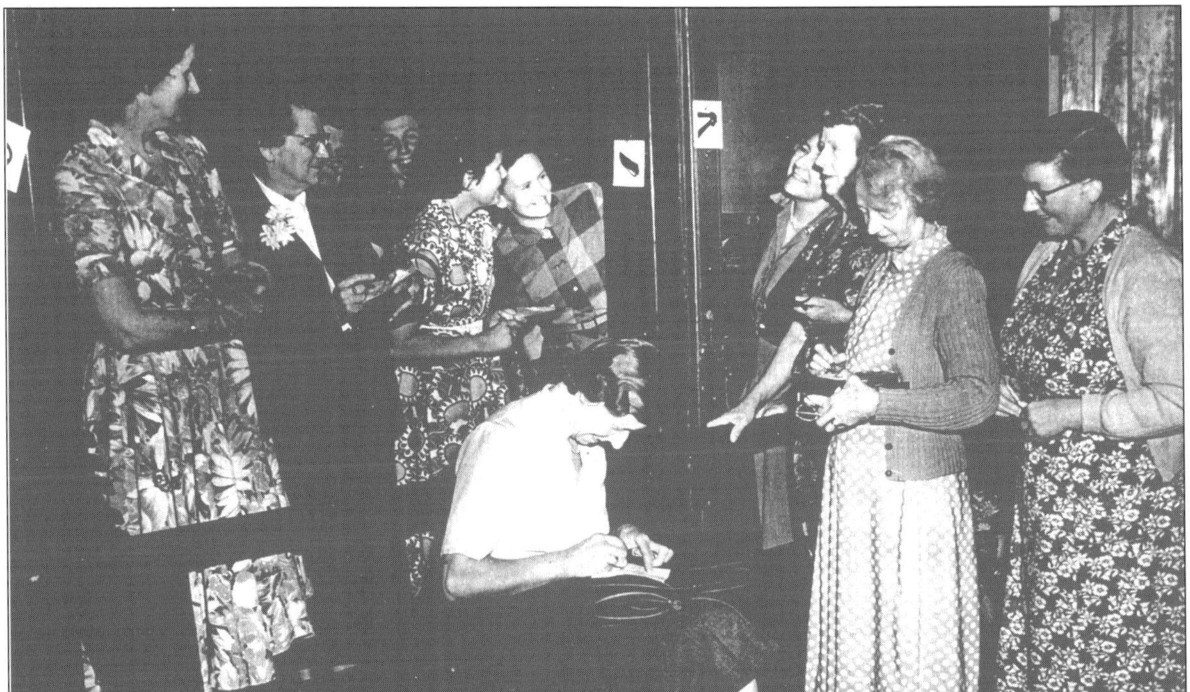

Sculthorpe Women's Institute holding a competition in the reading and lecture room during the 1950s. Second from the left: *Miss Elsie Greeves;* centre: *Jean Allison;* second from the right: *Miss Ethel Filby.* (From the collection of Mrs Jean Allison. Reproduced by kind permission of the *Dereham & Fakenham Times*)

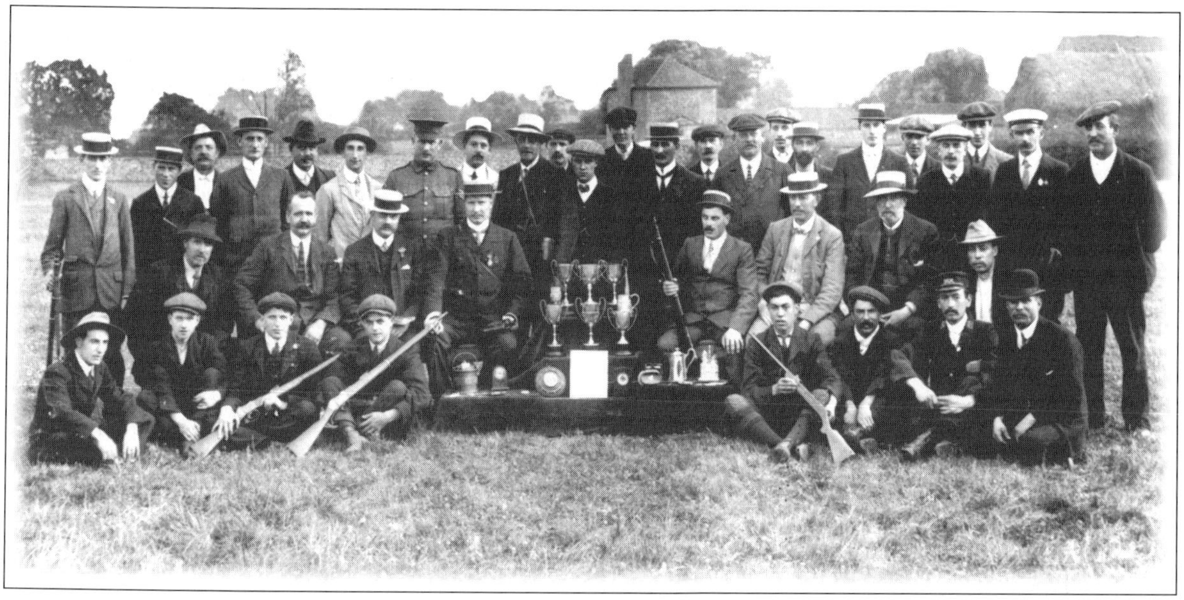

Sculthorpe Rifle Club shoot to mark the coronation of King George V and Queen Mary, 1911. Seated to the left of the trophies is Mr George Grant Lockhart Ross, the tenant of Cranmer Hall and founder president of the Rifle Club. He was an excellent shot but once caused great controversy by shooting a bittern nesting on Sculthorpe Fen. Seated on the right in a straw boater is Mr Ernest Syder, the cattle-dealer from Shrublands in Moor Lane. Next to him, in a large straw hat, is 'Grandpa' Crane. Back row, second from the right: *Billy Crane (chauffeur to Mr Lockhart Ross);* sixth from the right: *Mr Keeble (butler to Mr Lockhart Ross).*
(From the collection of the late Mrs Eleanor Crane. Reproduced by kind permission of Mr Richard Land)

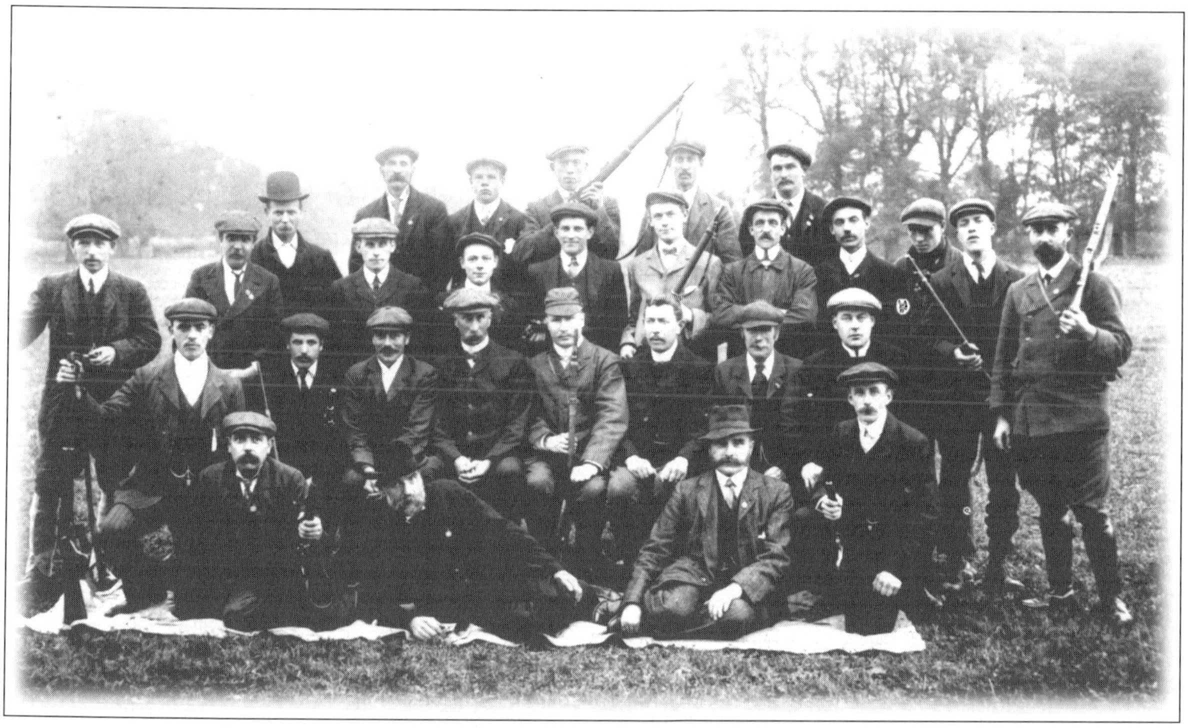

Sculthorpe Rifle Club, c.1914. Mr George Grant Lockhart Ross is seated in the centre. On his left is Dick Harris, tenant of Grange Farm. On the right are Mr Ernest Syder, Ted Owen of Grove Farm and the Revd John Labouchere. In front of the Revd Labouchere is Billy Crane and to the left Mr Short, gamekeeper on the Cranmer Hall estate. Others included in the photograph are: *Charlie Cornwall, 'Dimshy Winn', Jack Lingwood, Mr Schofield, Charles Tuck, Mr Mallom, the Layton brothers, Bob Lingwood and Mr Jarmany.*
(Reproduced by kind permission of Mrs Joyce Lingwood)

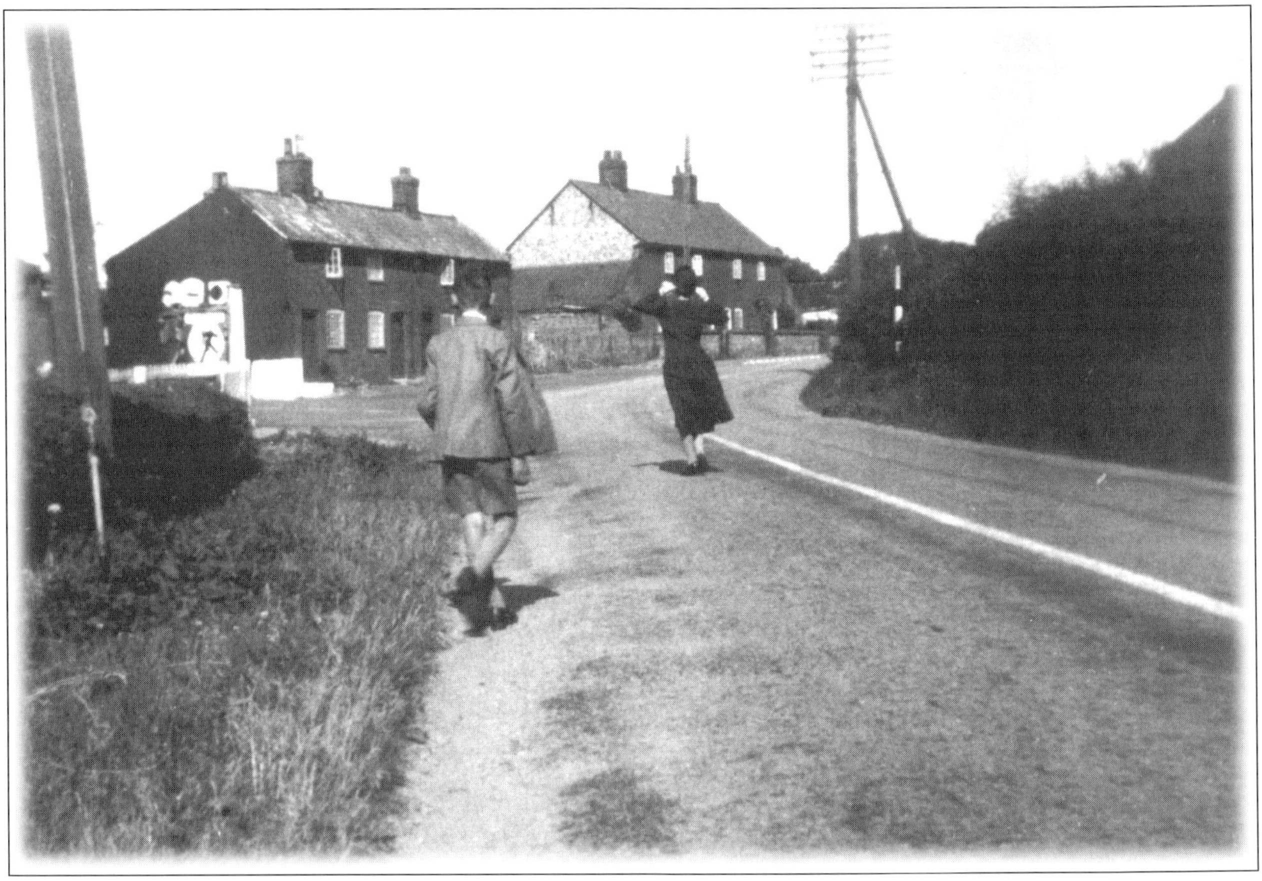

The Street near Rumbelow's Bridge and Crane's Corner during the late 1930s. The people with their backs to the photograph are thought to be Kenneth Boast and his mother, Mrs Winifred Boast.
(Reproduced by kind permission of Mr Kenneth Boast)

blend of tea which we all know and love as Earl Grey.

The Major and Lady Evelyn undertook a substantial refurbishment of Cranmer Hall in 1929, the plaster-barrel ceiling and panelling were removed from the Philip Webb drawing-room and many of the original Georgian features of the house were carefully restored. The Major and Lady Evelyn employed a full compliment of domestic staff – Bertie Hood was the butler, Miss Reinhardt was Lady Evelyn's personal maid and Stanley Gathercole was the chauffeur.

The hall was filled with the sound of chatter and laughter from the Major and Lady Evelyn's young daughters: Nancy, Dinah, Vivien and Lavinia. Nancy and Dinah were the elder sisters, hosting weekend house parties and games of charades. Lady Harrod vividly recalled those 'wonderful parties' when, as a young, vivacious Billa Cresswell, she motored over to Cranmer from her family home at Snettisham Old Hall: 'Nancy was very striking, of course, and Dinah so arresting!' The younger daughters, Vivien and Lavinia, cherish their happy memories from the nursery and the schoolroom, entrusted to the devoted care of their much-loved Nanny Fox and later to the tutelage of their French governess, the lively Mademoiselle Behm.

Lady Evelyn and her daughters took a very great interest in the life and activities of the village. During the early 1930s Lady Evelyn, together with her maid, Miss Reinhardt, and many village ladies including Mrs Eleanor Crane, Mrs Rose Applegate, Mrs Hood, Mrs Jessie Lingwood, Miss Ethel Filby, Mrs Minnie Woodhouse, Mrs Darby Greeves, Mrs Harriet Short and others, established a flourishing branch of the Women's Institute in Sculthorpe. This proved to be tremendously successful and gained an impressive membership roll. Sculthorpe Women's Institute Choir, which was later founded under the talented musical direction of Miss Nancy Jones, enthusiastically participated in many musical concerts and choral festivals at St Andrew's Hall in Norwich. The Institute also formed an amateur dramatic group which saw Norah Armiger, Rose Applegate and Doris Greeves star in such productions as *Farmhouse Teas* and *When Aunt's Away*.

Nancy and Dinah Jones, assisted by their friends from Cambridge, staged a production of A.A. Milne's play *Belinda* in the reading room at Sculthorpe during January 1937 to raise funds for the village nurse, Sister Green, and a new village hall. Nancy Jones, with the Revd Christopher Chitty, cast and directed a wonderful Nativity play in the Parish Church, based upon the Coventry Mystery Play and acted by many people from the village including

Stanley Gathercole as a shepherd and Mrs Gray's daughter from Sculthorpe Mill who wore golden wings and stood up in the pulpit for her role as the Archangel Gabriel.

The gardens at Cranmer Hall were the setting for the annual Women's Institute garden fête, and there were also open days when the public were invited to wander around the rose gardens, the walled kitchen garden and the Victorian greenhouses filled with succulent grapes, peaches and a huge fig tree. The children from the village attended their annual sport's day on the lawn in front of the hall with a tug-of-war, a greasy pole, pillow-fights, an egg-and-spoon race and relays – prizes were given and a splendid tea served. At Christmas the children returned for a magical party at which presents were distributed around the decorated Christmas tree standing in the entrance hall.

During the summer of 1938, with Hitler's annexation of Austria increasing the threat of war, the Major and Lady Evelyn received Her Majesty Queen Mary for afternoon tea at Cranmer Hall. There was tremendous excitement in the house as the royal Daimler swept up the Avenue along the drive, the Jones girls were all terribly nervous at the prospect of being presented to the regal Queen-Dowager. A number of Austrian Jews, refugees rescued by Lady Evelyn's efforts from Hitler's advance into their homeland, were staying at Cranmer Hall and were rather amused and surprised at the chaotic preparations being made to receive and entertain the important royal visitor. During the tea party a stray wasp from the garden flew into the drawing-room and proceeded to pester Queen Mary. Bertie Hood, the butler, instantly stepped into the fray and unflinchingly killed the wasp with a sharp clap of his hands. The offending corpse was removed from the royal coat with the aid of a tea napkin – Queen Mary was delighted!

The Second World War saw vast changes in Sculthorpe. Lady Evelyn organised the Women's Institute into working parties, producing woollen comforts for the troops and, as a Red Cross Commandant, supervised the conversion of part of Cranmer Hall into a Red Cross convalescent hospital for wounded servicemen which was fully staffed by Red Cross nursing sisters under the eagle eye of Matron Alexander. The Major was the local Home Guard commander and the hall served as the company HQ. There were dances and theatricals staged by the Women's Institute at the hall and in the village lecture room to entertain the troops.

Cranmer Hall narrowly escaped damage when an unexploded German bomb fell in the park in 1940. This was located by Susie Fox and Jack Lingwood and the bomb-disposal unit were summoned to the scene.

In November 1941 Nancy Jones married Dr David Morse at Sculthorpe Church, the Revd Christopher Chitty and the bridegroom's brother, the Revd Hilary Morse, conducting the ceremony. The whole village turned out to see Billy Crane driving the bride to church in his wedding car. Due to rationing and wartime austerity, the bridal dress of brocade had been created by Miss Reinhardt, Lady Evelyn's personal maid, from material inherited from the bridal trousseau of Lady Evelyn's mother, Alice, Countess Grey of Howick. During 1942 Vivien Jones married Simon Asquith, grandson of the Liberal Prime Minister and the inspiration for several plays penned by J.M. Barrie, the author of *Peter Pan*. The happiness generated by these joyful family weddings was sadly clouded by the tragic death of Dinah Jones on Christmas Day in December 1942.

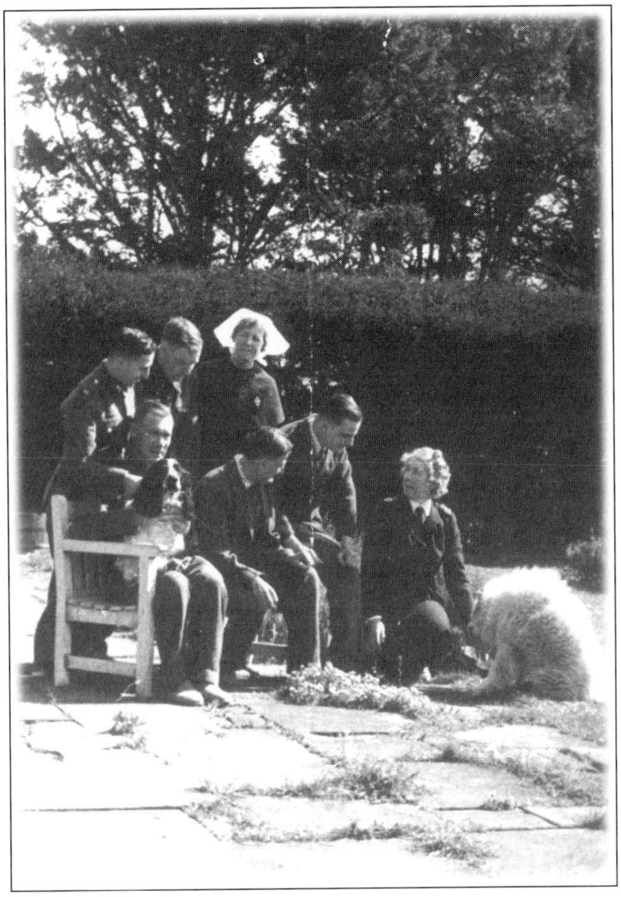

Lady Evelyn Jones, Matron Alexander and patients at the Red Cross hospital, c.1942. The dog was called Pushkin. (From the collection of the late Hon. Nancy Morse. Reproduced by the kind permission of Mrs Vivien Asquith and Mrs Lavinia Monaco)

Some 200 years of family history ended in 1946 when the Major and Lady Evelyn Jones left Cranmer Hall and the house was put up for sale. Much of the outlying estate had already been sold to sitting tenants and individual cottages in the village were purchased for the price they had originally cost to build. The hall was bought by a farmer, Mr W.J.T. Crossman. In 1947, amidst considerable controversy and opposition from both the Georgian Group and the Local and County Councils, plans

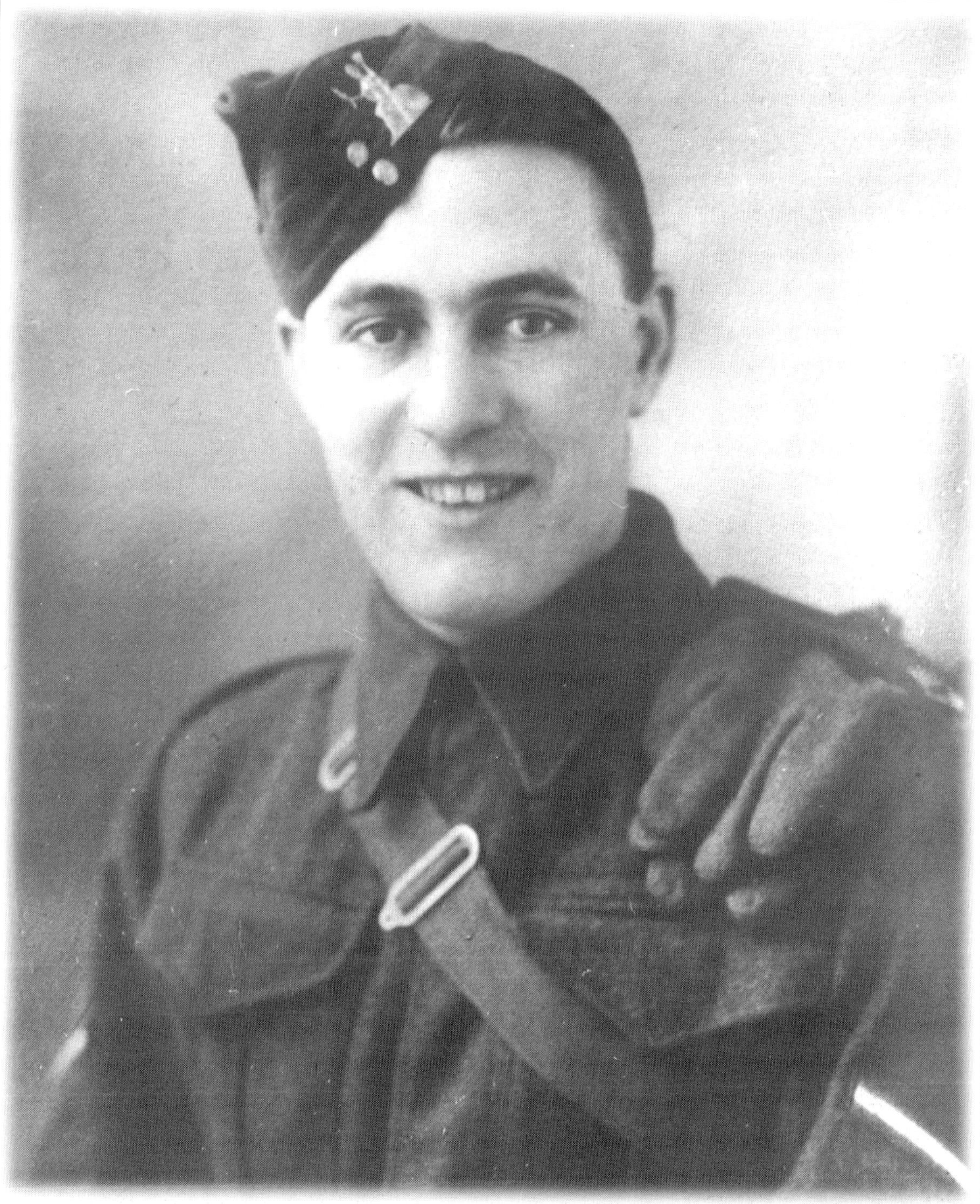

Lance Corporal Leslie Lingwood of the Royal Norfolks was captured by the Germans at St-Valery in the summer of 1940 following the Dunkirk episode. He recalled the long march through Northern France, Belgium and Holland, including three days without food, and the voyage down the Rhine on a barge into Germany. Here the men were herded onto a cattle train and then subjected to a further march into Poland and the privations of a series of German prison camps. In May 1945 the men were liberated and Leslie's return flight from Lubeck was on a Lancaster bomber, flying low over the bombarded cities of Hamburg and Arnhem, immortalised in the film A Bridge Too Far. *The Revd Claude Cotter, rector of Sculthorpe, wanted Leslie to publish his memories as a prisoner of war in German camps but Leslie always felt this to be far too painful to recount.* (Reproduced by kind permission of Mrs Joyce Lingwood)

were submitted for substantial alterations to be made to the house, which included the proposed removal of the top storey and conversion into three individual houses. In May 1948 a fire badly damaged the top storey and the roof of the house, the fire service successfully contained the blaze and the rest of the house was saved from serious damage.

By the 1950s the hall had lost both its top storey and the 1875 clock tower. The north wing, dating from 1853, had also been demolished. The walled kitchen garden and the greenhouses were derelict and most of the beautiful trees in the Avenue and former parkland setting had been cut down. Part of the hall was let as flats for United States Air Force personnel based at nearby RAF Sculthorpe. When John and Louise Hurst purchased the hall in 1965 it was fast becoming a derelict building.

The Hursts immediately set about restoring the house and successfully recaptured much of its former glory. In 1971 they sold the hall to Mr Seymour Collins, a London solicitor who subsequently sold the house in 1976 to Dr and Mrs Edward de Bono.

Dr Edward de Bono, the distinguished philosopher, prolific author and pioneer of the concept of lateral thinking, continued with the restoration of Cranmer Hall and re-established its prestige as a country residence and family home. Much of this development was achieved due to the artistic talents of his wife, Josephine de Bono, an art historian who drew upon the expertise of both the National Trust and the Victoria and Albert Museum in the furnishing and décor of the principal apartments.

The Jones family have maintained strong links with the village of Sculthorpe and, despite the end of the Cranmer Hall estate, have retained the titular lordship of the manor. In the event of the death of Sir Lawrence John Jones in 1954 his son inherited the title as Sir Lawrence Evelyn Jones, 5th Baronet. His memories of life at Cranmer Hall are related in his autobiographical memoirs *A Victorian Boyhood* and *Georgian Afternoon*, published during the 1950s. At his death in 1969 the family baronetcy passed to his nephew, Sir Christopher Lawrence Jones, 6th Baronet, who still receives a traditional peppercorn rent for the use of Fakenham market square. Lady Evelyn Jones and her daughters, the Hon. Nancy Morse, Vivien Asquith and Lavinia Monaco, maintained old friendships and links with the parish.

At the time of writing, magnificently restored, surrounded by new plantations of trees and steeped in rural history, Cranmer Hall has re-emerged as an important country house.

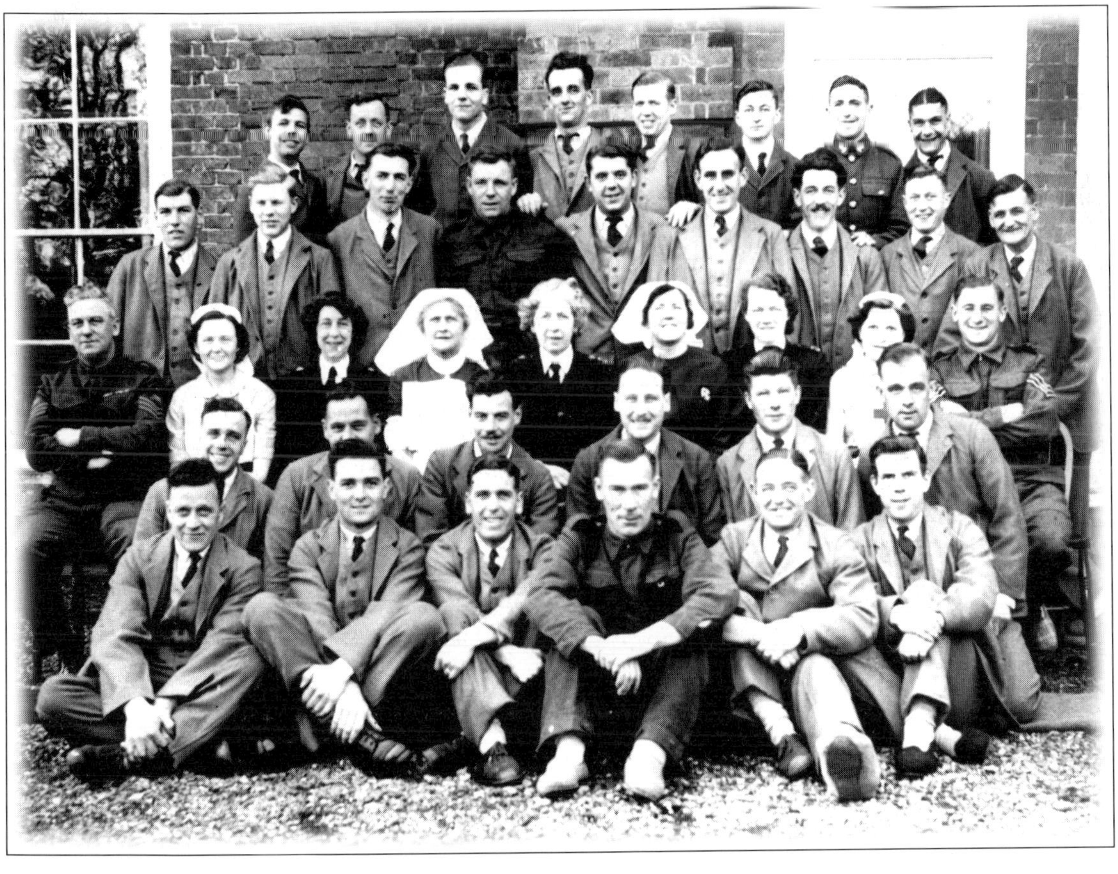

During the Second World War Cranmer Hall became a Red Cross convalescent hospital. Lady Evelyn Jones was Red Cross Commandant. She is pictured here, in 1942, with her daughters, Nancy and Dinah Jones, Matron Alexander, Red Cross nursing sisters and many of the patients who had been wounded in action during the early stages of the war. (From the collection of the late Hon. Nancy Morse. Reproduced by kind permission of Mrs Vivien Asquith and Mrs Lavinia Monaco)

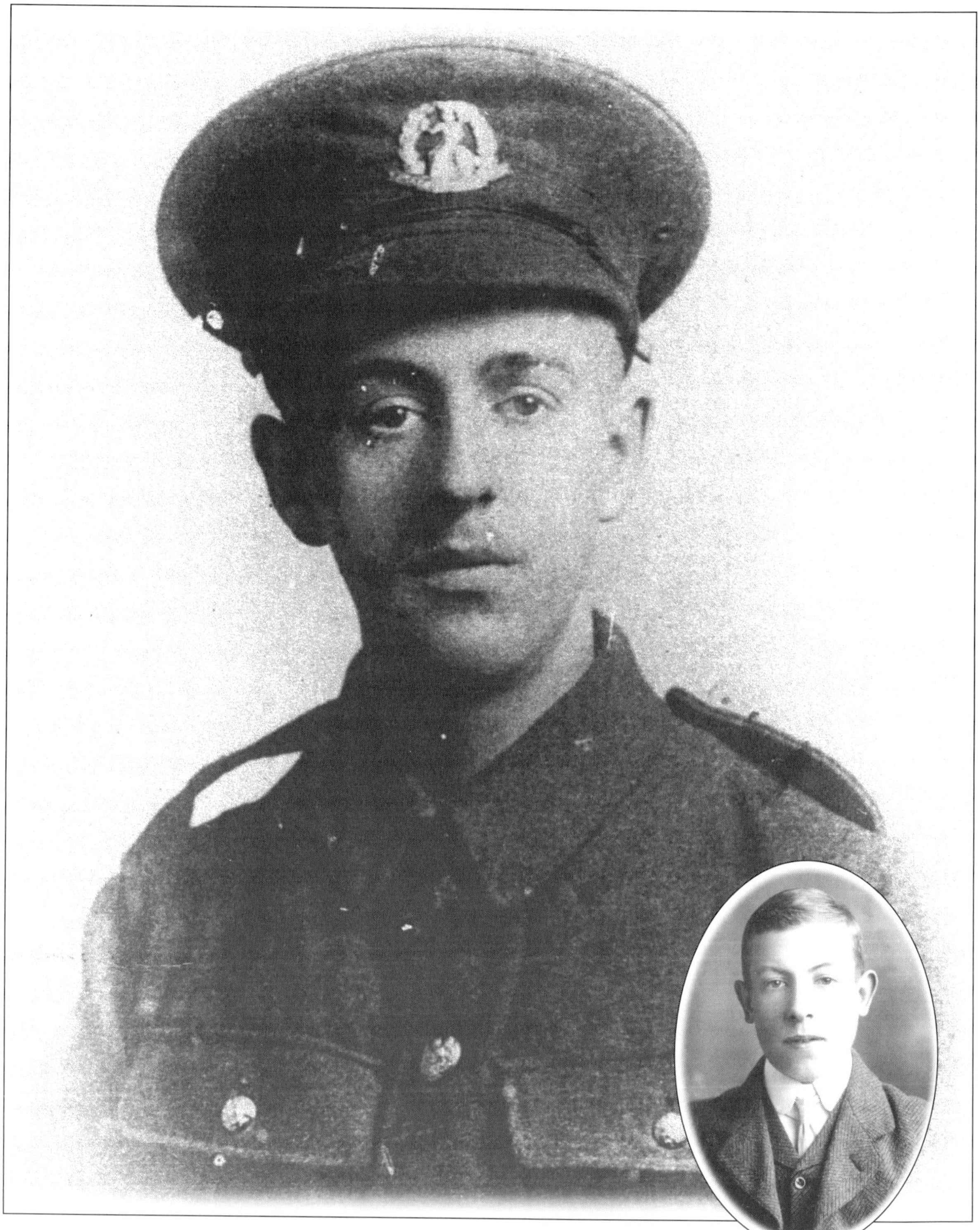

Above: *Private Wilfred Rutland of the Royal Norfolk Regiment who was tragically killed on active service in France during the First World War. His name appears with others on the war memorial in the church porch which was dedicated by the Revd John Labouchere and unveiled by Sir Lawrence John Jones, lord of the manor of Sculthorpe, in 1920.* (Copyright: Norfolk County Council Library and Information Service)

Inset: *John Woodhouse (1897–1967) was the younger brother of Eleanor and Marion Woodhouse. He lost an arm during the First World War.* (Reproduced by kind permission of Mr Richard Land)

RAF Sculthorpe

Much has been written and recorded about RAF Sculthorpe, once home to the United States Air Force and known as Little America in this part of Norfolk. Strictly speaking the base is beyond the parish boundaries of the village, situated on what was once Hall's Patch, Dunton, Brazen Hall Farmhouse and land which was formerly part of the Pinkney Hall estate in nearby Tattersett, but its influence, particularly during the 1940s and '50s, was enormous. In December 1954 Anthony Brown of the *Daily Mail* ran a front-page spread about the 'Atom Bomb Village' and Billy Pointer, chairman of Sculthorpe Parish Council, Eric Williamson of Home Farm at Cranmer, Constance Catlin, headmistress of Sculthorpe School, and Fred Woods, landlord of the Horse & Groom public house, were all interviewed about their personal reactions to living in the shadow of RAF Sculthorpe. The Silver Pheasant, presented by the people of Norfolk to the 47th Air Bombardment Wing based at RAF Sculthorpe for their heroic rescue work during the east-coast floods in 1953, was later presented to the USAF memorial library within the central library at Bethel Street in Norwich. This library was destroyed during a disastrous fire in August 1994 and a splendid new Silver Pheasant can now be seen in a glass showcase within the new American memorial library, part of the Norfolk and Norwich Millennium Library.

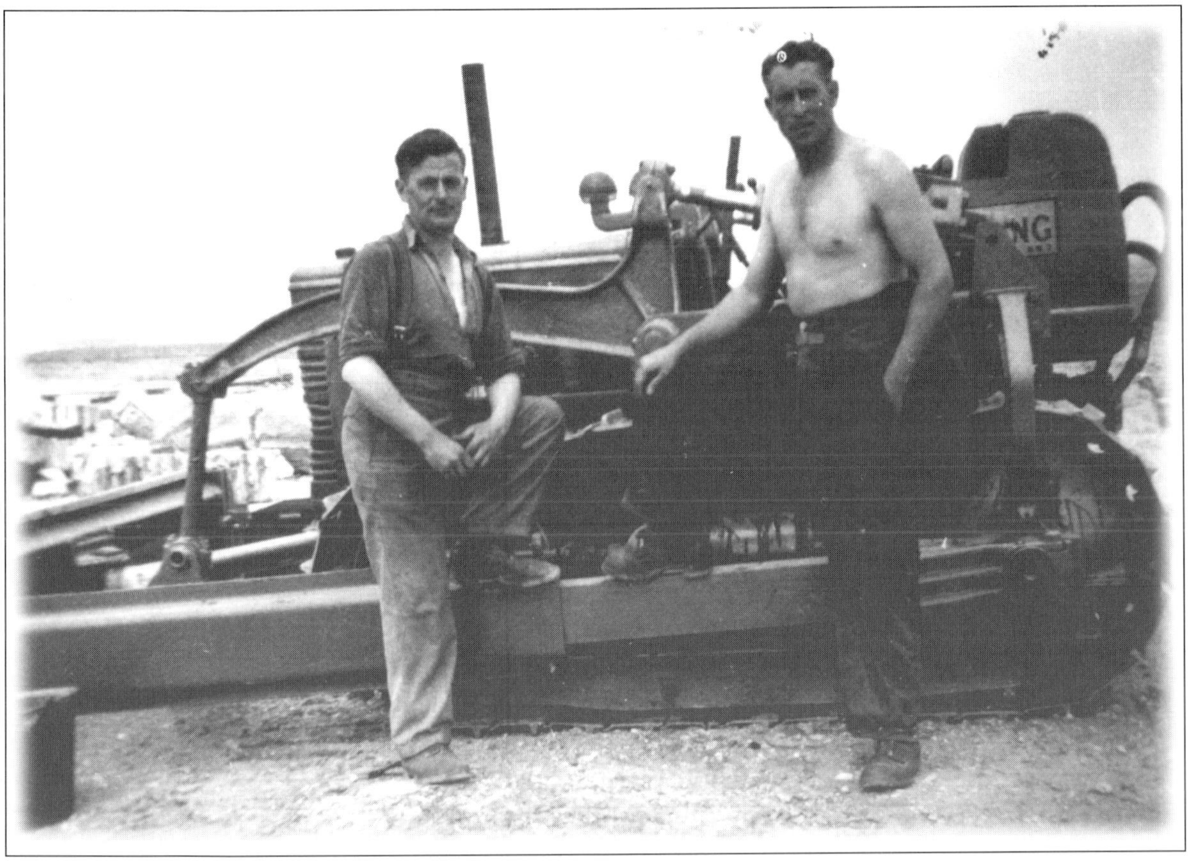

Extending the runway, 1945. This photograph shows employees of John Lang & Sons, building contractors. On the right is Mr Geoffrey Minns who came from Pulham St Mary in South Norfolk and had worked at Manston aerodrome in Kent. He lodged in Sculthorpe during his time at the base in the mid 1940s.
(Reproduced by kind permission of Mrs Gwen Windeler (née Lingwood))

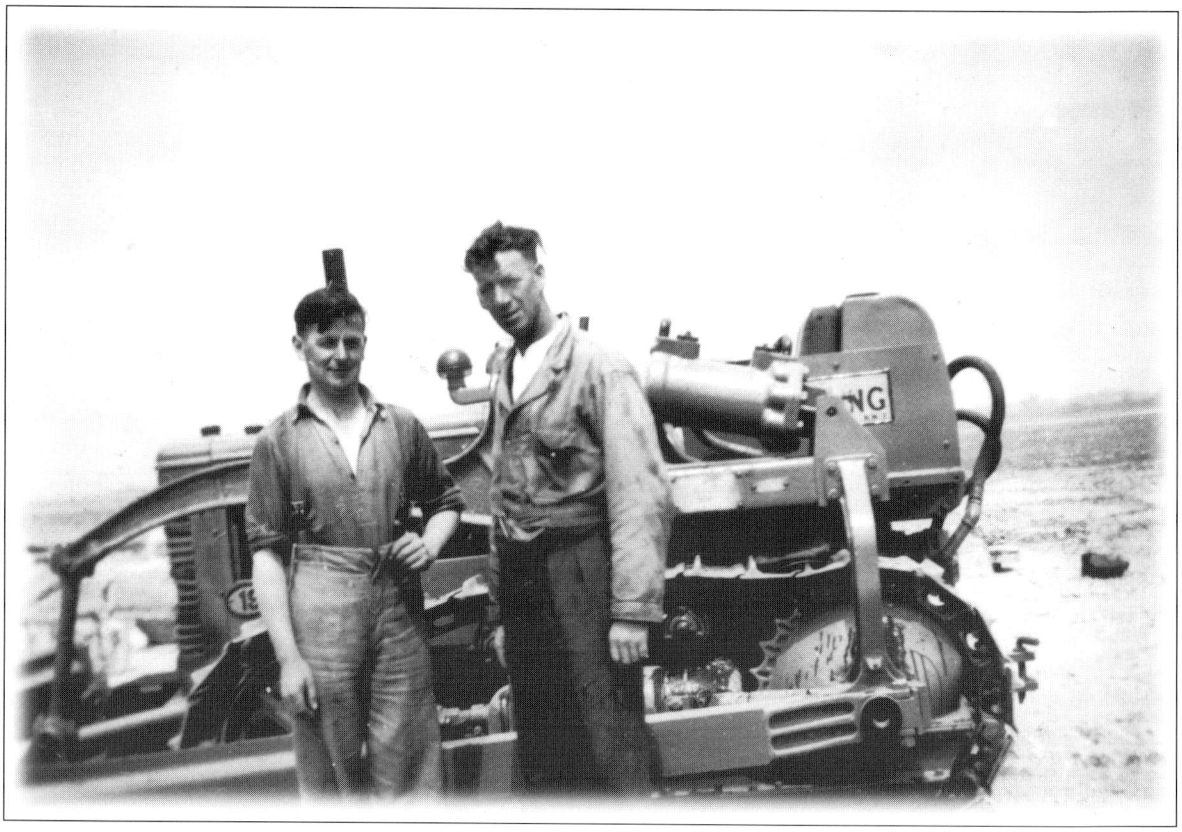

Extending the runway at RAF Sculthorpe, 1945. Employees of John Lang & Sons, building contractors. (Reproduced by kind permission of Mrs Gwen Windeler (née Lingwood))

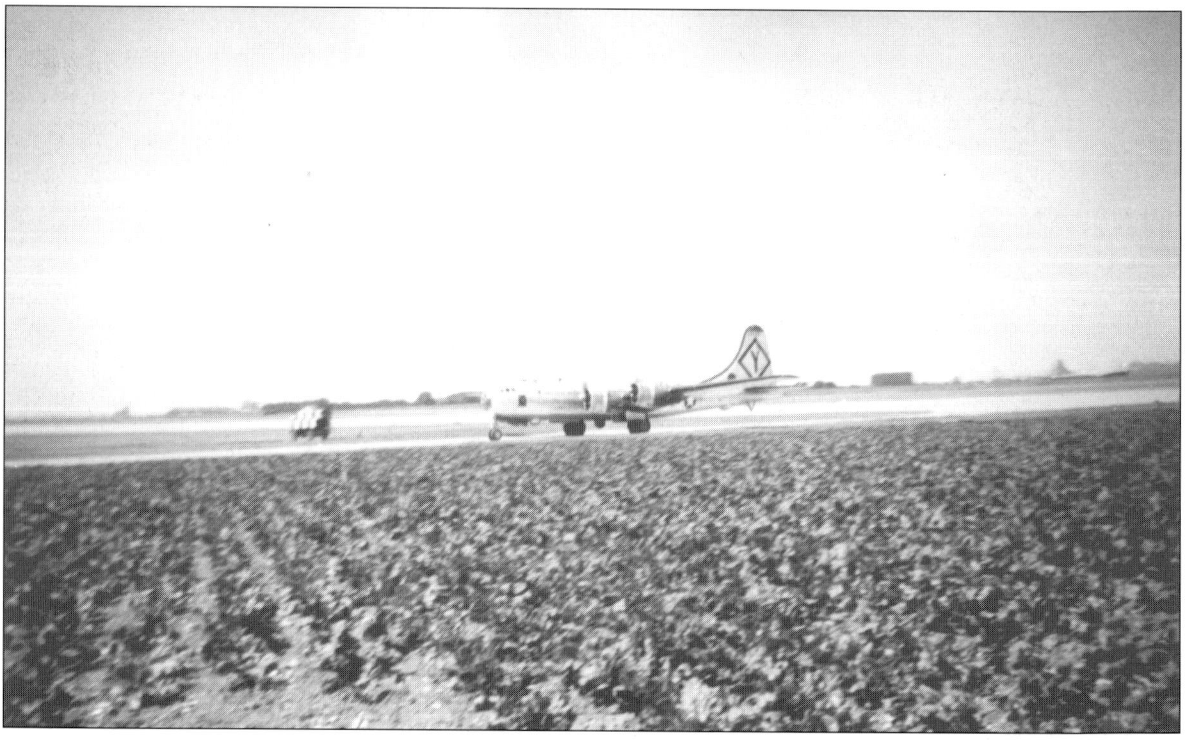

This photograph, taken during the early 1950s by an amateur photographer, shows a field of Norfolk sugar beet next to the famous runway of RAF Sculthorpe. On the horizon aircraft hangars and the VHB control tower are visible. (Reproduced by kind permission of Mr Bob Hood)

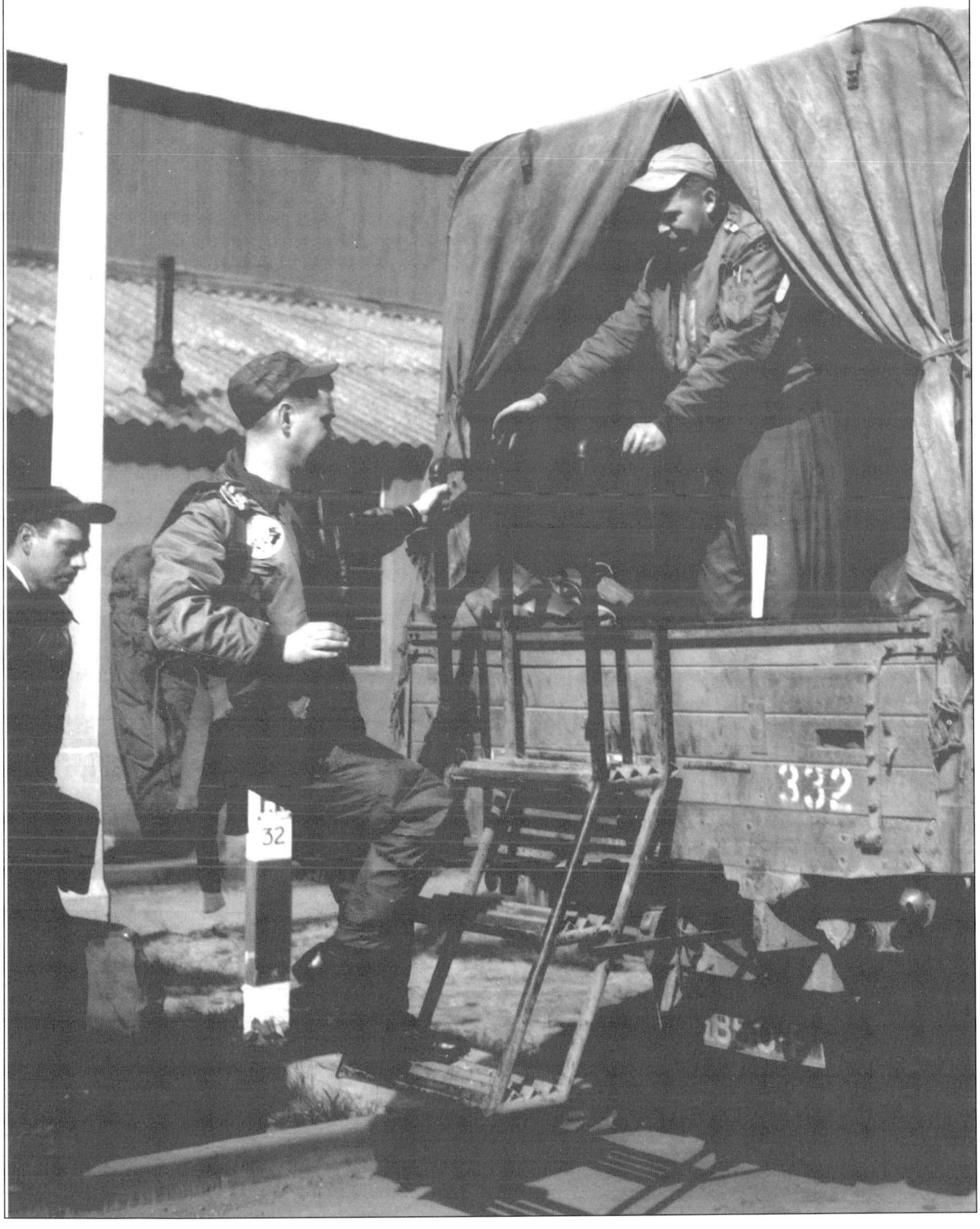

United States Air Force personnel at RAF Sculthorpe, early 1950s.
(Reproduced by kind permission of the *Eastern Daily Press*, Archant Norfolk Ltd)

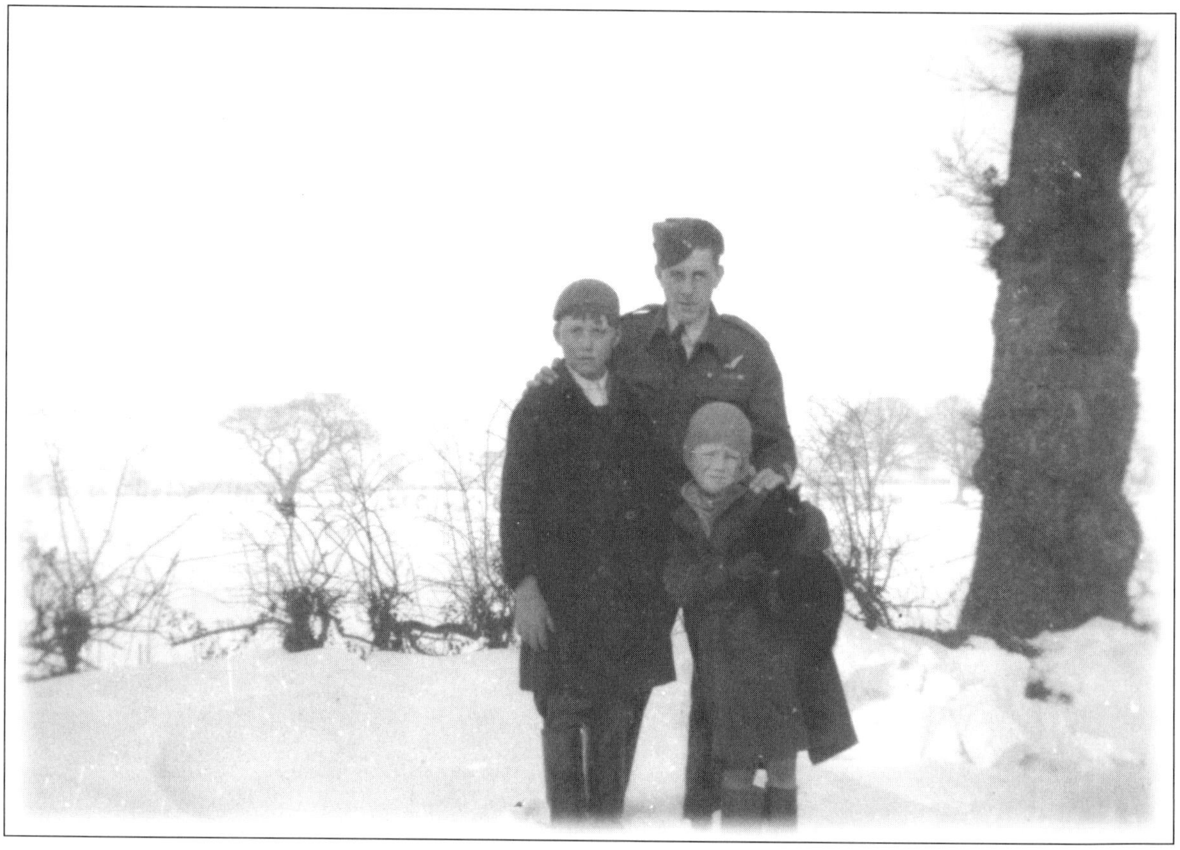

RAF warrant officer Ronnie Lingwood had just returned from flying with Liberators in Burma and must have found the heavy snows of 1947 a raw shock! Here he is pictured with his nephew, John Greeves, and Brian Groom in the snowdrifts at Cranmer. (Reproduced by kind permission of Mrs Gwen Windeler (née Lingwood))

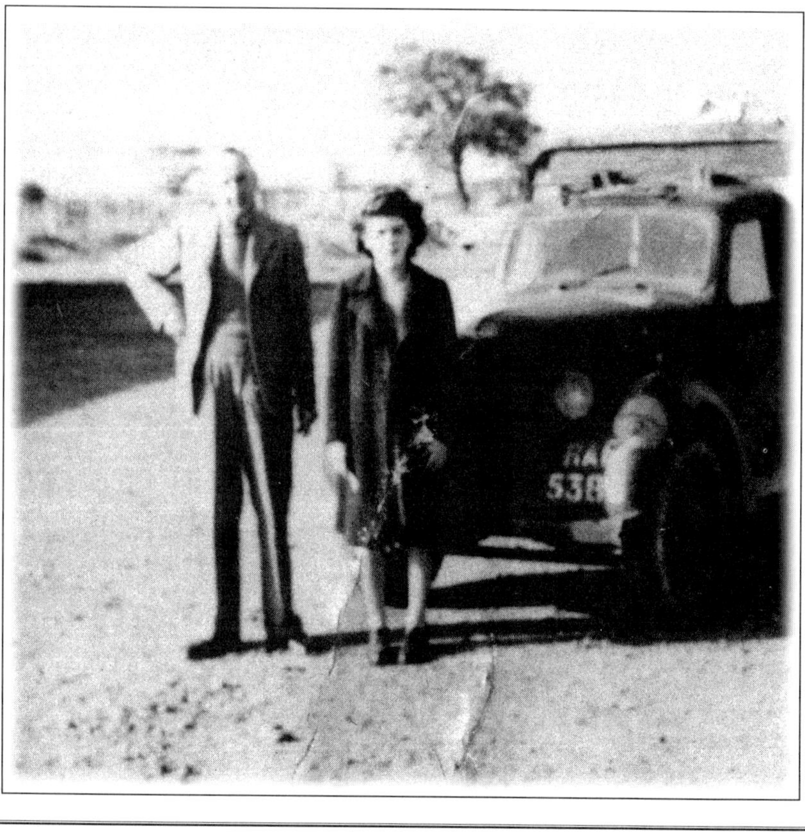

Left: *RAF Sculthorpe in the summer of 1945. Mr Parrish from Heacham, office clerk for the Air Ministry Works Directorate, with Miss Gwen Lingwood, junior typist. The VHB control tower was being built at this time by John Lang & Sons, building contractors, and the runway was also extended.* (From the collection of Mrs Gwen Windeler (née Lingwood))

Winter 1947

The harsh winter of 1947 is still vividly remembered by many in Sculthorpe. The heavy snowdrifts physically cut off the village from outside contact for three days. Roads were inaccessible and people were forced to walk across the fields to outlying farms and into Fakenham to collect provisions. In these photographs attempts are being made to clear the New Road of 1829 near Cranmer Park.

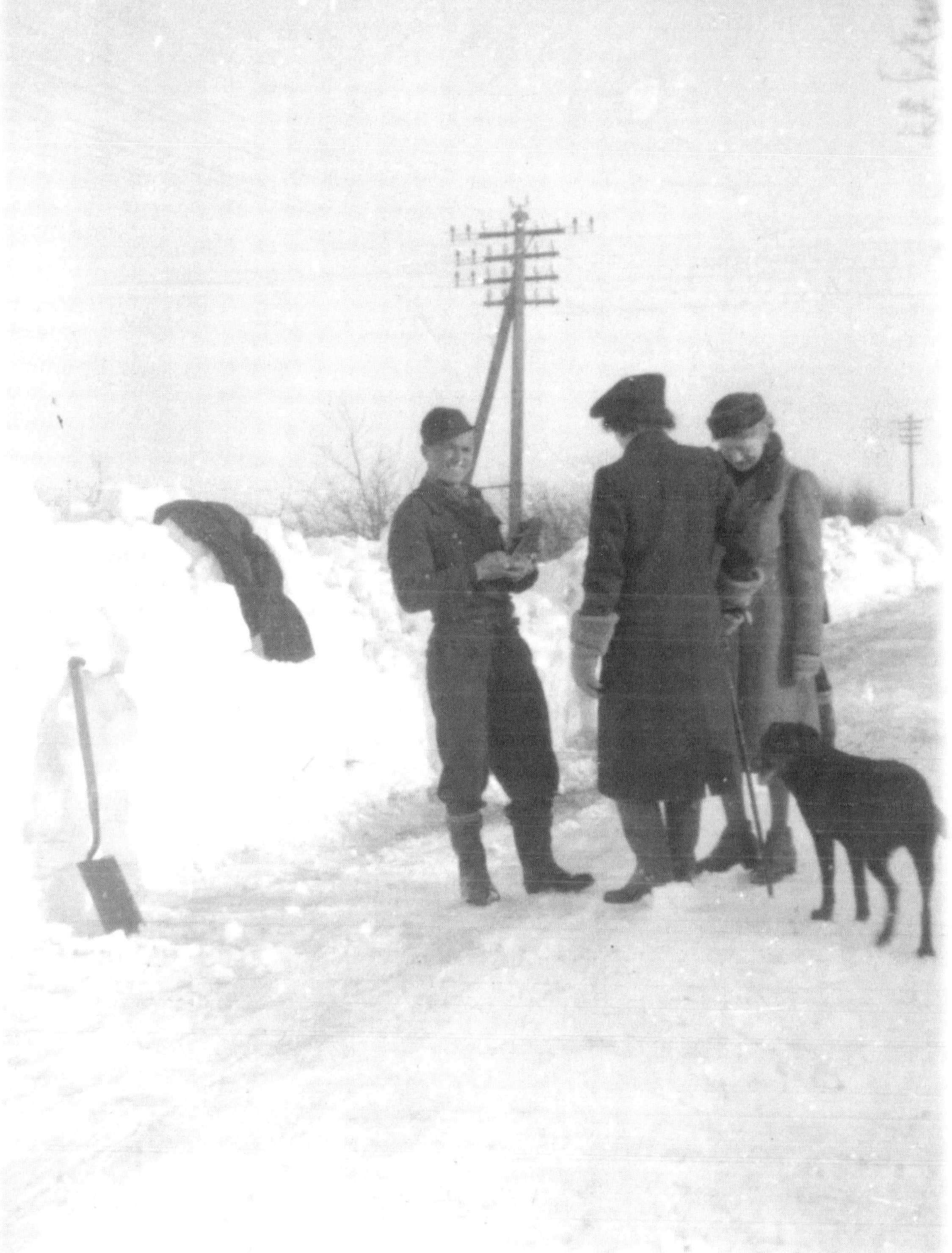

Arthur Lingwood, Agnes Lingwood and Mrs Kathleen Keith from West Barsham Hall on the New Road near Cranmer Hall during the heavy snowdrifts in 1947.

A LETTER FROM THE RECTOR.

SCULTHORPE RECTORY.

EASTER 1947.

My dear friends,

Only old folk like myself can remember such a winter as we have had this year happening before and I very much doubt if anyone can really remember one so bad.

I am afraid that some of you have been very cold through lack of firing and proper food, and I know it has been very trying for those who were ill.

I know also what a blow it has been to the farmers and all who work on the land, a blow from which it will take a long time to recover.

Coming on top of bad weather in the harvest and in autumn, they have had a very hard time and deserve all the sympathy we can extend to them.

Church life has been difficult too, as the roads were too bad to ask people to come out for more than one service a Sunday let alone on weekdays, and it has hampered us in every way.

Dunton has been in the worst plight of all, cut off from the outer world by huge snow-drifts as it was, and we have not been able to get up to them to try and cheer them up.

Here I should like to say a word of thanks to the tradesmen, bakers, milkmen, postmen and others, who, in spite of all the obstacles they had to meet, kept us supplied with the necessities of life, and letters, papers, etc.

The way which neighbours helped each other, too, was beyond praise, but I have always felt that Sculthorpe and Dunton were two of the most neighbourly places I have ever known in my long life.

Some old folk whom we can ill spare have died during this time and we should like to assure their relatives that we feel for them very much in their sad loss.

Fortunately there has been only one serious accident due to the frost, but we are glad to say that he, Raymond Jolliffe, is making a good recovery.

Now we can all start afresh.

Easter speaks of new life and new beginnings, and should find us ready to begin again.

I trust that we shall all try to come to church on Easter Sunday.

The services will be :—

SCULTHORPE. Holy Communion at 8-30 and noon.
Morning prayer at 11 a.m.
Evening prayer at 6-30 p.m.

DUNTON. Service at 3-30 p.m.

I need hardly remind you that the Prayer Book says that every confirmed person should come to Communion on Easter Day so I am sure that we shall all be there.

I have been very struck on each of the three Easters I have been here by the number of people at the 8-30 service, it has been quite remarkable and we hope it may be so this year.

Dunton folk will make a special effort too I know.

They are so friendly to me that I have been sometimes disappointed when I hoped to find them in church, but I am certain I shall not be disappointed this year.

One ***great event.***

On Easter Sunday at 6-30 p.m. a band of twenty German prisoners are coming to sing their special music to us. They love singing and we shall be very glad to welcome them. Their Padre will give a short address, first in English, then translated into German.

Let us come to hear them.

God bless you all in your homes and in your work.

Yours very sincerely,

C. R. Cotter, Rector.

Left: *A parish letter from the Revd C.R. Cotter, rector of Sculthorpe, in which he mentions the harsh winter of 1947.*

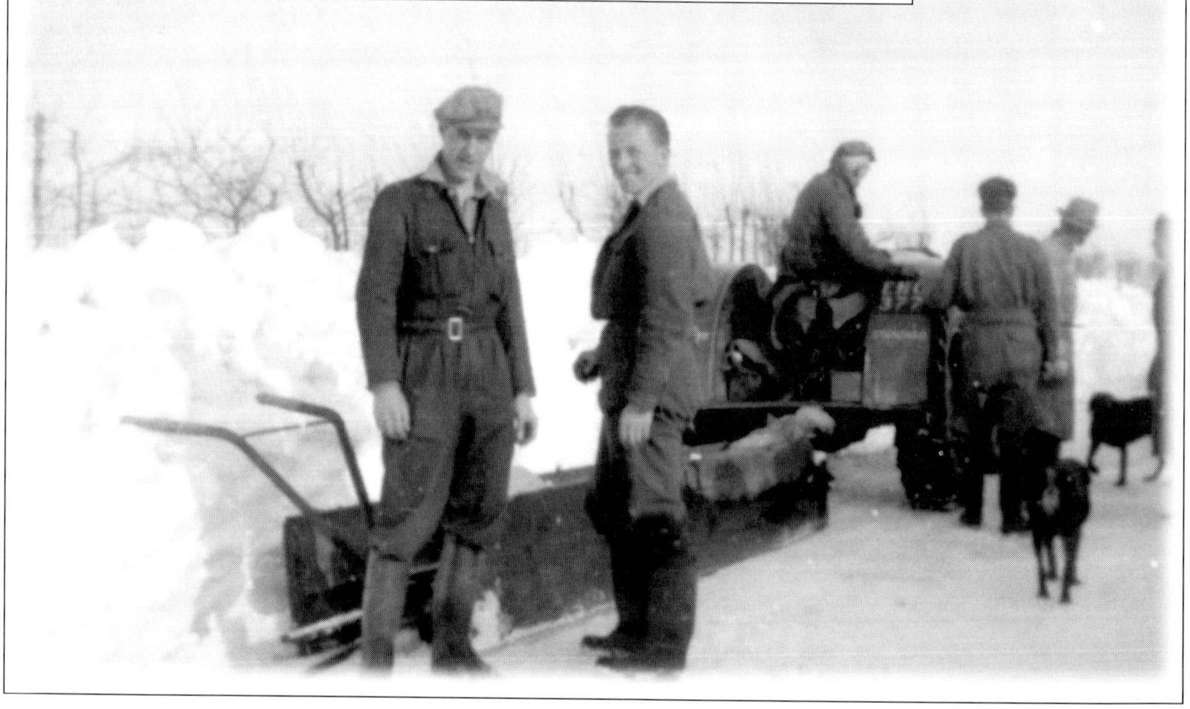

Below: *Winter, 1947.* Left to right: *Leslie Lingwood, Arthur Lingwood, Walter Clarke* (in the background)*, Jack Lingwood, Mrs Kathleen Keith of West Barsham Hall* (just visible). (Reproduced by kind permission of Mrs Gwen Windeler (née Lingwood))

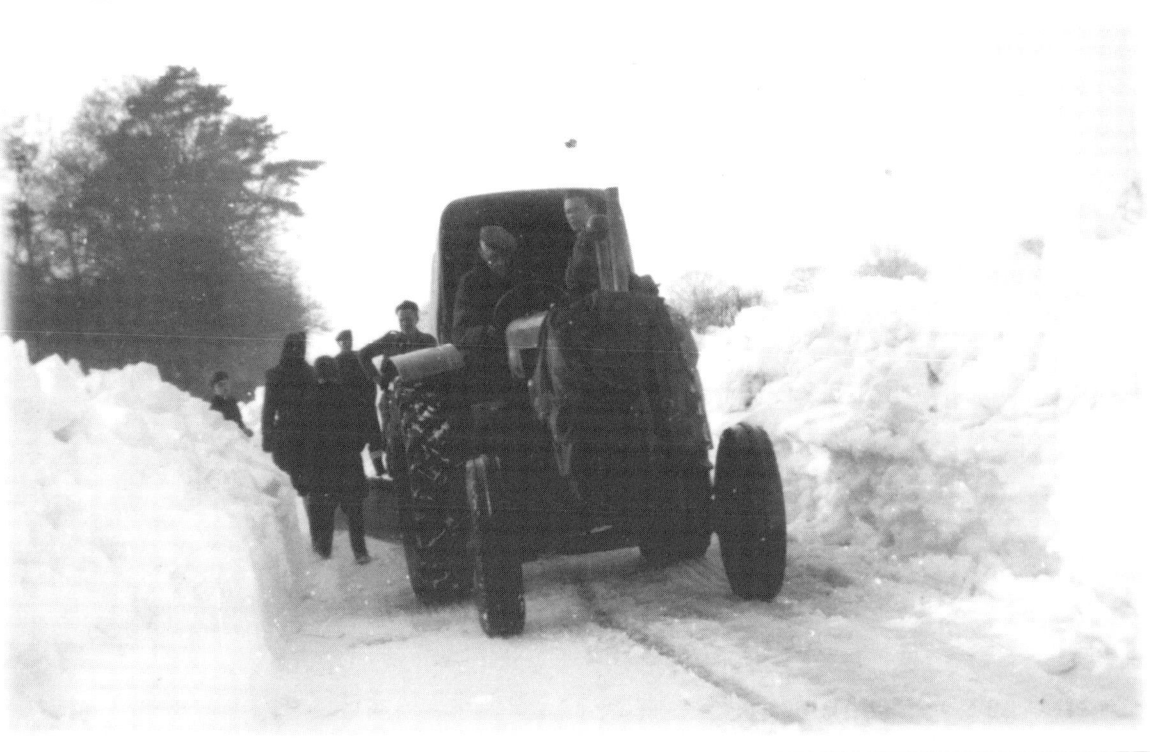

The New Road at Cranmer in the winter of 1947.

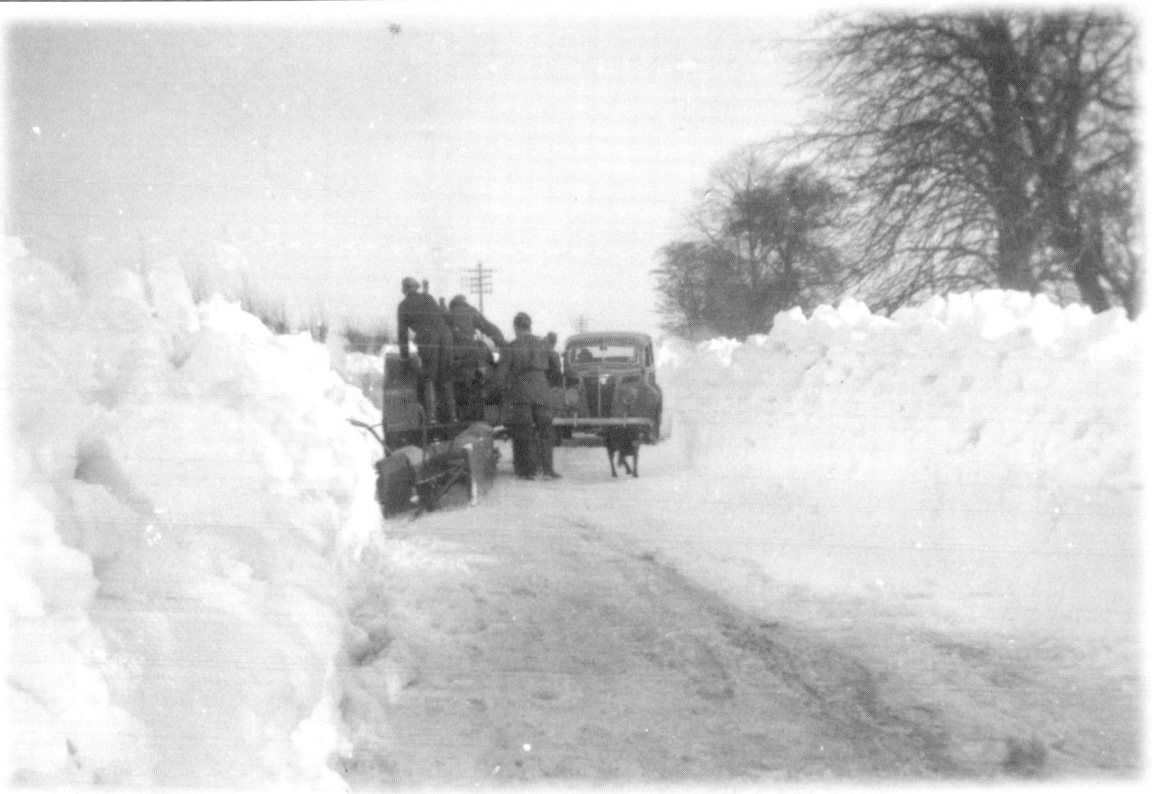

Clearing the snow from the New Road at Cranmer in the winter of 1947.

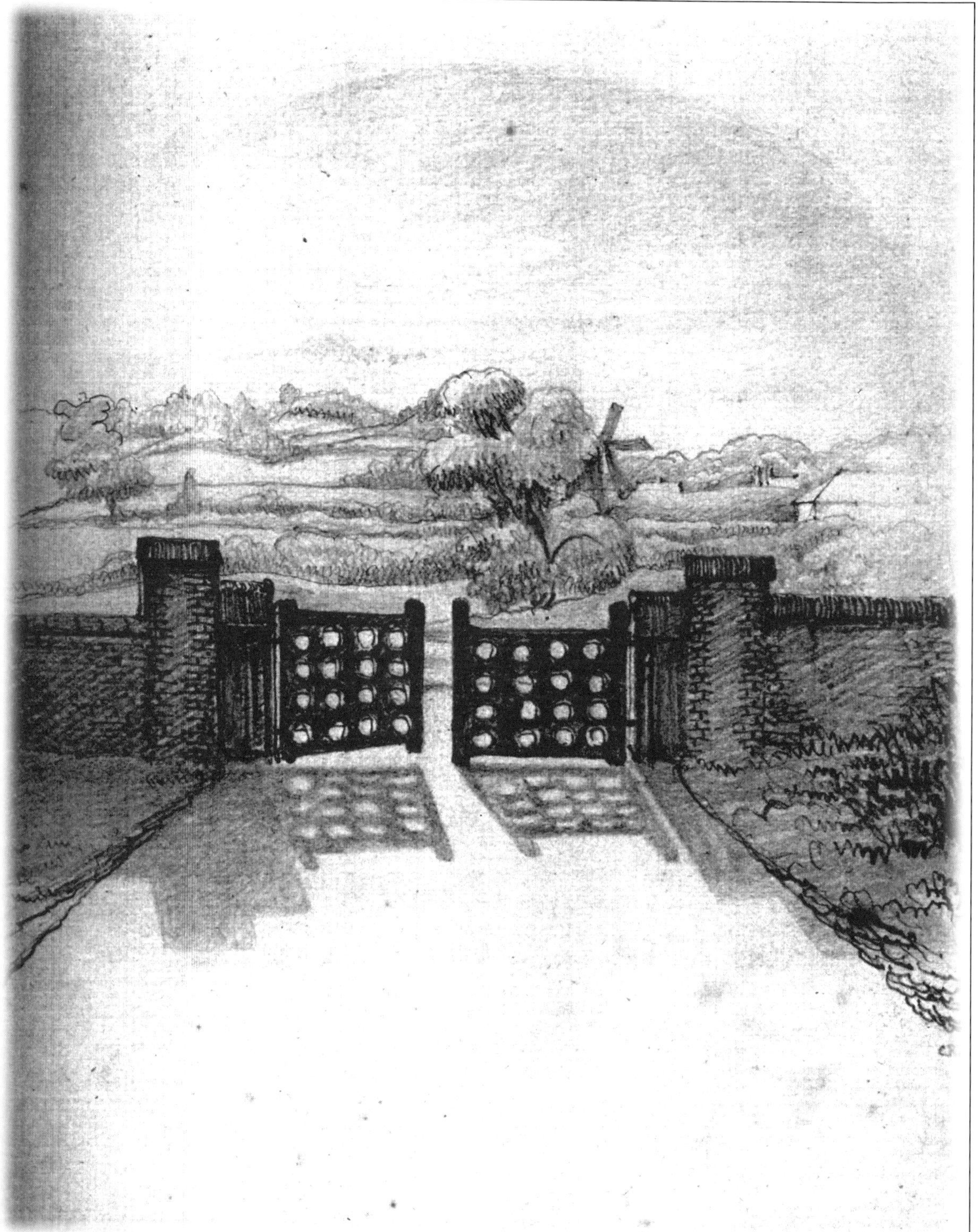

A charming pencil sketch by Mrs Herbert Jones – initialled 'CRJ' for Catherine Rachel Jones and dating from 1870 – which shows the Tower Windmill on the horizon, also the tall ash tree near Crockley Pit, which was felled by a thunderbolt in 1968. This picture was the frontispiece to An Account of Sculthorpe Church *by Mrs Herbert Jones.* (Reproduced by kind permission of Father Andrew Thomson, rector of Sculthorpe)

Chapter Ten

THE WINDMILL

In her 1870 manuscript history of Sculthorpe Church Mrs Herbert Jones included one of her pencil sketches of the village as a frontispiece. The sketch shows the Tower Windmill, which once dominated the skyline at Sculthorpe.

Bryant's 1826 map of Norfolk showed a windmill in Sculthorpe which was positioned on the Great Common nearer the River Wensum. This may have been a drainage pump, rather like the polder mills in Holland, which are essential in marshy fenland. The Ordnance Survey map of Norfolk, dated 1838, clearly marked the site of the Tower Windmill as being in the yard off Moor Lane next to Shrublands, originally a seventeenth-century farmhouse and possibly the 'Mill-field farm house' mentioned in the church register in 1738. The southern lower stretch of the field in the centre of the village was traditionally known as Mill Field and the big marl pit as Mill Field Pit. Older generations in the village referred to the yard where the windmill once stood as Mill Piece and described the right of way, which is now Chapel Lane and was previously Jodrell's Drift, as being anciently called Mill Lane.

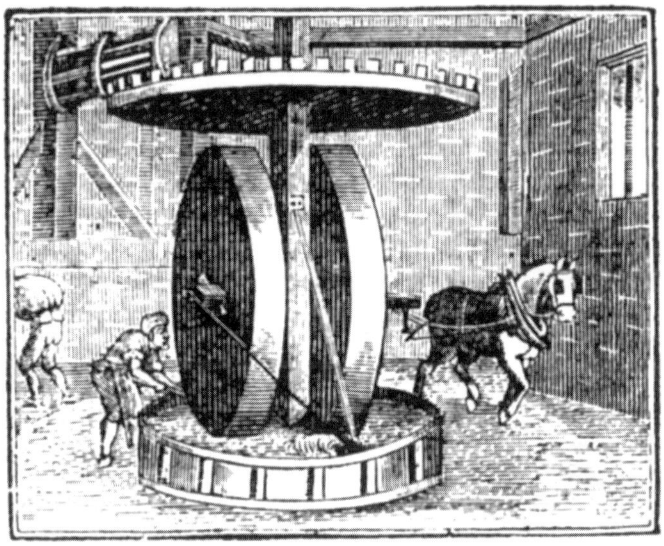

White's Directory and Gazeteer, dated 1836, mentioned Jonathan Williamson as the miller whilst the Tithe Award in 1839 described the owner as Daniel Thompson and the working miller as John Seals. Advertisements for letting the windmill frequently appeared in the *Norfolk Chronicle* newspaper during the nineteenth century and these provided detailed descriptions of the Tower Windmill and its six sails. According to the late Harry Apling, the historian of Norfolk windmills, Sculthorpe Tower Mill was one of only six in the county to be equipped with six sails.

The trade directories of Norfolk and census returns during the 1840s and '50s described Thomas Barker as miller, followed by Thomas Eagle and Mrs Sarah Eagle. The 'Scoulthorpe' Poor Rate books, dating from 1833, provided 'a rate and assessment for the necessary relief of the poor' and included frequent references to the windmill. The Poor Rate book of 1866 described the 'Tower Windmill and cottage, House and garden' and the owner-occupier as 'John Martin, senior'. By 1873 Charles Horsley, tenant of Grove Farm in Sculthorpe, had hired the lease on the windmill.

Following the death of John Martin in 1882 the *Norfolk Chronicle* newspaper featured the sale by auction of the windmill in the Crown public house at Fakenham. The details described a flourishing windmill, equipped with French burr millstones, flour-mill, bone crusher and two steam engines.

By 1900 the windmill had ceased functioning, its cap and sails had been removed and the brick tower was left ruinous and was eventually levelled to the ground. Fortunately many of the mill's outbuildings survive and Stable Cottage, representing the mill's cart stable and loose boxes which once housed four horses, is a remarkable seventeenth-century structure with the date '1649' cut into the brickwork. The Pightle, the neighbouring brick cottage with blue-glazed tiles, was the original miller's cottage and retains many period features.

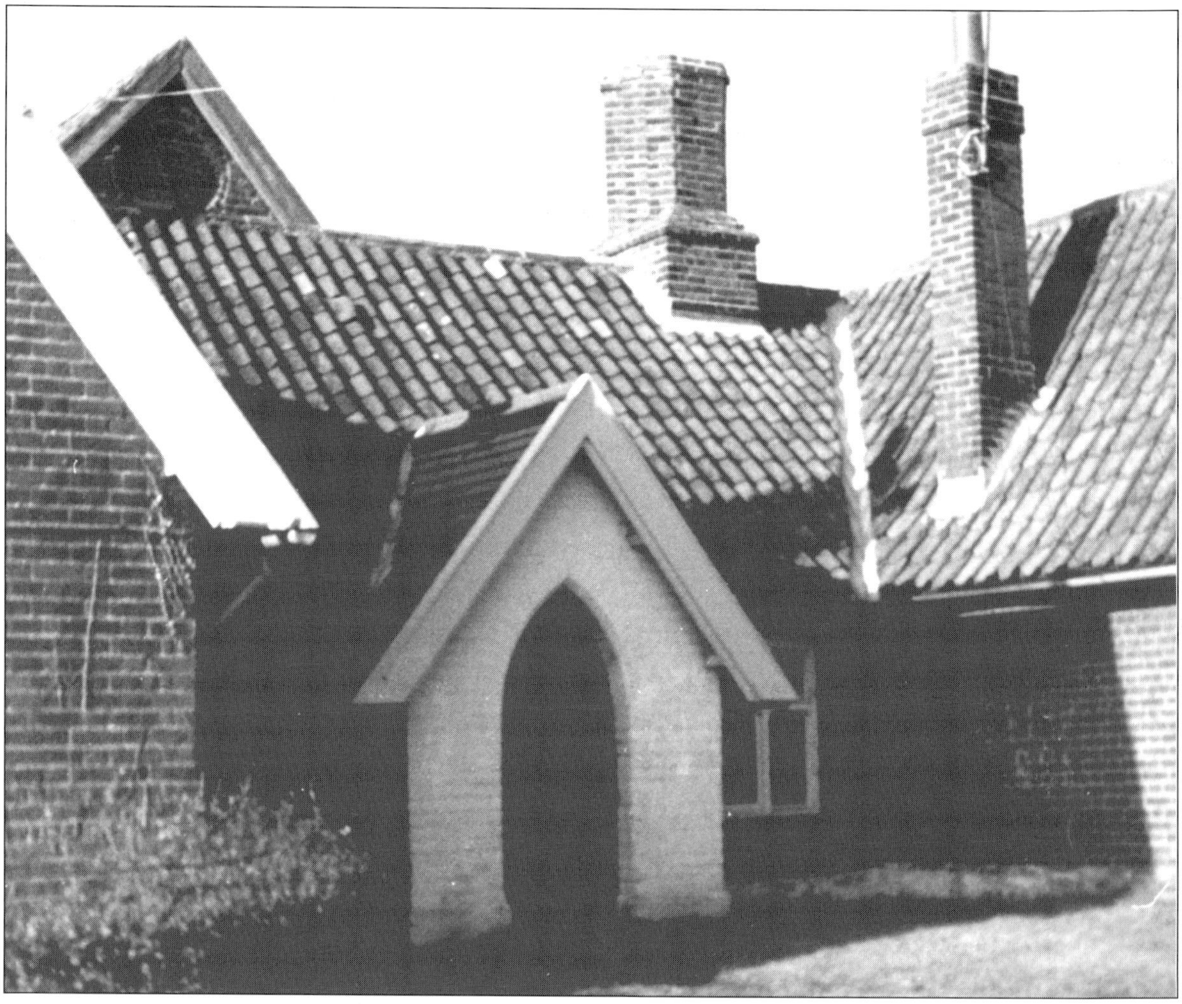

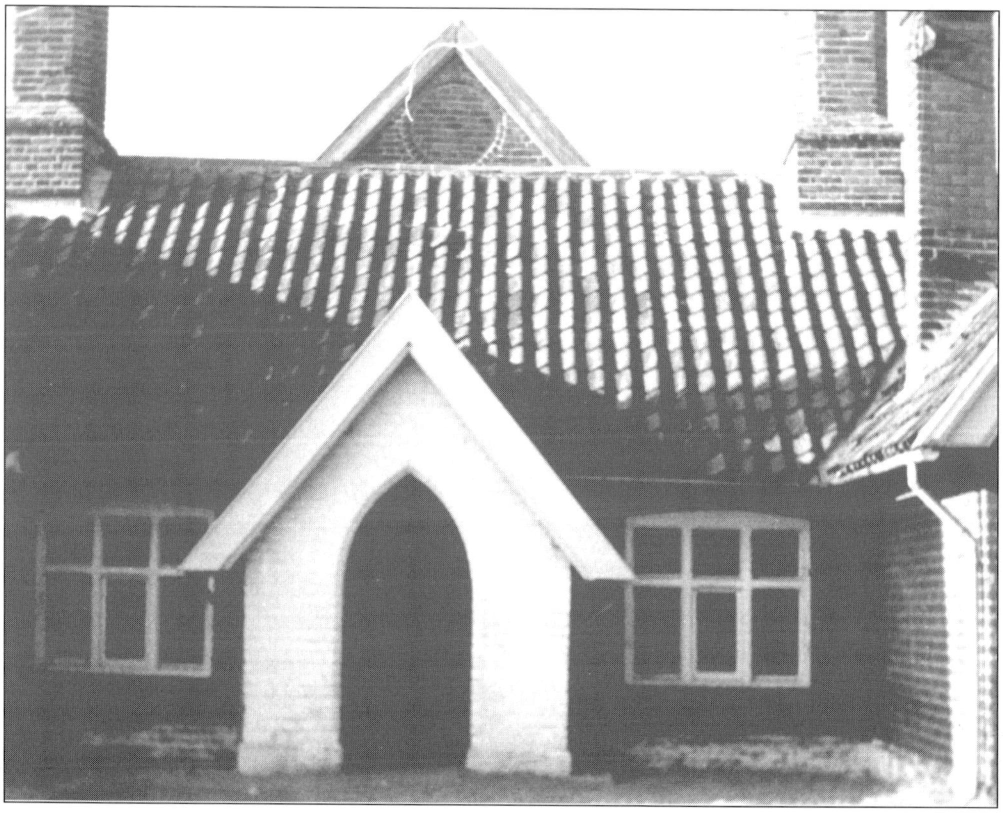

Above: *The reading room flanked by the Beckham Almshouses in Moor Lane, Sculthorpe.*

Left: *Another view of the old reading room in Moor Lane.*

Chapter Eleven

The Almshouses and Turf Moor

The Beckham Almshouses in Moor Lane were a gift made by Francis Beckham in 1686 to the poor of the parish. The Church Terrier of 1784, inscribed in the hand of the Revd Matthew Jones, refers to 'one small cottage situated upon the Common of the said Town and inhabited by poor people for which no rent is paid.' Faden's 1797 map of Norfolk clearly showed the extent of the Great Common where the almshouses were situated. *White's Directory and Gazeteer*, dated 1845, also referred to this 'double cottage and garden, occupied rent free.'

The present almshouses date from the Victorian period. In the flyleaf of the nineteenth-century church register is an entry for the year 1859 in the hand of the Revd Herbert Walsingham Jones:

> *This year the 2 cottages given the poor by Francis Beckham (inhabited by old Groom and Widow Armiger) were pulled down and the present buildings erected at the charges of my mother Lady Jones.*

Catherine Maria, Lady Jones of Cranmer, died in December 1859 and is commemorated by the stained-glass east window in the Parish Church. Mrs Herbert Jones in her 1870 *Account of Sculthorpe Church* wrote of her mother-in-law, '(she) did not pass away without leaving to the poor and destitute an abiding trace of beneficent kindness.' The four almshouses built on the site of the two seventeenth-century cottages were usually inhabited by poor widows. In 1865 a central reading room was added to these and to the rear, divided by a wooden partition, was a church mission room which was chiefly used as the Church infants' school and later as the parish lecture room.

The Francis Beckham Charity Trustees form one of the oldest charitable trusts in Norfolk and remain a vigorous body. In 1996 a substantial National Lottery grant of £10,000 and an additional cash grant from North Norfolk District Council enabled the trustees to embark on an ambitious project. The four almshouses, later adapted as two dwellings, required modernisation whilst the badly derelict lecture and reading room was earmarked for conversion into three new almshouses. The splendid new almshouse complex reflects the historic character of the Victorian buildings and perpetuates the original intention of its founder in the seventeenth century.

The trustees are also responsible for another charitable endowment in the parish, the Turf Moor, which was the fuel allotment of 30 acres near the River Wensum, awarded to the poor of Sculthorpe in 1830 after the Inclosure Act of 1829 had eradicated the ancient common lands from the face of the village. The Inclosure Map of 1830 in the Norfolk Record Office identifies the drift way to the fuel allotment as Turf Moor Road and clearly shows the boundary fences and the Middle Drain running through to the river.

Turf Moor is situated on what was once the vast expanse of Sculthorpe Common, called the Great Common in the Sculthorpe Field Book of 1766 and shown to its full extent on Faden's map of Norfolk (1797) and Bryant's map (1826). This ancient stretch of common land is thought to have originally included a medieval deer chace. Entries in the Calendar of Patent Rolls for the years 1302–06, in the Public Record Office, made frequent reference to the chace and warren in 'Sculthorp' which belonged to John de Warenne, Earl of Surrey, and to the band of armed robbers who made daring raids on horseback into this and other deer chaces held by him to hunt rabbits, hare and deer whilst the Earl was serving his kinsman, King Edward I, in the Scottish Wars.

Aerial photography over this stretch of moorland has revealed traces of a moated site, possibly the remains of a boundary ditch dating from the period of the deer chace. The Moor Plantation with its ancient trees of alder and oak is believed to trace its origins from the Middle Ages and today the wild native roe deer can still be found in this place as well as the muntjac and Chinese water deer.

Turf Moor, originally providing the poor of the parish with turf and peat for fuel, was in later times let, the money from the rent paying for coal to be distributed to the poorest families. In recent years the shooting rights have been particularly popular. In his autobiographical book *Georgian Afternoon* Major Lawrence Evelyn Jones described his shooting parties during the 1930s across Sculthorpe Fen and the valuable reserves of wild duck and game to be bagged including teal, shoveler, mallards, snipe and woodcock as well as partridges and pheasants.

In recent years Turf Moor has come under increasing scrutiny as a site of special scientific interest because of its rich and valuable reserves of rare fenland vegetation as well as being a haven for wildlife.

During the 1920s and '30s the children of Sculthorpe had been encouraged to gather wild flowers here including flag iris, meadowsweet, ragged robin and marsh orchids. There are still many of these flowers here and also wild foxgloves and cowslips. The fenland fauna includes the nationally-rare marsh fern as well as slender sedge, black bog rush, creeping willow, meadow thistle, liverwort, marsh lousewort and sawsedge, which was traditionally used for thatching roofs.

Although the bittern no longer nests here, the number of owls and birds of prey which frequent the upper reaches of the Wensum valley have greatly enhanced the importance of the site. Barn owls hunt at dusk and there are little owls, tawny owls and long-eared owls in the area too. Sparrowhawks, hobbys and peregrine falcons have been sighted and the marsh harriers annually nest in the reedbeds. The osprey has also been noted as an occasional visitor.

In 2001 the Hawk and Owl Trust was granted the lease of Turf Moor by the Francis Beckham Charity Trustees and is currently engaged in clearing scrub and undergrowth in an attempt to establish an important nature reserve on the 30-acre site. There are extensive plans for boardwalks and bird hides, a small visitor centre and educational facilities for scientific and ornithological research. A nature trail and woodland walk are also envisaged as well as Monet-style bridges over the deep-water drains to improve access. Much of this exciting project is being co-ordinated by the trust's new warden Nigel Middleton.

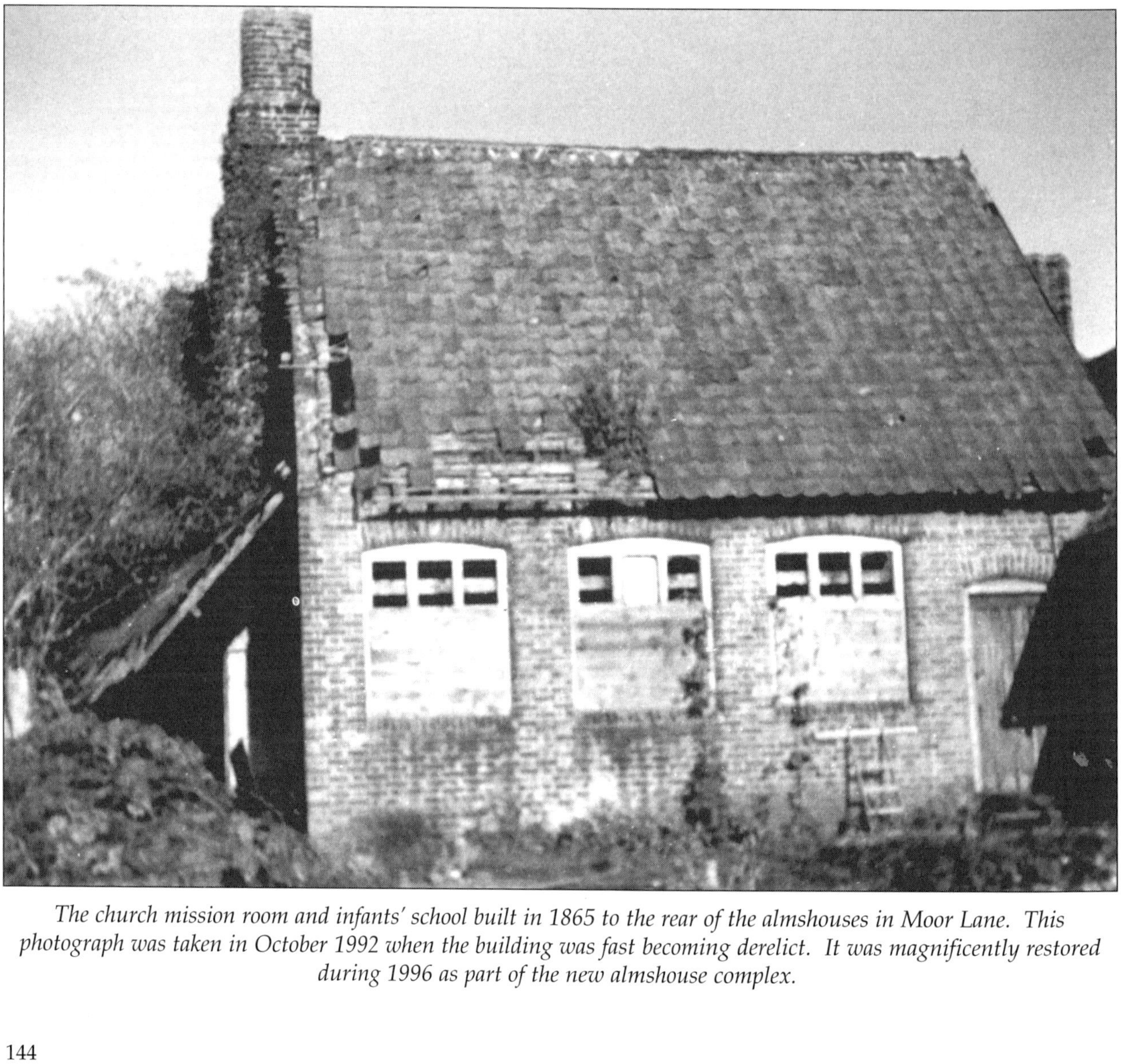

The church mission room and infants' school built in 1865 to the rear of the almshouses in Moor Lane. This photograph was taken in October 1992 when the building was fast becoming derelict. It was magnificently restored during 1996 as part of the new almshouse complex.

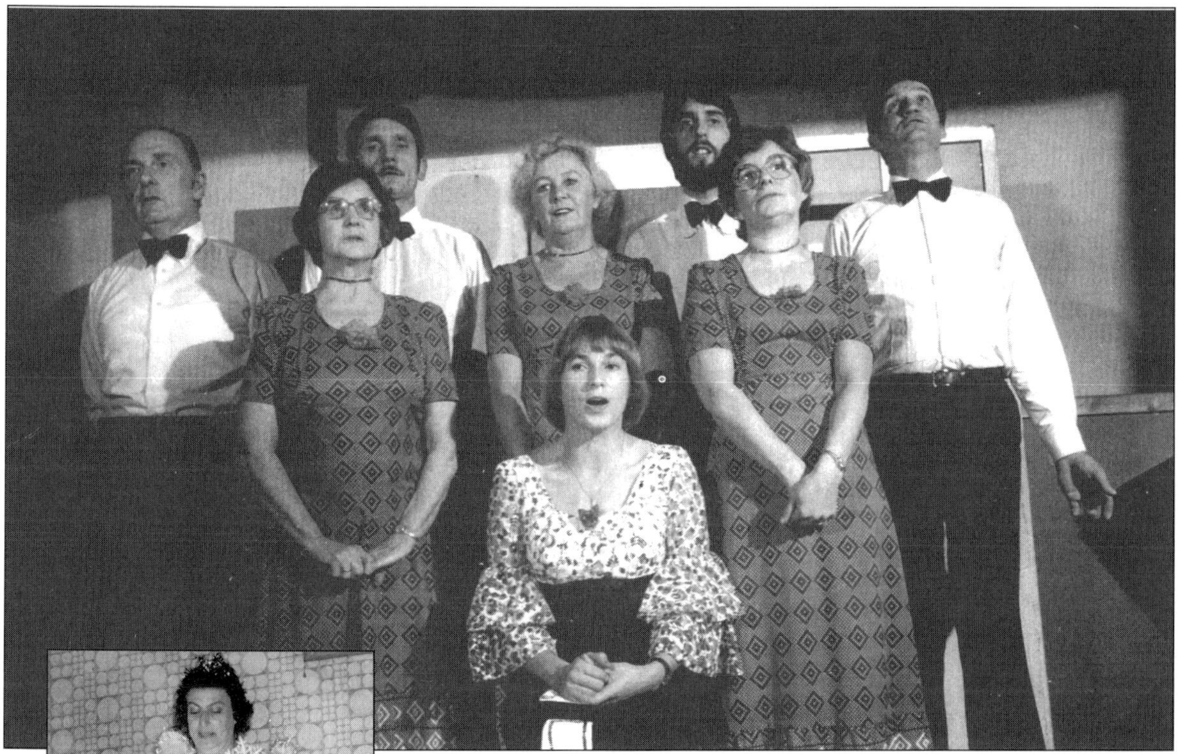

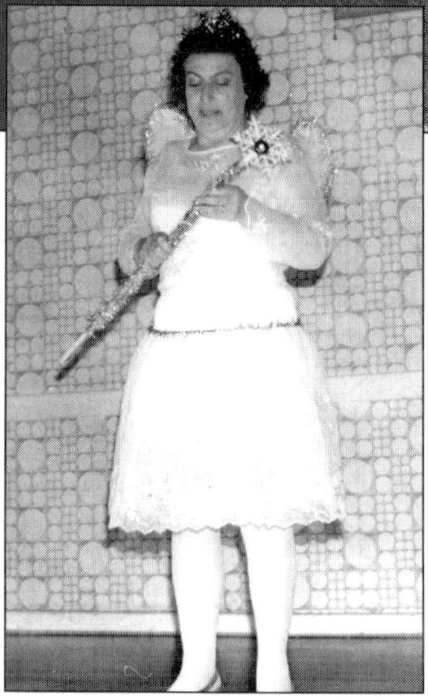

Above: *Sculthorpe Merry Makers were founded in 1969 and staged concerts of musical and comical sketches in the village until 1999. This photograph shows some of the best-remembered members of the cast.* Left to right, standing: *John Smith, Norah Armiger, Edwin Norman, Doris Mitchell, Ray Norman, Jean Edge, Bernard Edge;* front: *Margaret Walters.* (Reproduced by kind permission of Mrs Doris Mitchell)

Left: *Sculthorpe Merry Makers. Muriel Norman as the Christmas fairy.* (Reproduced by kind permission of Mrs Doris Mitchell)

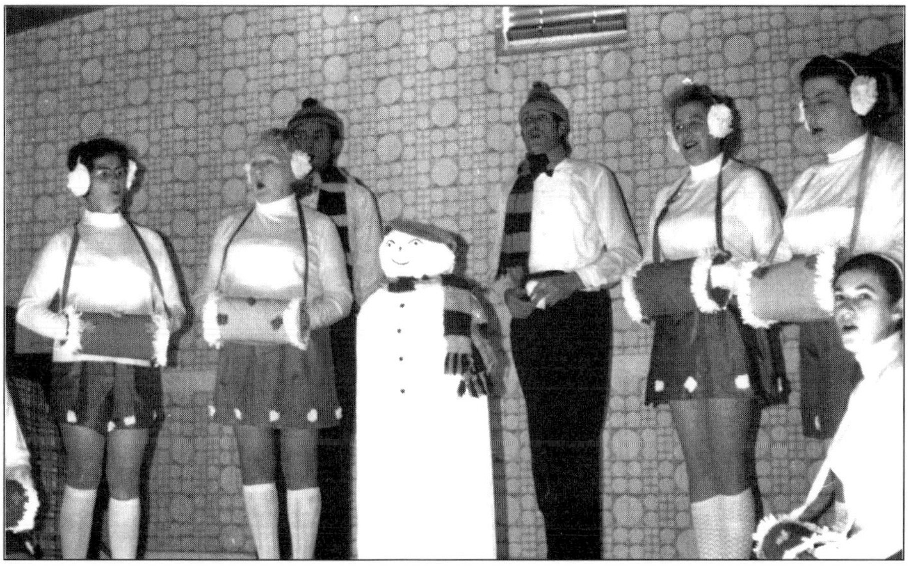

Right: *Sculthorpe Merry Makers at the Christmas show, 1972.* Left to right: *Norah Armiger, Bobby Westwood, Edwin Norman, Bernard Edge, Doris Mitchell, Muriel Norman, Margaret Walters.* (Reproduced by kind permission of Mrs Doris Mitchell)

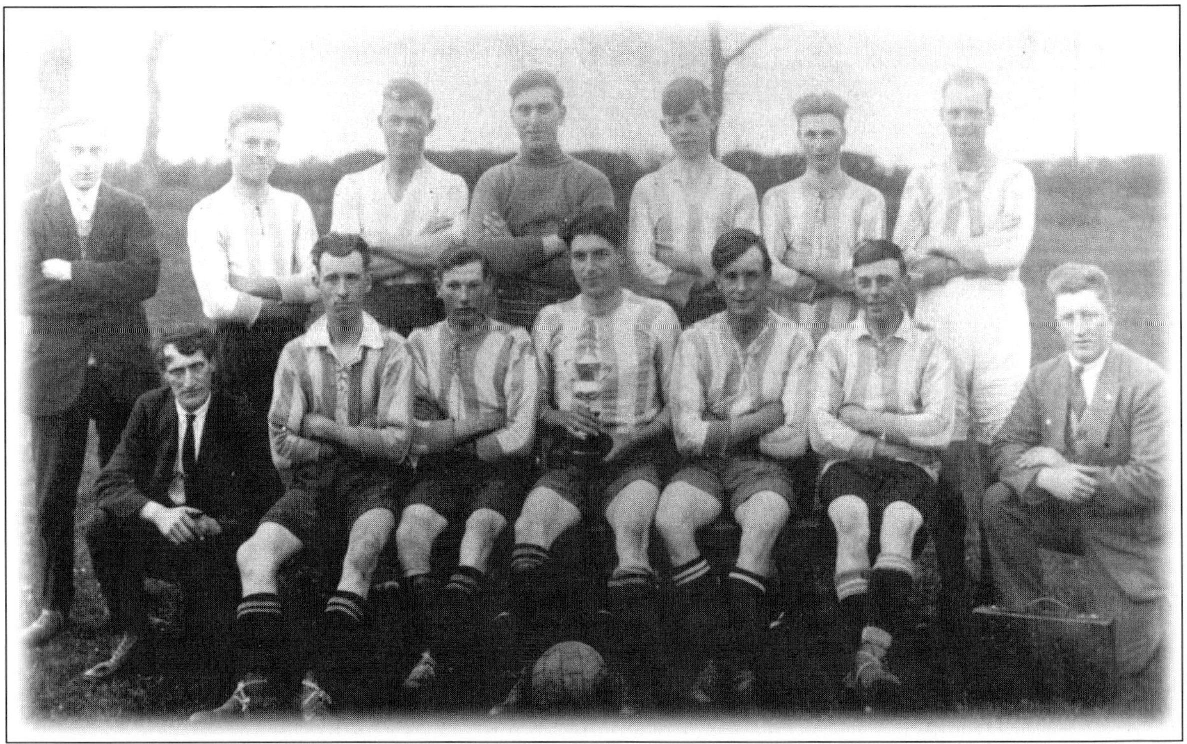

Sculthorpe Football Club, c.1929. The club was started during the 1920s. Among those pictured are: *Willy Sewter, Ernie Stapleton, Ken Southgate, Philip Armiger, Victor Fuller and, holding a prize trophy, John Bancroft* (centre), *the loveable rogue whose father was the vicar of St Peter's Church in neighbouring Dunton.* (From the collection of the late William Sewter. Reproduced by kind permission of Mrs Jean Benstead)

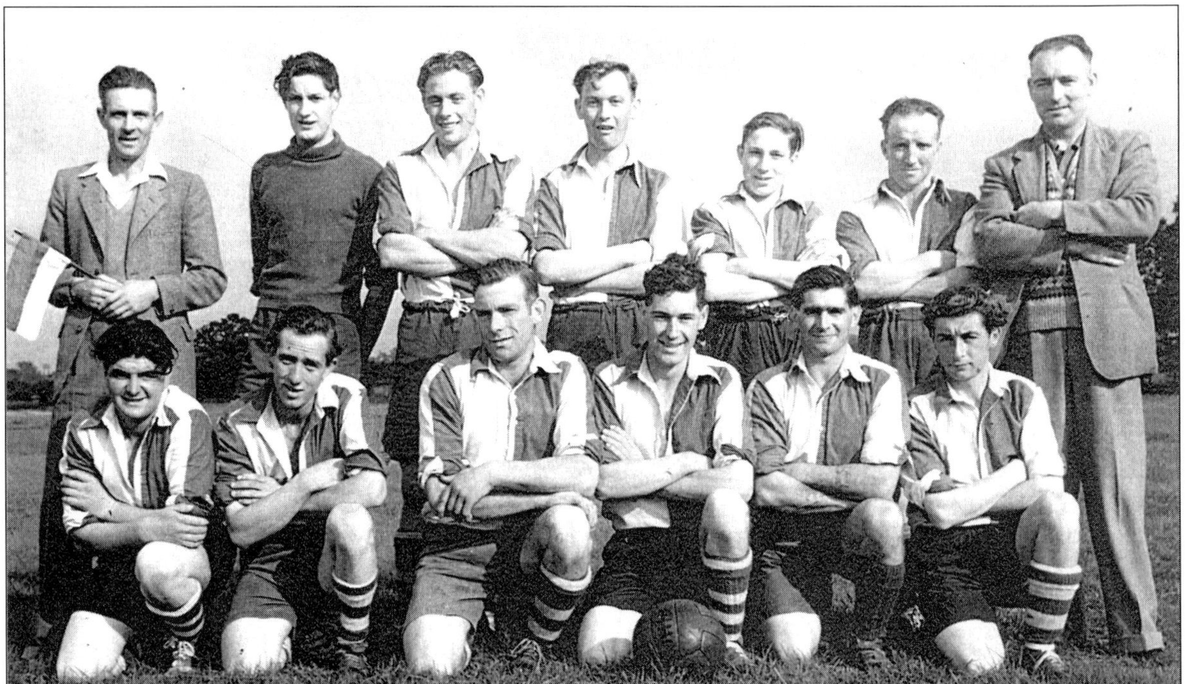

Sculthorpe Football Club, early 1950s. Left to right, back row: *Lou Norman, Bernard Edge, Derrick Barber, Austin Cornwall, Paddy Hammond, Sid Todd, Clifford Armiger*; front: *Douglas Leete, Dick Barrett, John Galer, Donny Clarke, Ernie Parker, Leslie West.* (From the collection of Mrs Joyce Harrison. Reproduced by kind permission of the *Dereham & Fakenham Times*)

Village Sports

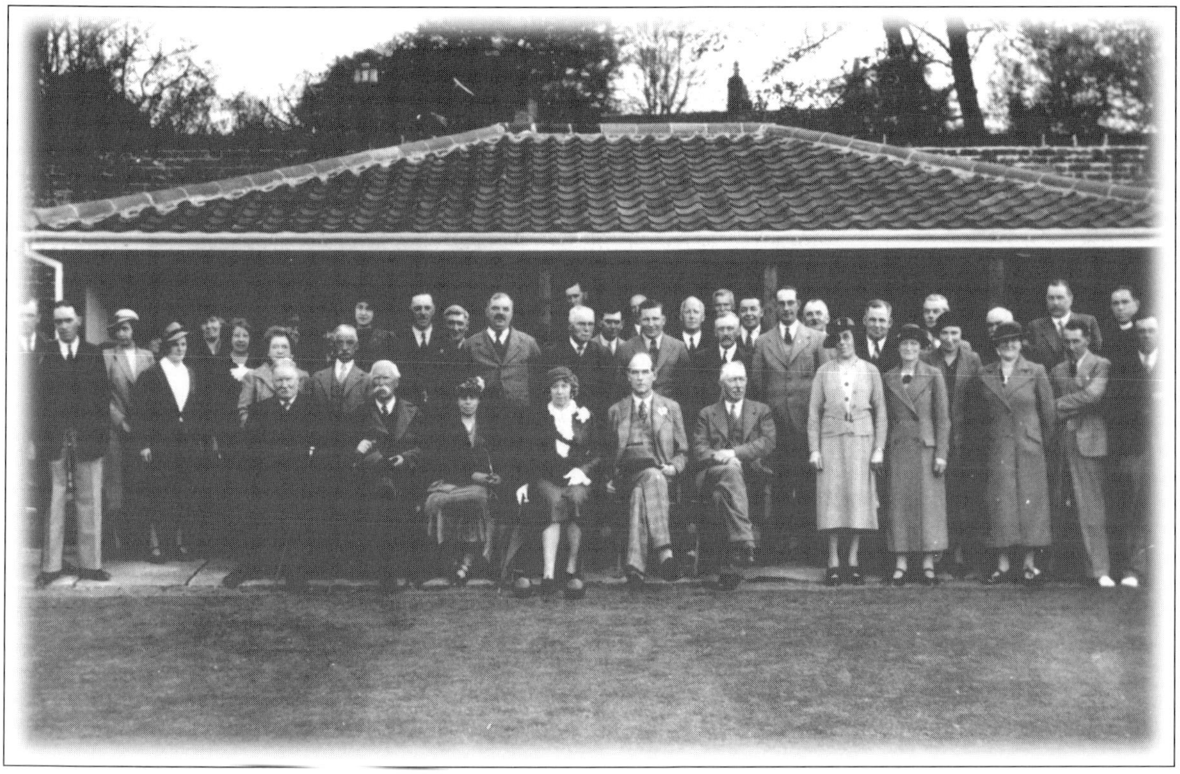

The grand opening of the new village bowling green (the former walled kitchen garden at the rectory) in 1939. Left to right, seated: *Mr George Grant Lockhart Ross, Sir Lawrence John Jones 4th Baronet of Cranmer, Paula, Lady Jones, Lady Evelyn Jones, Major Lawrence Evelyn Jones, Mr Ernest Syder, president of Sculthorpe Bowl's Club and chairman of Sculthorpe Parish Council.* Others included in the photograph in the back row, left to right: *May Gathercole, Enid Pointer, Nanny Fox, Millicent and Willy Woodhouse, Miss Reinhardt, Miss Dinah Jones, Bob Lingwood, George Patfield, George Armiger, Billy Pointer, Mr Smith, Billy Crane, Minnie Woodhouse, Jessie Lingwood, Rose Applegate, Harriet Short, Stanley Gathercole and the Revd Christopher Chitty, rector of Sculthorpe.* (Reproduced by kind permission of the *Eastern Daily Press* and the *Dereham & Fakenham Times*, Archant Norfolk Ltd)

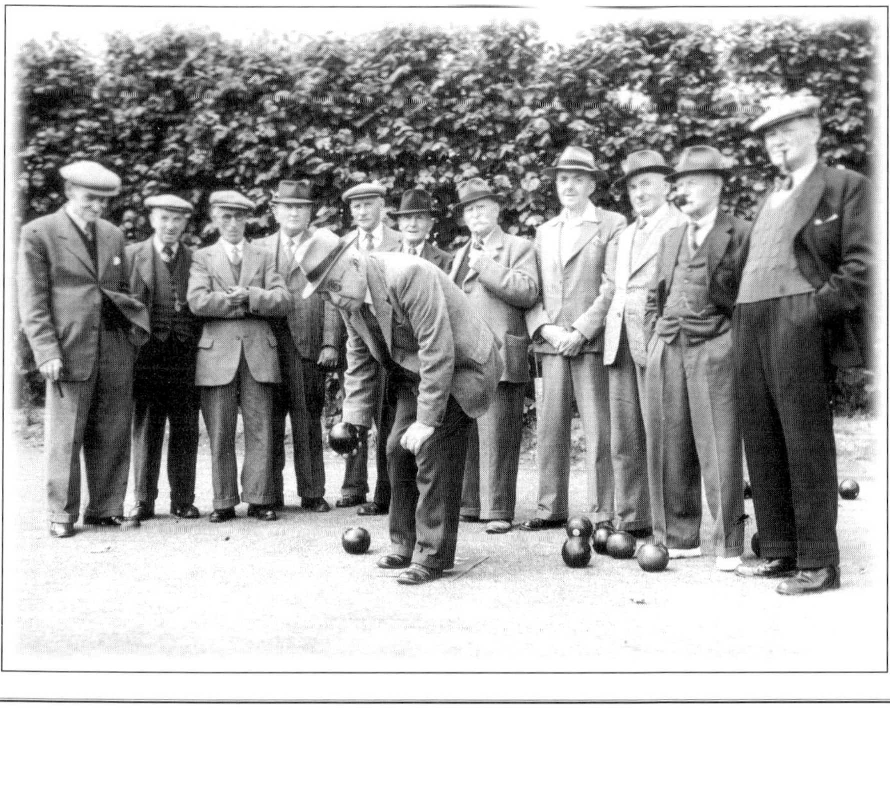

Left: *Sculthorpe Bowls Club, 1940s.* Among those pictured are: *Billy Barnes, Bob Lingwood and Billy Crane.* (Reproduced by kind permission of Mr Richard Land)

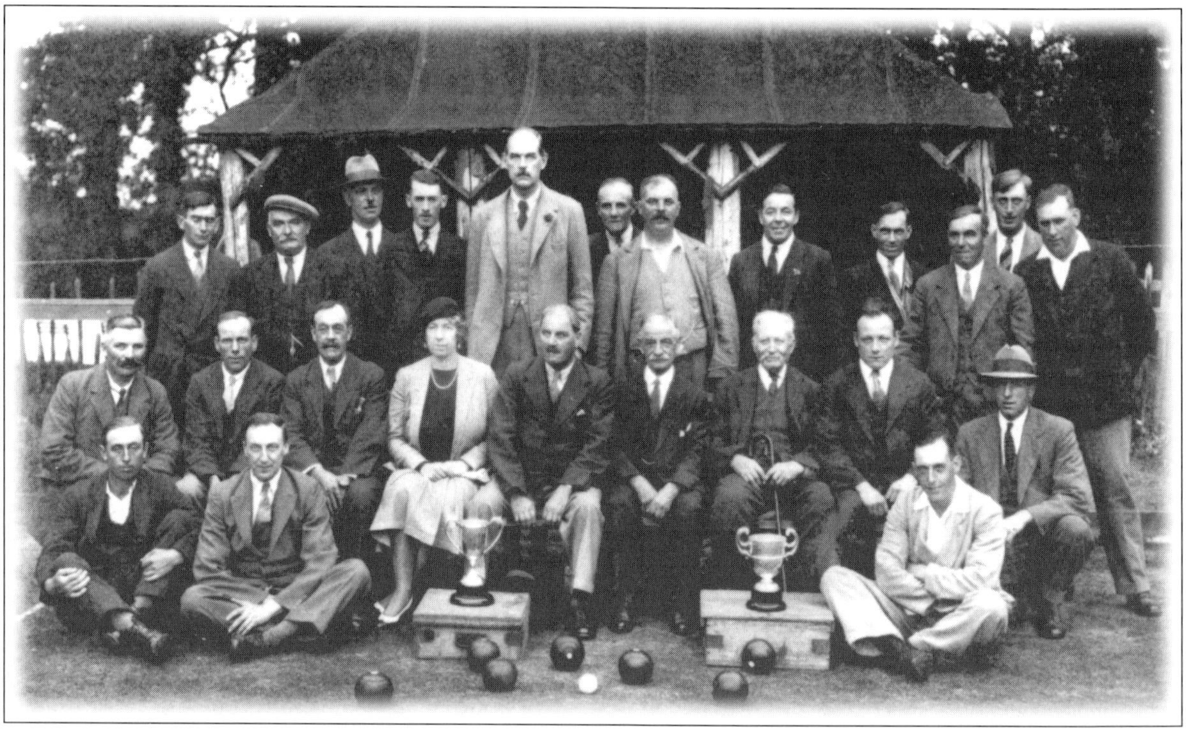

Sculthorpe Bowls Club started in c.1922 and, before the opening of the present bowling green in 1939, games were played on a small green on Home Pasture behind the Parish Church. The club president, Mr Ernest Syder, also had a private green in his garden at Shrublands, Moor Lane. This photograph shows Major Jones and his wife, Lady Evelyn Jones, at a prize-giving during the early 1930s. Among those photographed are: *George Armiger, Charlie Cornwall, Bob Lingwood, Archie Vertigans, George Patfield, Alfred Smith, Ted Lingwood, Alfred Webster, Horrie Greeves, Mr Short, Mr Mallom, the Layton brothers, Willy Woodhouse and Mick Barnes.* (From the collection of the late Mrs Eleanor Crane. Reproduced by kind permission of Mr Richard Land)

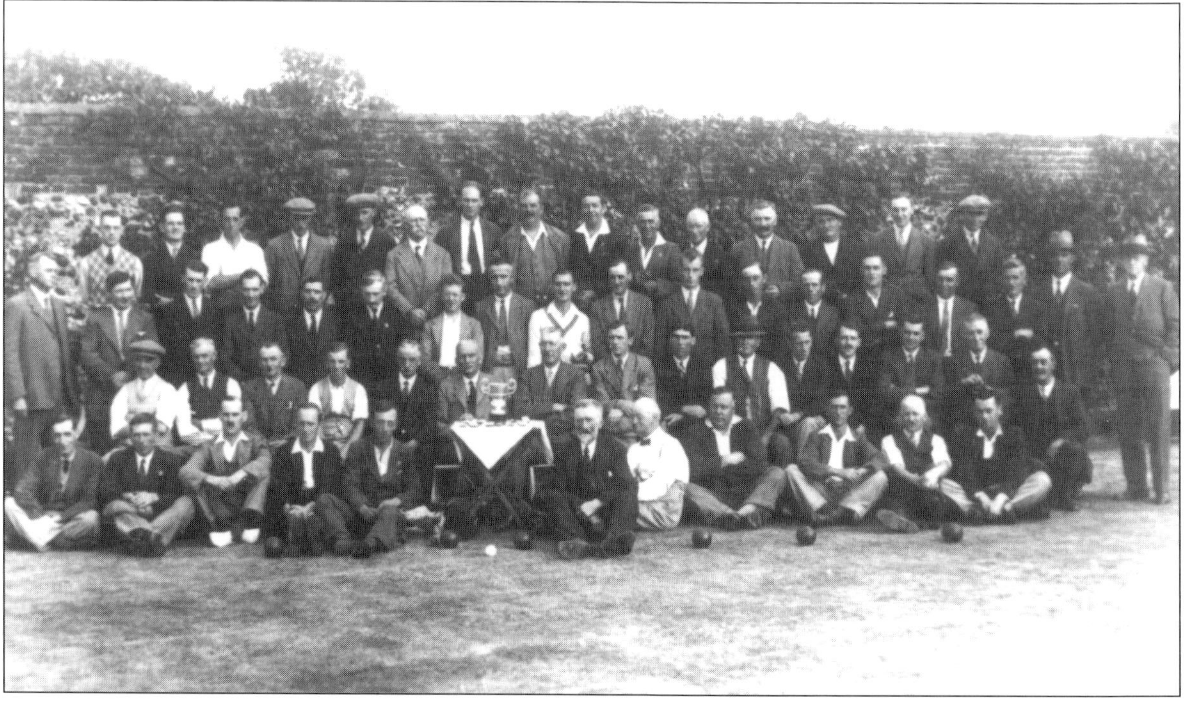

Sculthorpe Bowls Club on their new bowling green in Creake Road, 1939.
(Reproduced by kind permission of Mrs Audrey Jordan)

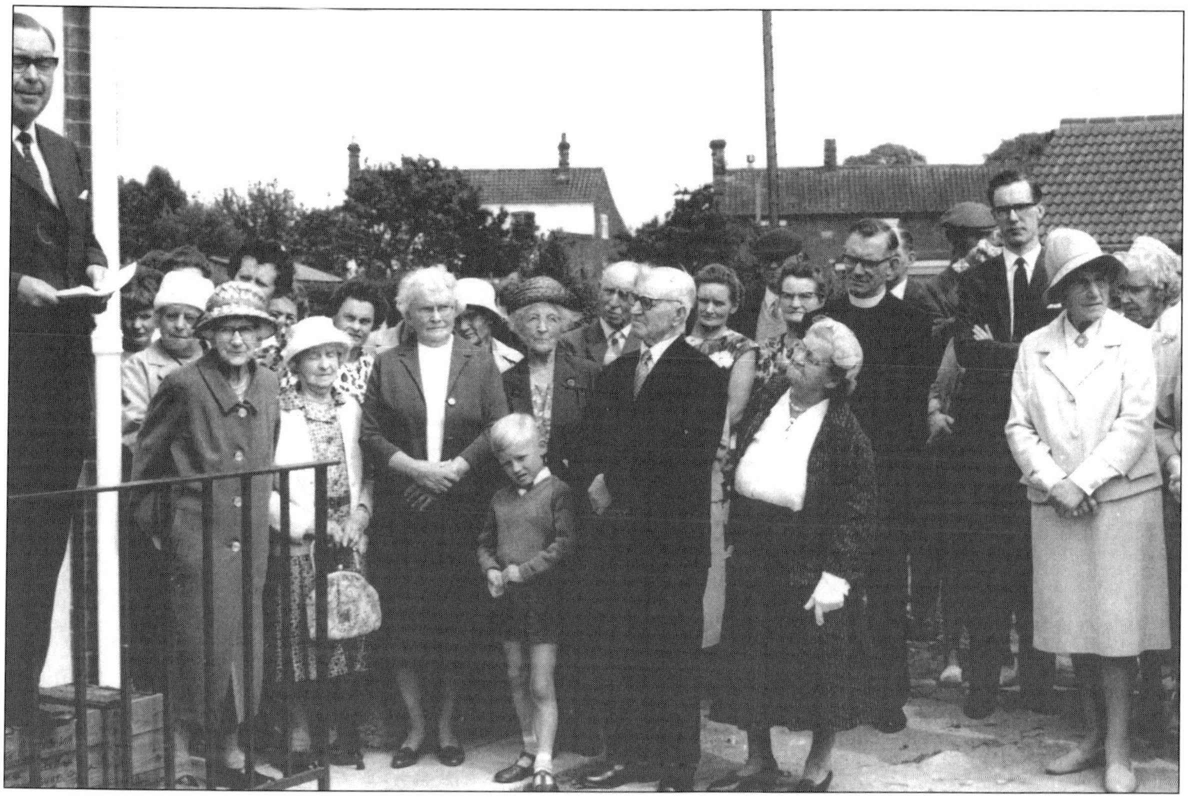

In June 1966 Dick Joice of Anglia Television officially opened Sculthorpe's village hall. He was an appropriate choice because Dick's uncle, Mr George Joice, had been tenant farmer at Grange Farm in Sculthorpe during the 1930s. The Village Hall Committee had been actively fund-raising since March 1960, originally under the chairmanship of Mr Derrick Boyce. The hall was built on the site of the old Parish Pound, later Pound Close or Pound Yard, with its ancient cottages, deep well and tiny cobbler's shop. Commemorative plaques are inscribed with the names of the original chairman Derrick Boyce, the treasurer Archie Filby and Colonel Peter Labouchere, who all sadly died before the project was completed. In 1999 generous grant aid from both the National Lottery Fund and Norfolk County Council enabled the present Village Hall Committee to carry out refurbishments and add a new extension to mark the millennium. Some of the people depicted in this photograph of the official opening in June 1966 are: Dick Joice, Julia Seaman, Mrs Harrowen, Dorothy Mace, Miss Ethel Filby, Dorothy Heyhoe, Mabel Boyce, Roger Allison, Eleanor Crane, Horace Boyce, Mr Harrowen, Jean Allison, Mrs Allison, Mrs Betts, the Revd Fred Gunn, John Gunn, Miss Constance Catlin, headmistress of Sculthorpe School.

(From the collection of Mrs Jean Allison. Reproduced by kind permission of the *Lynn News*)

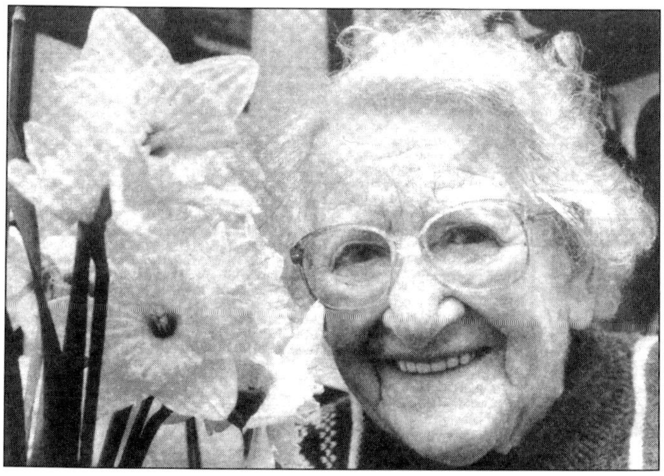

Left: *Mrs Violet Skippon (1902–98) was one of the famous characters of Sculthorpe in recent times and was affectionately known as 'Skippy'. Mrs Skippon remembered the day during the early 1950s when a uniformed chauffeur knocked on her cottage door asking for directions to West Barsham Hall. Mrs Skippon went outside, only to find the royal Daimler containing the Queen, the Queen Mother and Princess Margaret. The royal party were on their way to take afternoon tea with Mrs Kathleen Keith at West Barsham Hall and the chauffeur had lost his way!* (Reproduced by kind permission of the *Lynn News*)

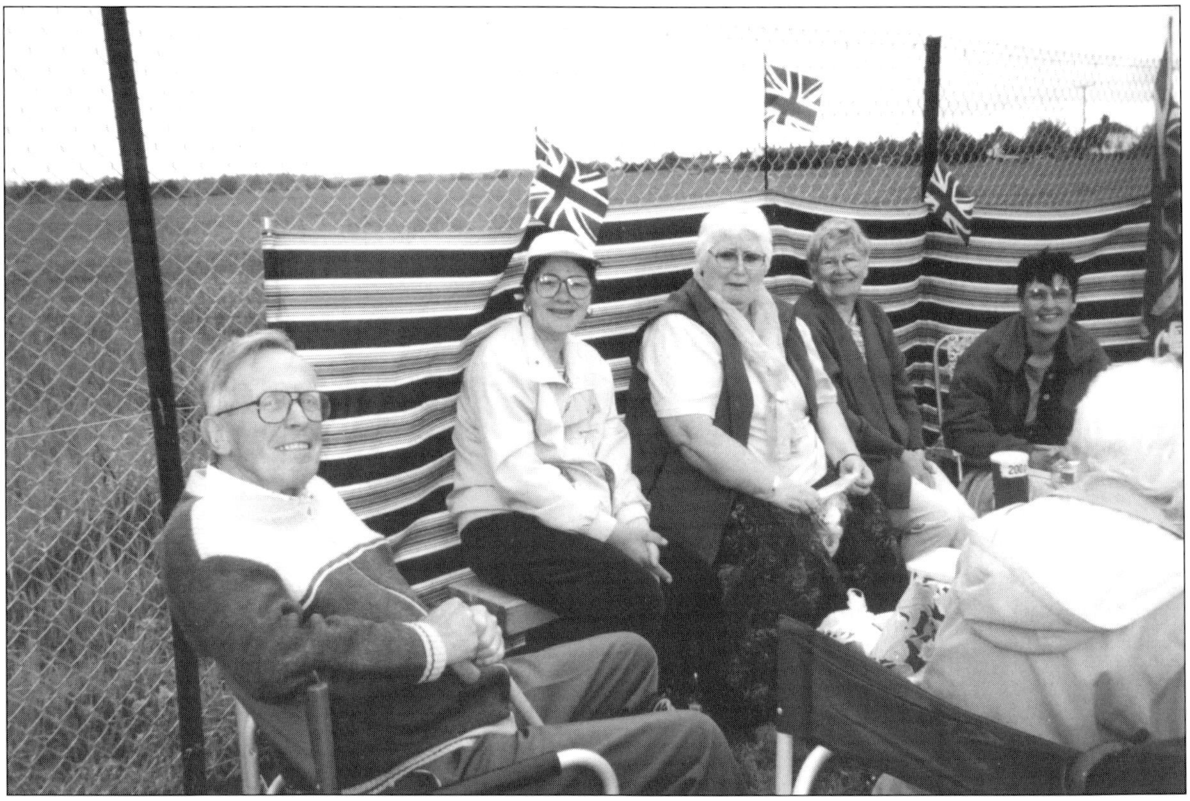

Celebrating the Queen's Golden Jubilee, June 2002. Left to right: *Harold Lingwood, Stephanie, Anne Lingwood, Jean Edge and Sally Norman.*

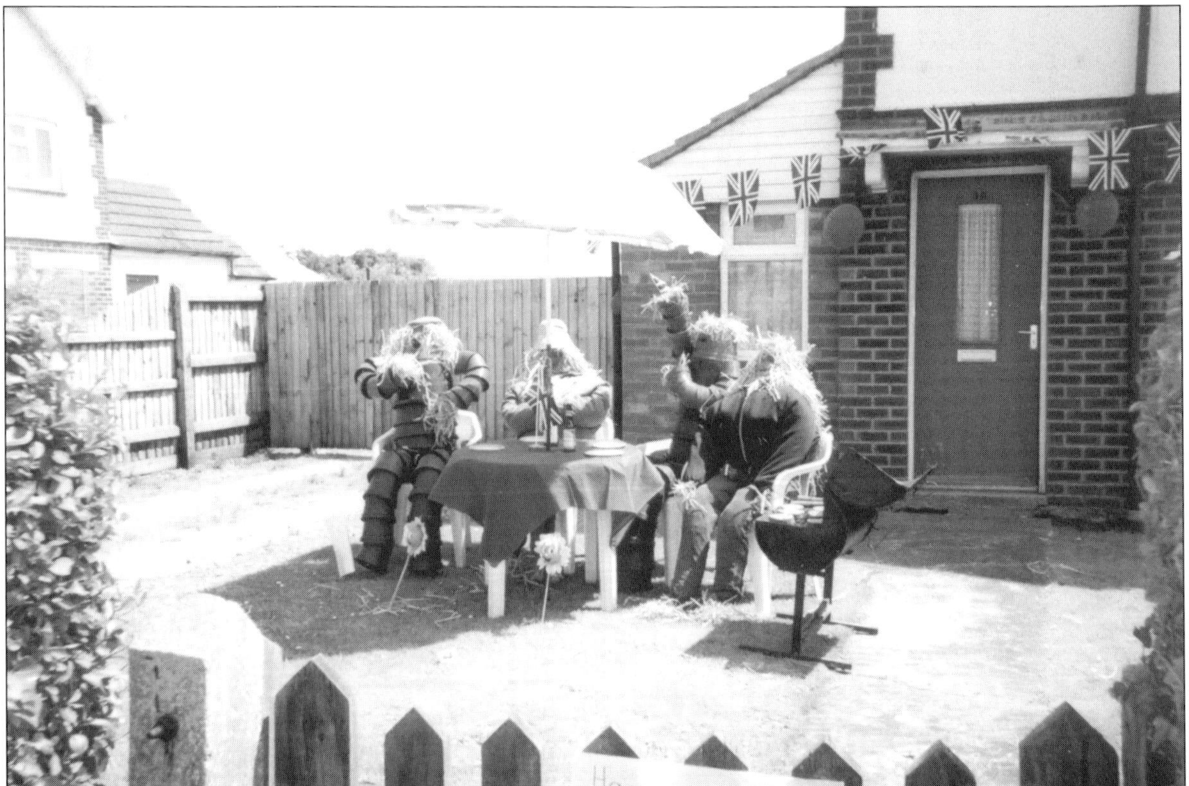

'Bill and Ben' and scarecrow friends celebrate the Golden Jubilee in Moor Lane, June 2002.

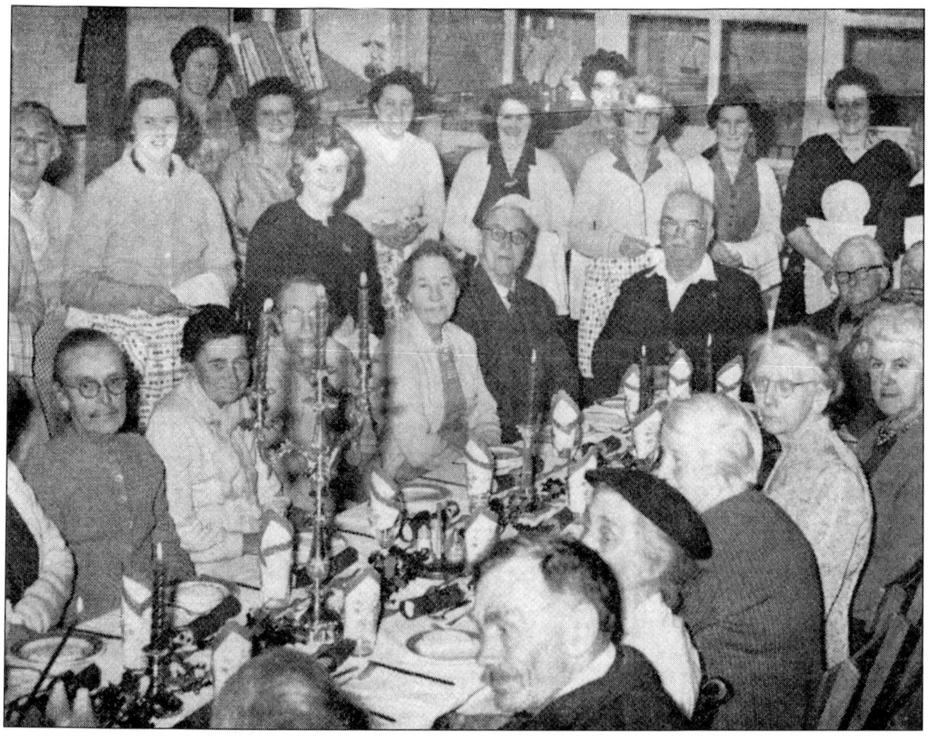

Left: *The Good Companions Over-60s Club was founded in 1962 and this photograph shows their first Christmas dinner served by helpers in Sculthorpe School.* Left to right, back row: *Rose Applegate, Hettie Hipkin, Peg Labouchere, Chrissie Fuller, Enid Pointer, Joan Howes, Marjorie Playford, Ann Lingwood, Mrs Gunn, Josie Lingwood, Dorothy Mace;* seated, clockwise: *Mrs Shorten, Mrs Galer, Agnes and Ted Lingwood, George Palfield, Mr Hole, May Lingwood, Mrs Cornwall, Mrs Woodhouse, Mrs Taylor.*
(Reproduced by kind permission of the *Eastern Daily Press* and the *Dereham & Fakenham Times*)

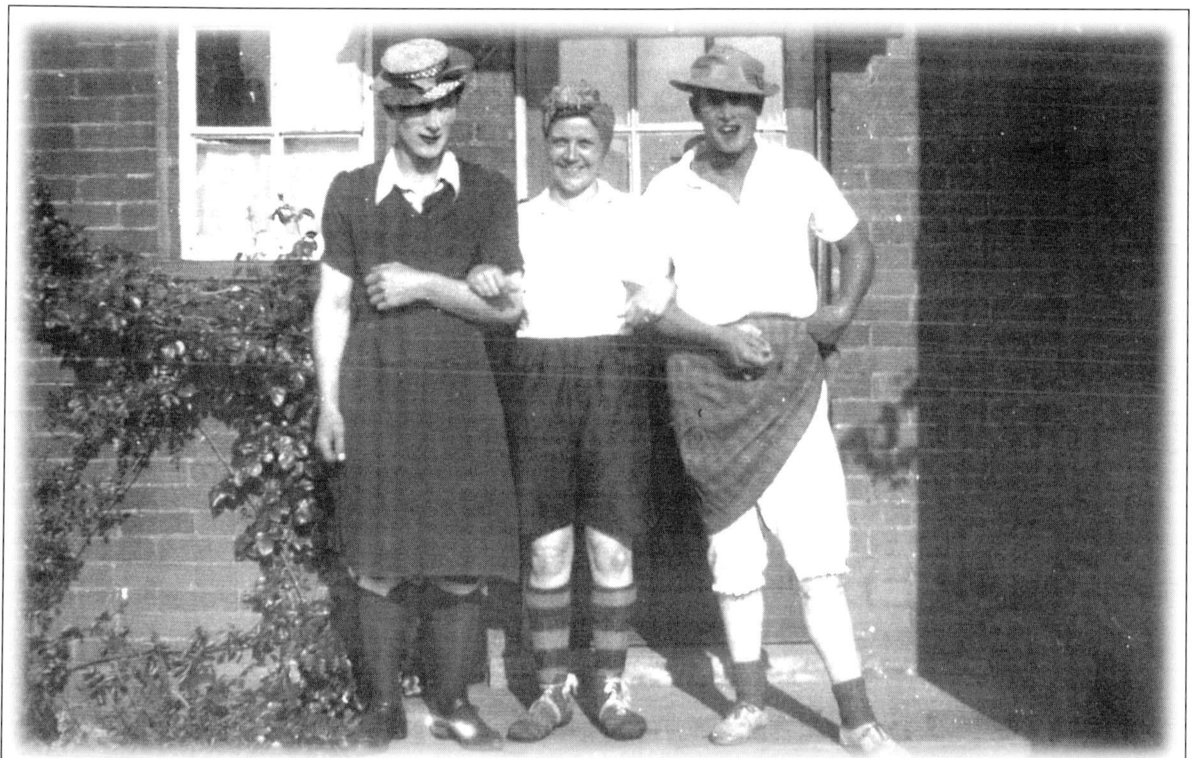

A charity football match was held in Sculthorpe during the summer of 1945 to raise funds for troops returning home at the end of the Second World War. Photographed on the doorstep of 60 Moor Lane, then No.1 Council House, are (left to right): *Arthur Playford, Doris Greeves, Geoffrey Minns.*
(Reproduced by kind permission of Mrs Joyce Harrison)

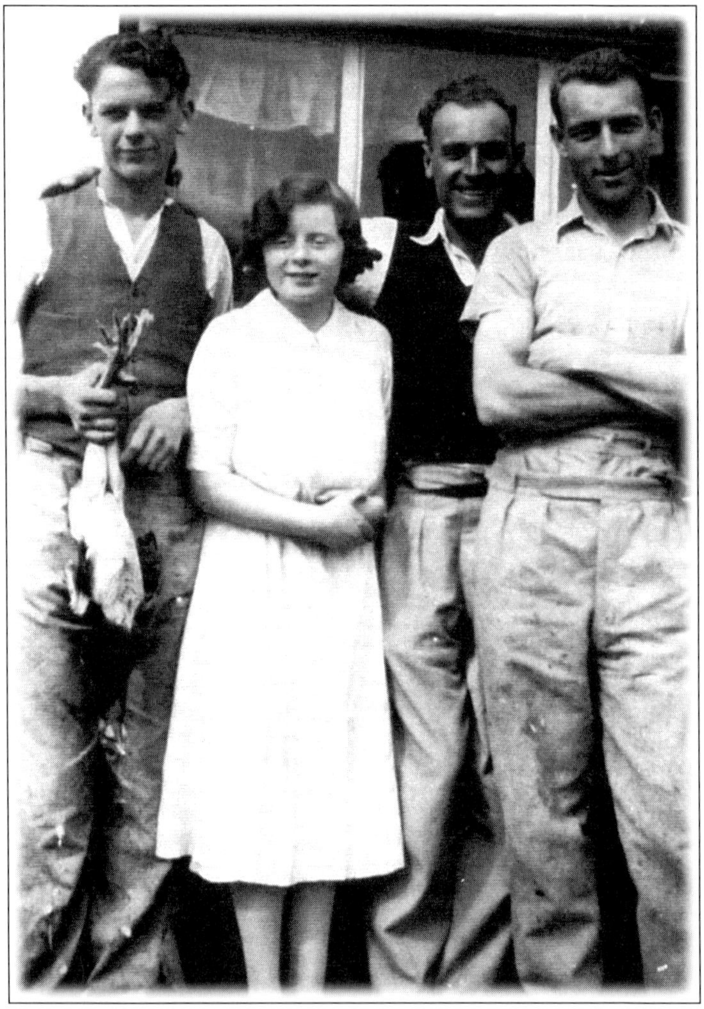

Left: *The former Primitive Methodist Chapel to the rear of the Greyhound pub was, for many years, used as a cart house and plucking shed. This photograph of chicken pluckers was taken during the 1930s.* Left to right: *Arnold Howes, Phoebe Shackcloth, Aubrey Wright and Clifford Armiger from the Greyhound.* (Reproduced by kind permission of Mrs Joyce Harrison)

Below: *The Sculthorpe chicken pluckers, 1930s. This photograph was taken by Miss Joyce Lingwood with her Brownie-box camera.* Left to right: *Fred Armiger, Arnold Howes, Aubrey Wright, Clifford Armiger and Ray Howes. Ray Howes was tragically killed on active service in Italy during the Second World War. The breeding and rearing of poultry in Sculthorpe was commonplace before the Second World War and there were several plucking sheds in the village providing employment for both men and women.* (Reproduced by kind permission of Mrs Joyce Harrison)

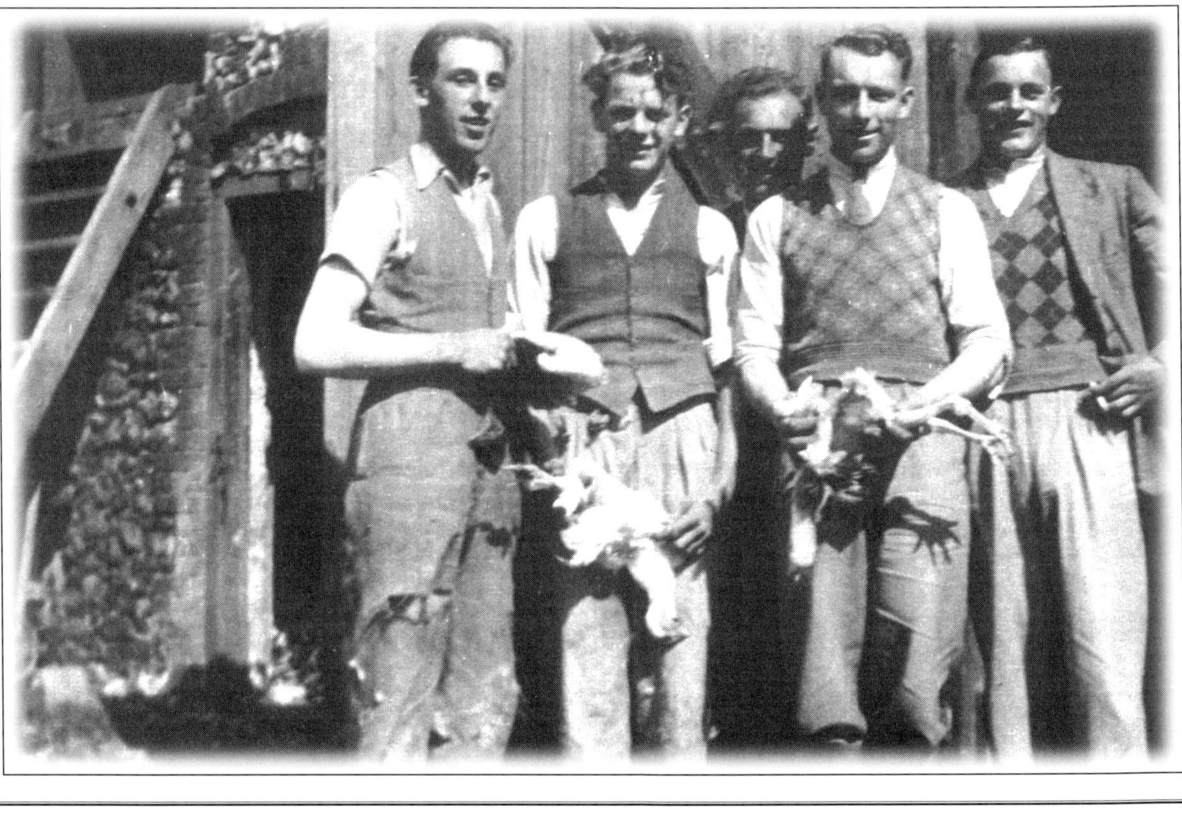

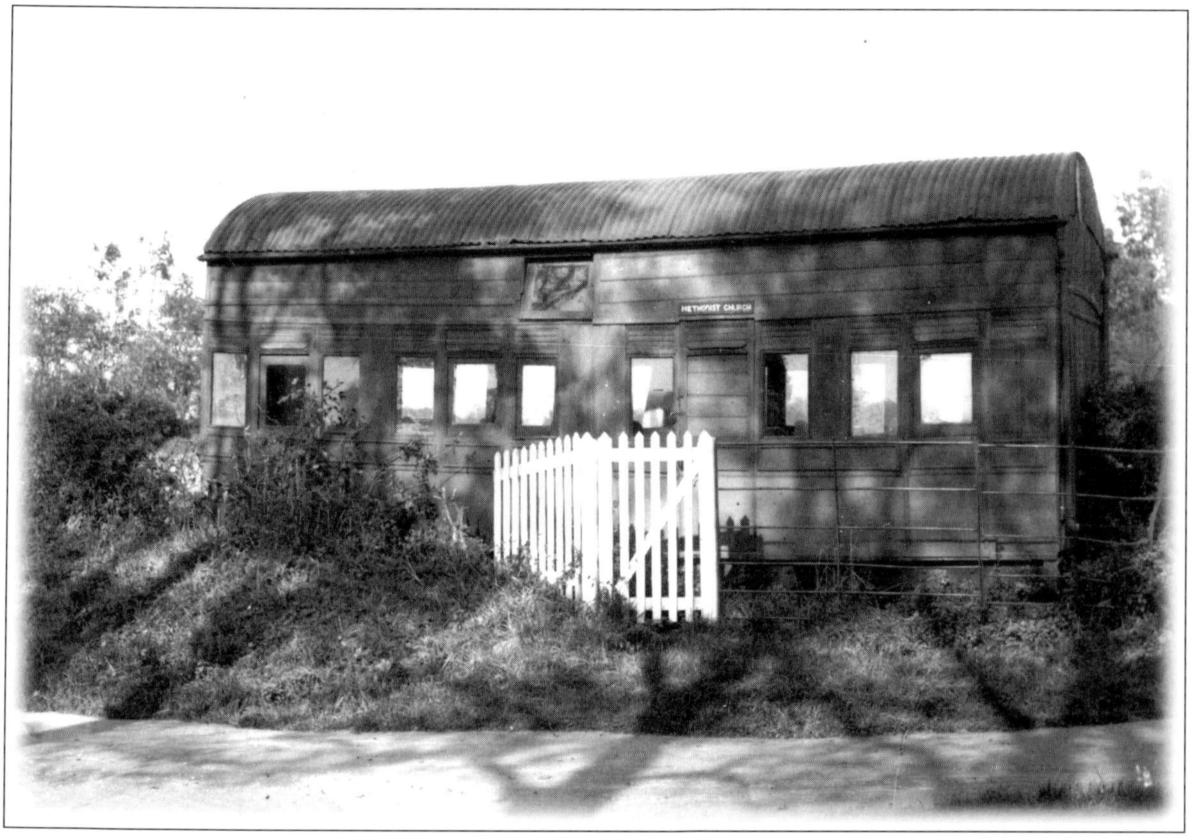

The tiny Primitive Methodist Chapel at Doughton hamlet near Sculthorpe was adapted from a disused railway carriage from the Midland and Great Northern Railway in 1891. During the 1930s Mr George Boast and Mr George Howes from Sculthorpe, active Primitive Methodist lay preachers within the Fakenham-Wells Circuit, frequently conducted services here. The tiny congregation from Dunton-cum-Doughton was considerably swelled by members of the Sculthorpe faithful who also attended. (Reproduced by kind permission of the Norfolk Rural Life Musuem at Gressenhall)

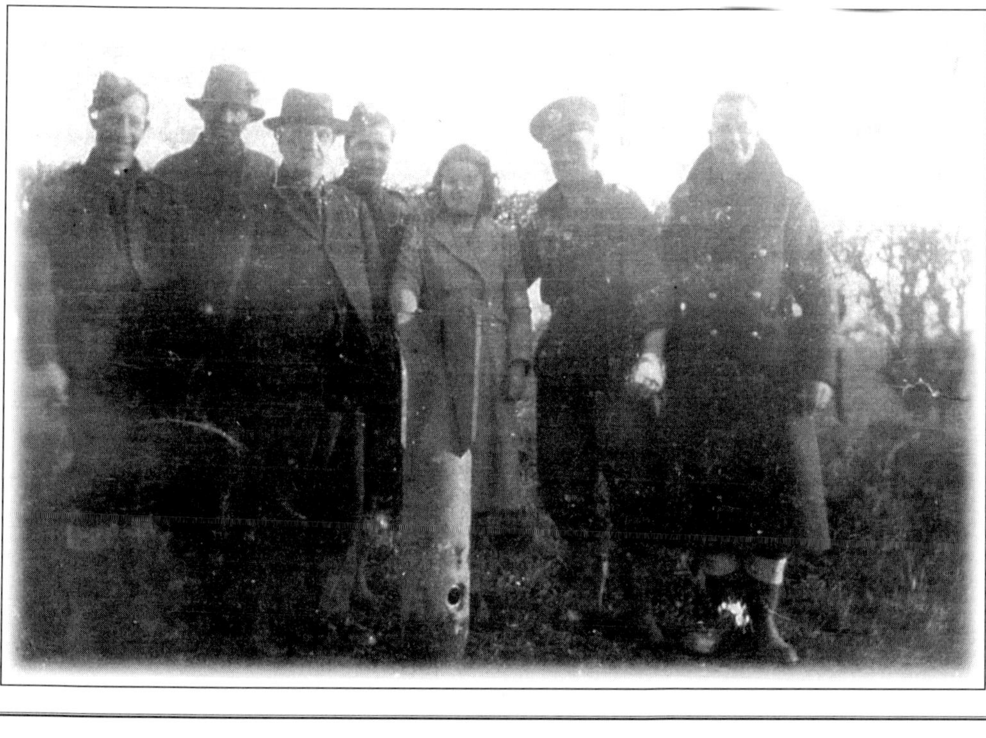

Left: *Cranmer Park, 1940. The unexploded German bomb was dealt with by the Army bomb-disposal unit.* Pictured with them are: *Jack Lingwood* (second from left), *Mr Girling* (third from left) *and Susie Fox* (centre). (Reproduced by kind permission of Mrs Joyce Harrison, née Lingwood)

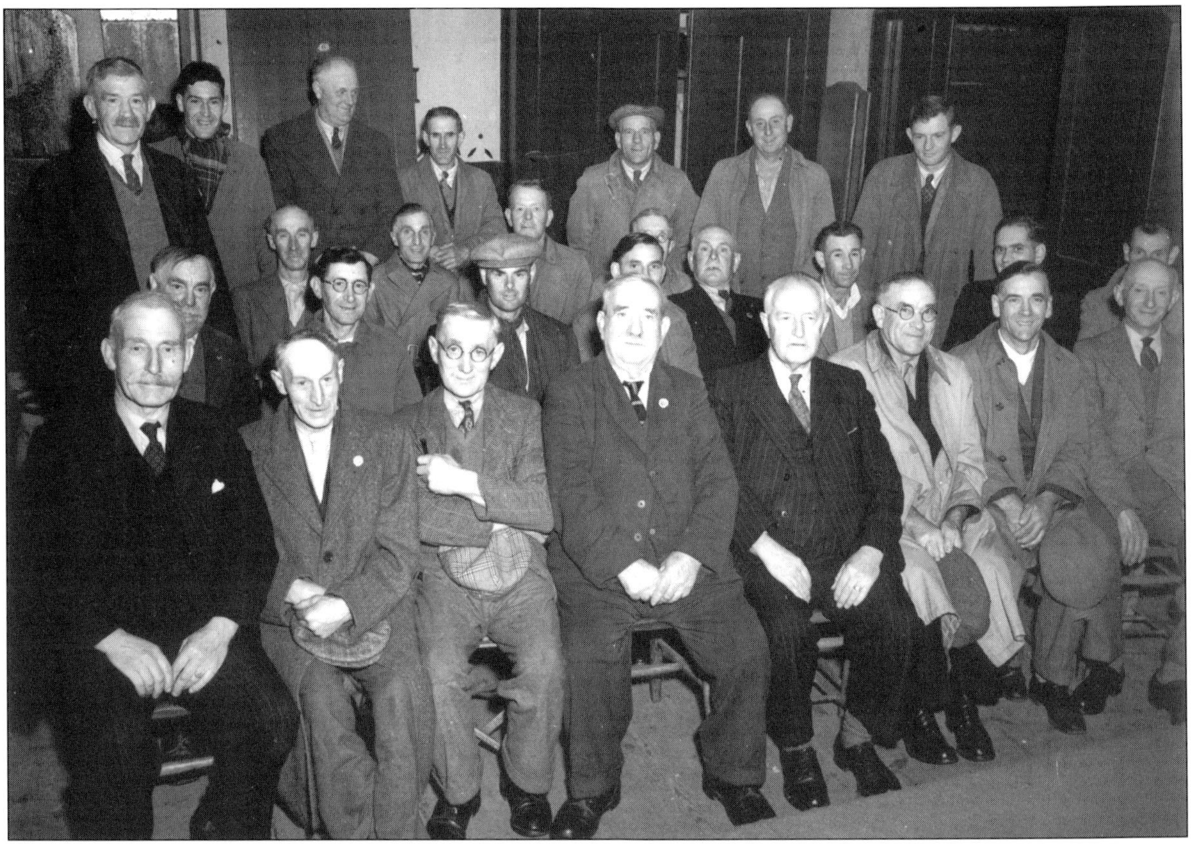

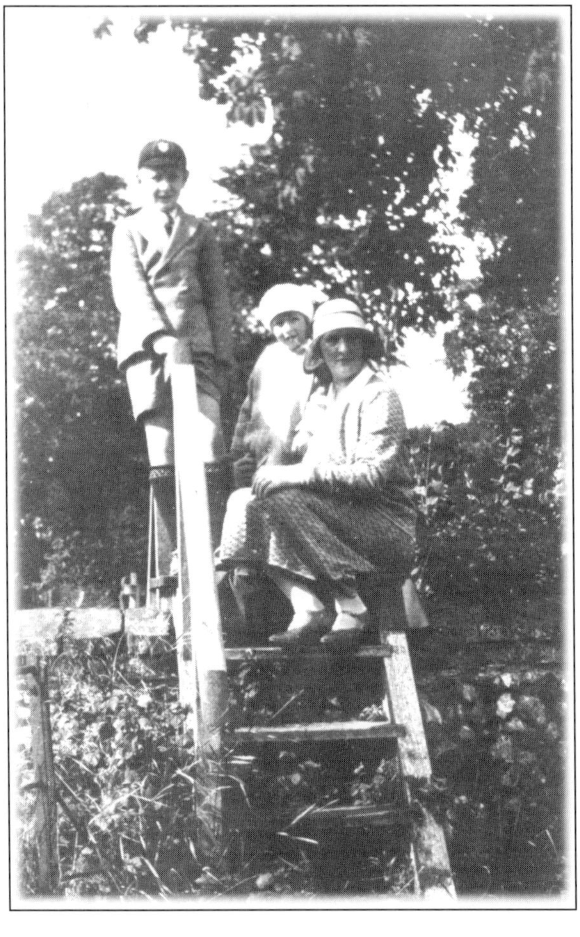

Above: *A meeting of Sculthorpe members of the National Union of Agricultural Workers held in the lecture room at Sculthorpe during the early 1950s. The large gentleman seated in the centre of the front row is Mr 'Friday' Layton, great friend and supporter of Sir George Edwards. Back row, first from the left, is Mr George Howes, Methodist lay preacher in the Fakenham-Wells Circuit. His son, Mr Alan Howes, is pictured in the back row, first from the right. Alan Howes was chairman of Sculthorpe Parish Council for many years and was also Justice of the Peace and was decorated with the British Empire Medal.* Among those pictured are: *Victor Fuller, Billy Barnes, Mick Barnes, Tom Gathercole, Mr Prior, Austin Bacon, Peter Barrett, three of Friday Layton's sons and Donny Clarke.* (Reproduced by kind permission of the Norfolk Rural Life Museum at Gressenhall)

Left: *The stile into the churchyard was only replaced with a gate during the late 1960s. This photograph dates from the late 1920s.* (Reproduced by kind permission of Mr Kenneth Boast)

Bibliography

Articles, Dictionaries, Directories

Bryant, T.H., *Churches of Norfolk: Hundred of Gallow*, (*Norwich Mercury*, 1900)

Craven's Trade Directory of Norfolk, 1856

The Concise Oxford Dictionary of English Place Names, (Various)

The Dictionary of National Biography (Various)

Groves Concise Dictionary of Music

Jones, Mrs Herbert, *An Account of Sculthorpe Church*, 1870 (An unpublished manuscript history belonging to the Parish Church of the Blessed Virgin Mary and All Saints, Sculthorpe)

Religious Worship in Norfolk: The 1851 Census of Accommodation and Attendance at Worship, edited by Jane Edge/Norma Virgoe, published by the Norfolk Record Society, Vol. LXII, 1998.

Watkin OSB, Dom Aelred (transcriber), *Norwich Archdeaconry: Inventory of Church Goods 1368*, published by the Norfolk Record Society, Vol. 19, 1948

William White's Directory of Norfolk, editions 1836 and 1845

Books

Armstrong's History of Norfolk

Blomefield, Revd Francis, *The County of Norfolk* (2nd edition), 1808, Charles Parkin

Bryant, Sir Arthur, *The Age of Chivalry: The Story of England*, published by Collins, 1963

Burke's Peerage (Various)

Coote, Stephen, *William Morris: His Life and Work*, published by Past Times/CLB Publishing Ltd, 1995

Cozens-Hardy, Basil, *Norfolk Archaeology: Vol. 33, Part 3 – Norfolk Lawyers*, published by the Norfolk & Norwich Archaeological Society, 1964

de la Rochefoucauld, Francois, *A Frenchman in England*, 1784, English edition translated by S.C. Roberts, published by Cambridge University Press, 1933

Doubleday, H.A., and Page, W. (editor), *Victoria County History of Norfolk: Vols. I & II*, 1901–06

Froissart, Jean, *The Chronicle of Froissart*, published by Penguin Classics

Gough Nichols, John, *The Unton Inventories*, 1841

Gunn, Revd Frederick, *The Church of St Mary & All Saints, Sculthorpe*, published by Graham Cumming Ltd, Ramsgate, 1958

Harrison, Martin, *Victorian Stained Glass*, published by Barrie and Jenkins Ltd, 1980

Harrod, Wilhelmine, *The Norfolk Guide*, published by the Alistair Press, 1988

Haward, Birkin, *Nineteenth Century Norfolk Stained Glass: An Account of Norfolk Stained Glass Painters*, published by Geo books and the Centre of East Anglian Studies, 1984

Haythornthwaite, Philip J., *Who Was Who in the Napoleonic Wars*, published by Arms & Armour/The Cassell Group, 1998

Jarvis, Rupert, *The Ceremony of the Knollys Rose*, published by All-Hallows-by-the-Tower, London

Jones, Mrs Herbert, *Notes on Sculthorpe Church*, published by the Norfolk & Norwich Archaeological Society, 1872

Jones, Mrs Herbert, *Sandringham Past & Present*, (2nd edition 1888), published by Jarrolds

Jones, Mrs Herbert, *Some Norfolk Worthies*, published by Jarrolds, 1895

Jones, L.E., *Georgian Afternoon*, published by Rupert Hart-Davis, 1958

Jones, L.E., *A Victorian Boyhood*, published by Macmillan & Company Ltd, 1955

Ketton-Cremer, R.W., *Norfolk Assembly*

Ketton-Cremer, R.W., *Norfolk Portraits*

Labouchere Thorold, Algar, *The Life of Henry Labouchere*

Margary, I.D., *Roman Roads in Britain*, 1967

Messent, Claude, *Old Norfolk Watermills*, 1938

Parker, R.H.C., *Coke of Norfolk and the Agricultural Revolution*, 1975

Pearsall, Derek, *The Life of Geoffrey Chaucer: A Critical Biography*, published by Blackwell, 1994

Pevsner, Sir Nikolaus, *The Buildings of England: Northwest & South Norfolk: 1962*

Porter, Enid, *The Folklore of East Anglia*, published by Batsford Ltd, 1974

Rye, Walter, *Norfolk Families*

Townshend, Lt-Col, CVF, *The Military Life of Field-Marshall George, 1st Marquess Townshend of Raynham*, published by John Murray, 1901

Troubridge, Laura, *Life Amongst the Troubridges – The Journals of a Young Victorian*, edited by Jacqueline Hope-Nicholson, published by John Murray, 1966

Whatmore, Father Leonard, *Highway to Walsingham*

Wade Martins, Susanna, *A History of Norfolk*, published by Phillimore & Company Ltd, 1984

Willett, Peter, *The Story of Tattersalls*, published by Stanley Paul and Company Ltd, 1987

Young, Arthur, *A General View of the Agriculture of the County of Norfolk*, 1804, reprinted in 1969 by David & Charles Publications Ltd

Magazines, Newspapers and Maps

Bryant's map of Norfolk, 1826, Larks Press edition, 1998

Country Life magazine article, 'In Sculthorpe Church', March 1907 edition

Faden's map of Norfolk, 1797, Larks Press edition, 1989

The Illustrated London News, May 1845 edition

Ordnance Survey map, 1838, reprinted by David & Charles Publications Ltd

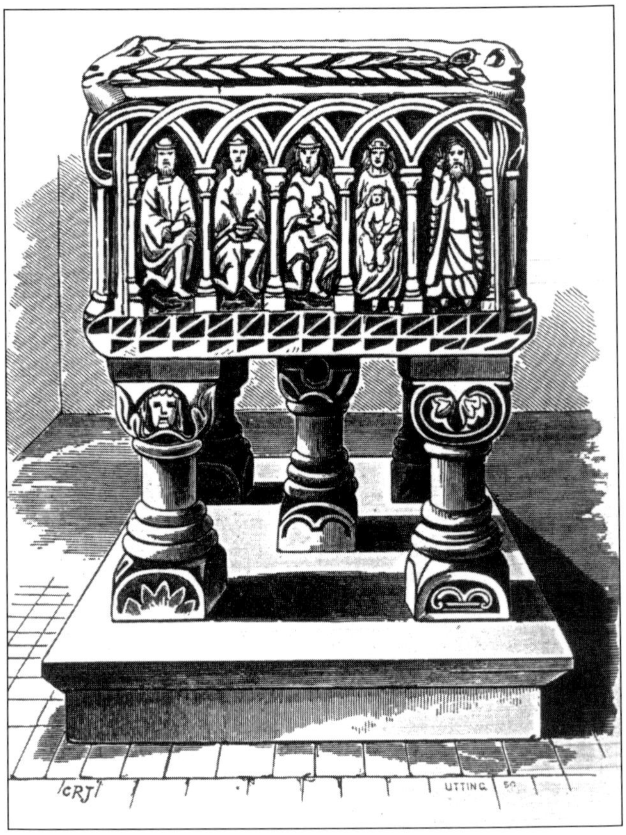

Above: *A drawing of the ancient Norman font in Sculthorpe Church taken from* Notes on Sculthorpe Church *by Mrs Herbert Jones, published in 1872.* (Reproduced by kind permission of the Norfolk & Norwich Archaeological Society)

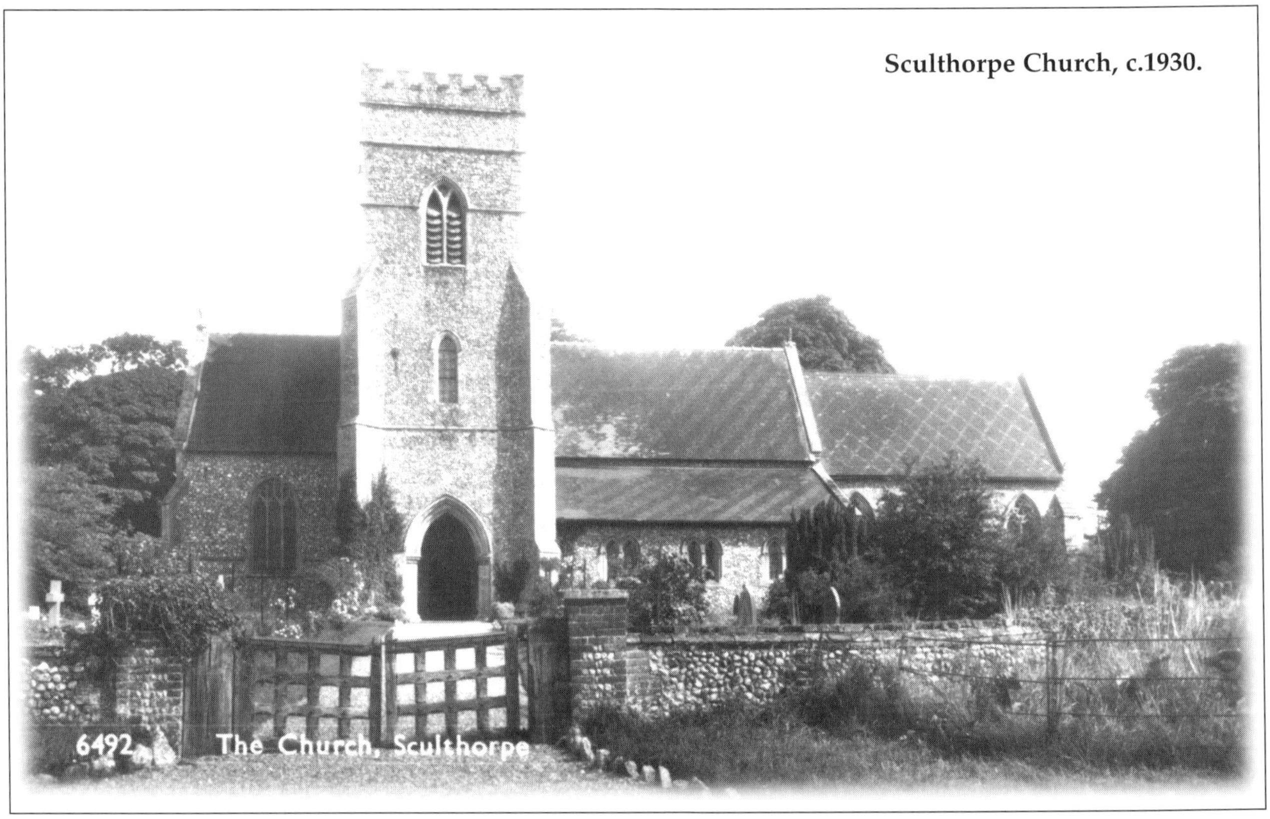

Sculthorpe Church, c.1930.

Subscribers

J.M. Allison (née Boyce), Sculthorpe, Norfolk
Freda M. Andrews, Fakenham, Norfolk
Mr John, Mrs Jacqueline and Mr Dale Archer, Sculthorpe, Norfolk
Robert F. Armiger, Sculthorpe, Norfolk
Trudy Dawn Armiger, Sculthorpe
Mr D.C. Armiger, Creake Road, Sculthorpe
Ronald and Richard Avis, Hornchurch, Essex
Austin Bacon, Sculthorpe, Norfolk
Jennifer Bacon-Hilton, Fakenham
Mr and Mrs G. Banham, Sculthorpe, Norfolk
Kenneth Clive and Debra Anne Barnes
Ellen L. Barnes, Doughton, Norfolk
Jack Barrett, Fakenham, Norfolk
Dale Bassham, Arkansas, USA
Alan Bassham, Knaresborough, North Yorkshire
Joyce and Ruth Batchelor, Sheringham, Norfolk
John and Grace Baxter, Earsham, Norfolk
David and Sue Beale, Sculthorpe, Norfolk
Mrs Fay E. Bell (née Pearson), Hempton, Norfolk
Miss L.J. Boswell, Waltham Forest, London
Miss D. Bowles, South Raynham
Philip Brett and Amanda Whitton, Foulsham, Norfolk
Mrs Linda Bubbear, Fakenham, Norfolk
Mrs A. Cain, Fakenham, Norfolk
The Clifford's, The Street, Sculthorpe
Anthony J. Clifton Brown, Congham, Norfolk
Ursula M. Clifton Brown, Congham, Norfolk
Peter C. Clifton Brown, Cashel, Tipperary
Conway and Family,
Mr Fabian John Cooper, The Street, Sculthorpe, Norfolk
Mrs Thomas Corbin (née Quarles), Greenville, USA
Chris Cornwall
Austin Cornwall, Sculthorpe, Norfolk
Margaret Crane, Shrewsbury
Arthur F. Cubitt, Sculthorpe, Norfolk
Arthur and Peggy Cubitt, Moor Lane, Sculthorpe
Peter Davis, Sculthorpe, Norfolk
William and Daphne Dawkins, Sculthorpe, Norfolk
Mrs Josephine De Bono,
D. Delaney, Fakenham, Norfolk
Margaret Durrant (née Large), born Sculthorpe 1932
Chris Edge, Bicester, Oxon
Colin Edge, Northampton
Conor and Gavin (sadly missed) Fenn, Sculthorpe
Mrs M.J. Flanagan, Hemel Hempstead, Hertfordshire
Janet Flower (née Greeves), Swainsthorpe
Julian, Christina, Hilary and Helena Foord, Sculthorpe, Norfolk
Richard Foster, Colkirk
Janice Fowle, Sculthorpe (Colkirk)
Mr R. Francis, Sculthorpe, Norfolk
K.W. Francis, Creake Road, Sculthorpe
Rosemary French (née Land), family originated Sculthorpe
Dorothy Frost, Sculthorpe, Norfolk
Mr Brian Frost, Sculthorpe, Norfolk
Peter and Patricia Futter, Sculthorpe, Norfolk
Raymond Futter, Little Snoring, Norfolk
Valerie May Futter, Sculthorpe, Norfolk
Patricia A. Futter, Colkirk, Norfolk
Terry (Buster) Futter
Angela J. Futter, Sculthorpe, Norfolk
Aidan Goward-Pearce, Gary's Godson
Mrs J.F. Grace, Mundesley, Norfolk
John G. Greeves, Grimston, Norfolk
Michael Horace John Hammond, Fakenham
Joyce M. Harrison, Sculthorpe, Norfolk
Rosina A. Haws, Sculthorpe, Norfolk

Josie Hingley (née Mitchell), Melton Constable
Ray Hipkin, Gt Massingham, Norfolk
Mrs Joan Howes, Sculthorpe, Norfolk
Janice Howes, Sculthorpe, Norfolk
Sheila Jarrett, Sculthorpe (Rudham)
Barbara and Richard Jermy, Sculthorpe, Norfolk
Terence M. Knights, Sculthorpe, Norfolk
H.D. Labouchere, Blue Tile Farm, Field Dalling, Holt, Norfolk
David H. Labouchere, North Elmham, Norfolk
John P. Labouchere, North Elmham, Norfolk
Colin M. Labouchere, Kington St Michael, Wiltshire
Dinah G. Labouchere and David R. Potts, North Elmham, Norfolk
Richard Land, family originated Sculthorpe
John Land, Hornchurch, Essex
Susan Lane (née Mitchell), Warham
Mr David Lingwood, Harlow, Essex
Mr Philip Lingwood, Old Colwyn, North Wales
Harold and Anne Lingwood, Sculthorpe, Norfolk
Colin Lingwood, Fakenham, Norfolk
Ray Lingwood
Ron and Margaret Lingwood and Family,
Frank Lingwood and Family, Anglesea
Mr Michael Linswood, Northolt, Middlesex
Ian Liston-Smith, April Cottage, Sculthorpe
Roger and Tricia London, Sculthorpe, Norfolk
B.D. Mace (née Boyce) SRN, SCM, Sculthorpe, Norfolk
Colin B. Mack, Gosnells, West Australia
Ginny Magee, Norwich
Christine Massingham (née Francis), Pudding Norton
J.O. and G.G. McMasters, Farnham Royal, Buckinghamshire
Susan H. Mennie, Portishead, North Somerset
Bethany E. Mennie, Portishead, North Somerset
Sophie E. Mennie, Portishead, North Somerset
John Mitchell, Fellbeck, York
Thomas Mitchell, Australia
David Mitchell, Fakenham
Doris Mitchell, Sculthorpe, Norfolk
Stuart Mitchell, Whissonsett
Stanley and Christine Neale
Mary, Sid and Simon Negus
Ray Norman, Fakenham, Norfolk
Edwin P. Norman, Sculthorpe, Norfolk
Muriel Norman (née Wicks)
Lady Norris (née Pamela Crane), Steyning, West Sussex
Phyllis J. Palmer, Fakenham, Norfolk
Patrick A. and Heather M. (née Playford) Pearce, Sculthorpe, Norfolk
Dennis J. Playford, born 1935 Sculthorpe/now Hingham, Norfolk
David G. Playford, Sculthorpe, Norfolk
Dulcie Rawlings (née Tuck), Fakenham, Norfolk
Eva and Richard Read, Dunton Rectory
Maurice, Sabina and Mark Roberson, Beetley
Jean and Derek Rouse, Shop - Post Office
Mrs Geraldine S. Ryder (née Palmer), Rosh Pinny, Sculthorpe, Norfolk
Julia Seaman (née Watson), Sculthorpe
Mrs E.M. Sibley (née Skippon), Streatham, London
Robert A. Snowball, Chelsea, Sculthorpe, Fakenham
Ann Stephenson, Sculthorpe, Norfolk
Jill Stone, Garforth, Leeds
Revd Andrew Thomson, Rector of Sculthorpe
William Tuck, Freeman of Norwich City. Saltdean, Sussex
Denton Tuck (Joe), Fakenham, Norfolk
Stella E. Vertigan (née Cornwall),
Patricia Vertigan (née Harper), born Sculthorpe 1942
Mrs Elizabeth Walden (née Howes), Fakenham, Norfolk
Tony and Margaret Walters, Sculthorpe
Keith Walton, Clyst Honiton, Exeter, Devon
Guy Myles Warren, Wells-Next-The-Sea, Norfolk
Mrs Tracey Waters, Sculthorpe - granddaughter of Jack & May Lingwood
S. Waters, Sedgeford
Peter West, Fakenham, Norfolk
Mr Philip West, Hindringham, Norfolk
Mrs M. West, Sculthorpe
Jacqueline White, Sculthorpe
Sue Williams (née Labouchere), Brecon, Wales
Michael R. Williamson, Fundenhall, Norfolk
Mrs Gwen Windeler (née Lingwood)
Patricia Wright, Adelaide, South Australia (descendants of Rev John Gibbon Wright
Christine Wright (née Mitchell), Heacham
Jean M. Youngs, Fakenham, Norfolk

Community Histories

The Book of Addiscombe • Canning & Clyde Road Residents Association & Friends
The Book of Addiscombe, Vol. II • Canning & Clyde Road Residents Association & Friends
The Book of Axminster with Kilmington • Les Berry and Gerald Gosling
The Book of Bampton • Caroline Seward
The Book of Barnstaple • Avril Stone
The Book of Barnstaple, Vol. II • Avril Stone
The Book of The Bedwyns • The Bedwyn History Society
The Book of Bickington • Stuart Hands
Blandford Forum: A Millennium Portrait • Blandford Town Council
The Book of Bramford • Bramford Local History Group
The Book of Breage & Germoe • Stephen Polglase
The Book of Bridestowe • R. Cann
The Book of Bridport • Rodney Legg
The Book of Brixham • Frank Pearce
The Book of Buckfastleigh • Sandra Coleman
The Book of Buckland Monachorum & Yelverton • Hemery
The Book of Carharrack • Carharrack Old Cornwall Society
The Book of Carshalton • Stella Wilks and Gordon Rookledge
The Parish Book of Cerne Abbas • Vale and Vale
The Book of Chagford • Ian Rice
The Book of Chapel-en-le-Frith • Mike Smith
The Book of Chittlehamholt with Warkleigh & Satterleigh • Richard Lethbridge
The Book of Chittlehampton • Various
The Book of Colney Heath • Bryan Lilley
The Book of Constantine • Moore and Trethowan
The Book of Cornwood & Lutton • Compiled by the People of the Parish
The Book of Creech St Michael • June Small
The Book of Cullompton • Compiled by the People of the Parish
The Book of Dawlish • Frank Pearce
The Book of Dulverton, Brushford, Bury & Exebridge • Dulverton & District Civic Society
The Book of Dunster • Hilary Binding
The Book of Edale • Gordon Miller
The Ellacombe Book • Sydney R. Langmead
The Book of Exmouth • W.H. Pascoe
The Book of Grampound with Creed • Bane and Oliver
The Book of Hayling Island & Langstone • Rogers
The Book of Helston • Jenkin with Carter
The Book of Hemyock • Clist and Dracott
The Book of Herne Hill • Patricia Jenkyns
The Book of Hethersett • Hethersett Society Research Group
The Book of High Bickington • Avril Stone
The Book of Ilsington • Dick Wills
The Book of Kingskerswell • Carsewella Local History Group
The Book of Lamerton • Ann Cole & Friends
Lanner, A Cornish Mining Parish • Sharron Schwartz and Roger Parker
The Book of Leigh & Bransford • Malcolm Scott
The Book of Litcham with Lexham & Mileham • Litcham Historical & Amenity Society
The Book of Loddiswell • Reg and Betty Sampson
The New Book of Lostwithiel • Barbara Fraser
The Book of Lulworth • Rodney Legg
The Book of Lustleigh • Joe Crowdy
The Book of Lyme Regis • Rodney Legg
The Book of Manaton • Compiled by the People of the Parish
The Book of Markyate • Markyate Local History Society
The Book of Mawnan • Mawnan Local History Group
The Book of Meavy • Pauline Hemery
The Book of Minehead with Alcombe • Binding and Stevens
The Book of Morchard Bishop • Jeff Kingaby

The Book of Newdigate • John Callcut
The Book of Nidderdale • Nidderdale Musuem Society
The Book of Northlew with Ashbury • Northlew History Group
The Book of North Newton • Robins and Robins
The Book of North Tawton • Baker, Hoare and Shields
The Book of Nynehead • Nynehead & District History Society
The Book of Okehampton • Radford and Radford
The Book of Paignton • Frank Pearce
The Book of Penge, Anerley & Crystal Palace • Peter Abbott
The Book of Peter Tavy with Cudlipptown • Peter Tavy Heritage Group
The Book of Pimperne • Jean Coull
The Book of Plymtree • Tony Eames
The Book of Porlock • Denis Corner
Postbridge – The Heart of Dartmoor • Reg Bellamy
The Book of Priddy • Albert Thompson
The Book of Princetown • Dr Gardner-Thorpe
The Book of Rattery • By the People of the Parish
The Book of St Day • Joseph Mills and Paul Annear
The Book of Sampford Courtenay
with Honeychurch • Stephanie Pouya
The Book of Sculthorpe • Gary Windeler
The Book of Seaton • Ted Gosling
The Book of Sidmouth • Ted Gosling and Sheila Luxton
The Book of Silverton • Silverton Local History Society
The Book of South Molton • Jonathan Edmunds
The Book of South Stoke with Midford • Edited by Robert Parfitt
South Tawton & South Zeal with Sticklepath • Radfords
The Book of Sparkwell with Hemerdon & Lee Mill • Pam James
The Book of Staverton • Pete Lavis
The Book of Stithians • Stithians Parish History Group
The Book of Stogumber, Monksilver, Nettlecombe
& Elworthy • Maurice and Joyce Chidgey
The Book of Studland • Rodney Legg
The Book of Swanage • Rodney Legg
The Book of Tavistock • Gerry Woodcock
The Book of Thorley • Sylvia McDonald and Bill Hardy
The Book of Torbay • Frank Pearce
Uncle Tom Cobley & All:
Widecombe-in-the-Moor • Stephen Woods
The Book of Watchet • Compiled by David Banks
The Book of West Huntspill • By the People of the Parish
Widecombe-in-the-Moor • Stephen Woods
The Book of Williton • Michael Williams
The Book of Witheridge • Peter and Freda Tout and John Usmar
The Book of Withycombe • Chris Boyles
Woodbury: The Twentieth Century Revisited • Roger Stokes
The Book of Woolmer Green • Compiled by the People of the Parish

For details of any of the above titles or if you are interested in writing your own history, please contact: Commissioning Editor Community Histories, Halsgrove House, Lower Moor Way, Tiverton Business Park, Tiverton, Devon EX16 6SS, England; tel: 01884 259636; email: katyc@halsgrove.com